# JOHN MASEFIELD'S
# LETTERS FROM THE FRONT

25 March. 1915. Arve.

My beloved Lou,

Bobby is having a long collogue tonight with Tonks to discuss my idea, that we should start an Authors' & Artists' Hospital in the Vosges, & spend May in drumming up money for it. He is very keen indeed on having you on the staff & suggests that the dear babes should come, too. He is quite hopeless beyond his level, you see, like the rest of us. The result of the collogue won't be clear tomorrow, as Tonks has a toothache and is inclined to curse the world.

While I was packing up some sackings in the Hall today, the lad who is so like Cross came in. He was only lightly hit in the arm & is now at the Hospice convalescent & about to go altogether for his forty days leave before returning to the war. He speaks a cruelly difficult patois, very rapidly, but, as in reading aloud to you sometimes, I often feel a Kind of Holy Ghost coming down on me, when I listen to these people, & when that happens I can understand every word & they me. I got him to talk about the war & his own feelings. He is an orphan, & has one brother a year younger than himself, & he himself is 18, & looks three years younger, a merry, cheery, honest, hard working country boy with very warm affections & good hearty animal recreations, with much that country way which some of the lads in Hereford used to have when I was a boy, a sort of brisk emphasis. He said that his first coming under fire was in an attack with the bayonet, & that the fire confused him & all the other new comers till they were like dazed people, but that one got used to it. He said that the trenches were not so bad; you had little

# JOHN MASEFIELD'S
## ——LETTERS——
# FROM·THE·FRONT
## ——1915–1917——

### EDITED BY
# PETER VANSITTART

CONSTABLE·LONDON

First published in Great Britain 1984
by Constable and Company Limited
10 Orange Street London WC2H 7EG
Letters and quotations from John Masefield's work
Copyright © 1984 by The Estate of John Masefield
Editorial matter copyright © 1984 by Peter Vansittart
Set in Linotron Plantin by
Rowland Phototypesetting Limited
Bury St Edmunds, Suffolk
Printed in Great Britain by
St Edmundsbury Press
Bury St Edmunds, Suffolk


British Library cataloguing in publication data

Masefield, John
John Masefield's letters from the front
1915–1917
1. World War, 1914–1918 – Campaigns –
Western   2. World War, 1914–1918 –
Personal narratives, British
I. Title     II. Vansittart, Peter
940.4'144'0924       0544

ISBN 0-09-465860-9

TO JUDITH MASEFIELD

## LIVERPOOL 1890

Gray sea dim, smoke-blowing, hammer-racket, sirens
Calling from ships, ear-breaking riveting, the calthrops
Of great gray drays, fire-smiting on the cobbles, dragging
The bales of cotton.

The warehouse roofs, wet-gleaming, the ships bedraggled,
Awry-swung yards, backt on the main, the jib booms
Run in, the winches clanking, the slings of cargo
Running up, jolt.

There lie the ships, paint-rusted, each as a person
In rake or sheer or rig, coulters or counters,
Sea-shearing bows, those swords of beauty that thrust
The heart with rapture.

All fair ships, man-killers some, sea-eagles, sluggards.
Tall, too, many: lofty, a dread to look at, dizzy thus:
Among them always one more sky-aspiring queen,
Remembered always.

JOHN MASEFIELD

# Acknowledgments

The Publishers would very much like to thank the following for their help in preparing this book: Judith Masefield and Jack Masefield, Mrs Roma Woodnutt of The Society of Authors, Professor Corliss Lamont, and Mr Kenneth A. Lohf, Librarian for Rare Books and Manuscripts at Columbia University, New York, who now own the 1917 letters; and finally Mr Roderick Soddaby, Keeper of Documents at The Imperial War Museum.

We should also like to thank the following publishers for use of short extracts: Messrs William Heinemann Ltd for Masefield's *Liverpool 1890*, *Grace before Ploughing*, *The Conway*, *New Chum*, *Dauber*, *In the Mill*, *A Book of Both Sorts*, *Gallipolli*, *The Old Front Line*, *The Everlasting Mercy* and *Gautama the Enlightened*; Messrs Buchan & Enright for Masefield's *Letters to Reyna* and their forthcoming *Letters to Margaret Bridges*; Oxford University Press Ltd for Constance Babington-Smith's *John Masefield*; The Bodley Head for Marjorie Fisher's *John Masefield*; Messrs Macmillan & Co Ltd for Masefield's *Letters to Florence Lamont*; finally Messrs Faber & Faber Ltd for Ezra Pound's 'Hugh Selwyn Mauberley'.

# Contents

# Introduction

John Masefield was born in 1878, at Ledbury, Herefordshire, land of orchards, waters, hills, the remains of a great forest, and a fine cathedral: it was a land also of roses, corn, hops, and a particular breed of cattle which, seen on his American travels, always made him immediately nostalgic. The daffodils still grow, as he saw them in *The Daffodil Fields*. And, nourishing the future *Reynard the Fox*, he could remember 'as I was much in the woods as a boy, I saw foxes fairly often, considering that they are night-moving animals. Their grace, beauty, cleverness and secrecy always thrilled me.' (*Recent Prose*, 1926.) Years later, a stopped-up fox's earth quickened his sympathy and raised his anger.

He was one of six children. His mother had rich narrative skills, his father was a prosperous solicitor. The children had abundant love, relative freedoms, and apparent security.

Young John was a roamer, a seeker, from the start. Flowers, beasts, trees and spaces, his mother's stories, old folks' lore – they all absorbed him. By the Avon, or the Hereford and Gloucester canal, he would watch the slow barges, their brass gleaming, painted with flowers, castles, nymphs, and with amiable families who invited him aboard. Down-river were wooden warships; horse-drawn fire-engines sped between villages, urged by the huge Ledbury fire-bell.

For some years, like many children, I lived in Paradise, or rather, like a specially lucky child in two Paradises linked together by a country of exceeding beauty and strangeness. In one extreme I was told that the ancient joy of Britons, the woad plant, grew; and in another extreme there was the wonder, where a hill moved for three days screaming as though it hurt.

*Grace before Ploughing* (1966)

Paradises are more often visions and glimpses than enduring facts and his mother's early death and his father's decline into indigence and insanity passed the children into the care of an uncle and aunt, conscientious, but philistine, unimaginative, strict in the bleaker manner of Victorian piety. Masefield was to undergo disillusion, and his subsequent childhood, like most others, bristled not only with stories, discoveries and secrets, but also with misunderstandings and harshness. All contributed to both his fantasies, myths, legends, and to his limitless store of facts observed and felt. The acerbic witch in *The Midnight Folk* may derive from youthful distress and harshness. Echoes of wretchedness from a governess and his aunt are discernible in his play *The Tragedy of Nan*. It must be added that he experienced no cruelty of the sort inflicted on the young Kipling and Saki, merely from the disposition of those who distrusted the imagination, and leagued poets and story-tellers alongside gypsies, tinkers, the idle, the errant and the mischievous.

A strong sense of history pervades Masefield's work, but not the graphs and statistics of sociologists, or even the sustained capacity for making large-scale judgements or political calculations. His romantic loyalties to losers, often Arthurian Celts, made him undervalue the Anglo-Saxons, and readers of the letters may jib at his wholesale indictment of Germans. What he could grasp, and grasp powerfully, was the raw living moment, residue of an event long vanished, the period details in the lives of men, women, children, fiercely independent, many of them of singular character, often forced from home and land through poverty, or from the inescapable needs of curiosity and the impulse towards adventure, social betterment, or impatience with inherited routine.

His daughter Judith recalls his empathy with ages even more distant, the time of silent stones, lonely barrows, carefully ridged hills and forgotten forts:

> I think he did at times see the past. Once we went up a hill in Gloucestershire with his great-aunt, looking for a vanished chapel to St Catherine. He pointed to a wide spot and said 'It was there.' 'It could not *possibly* have been there,' said the old lady, but the next year a rabbit tossed up a tile and the floor was uncovered exactly where he said.

As a boy, Masefield not only spoke with a man who had seen the Shropshire coach arriving with news of Waterloo but encountered survivors from the battle.

In barely literate communities, memories are long, and Hereford-shire passions aroused by the Civil War still glowed. Old mementoes could be sought. Here Prince Rupert charged, or was said to have charged, there a cannon-ball had recently been dug up. The Welsh were still foreigners; the Irish almost worse. Old tales abounded: tales of smugglers, highwaymen, old murders, black and white magic were eagerly absorbed by a future writer, who was to tap an England by now almost extinct.

It was an England of busy canals, unquestioned hunts – Masefield's poem, *Reynard the Fox* (1919), did for the Edwardian hunt what Surtees and Trollope did in prose – hiring fairs, forges, wagonettes, charcoal-burners, gypsies supposed to be lurking to 'nap' a passing 'kid', and small family circuses, recalled in *King Cole* (1921), in one of which he saw a caged lion, advertised as 'The Same Lion What Ate Poor Miss Baker'. Fairs had fighting booths, in one of which The Lambeth Pop guaranteed to knock out all comers within two minutes. There were mummers with helmets, swords, lanterns, dressed as giants or St George fighting the Turkish Knight; tramps with their secret signs and mysterious motives; itinerant tinkers; revivalist preachers perhaps giving forebodings of *The Everlasting Mercy*; seasonal festivals, with scraps of paganism lingering, sometimes unnoticed, in church, chapel, manor and hedgerow; stentorian towncriers, as at Shrewsbury and the one at Ledbury station who chanted the announcements; dandies in moleskin waistcoats and, in towns, with rings worn outside their gloves. Lower voices, by kitchen range and tavern bench, spoke of old horrors, the witch hangings, torture, the deportation to slave plantations of the losers and the poor.

Transmuted into a sort of realistic fantasy, such memories, with fragmented ballads and old sayings, saturate Masefield's narratives, notably his favourite, *The Midnight Folk*, for children, but not for children only.

Significantly, on the roads, were boys and men trudging to Bristol, or to Liverpool, seeking a brigantine, barque, clipper, in which to sail the future. They would be passed by the horse-coaches, each with some fabled pedigree. Near Ledbury is Chance's Pitch, a steep hill where a coach-and-four was wrecked in the snow, with no survivors. Their ghosts troubled the hill, also the spectral coach itself, trying to collect new passengers. On his 86th birthday, Dr John Masefield, OM, Poet Laureate, returned to that hill, and revived ancient memories of simple delights and unfolded secrets.

If one went upon that road toward the time of the coach's arrival, one saw an unusual stir near the roads: people were coming to the road by every lane or field-path, for the coach carried the mails and the Gloucester and London papers. The guards had sorted these, and had them ready to fling to the trusty messengers who would be there to collect them. Presently, away in the distance there would come the note of the guard's horn, his 'yard of tin' or key-bugle. Then one would hear welcoming shouts, and then the beat, the measured, unvarying beat which is in my mind as the 'tantivy trot' of the four-in-hand drawing closer.

As it swept past the waiting messengers and the guard flung the mail-packets to the watchers, there would be a shout, a cheer, a swift greeting, then the coach would be past, and the guard would give a note of the horn and the moment of the day would be past.

It was a great moment. There was something most noble in that balanced slither that was not a slither, but an exquisite controlled motion. The perfection of the team, the driving, the build and colour of the coach, a triumphant work of art in itself; the exhileration of the horn, and the certainty of the delivery of the packets, all these things were the wonder of man, and each a credit to us.

*Grace before Ploughing*

Poet originally meant 'maker', and, throughout, Masefield cared for man as a craftsman, a doer, as much as a dreamer – both were essential – and in the objects he creates: a barge, a chair, mast, wagon-wheel, flute.

The sailor, the stoker of steamers, the man with the clout,
The chanty man bent at the balliards putting a tune to the shout,
The drowsy man at the wheel and the tired look out.

'A Consecration'

His pages are thronged with the smith, mechanic, timber-carter, songster, ploughman. He could say, like Kipling – whose influence he denied with some heat, adding that he hated Kipling's verse – 'I love watching the skills of men.' (Muriel Spark considers that his early ballads did owe much to Kipling in form, but had a radical difference of outlook.) Such people were in touch with the elements and minerals, the organic, with plant and star, tree and beast, the weather, the community, history. He describes the building of the Trojan Horse: exact, complete, original:

The pinewood workers made neck, head and legs.
Then all the parts were tenoned to each other
And tree-nailed fast, and shod to the wheeled stand,
Then the rough wood was polished with sea-sand
As smooth as ivory; then the bronze workers
Plated the wood with bronze from battle gear
And ran fine gold work over all the seams,
And horse-hair helmet-plumes made mane and tail.

*A Tale of Troy* (1932)

Or Arthur and Lancelot burying the Dragon ships in *Badon Hill* (1928):

First the wind bowed it down, then at a gust,
The flame that had been greedy, became lust.

On the *Conway* he was enraptured by carvers, riggers, wire-splicers, draughtsmen, painters, carpenters, netters, tugmen, with their delicate expertise and inherent sense of form and balance. Even swabbing a deck, polishing staunchions had glamour, and he remembered a little dancing master who had perfected his job amongst even the toughest, unruliest apprentices.

Masefield made a reputation by chronicling such types: the clipper crew working the China tea-race in *The Bird of Dawning* (1933); maintenance and trading personalities in *The Wanderer of Liverpool* (1930); grain-racers from Australia in *The Hurrying Angel* (1935). In his long writing life he describes lifeboatmen under tempest; men smashed in the Somme trenches, waiting at Gallipoli, at Dunkirk; the sensations of climbing aloft in a nor'easter; cargoes being shipped, oil-bags unloaded; weapons scoured; a ship manipulated through narrows; chariot racers; murderous Byzantine circus factions; a ship's bedraggled floor 'linked with raving and ruin'; the intricacies of rigging; deployment of troops; wartime political tactics. Men at work, men in action – Muriel Spark has written about his pronounced use of the verb, the active principle, often at the expense of the adjective.

His own attitude to literature must, in large part, have been derived from such personal observations. 'Well-made' currently incurs critical contempt, like 'do-gooder', with the disturbing implications that the badly-made and do-harmer are preferable. Masefield would have sympathised too, with Philip Toynbee's perplexity at the acclaim for the

'Theatre of Cruelty' and the derision to be expected for a 'Theatre of Kindness'.

In these letters, Masefield shows modest pride in swiftly constructing a table on the Western Front, then crutches and sticks, and also helping amputate a leg, an arm, cutting out 'great hunks of splintered bone'. He always loved carving and rigging model ships, and once made one for Thomas Hardy, though thinking very little of it.

Ships, particularly sailing ships, engrossed him until the end of his life. In boyhood he saw upon the *Conway* the remains of the *Great Eastern*, once the largest ship in the world. A mess-mate told him: 'She was a wonder in her day. She was built with a double-bottom; so that she could not be sunk; and a riveter got riveted in between the two skins; and he knocked and he knocked, to call attention; and for years afterwards his ghost used to knock. The crews couldn't stand it; and she was always an unlucky ship. Well, when they opened her up, on the beach, they found his skeleton between the skins, with a hammer tight in his finger-bones, and the head of the hammer all worn away with knocking.' (*New Chum*, 1944).

Sail was already doomed, but, describing a ship, he continues that she was 'elegant in the English style, and being almost new had all the latest sailors' blessings; nothing above her royals, double-top gallant yards, a spike-jib boom and no spanker gaff. She had donkey engine, deck capstans and fiferail winches for the braces. You could see at a glance that a lot of thought and love had gone to her building and fitting.'

What J. B. Priestley has done in recording the pre-1914 popular culture of northern towns, Masefield did for the rough life on ships, and, like Hardy, for the countryside, where, in his youth, people said that the test of spring's arrival was to be able to tread on nine daisies at once. He always remembered the fairs:

> Stalls of hardbake and galanty shows,
> And cheapjacks smashing crocks and trumpets blowing,
> And the loud organ of the horses going.
>                          'The Widow in the Bye Street'

Men wrestling with rams, swingboats straining for the sky, and 'The Murder in the Red Barn with Real Blood'.

Nevertheless, his romantic love of the sea and countryside – and his own past – seldom permitted him to romanticise the hideous, the petty criminal and sordid cottage:

I'll tell this sanctimonious crowd,
This town of window-peeping, prying,
Maligning, peering, hinting, lying,
Male and female human blots
Who would but daren't be whores and sots,
That they're so steeped in petty vice
That they're less excellent than the lice
That they're so soaked in petty virtue
That touching one of them will dirt you,
Dirt you with the stain of mean
Cheating trade and going between,
Pinching, starving, scraping, hoarding,
Spying through the chinks of boarding
To see if Sue the prentice lean
Dares to touch the margarine.
Fawning, cringing, oiling boots,
Raging in the crowd's pursuits.

*The Everlasting Mercy*

In such novels as *Dead Ned* and *Alive and Kicking Ned*, he depicted the gallows grin of the Good Old Days. Like his friend Synge he knew that beauty can accompany savagery: he had seen very early those he called the starved, stunted, ill-clad and untaught, and he rounded on those who forget that the sailor was usually badly paid by greedy employers and, cold and diseased, swiftly discarded and forgotten. In *Sea Life in Nelson's Time* he recorded the sufferings of 'barbarously maltreated men'.

Still a boy, he was dismayed by the fo'c's'le of a filthy steamer, and by the men, who, far worse than pigs and dogs, lived in 'a small frowsy, bare iron box, with a wet floor and a few wooden shelves.' He recalled the savagery of old whalers, and an American Captain: 'All I ask of officers and men, Sir, is common servility, and that of the most dog-goned sort.' The cruelty to long-dead crews haunted him, and the imbecility of naval and political authorities condemning them to bungled campaigns and venal transactions. In 1957, he wrote to Audrey Napier-Smith on the execution of Admiral Byng:

It is easy to be wise and cocksure 200 years after the events that I hesitate to write yet; I do not know enough; but I do know that skunks in power made him a scapegoat and murdered him for their own dirty skunkery and its results. It is a terrible tale: and it is terrible also to find, *in this century*, members of the guilty families writing deliberately lying books to clear their dirty forbears, who did not shrink from falsehood, forgery, theft and inconceivable baseness to hide their guilt – and make Byng die for it.

Years before, he had reflected:

> The ships were beautiful; their building and rigging were wonderful to me. It was, however, quite clear to me that something was very much amiss somewhere; there was too much grab, too much snatch, and I knew very well that I did not want to belong to it. I wanted to be clear of the type of man who gave iron walls and a shelf and a little daily offal in exchange for a life's work.
>
> *New Chum*

This should be noted by those who remember John Masefield only for *Cargoes*, and 'I must go down to the seas again'. In a typical sentence he once wrote: 'The hound has boiled horse. God knows what it was that the seamen had.'

Tenderly observant of landscape he could sometimes be lush, very occasionally sentimental, but violation of landscape – and people – stung him to measured anger. Here he describes a Great War mine-crater at Beaumont Hamel:

> It is like the crater of a volcano, vast, ragged and irregular, about one hundred and fifty yards long, one hundred yards across, and twenty-five yards deep. It is crusted and scabbed with yellowish tetter, like sulphur or the rancid fat on meat. The inside has rather the look of meat, for it is reddish and all streaked and scabbed with this pox and with discoloured chalk. A lot of it trickles and oozes like sores discharging pus, and this liquid gathers in holes near the bottom, and is greenish and foul and has the dazed look of eyes straining upwards.'
>
> *The Old Front Line*

Masefield felt passionately about cruelty: the cruelty of Shakespeare's Henry V, as prince and king: the cruelty to frogs and worms which made him unable to read *The Compleat Angler*. His earlier ambiguity towards fox-hunting, eventually hardened into revulsion. Near the end of his life he wrote: 'I saw the old England of 80 years ago: a dreadful land, so starved, so drunken, so untaught, so cruel, and now I cannot see any child unfed or lousy or beaten or set off to beg, and thrashed if unsuccessful, or sewn into clothes already ragged.' (*Letters to Reyna*, 1983)

*Lost Endeavour*, the title of his 1910 novel, came easily to this romantic but brooding outlook. As a countryman he knew well what could be concealed by the thatched cottage, prim window and the field too distant for cries to be heard. *The Daffodil Fields* promises a Wordsworthian pastoral but reveals the atrocious.

> She had two children as the fruits of trade
> Though she drank bitter herbs to kill the curse,
> Both of them sons, and one she overlaid,
> The other one the parish had to nurse.
> Now she grew plump with money in her purse,
> Passing for pure a hundred miles, I guess,
> From where her little son wore workhouse dress.

In *Reynard*, 'over which I took great pains and much red paint,' the fox escapes for another day, but much of the longer narrative verse, within settings of postcard beauty, tell of lust and squalor, violence and the gibbet, though never of the irredeemable. The parricide in *No Man takes the Farm* derived from an actual event.

Nothing is permanent, in nature, in man. During the Great War, Masefield visited Hébuterne, quite dead, grass growing in the street, ruined by war as once it might have been by Plague.

> The bells are silent; the beasts are gone from the byre and the ghosts from the church. Stealing about among the ruins and the gardens are the cats of the village, who have eaten too much man to fear him, but are now too wild to come to him. They creep about and eye him from cover and look like evil spirits.

> *The Old Front Line*

Again, like Priestley, Masefield recorded the Western Front, and here both writers have been under-valued. On the Somme, Masefield noted two graves in No Man's Land.

There are many English graves (marked, then, hurriedly, by the man's rifle thrust into the ground) in that piece of the line. On a windy day, these rifles shook in the wind as the bayonets bent to the blast. The field testaments of both men lay open beside them in the mud. The rain and the mud together had nearly destroyed the little books, but in each case it was possible to read one text. In both cases, the text which remained read with a strange irony. The one book beside a splendid youth, cut off in his promise, was open at a text which ran 'And Moses was learned in all the wisdom of the Egyptians and mighty in word and in deed.' The other book, beside one who had been killed in an attack which did not succeed at the moment, but which led to the falling back of the enemy nation from many miles of conquered ground, read even more strangely. It was open at the eighty-ninth Psalm, and the legible words were 'Thou hast broken down all his hedges; thou hast brought his strongholds to ruin.'

Those who associate Masefield exclusively with the Georgian lyric might examine his war-writings. From the Somme he wrote:

Sometimes in winter storms, the Atlantic is heaved aloft and tossed and tumbled under an evil heaven till all its wildness is hideous. This hill-top is exactly as though some such welter of water had suddenly become mud. It is all heaped and tossed and tumbled as though the earth there had been a cross-sea. In one place some great earth wave of a trench has been bitten into and beaten back and turned blind into an eddy by great pits and chasms and running heaps. Then in another place where the crown of the work once reared itself aloft over the hill, the heaps of mud are all blurred and pounded together, so that there is no design, no trace, no visible plan of any fortress, only a mess of mud, bedevilled and bewildered. All this mess of heaps and hillocks is strong and filthied over with broken bodies and ruined gear. There is nothing whole, nor alive, nor clean, in all its extent; it is a place of ruin and death, blown and blasted out of any likeness to any work of man, and so smashed that there is no shelter on it, save for the one master-gunner in his box. On all that desolate hill our fire fell like rain for days and nights and weeks, till the watchers in our line could see no hill at all, but a great, vague, wreathing devil of darkness in which little sudden fires winked and glimmered and disappeared.

That was written in 1917, but the years did not weaken Masefield's sense of outrage on nature and man, nor limit his human concerns to the merely topical. In a letter to Miss Napier-Smith, in 1957, he mentions Cervantes.

It is strange: I do not feel the greatness of the plots and the power of the telling, as formerly, when they laid me low: but I feel more and more the greatness of the man and power of his spirit: And the privilege and also, perhaps, a little of the terror, of being such a one.

Perhaps the terror is that of being brought into that time with him, when all men had seen men and women burned, when pestilences walked by noonday, and every alley had its murder and every parish its gallows.

John Masefield never ran away to sea, as legend used to have it. Dreams of becoming painter or writer wilted before Aunt Kate's stern outlook, and, at the age of 13, after a brief sojourn at Warwick Grammar School, he was, in 1891, a cadet on the *Conway*, the Merchant Navy training ship in the Mersey.

In an age of ever-encroaching steam, and when ships, without radio, could be abruptly lost with all hands, the *Conway*'s routine, like herself, was outdated, even anachronistic. Masefield appreciated more the discipline, the newness, the liveliness of the Mersey with its long lines of steamers and sailing ships, the latter 'in their last, strange, beautiful perfection.' Four-masters, grain-bearing barques, schooners, brigantines, red-sailed barges, yawls, ketches, polaccas. He told, and heard, ghost stories; absorbed manifold human types, the lore and songs of ships; realised the daily transformations of water and sky: he also saw the feuds and violence, the unexpected generosities and goodwill. The ship was a microcosm: passion, obsession, tyranny and hazard, danger and rescue, concentrated within several hundred feet of plank and canvas, a life of shovings and kickings, obscenities, painful practical jokes, 'roastings', pacing and scrubbing decks of African oak, 'white as a hound's tooth', learning to pass the tucks of an eye-splice, to tack ship, to go aloft to the tops.

I knew now that the sails were sheeted home and hoisted; and looked superb, when set; but that just as they were beginning to send the ship ahead, to ease her moorings a little, an order sent us all to the braces. 'Weather topsail braces,' came the order. I did not know what

they did nor where they were, but I was hurried aft to their cleat;
again we hauled; and had hardly finished, before some other devilry
had begun; reefs had to come in; I had to hop to the reef tackles. I had
some glimpses of wonders aloft, devil-may-care men at the yardarms,
with one foot free, outside the yards, handling the ear-rings like the
leading seamen they were. Orders were shouted about dog's lugs, and
to lay in: and then to me, not to stare aloft but put my weight on the
halliards. We had scarcely got the sail rehoisted, when more reefs had
to come in; then the sails were furled; most of the men came down
from aloft; and there came a minute during which ropes were coiled
up or down, so as to leave a clear deck.

Such adventures are now drained from the European experience, even
consciousness, but they gave rewards. He added later:

I have told of my joy in being aloft. That heart would have been dead
indeed who could not find beauty in the River, at all seasons, at all
states, the River was beautiful. At dead low water, when great
sandbanks were laid bare, to draw multitudes of gulls; in calm, when
the ships stood still above their shadows; in storm, when the ferries
beat by, shipping sprays, and at full flood when shipping put out and
came in, the River was a wonder to me. Sometimes, as I sat aloft in the
cross-trees, in those early days, I thought how marvellous it was, to
have this ever-changing miracle about me, with mountains, smoky,
glittering cities, the clang of hammers, the roar and hoot of sirens; the
miles of docks, the ships and attendant ships, all there for me,
seemingly only noticed by me, everybody else seemed to be used to it
by this time, or to have other things to do.

*New Chum*

In *Dauber*, experience, description, become tauter:

Which three will furl their sail first and come down?
Out to the yard-arm for the leech goes one,
His hair blown flagwise from a hatless crown,
His hands at work like fever to be done.
Out of the gale a fiercer fury spun.
The three sails leapt together, yanking high,
Like talons darting up to clutch the sky.

To a more sophisticated generation, the contrasts in all stages of Masefield's work may seem simple, though they were stark enough. Still in his teens he knew that there might await him San Francisco, the old, roaring Barbary Coast, where seamen 'were drugged, slung-shotted, and sold out at forty dollars a head,' and, on Liverpool quaysides, he would see the crimps, dreadful predators of both sexes or neither, awaiting men to emerge from ships with perhaps a year's pay in their pockets, to tempt and rob them.

Masefield never 'served before the mast', in the fo'c's'le, with the regular crew, but below deck with fellow apprentices. His sea career was brief, though it pervades his work. He watched much, and remembered more; tales, techniques, slanting seas and clouds, routines:

Spunyarn, spunyarn, with one to turn the crank,
And one to slather the spunyarn, and one to knot the hank;
It's an easy job for a summer watch, and a pleasant job enough,
To twist the tarry lengths of cloth to shapely sailor stuff.

Life is nothing but spunyarn on a winch in need of oil,
Little enough is twined and spun but fever-fret and moil.
I have travelled on land and sea, and all that I have found
Are these poor songs to brace the arms that help the winches
    round.'

'Spun yarn' (1902)

He sailed, in 1894, on the four-masted barque *Gilcruix*, for Chile, and, like Dauber, rounded the Horn and went aloft in towering gales and toppling seas. His companions, as for Dauber, proved brutally coarse, art-hating, unsympathetic. Like Nelson, like George V, 'the Sailor King', he was endlessly seasick. On shore, ill and exhausted, tubercular, almost broken by the unnerving voyage, by horror, danger, illness, he was hospitalised, and discharged. From such an unromantic beginning, the romancer struggled home, only to be accused of gutlessness and failure. His desire to write was probably reinforced by this harsh subject-matter, but, forced back to sea in 1895, he sailed again across the Atlantic, and, shedding any last illusions, deserted ship for ever, confessing in 1953 that, as a sailor, he was never 'worth a cent', but loved ships, 'in a way'. Years later, he still welcomed the chance to climb a rigging.

He had accumulated a trove of stories, memories, images, cruel, grotesque and comic: a huge nautical vocabulary, experience of himself and others under extremes, swift but unforgettable encounters with man and nature, a heap of old songs.

> Don't put your feet in the port wine, Joe,
> There's plenty of stale old beer.

He had already read Marryat, Dana, Ballantyne, but not Chaucer, Malory, Melville. Like most of us – one remembers Graham Greene's evocative essay on his early reading, *The Lost Childhood* – he remained in lifelong communication with his first books. At fifteen 'I had never read *Huck Finn*, but I must have read it at least once in every year since then, as I have read *Peter Simple*, *Treasure Island* and *Frank Mildmay, Naval Lieutenant*. I cannot read them today without some ghost of the old original joy coming back to me, in a memory of the scene, the old orlop deck, with the lines of chests, some men sitting in them, others changing clothes, or hanging around some whistler or fiddler, or playing the fool in some way, or tormenting a new chum who was ass enough to mind, or netting, or perhaps doing a neat job in seamanship, strop, point or becket, or mending a trouser crutch, or only passing by calling, 'Top, please.' (1944)

With £1 in his pocket, at seventeen, he was jobless, homeless, disowned by aunt and uncle, possibly ruined in health. All that remained was a dogged, untutored concern for life and an imperturbable courage.

Like Maxim Gorky, Dickens, H. G. Wells, and his friend Bernard Shaw, Masefield did not come from a bookish home, and was to find that 'the university of life' recompensed his lack of degrees and diplomas.

> I have seen flowers come in stony places
> And kind things done by men with ugly faces,
> And the gold cup won by the worst horse at the races,
> So I trust, too.
>
> poem from *Odtaa*

He revelled in old New York and its rural environs. 'Beauty all around me, leisure, such as I had not thought possible, books so cheap that I could have a library of them, and a great, vivid, romantic Capital City only half an hour away'. He wandered the Battery, South Street, West Street, and 'in places you could walk under jibbooms and figureheads, and trip over hausers.' (*In The Mill*, 1941). The sight of a single mast could absorb him for hours. There were music halls, sunset on the Palisades, woods made golden by Fall, the brisk theatre of the streets; 153rd Street ended in ancient woodlands the Indians had known. In Greenwich Village he worked and lived alongside men with a knife in their boots; one told him that his acquaintances in Yonkers included ten murderers. Discovery of Irish and American history widened his sympathies, imagination, curiosity.

He was, in turn, vagrant, gardener, bar-tender, dogsbody in a dubious hotel, a dynamiter of rocks, farm hand – looking back with regret to 'the exquisite days, the poultry, the cattle, the magnificent ploughing-oxen, and the exhileration of the earth.' He drudged in a bakery and in a livery-stable. More substantially, he worked in a Yonkers carpet mill.

> Deep in myself was a longing to be a writer; but this longing was very deeply buried, under the more immediate longing to read and read, and not to be so ignorant; I wanted to know all that men had thought and done.

And, with a few books of poetry now within him:

> I meant to get into poetry somehow before the mill got me. Very likely I wasn't good enough for poetry, but the extraordinary beauty of that promised land was enough to call out all my hope and all my courage.

He bought a 75 cents Chaucer:

> On that Sunday afternoon, after lunch, I decided not to walk but to read Chaucer. It was a hot, beautiful day, and it seemed a pity to go into the woods while there were still so many mosquitoes. I stretched myself on my bed, and began to read 'The Parliament of Fowles'; and with the first lines entered into a world of poetry until then unknown to me.
>
> Many years before, when I was still a little child, I had had delight, from the early poems of Milton; Latterly I had had delight from 'The Piper of Arll'. Now I tasted something deeper; I was taken into

another world, unlike this in its excitement and beauty; it was a new experience. It seemed to me, that evening, that very likely there was no limit to the world opened by such poetry; it seemed boundless in liberty, inexhaustible in riches, deathless in beauty, eternal in delight.

*In The Mill*

Chaucer remained inexhaustible, his descriptive tones, love of nature, grasp of human oddity. In a letter, 1956, Masefield wrote of the Knight's Tale that Chaucer 'is at his freshest and loveliest in it, and writes with poetry, from poetry, not as a translator at all, but as a man who had been in April and meant to bring April to England, and then did it, dew and primroses, and wild daffodils and young men in love with womanhood.'

Thenceforward he read insatiably: Malory, the Romantics, Villon, Rossetti, Hardy, Swinburne. From these he realised that life is brief and entails discovery of the laws of one's being. All people have interesting lives but too few give proof of it. For him, it was not carpet-making nor bottle-washing, not even science and doctoring, that was essential, but to follow poetry, even if he died for it. Initially, he was in some danger of doing just that. Shelley led for a time, to vegetarianism and total abstinence, again wrecking his health. But he recovered, read on: Pope and the Augustans, Dumas, Sterne, Molière, Langland, Melville, the Sagas, myths and Ballads . . . Baudelaire, Johnson, Maupassant, Rabelais, Voltaire, Blake, Housman, Ronsard, Crabbe . . . Smollett, 'who saw a frightful thing (the Cartagena Campaign), and said that it was frightful.' He was to rate Aeschylus's *Agammemnon* the greatest of all plays, revered Herman Melville, rated Verlaine a lively, sentimental thug; he always disliked Wilde and most of Byron, respected Ben Jonson, without much love, and, rather surprisingly, judged Fletcher 'the nearest to me in all whom I read'. He admired Ruskin, and more so, William Morris, whom he came to believe the one sensible man of the century. Much later, he wept when Morris' daughter told him that he always reminded her of her father. Morris' verse gave him 'particular thrills and special lurings into special ways', but he lived to appreciate Rilke, Lorca, W. H. Auden. *Macbeth* remained his favourite Shakespeare. By the time he returned to London in 1897, even more than Morris and Rossetti, he admired W. B. Yeats. He never ceased: Alain-Fournier, Hugo, Borrow, Fielding, Browning, du Maurier, Tolstoy, Hazlitt, Stevenson, Disraeli . . . He began teaching himself French, examined Buddhism, fostering the hope, then the need, finally the determination to write, and began some verses, undeterred by discouragement.

His workaday backgrounds made him unlikely to write much in the somewhat thin, etiolated manner of London and Dublin *fin de siècle* petty masters. Though the myths of Arthur, Ossian, Tristan and Troy were permanently in his imagination, they were less often motifs for dream and etherealisation than narratives of action, quest and moral dilemmas. L. A. G. Strong was to assert that he transferred poetic narrative from romance to contemporary life.

In England, now married, he worked as a City clerk, a bank clerk, a journalist, a columnist on the Manchester Guardian. For a time he lived in Bloomsbury, though his work remains wholly at odds with the aura associated with that name.

His imagination and prospects magnified. In London he saw much of Yeats, who encouraged his writing, and at whose home he met Tagore, Laurence Binyon, Synge and Ezra Pound. He was befriended, then published, by the influential patron, Eddie Marsh, private secretary to Winston Churchill. His early feelings for painting expanded. First seen in the Walker Galleries, Liverpool, the Pre-Raphaelites enthralled him: then Velasquez, Turner, Breughel. He always loved the theatre and, years later, he founded the Hill Players and with his wife and daughter staged Shakespeare, Bunyan, Anatole France, Yeats, Molière, Greek tragedies, Jonson, his own versions of Racine and much else. Fokine's ballets delighted him. He enjoyed Chopin, Berlioz, Holst, with whom he collaborated in his play, *The Coming of Christ*. Characteristically, in old age, he wrote to Geoffrey Bush, 'I am ignorant of music and of so many other matters.'

Deeper absorbtion in the arts, however, never withdrew him from popular life, with its quirks and oddities, its unexpected details. He had heard the favourite chanteuse, Yvette Guilbert, and saw Adah Menken, Henry Irving, William Morris, Lillie Langtry. He spoke with a man who had met Napoleon, with another who had known Wellington, with an old lady whose life had been changed by hearing Dickens read. He had sat behind Jenny Lind in church, he saw a leper selling pigs' trotters outside Charing Cross station and opened a door for W. G. Grace. He missed a chance of meeting Lenin, then researching for *Materialism and Empiro-Criticism*, not a title to inspire a young romantic. Masefield wrote to Florence Lamont in 1964:

I often saw him in the British Museum Reading Room . . . and always said to myself 'I wonder who that extraordinary man is,' for anyone must have seen that he was an extra-ordinary man certain to make a mark on the wall. Once, as I was leaving the room, I saw that he was just behind me, so that I held the door open for him till he had passed. He smiled at me and muttered some words of thanks, and that was the nearest I ever got to him.

He wrote too a justly more celebrated description of Yeats:

When greeting or parting with a friend, he stood very erect and lifted his right hand above his head. This gesture of his he kept until the last time I saw him. It was a strangely beautiful gesture; the man himself; unearthly and beautiful, with a winning, and witty charm unequalled in our time.

*A Book of Both Sorts* (1947)

By 1914, Masefield was established, famous on both sides of the Atlantic. The work I shall detail a little later. On the outbreak of war, at 36, he volunteered for active service but, though placed on the reserve of officers, was rejected for health reasons. He did not, on that account, sit at home, write poetry and count his royalties.

Many writers were officially employed on war-service, on vaguely defined 'missions', in Intelligence, as propagandists, and in the Medical Services. They included A. E. W. Mason, Galsworthy, Ivor Novello, Harley Granville-Barker, Frederick Niven, Somerset Maugham, Compton Mackenzie, Hugh Walpole, John Buchan, Ian Hay, Arthur Ransome, Arnold Bennett, Kipling, E. M. Forster and Masefield himself. Ford Madox Ford wrote two propaganda books, before enlisting. H. G. Wells, usually free-lancing, wrote many noisy articles and pamphlets on the war, its conduct, motives, its many scandals and the world it should produce. Some of these he collected, in a book to which he gave a title that became famous, *The War that Will End War*.

In February, 1915, Masefield was in France as a British Red Cross orderly, serving French wounded. He had many shocks, which the letters reveal. Not the least involved women. He normally regarded women as remote, mysterious, superior, and once committed himself to a view, now fiercely discredited: 'One only sees the good things through women. Our hearts are "stables for beasts" and women bear the Christ there.' His correspondent, the subtle, Ibsenite actress and writer, Elizabeth Robins, must have smiled rather grimly at this, and it will be seen that the matrons, nurses, and certain hostesses he met in France and America, scarcely sustained this role.

He was back on leave in April, and, shocked by his experience, haunted by dreadful wounds and apparent official unconcern, planned to create a mobile field hospital operating much closer to the Front. In July, he was making journeys of inspection of French military hospitals, and his horror, anger, pity and incredulity increased. The French bureaucracy appeared unable to see men as more than 'cases'. His personal scheme never materialised, but in August he was back with the Red Cross at Gallipoli, working in a nautical ambulance service, with funds raised by himself. This experience, he afterwards told Mrs Lamont, 'made me very old'.

Out of this came his prose account, *Gallipoli* (1916). This was written partly as propaganda, notably for America, still neutral, but more than that impelled him. Poet and humanitarian were involved with the propagandist. His loathing of cruelty and waste and distortion, his feeling for courage and endurance, needed expression throughout his life, nowhere more urgent than in his war-time writings.

> They came from safety of their own free will
> To lay their young men's beauty, strong men's powers
> Under the hard roots of the foreign flowers
> Having beheld the Narrows from the Hill.

The Dardanelles campaign, historically still disputable, still disputed, he considered 'not as a tragedy, nor as a mistake, but as a great human effort, which came more than once, very near to triumph, achieved the impossible many times, and failed in the end . . . To myself, this failure is the second grand event of the war; the first was Belgium's answer to the German ultimatum.'

Masefield's grasp of the strategic and logistical problems was firm: the poet emerged on behalf of those who suffered and died, in the interpolations from *The Song of Roland*, and in descriptions of ships and landscapes. Censorship, and the war-time situation forbade plain speaking about official shortcomings and mistakes, however Masefield may have assessed them.

This book had followed a lecture tour in America, from January to July, 1916, ostensibly literary, but, more practically, to win support for the Allies and explain such setbacks or defeats as Gallipoli. His biographer, Constance Babington Smith, writes:

> Masefield's first American tour had unexpected results that deter-mined the course of his life for the next three years. Before it his war service had been practical rather than intellectual; after it he was to serve primarily as a writer, a recorder of the heroism of others. On his return to America in March 1916 he submitted a formal report to the Foreign Office in which he stressed that during his tour he had been persistently questioned (by hecklers who had obviously been under the influence of enemy propaganda) about the failure of the Dardanelles campaign. Might he not write an article which would dispose of the enemy's lies?
>
> *John Masefield* (1978)

The article became a book and, though it has scarcely proved to be the last word on Gallipoli, not least among Anzacs, 'the bewildered anger that had been seething in Britain over the whole episode was evidently mollified by Masefield's romanticism.' A reviewer wrote, 'there were times when, as I read, the sweat of pity and grief stood upon my face.' I quote the final page.

> 'Still,' our enemies say, 'you did not win the Peninsular.' We did not; and some day, when truth will walk clear-eyed, it will be known why we did not. Until then, let our enemies say this: 'They did not win, but they came across three thousand miles of sea, a little army without reserves and short of munitions, a band of brothers, not half of them half-trained, and nearly all of them new to war. They came to what we said was an impregnable fort, on which our veterans of war and massacre had laboured for two months, and by sheer naked manhood they beat us, and drove us out of it. Then rallying, but without reserves, they beat us again, and drove us farther; then rallying once more, but still without reserves, they beat us again, this time to our knees. Then, had they had reserves, they would have conquered, but by God's pity they had none. Then, after a lapse of time, when we were men again, they had reserves, and they hit us a staggering blow, which needed but a push to end us, but God again had pity. After that our God was indeed pitiful, for England made no further thrust, and they went away.'

Even so was wisdom proven blind,
So courage failed, so strength was chained;
Even so the gods, whose seeing mind
Is not as ours, ordained.

Twenty-five years later, in the masterly *The Nine Days Wonder*, Masefield wrote again of a British defeat, doing for the men at Dunkirk something, perhaps more, of what he had for their fathers at Gallipoli, a very proper work for a laureate.

He returned to France, in August 1916, on a suggestion of Sir Gilbert Parker, of Propaganda and Intelligence, that he should gather information about America's voluntary aid to the Allies: field ambulances, relief-units and hospitals. He was profoundly concerned with Anglo-American relations, and believed that the two peoples could jointly restore civilisation. He accompanied the American Ambulance Field Service to Verdun, where fighting continued, though the worst of that atrocious massacre was over. In general he was disappointed with the Americans despite their technical expertise, the exceptions being the volunteers in the field. In October, Lord Esher, chief of British Military Intelligence in France, proposed he write a book on the Somme campaign, and by the 17th he was on that river, deafened by the guns, and thought the battle 'the biggest thing that England has ever been engaged in.' He remained in France until June 1917, writing *The Old Front Line* (1917) as a preliminary to *The Battle of the Somme* (1919). Censorship and withholding of documents considerably curtailed the scope and design of both, making them personal impressions rather than coded history. The confusion of tactics, divergencies of personality and military outlook of the leading generals and politicians, and the indadequate preliminary survey of the terrain, Masefield could scarcely have known or been allowed to know. The letters, like the books, display his acute observation of significant details, his compassion, contempt and indignation. Even he could find small romance in the agonies of the Western Front, though in May, he wrote to Agnes Fry:

Here on this field there are perhaps seventeen or eighteen largish villages without inhabitants. Each village is utterly ruined and smashed and flung about and gouged into great holes without any living soul within a mile of it, and when you go into these places and find yourself the only person there in the midst of the desolation, with perhaps some tulips or currant bushes, green or in flower, in some ruined garden beside you, and some bent Christ in the church flung sideways by a shell, you get a feeling, not of horror, but almost of romance, as though any strange thing might happen or be discovered, and as though there were a kind of soul in it, trying to speak.

He could have made a fine poem from this inset of the Somme Battle:

Once in a lull of the firing a woman appeared upon the enemy parapet & started to walk along it. Our men held their fire & watched her. She walked steadily along the whole front of the Schwaben & then jumped down into her trench. Many thought at the time that she was a man masquerading for a bet; but long afterwards when our men took the Schwaben, they found her lying in the ruins, dead. They buried her there, upon the top of the hill. God alone knows what she was doing there.

*The Old Front Line*

He undertook a second American tour in January 1918. The initial, set-piece lectures were disappointing, but later he very successfully gave impromptu talks at army camps, to huge and enthusiastic audiences of young men. To reach youth, with his verses and conversation, always gratified him.

However saturated with the past, it is probably obvious that Masefield was no escapist recluse, and these letters show his resentment at irresponsible nationalism and inhuman negligence. He admired Jack Dempsey and W. G. Grace, appreciated Havelock Ellis, studied de Sade. 'Men trample women's rights at will,' he wrote, 1910, the year he published *My Faith in Women's Suffrage*. He wrote on prostitution, social injustice, war-time landworkers, colonial agriculture, and concerned himself with the repair of the bells of St Katherine's, Ledbury, the rigging of model ships – and the sufferings of men in world wars. Novels like *Odtaa* ('One Damn thing after Another'), *Sard Harker*, *The Taking of the Gry*, derive from terrorist Latin-American despotisms. His concern with the tragedies of Troy, Tristan, Arthur, did not prevent him from protesting at the notorious judicial injustice to the nine Scotsborough blacks, in Alabama in 1932. He visited Nazi Germany several times, 'short spells in hell'. He lectured in Scandinavia, Finland, Australia, Greece, Turkey and often in America, where he recited his ode for Harvard's tercentenary in 1936. Like D. H.

Lawrence, he lamented the developing ugliness and coarseness and standardisation of life, particularly after the Great War, and did what he could, as writer and public figure, to amend it, though not by violence. In his most debated poem, the parson had declared:

> . . . keep the existing social state;
> I quite agree it's out of date,
> One does too much, another shirks,
> Unjust, I grant; but still . . . it works.
> *The Everlasting Mercy*

He was more prone to spontaneous anger than sustained loyalty to dogmas, sects or parties. William Morris moved him, the Webbs did not.

> Alas, I am not an improving person. I have never improved anybody, not even the man I once lent 6 dollars to and he didn't pay, for he spent it all on drink and died soon afterwards.
> *Letters to Reyna*

He had his own ways. After being burgled, he considered that the thieves' prison sentence would only do them harm. Questions of right and wrong are prominent in his work, though he dispenses with Kipling's tendency to lecture, teach and moralise. The comment is in the power of the mood, the direction of the story and its people:

> You starve his soul till it's rapscallion,
> Then blame his flesh for being stallion.
> You send your wife around to paint
> The golden glories of 'restraint'.
> *The Everlasting Mercy*

He would not have written Kipling's 'Then who should come to tuck him up but his Mother! And she sat down on the bed, and they talked for a long time, as mother and son should, if there is to be any future for our empire.'

He disliked everyday politics. A government department was 'a skunkery'. Platforms, manifestoes, utopianisms, factional vendettas – all were trivial beside the sufferings in Flanders and on the seas, the lacerations inflicted both by the crook and the idealist. He did believe in the Monarchy, not as snob but seeing it as a link between people and authority, by-passing politicians, and undeniably rooted deep in popu-

lar tradition. He would not have supported violent changes in England.
He noted, in a letter to his wife, 28 November 1918, 'a lot of unrest in
Glasgow, of a syndicalist kind, aiming at ending the industrial system as
a whole. It is supposed to be mainly an Irish movement, but not wholly.
There is a good deal of blue funk about it.'
The parson continues:

> States are not made, nor patched; they grow,
> Grow slowly through centuries of pain
> And grow correctly in the main,
> But only grow by certain laws
> Of certain bits in certain jaws.

Of another parson, in *Reynard the Fox*, he wrote:

> He had a mighty voice to preach,
> Though indolent in other matters,
> He let his children go in tatters.

Romanticism could, nevertheless, distort his judgement. That Edward
VIII was 'the only King we have had who felt for the poor and spent
hours of every day with the down-and-outs', would have surprised the
down-and-outs, and not all would agree that Wallis Simpson was 'a
lovely woman'.

He despised the Anglican hierarchy. He possessed religious temperament, but he was more a seeker, the pilgrim on quest, than a pledged
believer. Christian references and images abound in his work, but
probably emerge more from their context than from his own convictions. He had Buddhist leanings.

> Desire, longing for life, and ignorance,
> Dropped from my mind like rags; I was set free,
> I knew that I need never live again,
> Save as a mind that with undying Peace
> Moves among mortals in their misery
> Showing a way from darkness into light.
>
> *Gautama the Enlightened* (1941)

Judith Masefield wrote, 'He told me he did believe in a future life, and
was convinced that one returns to earth for other incarnations in flesh.
He often told me this and also that he loved the Buddhist teachings, and

found them most acceptable.' Constance Babington Smith refers to his 'ruminations and spiritual gropings'. In the Sonnets he wonders:

> Is this green earth of many-peopled pain
> Part of a life, a cell within a brain.

Masefield himself wrote in 1954, 'In my own belief, in this life we meet and are helped or hurt by all that we have helped or hurt in other human lives, and that we shall all meet again until we touch perfection.' (*Letters of John Masefield to Florence Lamont*, edited by Corliss Lamont, 1979)

He also wrote, 'Men say that this or that is the enemy of life; I say that Death is the enemy; and he has many friends among men, in all those authorities in whom a debased sense of life is linked with temporary power.'

He had written in 1917, in another letter to Florence Lamont, 'Prayer, which is intense thought mixed with feeling, is the only power. That was what Christ meant when he said that faith moves mountains; faith is imagination, it is the nature of energy, of the Sun, of God himself.'

This is far from the Victorian Sundays and strict observances of his childhood, which he must have recalled in *The Everlasting Mercy*:

> You cogwheels in a stopped machine,
> You hearts of snakes, and brains of pigeons
> You dead devout of dead religions,
> You offspring of the hen and ass,
> By Pilate ruled, and Caiaphas.

Masefield, despite reservations about institutions, accepted public honours: honorary doctorates, surely well-earned, from Oxford, Cambridge, Wales, Aberdeen, Glasgow, Liverpool, St Andrews, Yale and Harvard; membership of the American Academy of Arts and Letters; President of the Society of Authors, as Tennyson and Hardy had been before him; first President of the National Book League. He accepted the Order of Merit, as had other writers including Galsworthy, C. V. Wedgewood, J. B. Priestley and T. S. Eliot. Bernard Shaw allegedly refused it, protesting that people would define it as 'Old Man'.

Appointed Poet Laureate in 1930, by Ramsay MacDonald and George V (who enjoyed his poems), he held the office until his death, the sixteenth since Dryden. His predecessor, Robert Bridges, had given the position dignity, though without the state poems which had so often trivialised it, in the manner of the eighteenth-century Mr Eusden:

Hail, mighty GEORGE! Auspicious smiles thy reign,
Thee long we wish'd, Thee at last we gain.
Thy hoary Prudency in green years began,
And the bold Infant stretch'd at once to Man.
How oft Transported, the great Ernest smil'd
With the presages of his greater child.

Masefield's offerings, modestly enclosing a stamped envelope in case of rejection by *The Times*, are conscientious rather than inspired, though his tribute to the murdered President Kennedy was much appreciated. But he also saw the office as the chance to exercise pressure and contact influential authorities on behalf of authors, theatres and libraries, notably the London Library. He involved himself with the Royal Academy of Dramatic Art, and successfully proposed the King's Gold Medal for Poetry, which he first awarded to Lawrence Whistler. He encouraged Robert Graves, rated W. H. Auden (who also gained the medal) as 'a man of genius'. He tried to help the young unemployed and, as he had at his Oxford Recitations (annual verse-speaking competitions) in 1923–29, wanted to break down barriers: barriers between the arts; between classes; between actor and audience; reader and author. He pulled strings, judged at verse-speaking festivals, lectured, recited and organised, almost to his death. Though no longer in the literary forefront, he remained a celebrity. His views of war, society and history, were more realistic than those of Yeats: his experiences of hardship and gradual acceptance, and his feeling for a thousand years of British events, enabled him to identify with popular feelings in national crises, rejoicings, bereavements. He had a vision of what the land had once been, and could be again, if feelings for beauty, craft and community could be recovered. His verse had always had some bardic quality, narrating the exploits, drama, tragedies, vigilance and simplicity, of the mythical heroes and heroines. His message disdained hierarchy, and addressed the wider public.

His poems of the Second World War, in *A Generation Risen* (1943), ignored by modern anthologists, show profounder understanding of the fighting men than some more fashionable poets showed in the Spanish Civil War, which they lamented, mostly from off-stage. They lose little compared to those of the younger men who fought the Nazis. Of *The Nine Days Wonder*, Marjorie Fisher writes:

> It is a short piece, utterly simple, every word considered and inevitable. It stirs a more reflective spirit than *Gallipoli*, which was a trumpet call to the arms of the spirit. *The Nine Days Wonder* speaks of weariness and anxiety with the voice of one who has known these feelings himself, who between the wars had hoped for peace to build a civilisation worthy of man, but it speaks too of the heroism of man.'

*John Masefield* (1963)

Personal virtue seldom induces major writing, and many – perhaps most – major writers have been scoundrels, though Chekhov, Shaw and Whitman, might seem to disprove this. 'Beautiful feelings,' André Gide wrote, 'make bad art.'

With whatever implications, Masefield was virtuous. In America, he had youthful ambitions to work amongst lepers, to be a doctor and 'lead a life useful to others', to combat yellow-fever, scourge of sailors, and discover 'its unseen, small but million-murdering cause'. Edward Thomas (1909) thought him 'a wonderful man', and, at Westminster Abbey, in 1967, Robert Graves spoke:

> Many of us forget how, at an otherwise dark period, the fierce flame of poetry had truly burned in him, or that he never lost what is the supreme poetic quality: an unselfish love for his fellow men. But I would never forget the days when I was a sixteen-year-old rebel and he my hero.

He was, Graves recalled, 'generous, courageous, unassuming, over-sensitive'.

He always enjoyed the young, was happy chatting with American students, mixing with, and tending, the soldiers in France, and entertaining Oxford undergraduates. He much admired the poetry of Charles Hamilton Sorley, an early victim of the Great War, and in 1922 he joined with Hardy and de la Mare in securing a pension for Charlotte Mew. In a letter to Margaret Bridges from France in 1917, he wrote:

> I have been seeing a lot of Anzacs up near the line and they are a fine lot of men, easily the finest men fighting on this front, and by much

the cleverest and most daring fighters. They are handsome, brave and clever and most beautiful on horses; you can tell them by their riding half a mile away. It is the kind of life they lead that makes such men. They are the likest men to sailors in their manliness, and much better than sailors in their generosity and niceness of mind.

This has an outmoded flavour, harking back to the poet's untutored, adventurous youth at sea, tramping an alien land, and 'in the mill', a useful pun, but those who sneer are the more grossly ignorant and unimaginative. In these days of demonstration, protest, youthful revolt, there is no disgrace in John Masefield grieving for savage, reckless destruction of youth, not least of his own son.

Dr Johnson, whom he admired, once stated that it is the business of the wise man to be happy, and Masefield himself liked to say that the days that make us happy make us wise. I feel that Masefield was a wise man but, to repeat Graves, was perhaps too sensitive to be consistently happy. Yet he experienced, and spread, rare intensity of happiness, and, of Graves himself, wrote, 'He has mirth, and I don't believe that people grow very far without mirth.' Others remarked on the quiet melancholy of his face, but he had humour, though, as W. S. Gilbert said of Shakespeare's, it was not 'rollicking'. Masefield referred to 'the fun and beauty' of Shakespeare. He relished, in America, his train stopping 'at a very matter-of-fact town called Mystic, with a hearse drawn up on the platform'. At the solemn lunch following the Oxford award of his honorary doctorate, he wrote:

With squeaky wit the light improper verse
Falls on the heavy lunch and makes it worse.

Having people to breakfast, he reflected, seems like smothering the day in its cradle. Which Belloc would have appreciated. Niagara Falls, he informed his wife, 'does, on the whole, convey a general impression of dampness.'

'Without curiosity,' reiterated Ezra Pound, one of his modernist supplanters, 'there can be no literature.' Masefield's curiosity never abated. In his last illness, Judith records:

When his leg got bad, the doctor said he must rest, but of course he didn't, and it grew agonisingly painful. The surgeon said he must have it off, or die. He said, 'I'll die,' and did. As he lay dying, he used to ask me to tell him about every archaeological discovery that had been made . . . A Greek chariot had just been found in a Greek lake. 'Were the axle trees of bronze or of cast iron?' he asked me, and to my shame I did not know. These were his last words to me.

John Masefield, mostly remembered as a poet, was actually an all-round man-of-letters, itself a title almost extinct. He wrote some hundred books, forty-five of them being verse.

> What am I, Life? A thing of watery salt
> Held in cohesion by unresting cells,
> Which work they know not why, which never halt,
> Myself unwitting where their master dwells?
>                     from *Lollingdon Downs*

The question marks are significant. He was always a questioner, the tentative expression in many pictures of him is not to be seen on his famous contemporaries, Shaw, Wells, Belloc, Russell, Yeats. One autobiography he called *Wonderings* (1943), aptly punning, for to him the world was filled with wonder and his own mind was prone not to dogmatise but to wonder. Indeed Miss Spark, probably perceptively, calls his expression that of wonder.

'I am no great shakes as a writer', he reflected in 1948. Another autobiography, typically, is entitled *So Long to Learn* (1952), reminiscent of Chaucer's 'The Lyfe so shorte, the crafte so long to lerne.' At 86, addressing the National Book League, he mentioned that he was still writing and hoped some day to write better. In 1953, he wrote to Audrey Napier-Smith, 'To the Victorian, like myself, modern verse is without any inner life; to which the modern writer retorts that my own verse is without any life at all: so there we rather stick.' In 1958, he observed that, of 300,000,000 English readers, three read him and four criticised him.

He was not a 'born writer', and has described his novicehood, imitating others, studying such methods as Rossetti's reading dictionaries to get 'stunning words for poetry'. He had to grapple with convictions of sterility. Success, if it came at all, would come not only from labour but drudgery.

Always a theatre-lover, he wrote on the Elizabethan Theatre and he adapted plays from France, Spain, Norway and Japan. Books on Shakespeare are usually long, and seldom give assurance that the authors have either written for, or trodden on, the stage. Masefield's

*Shakespeare* (1911), which John Wain, a much younger writer found 'full of illumination and wisdom', is very short, but written by a dramatist and producer, with deep experience of many human types. Elsewhere, he advises an actor, for *Macbeth*:

> Let him not play the earlier scenes like a moody traitor, but like Lucifer, star of the morning. Let him not play the later scenes like a hangman who has taken to drink, but like an angel who has fallen.

L. A. G. Strong wrote that Masefield's was 'the best book about Shakespeare which has been written in our time.' (1957)

He wrote on Ruskin, Yeats, Crabbe, Rossetti, Blake, Synge, Chaucer; ballet; the Pilgrim Fathers; a standard work on sea-life in Nelson's time, and much else on ships; he edited Herrick, the Restoration poets, Defoe, Jonson, books by Dampier, Hakluyt; he collected sailors' tales. Including the childrens' books, he wrote 21 novels. He translated from Spanish, Portuguese, French.

His plays were backed by Granville-Barker, *The Tragedy of Nan* appearing at the Court Theatre in a famous Vedrenne-Granville-Barker season, alongside work by Shaw, Galsworthy, Hauptmann, Schnitzler, Maeterlinck, Gilbert Murray, Yeats, and Granville-Barker himself. Shaw, whose early work he disliked, rated Masefield, around 1909, as the best of the younger dramatists, and the younger man found the formidable Irishman 'of an overwhelming and shattering generosity'.

Poetic drama was more practised than it is today. Tennyson, Beddoes, Hardy, Yeats, Gordon Bottomley, Stephen Philips, Binyon, Drinkwater, Isaac Rosenberg, wrote them, as did Masefield – though he felt that he never really mastered the stage. In 1928, seven years before T. S. Eliot's *Murder in the Cathedral*, his verse play *The Coming of Christ* was performed in Canterbury Cathedral, and E. M. Forster informed Eddie Marsh that it was 'wonderful, unquestionably great, there's nothing else one wants to say.'

After the Great War Masefield was experimenting more vigorously in his plays than in his poems, though his efforts were largely confined to his private theatre at Boar's Hill. He attempted to adapt Japanese dramatic techniques; wrote *Easter* for singers; wished for a drama combining the arts of dance, mime, speaking. He used painting and music; prose and verse; the seen and unseen; narrative and implication. His *The Trial of Jesus* had to be produced privately, it being then forbidden to depict Christ on the stage.

In 1966, Corliss Lamont's (Florence Lamont's son) suggestion that Masefield's sonnet against Determinism indicated that he was 'something of a philosopher,' elicited the reply, 'I am sorry to have to tell you that I am a very ignorant man and do not know what men mean when they talk philosophy. I am a storyteller, and am always drawn to narrative, seldom to drama or to pure thought. Now and again I have written a song or two, but my fancy is for stories.' Elsewhere he admitted, 'I just see, or fail to see.' Stories of racing clippers, of men working the mizzen 160 feet above a swaying deck, of the obsessions, impulses and injustices of youth; Arthurian romance, Chaucerian anecdote, squalid rural dramas, and national tragedies: he drew on his childhood for tales, dreams and reality, test and quest, initiation and discovery, suffering and redemption; on the old legends from countrysides stored with neolithic flints, Celtic torques and weapons, Roman coins, immemorial secrets. 'Always remember that a strong writer makes the fantastic real. A weak writer makes the real fantastic.' Like Saki, he could make a talking cat plausible, even ordinary; like Andersen and Kipling, he could make ships speak and kitchen tools move and have adventures; like T. H. White he recounted multiple magic transformations within a serious human theme.

In his days of fame he travelled at home and abroad telling stories and reciting verse, like a mediaeval goliard, and was one of the earliest writers to record for the gramophone, beginning with *The Story of Ossian* in 1959. Arnold Bennett, meeting him in 1918, had noted his fine voice with the precise diction of a public speaker. Masefield wrote in 1944, that he preferred narratives 'touched with beauty and strangeness; I like them to go on for a long time, in a river of narrative; and I like tributaries to come in upon the main stream, and exquisite bays and backwaters to open out, into all of which the mind can go exploring after one has learned the main stream.'

His childrens' books, notably *The Midnight Folk* (1927), which later won a huge radio audience, and *The Box of Delights* (1931), remain very readable, despite a few passages probably over-whimsical for modern tastes. They relive the ageless, mingling the natural extravagances and disconcerting directness, the curious yet acute angles of vision, of the child's imagination. Margery Fisher, experienced in modern childrens' reading, calls *A Book of Discoveries* (1910) 'as basic for children as *Bevis* or *Two Little Savages*.' *Victorious Troy* is as vivid as Kingsley's *The Heroes* and Rex Warner's fine reconstructions.

Naomi Mitchison, author of *The Corn King and the Spring Queen*, calls him 'an unsurpassed dealer in words . . . nobody tells an adventure story better than John Masefield,' and claims that in *Sard Harker* one scene 'beats most thrillers into a frazzle'. Books, fortunately, cannot be valued objectively, like livestock, football clubs, scholarship pupils, but *Jim Davis* (1911) must be as engrossing as Conan Doyle's *Rodney Stone*, and *Martin Hyde: The Duke's Messenger* (1910), I rate superior to Doyle's *Micah Clark*. Like Buchan, Rider Haggard, Kipling and Stevenson, Masefield combines adventure with quest, exotic backgrounds, and, perhaps, more serious personal relationships – though for a man who so valued and respected women, he was curiously ill at ease in depicting heroines. Perhaps he respected them too much. He never created a Mowgli, Kim, Sherlock Holmes, Alan Quartermaine or Long John Silver, but Kay Harker, Roger Mansel, Dead Ned, Dauber, Captain Margaret, Justinian and Theodora, are all substantial figures. Amongst them all, right and wrong are at work and expediency is condemned. The intuitive and magical are prominent in his own favourite, *The Midnight Folk* but, always, fate depends less on chance and astral forces, than on individual responses and personal character. His approach was never that of antiquarian or academic. Within physical adventure may be a scientific or spiritual dilemma; a failed marriage may harbour faults difficult to distribute. He can link a nineteenth-century sea adventure, *Victorious Troy* (1935), with the classical epic, as does the eighteenth-century *Live and Kicking Ned* (1939) with a great eighteenth-century city in decline, within an ominous and alien menace. His two Byzantine novels, *Basilissa* (1940) and *Conquer* (1941), concern the perennial nature of power, responsibility, faction, mob allegiances, ideals and religion corrupted, and the necessity of action, preferably right action, from rulers in crisis. Lancelot's single-handed fight on the wall in *Midsummer Night* (1928), taken from legend, is yet a real man set against credible enemies, former friends, each with his distinctive and plausible grudge: it is a passionate mixture of realism and fancy. Miss Fisher sees in the Arthurian *Badon Parchments* (1947) an ironical comment on the Maginot mentality and appeasement; there is also the contrast between heroic reputation and historical fact.

In 1902 Masefield wrote 'Poet I'm not, and never shall be, but one or two of my rhymes have technical merits. Genius I'm not, but I'm pretty sure that I've kept my talents unrusted under pretty tough circumstances, and, by God's gilt-edged clouds, I'll have another smack at the shams and humbugs of this wicked world before I've done.' For many years he did just that, with a flow and ebb of public attention.

Masefield was in spirit a romantic, who outlived romanticism. He refused to make concessions to the new, or was incapable of it. The murderous Great War reinforced his reverence for the classical heritage, the Celtic struggles, the solid achievements of Victorian England which were as patent as the injustices and cruelties. A story teller, he used simple modes, wished to be directly understood by live audiences, eschewed elaborate conceits and metrical devices, and, historically, together with Kipling and Housman, like Tennyson before him and Betjeman afterwards, he briefly restored poetry to a mass readership. Muriel Spark, in her book on Masefield, rightly detaches him from the Georgians, whom he ante-dated, outsoared, having different objectives, larger in scope, often more original in subject and technique, and first-hand experience of more varied life and lives. No Georgian could have written *Dauber*, and *Reynard the Fox* is no more Georgian than *Salt Water Ballads* or *Philip the King*. In poetic dialogue, notably in *Dauber* and *The Everlasting Mercy*, Miss Spark sees Masefield anticipating T. S. Eliot. Strong held that his longer poems 'brought violent gusts of energy to the polite, faintly countrified air of poetry in their day.'

Masefield believed that poetry was best spoken, not read, should enchant but not mystify nor stray far from natural speech: at its best, it might be mysterious, but was to be shared, not used to instruct and proselytise. 'Illusion is an artist's world: by charming sounds, pure lines, and the noble colours he makes an illusion, which may be truth, and will surely make truth easier to bear.' (1944). He would not have agreed with a recent dictum, in the *Times Literary Supplement*, asserted by a poet, that clarity is the death of language.

Constance Babington Smith wrote, of his neighbours, the Oxford dons, 'by their standards he was uneducated. Masefield was well aware that the Oxford scholars looked down on him and, with characteristic humility, he accepted their attitude as very reasonable.' Some readers of the Sonnets of 1916 and 1917 may consider his humility over-done.

The intellectualism, metaphysical structure and commentary of Hans Enzenberger's *The Sinking of the Titanic* was not for him, with his belief in beauty, adventure, courage, endurance. On such a theme he would have lavished lively description, of elemental nature, human behaviour, the contrasts between First Class and Steerage, complacency, then final horror, all doubtless harnessed to some personal conflict. But no co-ordination of philosophies and speculations. His

*Titanic* would have been a real ship, its physical workings carefully observed, its personnel scrutinised by an expert naval eye.

His forms and techniques were largely inherited – Constance Babington Smith mentions 'his jog trot metres and simplicity of style'.

> My school, that of the Romantics, who began with Gray, base their work on Chaucer, the early Shakespeare, and the early Milton; on choice books, that is, and a lovely general culture in which music is very important.

> I understand that much talent and good invention is with the moderns, and also the modern world. But what shone and seemed tempting, if unattainable, when I was 18, seems even more marvellous now; and I will not change; even if I could I wouldn't. I belong to the camp of Gray, Keats, Rossetti and Wm. Morris and the early Yeats.

> To Florence Lamont

Such a line as 'the windy gas-lamps and the wet roads shining' might confirm this.

Despite being an island people, the British have not learned to swim and have not produced a great sea literature. While cherishing rivers, pools, lakes, their poets have largely left the sea to the prose-writers: (Conrad), H. M. Tomlinson, Marryat. John Masefield's sea-poems are probably unrivalled, save by Coleridge and Falconer, and very few English poets had direct experience of ships, seas and crews. His *Salt Water Ballads* (1902), written in colloquial speech, did for sailors what Kipling's *Barrack Room Ballads* did for the soldier, and Synge did for the Irish peasantry. As he intended, they are effective when recited, and have made excellent songs. He wrote from personal knowledge. Similarly, he was no week-end countryman, like so many Georgians were accused of being. Observation and memory controlled his lyric. A second collection was often more literary, self-conscious, and more diversified, as Masefield developed his friendships and reading: sometimes slightly precious, but with instants of unusual power:

> There's sand-bagging and throat-slitting,
>     And quiet graves in the sea-slime,
> Stabbing, of course, and rum-hitting

Dirt, and drink, and stink, and crime,
   In Spanish port,
   Fever port,
   Port of Holy Peter.

*Ballads & Poems* (1903)

The pre-cinema, pre-radio and television age had encouraged narrative poetry. Following Tennyson, Browning, Arnold, Morris, Yeats, and Frederic Manning, whose *The Vigil of Brunhild* appeared in 1909, Masefield, 1911–21, produced several long verse narratives. In each, sombre and violent human drama is set in a wide landscape, capable of showing beauty but also horror. His recollections of fo'c's'le and tavern, of vagrancy and toil, and the promptings of his childhood, gave them force. *Reynard the Fox*, like *Right Royal*, a steeplechase tale, describes an animal under stress. *Reynard*, swift, kinetic, pungent, made exciting radio listening. A group of people, Chaucerian in range, observation and vividness, like the pilgrims, briefly discard class and status for a common enterprise, and Masefield superbly holds a balance between them and the fleeing fox.

An old bear in a scarlet pelt
Came next, old Squire Harridew,
His eyebrows gave a man the grue,
So bushy and so fierce they were:
He had a bitter tongue to swear.
A fierce, hot, hard, old stupid squire,
With all his liver made of fire,
Small brain, great courage, mulish will.

Strong called *Reynard* the finest narrative poem of the century and one of the finest in our language.

The sea-poem *Dauber* speaks for all minorities: the oppressed, the mocked, the outsiders, the failed, and the visionaries and artists, such as young Dauber himself, on his fatal voyage round the Horn:

'I cannot get it yet – not yet,' he said;
'That leap and light, and sudden change to green,
And all the glittering from the sunset's red,
And the milky colours where the bursts have been,

And then the clipper striding like a queen
Over it all, all beauty to the crown.
I see it all, I cannot put it down.'

He does his best, but later, when he goes to fetch his drawings:

He found them all obliterated, slimed,
Blotted, erased, gone from him line and note.
They were all spoiled: a lump came in his throat,
Being vain of his attempts, and tender-skinned –
Beneath the skylight watching reefers grinned.

Such poems have faults. Unassuming, he yet lacked strong powers of
self-criticism. Marsh considered some of *Dauber* 'abominably careless'; he had to curb excessive verbal energy, and did not always do so.
John Betjeman, in his 1978 selection of Masefield's poems, wrote,
'Masefield did not specialise in brevity. He obtained his effects by
direct, unadorned description. His canvas is as large as Brangwyn's. In
fact there is a likeness between that ebullient and inventive Welshman
and the shy Laureate from the borders of Herefordshire and Wales.'
His admirer, Strong, mentions his 'intermittent genius', and his
achievement is uneven.

   J. C. Squire had been caustic:

Dogs barked, owls hooted, cockerels crew
As in my works they often do
When flagging with my main design
I pad with a descriptive line.
                    *Collected Poems* (1959)

Dedication to regular metre and rhyme could induce monotony and
sometimes the doggerel. *No Man takes the Farm* I rate as high as
much in *A Shropshire Lad*:

They hanged Will
As Will said;
With one thrill
They choked him dead.

Jane walked the Wold
Like a grey gander;
All grown old
She would wander.

But his ear could lapse, as Housman's did not, and a dire and banal couplet had, earlier, almost ruined the poem, in which Muriel Spark goes further than I do, finding four deplorable verses stuck between the fine and the very fine. At his most laconic he achieves a cool mastery. In *The Rider at the Gate*, the ghost of Pompey visits the doomed Caesar:

'Out of the dark of the sands I come,
From the dark of death, with news for Rome.
A word so fell that it must be uttered
Though it strike the soul of the Caesar dumb.'

*Caesar turned in his bed and muttered,*
*With a struggle for breath the lamp-flame guttered;*
*Calpurnia heard her husband moan:*
            *'The house is falling,*
*The beaten men come into their own.'*

Masefield's abiding love of countryside aligned him too closely with Georgians of far less skill than his own, and who gave some force to Bernard Shaw's remark that the English mistake love of landscape for love of art. But there can be artistry in Masefield's selection and movement of words:

The loitering water flooded full,
Had yeast on its lips like raddled wool
It was wrinkled over with Arab script
Of eddies that twisted up and slipt.'
                    *Reynard the Fox*

His *The Wild Duck* wastes no words, and cuts finely:

Only the soul that goes.
Eager. Eager. Flying.
Over the globe of the moon,
Over the wood that glows.
Wings linked. Necks a-strain,
A rush and a wild crying.

A cry of the long pain
In the reeds of a steel lagoon,
In a land that no man knows.

In 1911 *The Everlasting Mercy* gave Masefield fame and caused a furore, with its scenes of bawdiness, drunkenness, violence, its earthy and blasphemous oaths, its introduction of 'low' characters, which, as Kipling had done, ripped away the gentility and sweetness of Tennyson, and early Yeats. Lord Alfred Douglas, from the loftiness of moral rectitude, pronounced it nine-tenths sheer filth, more wicked and licentious than Marlowe. Muriel Spark sees it as a historical poem, though it concerns a startling religious conversion. 'An inspired record of a powerful religious movement typified in the life of one man. It is also a good story.' This was mistaken for modernity, but the novel is not always genuinely new. Robert Graves, nevertheless spoke of it as 'a fresh wind that carried English poetry clear out of the Edwardian doldrums. Those pungent, urgent, violent lines, with their careless breaches of long standing taboos exhilarated us youngsters.' And, as Strong wrote, anyone who can make the British public argue about poetry has accomplished the feat of a lifetime.

Excited by a Post-Impressionist exhibition in 1910, Virginia Woolf declared that human nature had changed. Eighteen years before, Joachimides had announced from Berlin 'a radical change in the arts. The subjective, the visionary, the mythical have been brought back from exile.' The Great War swept away established assumptions, institutions, landmarks, in a mood from which Ezra Pound wrote:

> There died a myriad,
> And of the best, among them,
> For an old bitch gone in the teeth,
> For a botched civilization,
>
> Charm, smiling at the good mouth,
> Quick eyes gone under earth's lid,
>
> For two gross of broken statues,
> For a few thousand battered books.
>        'Hugh Selwyn Mauberley'

Masefield maintained, surely disputably, that when brains enter imagination, they poison it. He broke a contemporary mould, but was never a modernist. His work was visual and emotive, not cerebral. Or rather, he did not push his thoughts and convictions to extremes. This did not commend itself to newer readers, and the more sophisticated did not relish his freedom of words like 'Beauty' and 'April'. The age had learned to be wary of capital letters. His remark about Thomas Hardy, 'He spoke not from a brain but from a nature,' applied also to himself. 'Sonnets of Good Cheer' sounded Victorian. The Great War seemed to have innoculated the mind against adventures. He had no reverence for Freud: 'I don't think the soul can be explained by mucous membranes'. He still saw people whole: crises of identity, the fragmented ego, he scarcely recognised though he saw, sometimes tragically, the divisions within his characters, their fluctuating impulses, the pulses of conflicting tendencies. The ruffianly and rebellious Saul Kane, in *The Everlasting Mercy*, discovers Christian ecstasy, but this is the resolution of inherent opposites, present in people and ideas of all periods, the body-soul dichotomy, not a thesis on the nature of mind. Drawn from a real youth dashed to death on 'The Terceira', Dauber, with his fears and courage, is convincingly rounded.

Masefield, like others, used Arthurian themes for his own purposes, with an Arthur neither a Jungian archetype nor Tennysonian paragon, but Celtic warrior in a twilit era of violence and magic, creative ignorance and intelligent malevolence, when humans were reputed to raid the underworld, and, at queer peaks of the year, the dead returned, all frontiers dissolved, the unseen gleamed in uncanny radiance. 'Presences communed in the white owl's call.' A world less distant than, in the Twenties and Thirties, was often assumed. Comparison with Eliot's treatment of a Celtic theme in *The Waste Land* illustrates two very different visions and techniques.

As a man, Masefield accumulated a wisdom acknowledged even by so assiduous a modernist as Cyril Connolly, who would simultaneously have noted that, in technique and outlook Masefield did not develop. He cherished the broken statues and battered books, and lost much critical attention, reflecting in 1951, 'I thought it was long since decided that I am like the dodo and the great auk, no longer known as a bird at all.'

The truth of this must be decided by readers, today and tomorrow.

Masefield was a copious letter writer. His correspondence with Florence Lamont, for 35 years, produced some 2000 letters. During absences, he wrote daily to his wife. For his last 15 years he wrote weekly to the violinist, Audrey Napier-Smith, and extracts from these letters fill 500 pages (*Letters to Reyna*, 1983).

He was not a great, formal correspondent like the prodigious Rilke, with critical, aesthetic, confessional and descriptive set-pieces. He is conversational, reminiscent, informative, wryly humorous, very observant of detail, with a mass of anecdote, reflections on other writers, small choice phrases, bits of curious information. He always thought of himself as a wanderer, and his letters are gleanings of many journeys and sojourns in far lands of place and spirit, time and events.

He wrote to Margaret Bridges, 'Dostoievsky never exactly wins me, but he certainly haunts me, though not in the way of beauty; in the way, more, of the mad man one sees in a cell. Don't you think that the really haunting things come from the many (popular tales and traditions) suddenly made significant by the brooding of one great imagination? D strikes me as a hurt thing, who says "I don't know any tales or traditions; I only know this thing, whatever it is, called Human Life, with all these things called Human Institutions arrayed against it, and it hurts and hurts, & there is no escape from it; it is too wonderful to escape from; and this is how it has to live, and it is awful."'

Of Voltaire, he observed, 'His genius was not to give light, but to shatter darkness.' On Gerard Manley Hopkins, 'rather fresh and queer; and has a new kind of cock in it, & is as cheerful as a red-herring after a year of ship's provisions.' On America, feeling that '*Huck Finn* was the one masterpiece America has yet produced, the one wonderful book about boyhood.'

Assorted letters contain dozens of small notes, tiny essays, unsensational but shrewdly professional. He discusses the faulty nautical observation of Turner, Ruskin, Stevenson, Breughel; foxes as pets; the shape of mice's feet; public executions; Napoleon; Jesse James; Viking ships; the lonely Seven Barrows on the Ridgeway, 'each a great round grassy swelling in the nothing of nowhere'; Greek pottery; Apuleius, Irving; Henry Huggins's sea-paintings; Babylonian ziggurats; old crews and ships; *Macbeth*; reincarnation; fear of spiders; circuses; Bergson; Greek philosophers; Homer; Berlioz; Dr Porson drinking ink; a dying Spanish grandee murmuring that his killer had behaved like a perfect gentleman; Victor Hugo's 'marvellous tommy-rot' about Waterloo; Wagner in cloth of gold trousers; nightmarish ports and cut-throat occasions; the derivation of 'Dogger Bank'; the meaning of 'breaming', 'braving', 'bucko-boys'; a Dublin poltergeist; birds; Dickens; Hazlitt in a coach attacked by a lioness; Mr Mitford living in a gravel pit with 3d a day for food, 9d for gin. More than once he mentions a fox joining, undetected, the hounds pursuing him, and escaping. 'Cheer up about the fiddle,' he advised Miss Napier-Smith, in some crisis, 'most people would give 2 fingers and 4 toes to be able to fiddle even the first 2 lines of

*Alice Where Art Thou?* or *The Place Where the Old Horse Died*. Do reflect that with a fiddle you could go into any wild haunt anywhere and melt the maddest & the stoniest heart there in 17 seconds (less in England) and, I suppose, 3 in Africa.'

He wrote letters with a diffident awareness of immense stores of memory and knowledge, always very courteously offered, as if presenting a gift without absolute certainty that it would be appreciated. He always valued courtesy – courtesy rather than the chillier politeness – below deck, in an American hell-dive, in the Laureate's study. He once replied to a 'thank you' letter from Julie Bush: 'long since, I heard one of the great Victorians say: "Those who write a charming letter after only coming to tea are surely the Salt of the Earth".

These links with the lost – a lost England, a lost America, lost ships and livelihoods – make an unofficial social history, quirky, rambling, but consistent in tone and values. As an observer of war, he can be trusted, in his response both to the small but telling, and to the overwhelming. He notices two coltsfoots appearing on a desolate battlefield. To Margaret Bridges he wrote:

> Near the ruins of Hamel there is a little dwarf evergreen which somehow hasn't been destroyed. A soldier has put a notice on it: 'Kew Gardens. Please do not touch.'
>
> There was a telephone here, but some officer pinched it yesterday (cut it off and pocketed it): I can't think why; but some people are specially sensitive to certain things. Major Griffiths said that he once knew a thief who could be trusted with money and jewels, but could not be left alone with the garden roller.

### THE MASEFIELD FAMILY

Mrs Masefield was Constance de la Cherois-Crommelin, of Irish-French family, from County Antrim, and of very considerable intellectual powers and forceful personality. A. L. Rowse and Stephen Spender found her 'powerful'. A student of classics, mathematics, and English literature, skilled at tennis and swimming, she taught at Roedean, and later ran a small London school with Isabel Fry.

The Masefields had two children, often mentioned in the letters. Isabel Judith, born 1904, was – and is – an independent spirit, disliking orders and domesticity, a lover of horses, and, in the Hill Players, a fine amateur actress. She wrote for children, and illustrated books, including some of her father's. Some of her early difficulties, referred to in the letters, are tidily summarised by Constance Babington Smith:

> In Judith's life a difficult problem had arisen. For the school where she was boarded, St Felix's at Southwold, was on the Suffolk coast, it was frequently exposed to Zeppelin raids. Both her parents worried very much about this though for a time they made light of the risk and let her stay on . . . In the spring of 1917, however, at the time when America came into the war, and when it seemed likely that the east coast would be shelled, they decided that although Judith herself was most unwilling to leave, she simply must be moved; they would send her for the summer term to the 'farm school' that Isabel (Fry) had started near Aylesbury at Mayortorne Manor. Judith was much distressed, and in the Easter Holidays she poured out her misery to her father. He replied with wonderful tenderness . . .

Lewis Masefield, born 1910, was novelist, journalist, musician, lover of the countryside and birds. He was killled in North Africa in 1942, whilst serving in the Royal Army Medical Corps, in which, as a pacifist, he had enlisted. A music scholarship was later founded in his memory, and the first winner in 1946, was Geoffrey Bush, later Visiting Professor of Music at King's College London, and a distinguished composer.

# Part One

## Letters from France, 1915
(Letters 1 to 36, 1 March to 11 April)

Within five weeks of the murder of the Archduke Franz Ferdinand at Sarajevo by Slav nationalistists, the Great War had begun, involving all major European nations. Once Britain entered the war, Masefield's attitude was of simple patriotism, quickened by reports of German outrages in Belgium, invaded in defiance of a pledged treaty. A tolerant man, who never questioned his son's pacifism in the Second World War, he supported the war effort in all ways he could, and placed the blame squarely on the Germans. The war was:

This bloody smear on Time
Done by a devil.

He was totally at odds with the protests against British involvement reiterated by John Morley, Norman Angell, Bertrand Russell, Shaw and his fellow poet, Wilfrid Scawen Blunt, who wrote:

We are to fight for what? For Serbia, a nest of murderous swine which has never listened to a word of English remonstrance, for Russia, the tyrant of Poland, Finland, and all northern Asia, for France, our fellow brigand in North Africa, and lastly for Belgium, with its Congo record! And we call this England's honour!

Almost all had expected a short war, ending when the Germans reached Paris after a lightening dash through Belgium and the smashing of the French, so easily beaten in 1870, and the elimination of Britain's 'contemptible little army'.

The experts miscalculated. Despite initial German successes, the Allies regrouped; the German High Command, less impressive than it had been in 1870, made mistakes; the Russians, in the East, despite terrifying losses, proved more formidable than had been anticipated. After setbacks on the Marne, the Germans resolved on a defensive policy, digging themselves in behind a line of trenches, barbed wire, fortifications, stretching from Switzerland to the North Sea. Only German shells had reached Paris, the war had gone astray and, with millions of men now facing each other in virtual stalemate in the West, there seemed no prospect of an end.

By 1915 the costs, in lives, money, morale, were becoming ominous. After initial enthusiasm, civilians were beginning to grumble, at diminishing food and unending casualties. Huge frontal assaults were losing too much, gaining too little. A way must be found to reach victory elsewhere.

The Gallipoli campaign of 1915 seemed the solution, the winning of a free passage through the Dardanelles. Masefield wrote in *Gallipoli*:

> While the war was still young it became necessary to attempt this passage for five reasons: (1) To break the link by which Turkey keeps her hold as a European power. (2) To divert a large part of the Turkish army from operations against our Russian Allies in the Caucasus and elsewhere. (3) To pass into Russia, at a time when her Northern ports were closed by ice, the rifles and munitions of war of which her armies were in need. (4) To bring grain out of Southern Russia. (5) If possible, to prevent, by a successful deed of arms in the Near East, any new alliance against us among the Balkan peoples.

Masefield defended the campaign and wrote movingly, even passionately about it. He could romanticise men's courage, ardour, endurance, and relate them to the gallantry of Roland at Roncevalles, but not their sufferings. He knew, in his own blood and bones, that pain, disease, gangrene and rot and wastage are vile and cannot be disguised by literature.

The venture was plausible – perhaps had genius – but it failed, at grim cost to the youth of Australia, New Zealand, Britain and France, for reasons which are still argued. Major General J. F. C. Fuller wrote tersely, years later:

> No judgement; no clear strategical analysis of the initial problem; no proper calculation of its tactical requirements; and no true attempt to balance the means in hand with the end in view.

A fellow military expert, Captain Basil Liddell Hart, disagreed. The campaign was condemned by Lloyd George, 'the man who won the war,' and defended to the last by its chief inspirer, Winston Churchill, and by Clement Attlee, who fought in it, and indeed wrote verses about it.

The second attempt to end the stalemate was made by the Germans, in an all-out attack on Verdun in 1916, a battle which lasted for ten months of mass-slaughter: there were some 280,000 German casualties, and 315,000 French; the Germans captured a few square miles of ground and the French shot dozens of their men for mutiny.

The third attempt was largely British in concept – a full-scale assault on the Germans to relieve pressure on Verdun and assist a new Russian offensive in the east. The Battle of the Somme has passed into folklore as an instance of futility, gruesome carnage, criminal irresponsibility, but, here too, historians and survivors disagree. The losses were undeniably colossal: the stakes seemed momentous. One survivor is Dr Herbert Sulzbach, later a refugee from Hitler, decorated by George VI for anti-Nazi services. 'It would seem,' he wrote in his diary, 'that the fighting on the Somme is attempting to decide the outcome of the war.'

Though historians often end the battle in late November, 1916, Sulzbach was still fighting there on 6 December, when he noted: 'the battle of the Somme has already been going on for months; the aggressive spirit of the French and British still has not diminished.' Historically, the blood-letting has been defended, for showing the world, notably still neutral America, that the Germans were not unbeatable. Their loss of some miles on the Somme was scarcely a defeat, yet the blood and fury disquietened Germans of all ranks, including the Kaiser and his heir. The Allies lost some 700,000, the Germans about 450,000; and the controversy continues.

Masefield's two books and many letters are very visual, factual, and fiercely anti-German.

It was the biggest battle in which our people were ever engaged, and so far has led to bigger results than any battle since the Battle of the Marne. It caused a great falling back of the enemy armies. It freed a great tract of France seventy miles long, by from ten to twenty five miles broad. It first gave the enemy the knowledge that he was beaten.

*The Old Front Line*

The enemy wire was always deep, thick and securely staked with iron supports, which were either crossed like the letter X, or upright, with loops to take the wire and shaped at one end like corkscrews so as to screw into the ground. The wire stood on these supports on a thick web, about four feet high & from thirty to forty feet across. The wire used was generally as thick as a sailor's marline stuff, or two twisted rope-yarns. It contained, as a rule, some sixteen barbs to the foot. The wire, used in front of our lines, was generally galvanized, & remained grey after months of exposure. The enemy wire, not being galvanized, rusted to a black colour, and shows up black at a great distance. In places, this web or barrier was supplemented with trip-wire or wire placed just above the ground so that the artillery observing officers might not see it and so not to cause it to be destroyed. This trip-wire was as difficult to cross as the wire of the entanglements. In one place (was near the Y Ravine at Beaumont Hamel) this trip-wire was used with thin iron spikes a yard long, of the kind known as Calthrops. The spikes were so placed in the ground that about one foot of spike projected. The scheme was that our men should catch their feet in the trip-wire, fall back on the spikes, and be transfixed.

This, from *The Old Front Line*, is dryly informative, with an objectivity he sheds whenever German behaviour is to be described.

I have kept strictly to the letters as they were written, retaining minor inconsistencies of spelling, he seldom bothered with French accents, though I have omitted a few passages of wholly private interest. In the first batch, before his visit to America, he is writing from his post with the Red Cross. I have kept the footnotes to a minimum, generally explaining further only those characters and situations likely to be of interest today.

[1]                                                      1st March 1915

M.O.D.C.

I begin this first letter to you just as we leave Goring Station, with the train rapidly filling up with people, a battered traveller, who has been in the East, a lady in mourning and her husband who is a Liberal and is accoustomed to an indoor life. I think of the many people I shall have to travel with before I see my Dear Dears again. I keep thinking of you bravely facing the whole worry of it alone and that you are now going back to it across the fields, just about the style now, in the bog and I wish and wish I were with you, you who deserve the best man in the world and have only got me and now have not got me. Little Loo I can barely think of. The only pleasure is it has begun now and is therefore coming to an end.

We are at Reading now; war stores everywhere; 2000 tons of naval coal in the sidings and much compressed forage.

London – a great whirl of things to do and arrange.

                                                         2 p.m.

I must end this in the tube with Nana[1] going to Victoria again. Na is very well and sends her love and kiss to you and Lewis.

Bless you, dear heart, and forgive a hurried scrawl in a shifting train.
Your old love,

I hear it won't be possible to wire from Dieppe and perhaps not from Paris, as all wires have to be specially vised but if I can have time in Paris, as I am pretty sure to have a day, I'll get the vise there. I'm writing this in a taxi going to find Nana. I'm awfully late for her but I've a lot still to do. Lady S[2] is a minxy lady, of the type and bearing of Mrs R. McNeill, but too velvety and too gushy to be quite real. She's a pretty bad artist, I could gather. I've had a great to do, as there is now a doubt whether I can go by the 8 train, which is not supposed to be used by men in Khaki. Still I expect I can get a permit. It is a noisome wettish day here.

1. Sometimes Na, pet-name for Judith Masefield, at this time eleven years old.
2. Probably Kathleen Scott, Lady Kennett (1878–1947), sculptor, whose busts included those of Asquith, Prime Minister in 1915; Lloyd George, W. B. Yeats. She is not to be confused with Mrs Scott, who occurs later, wife of C. P. Scott, editor of the *Manchester Guardian*, for whom Masefield had worked as a reviewer and columnist.

---

[2]

1915
Tuesday, March 2nd. 8 a.m.

I'm writing this in the train on the way from Dieppe. We left Victoria in a sort of whirl. Mrs Rupell with baby, Rob Holland was there too, and we had some formalities to go thro, but off by 8.10 to Folkestone, where we took ship, the *Arundel*. A cold clear windy moonlit night, with a good big swell, the ship rolled a bit, and everyone was sick but myself, spuage universale, so to speak, but I kept on deck in a snug hole near a door, and sometimes slept, sometimes yarned with an engineer who came up from time to time I believe so as not to miss the submarine, which did not come however, as I suppose the devils are all gone off to have a go at the Dardanelles, which, if they do, will be one to them. We got to Dieppe at about 4, where we had scrutiny, douane, etc. coffee and a roll au buffet and then sleep for 2 hours, starting 6.10 at dawn (earlier than at Loll[1]) and by and by it was a light bright lovely day and the country a chalky wood like in Kent and now (after another coffee and roll) at 9 a.m., we wait at Pontoise where Francois Villon was born. We're off again now. Paris next stop. Odd to think Villon lived here and wandered about and was a little devil here, and probably stuck pins in frogs and was thought an interesting child. Strangely like the Wrotham country all this except the bottoms are wetter, and here in Oise which Daubigny[2] used to paint. I've had a long talk with a Frenchman here who has lost one son at La Bassee, but has still the other twin alive, fighting in the Argonne. He gives the war till July, but I say alas, no such luck (nos armées seront en retard; or will the miracle happen?) Plenty of signs of war here, women doing work in the fields, red X trains, with their brancards all disordered, and troops everywhere looking partly like game keepers partly like border freebooters, which I suppose sums up the Napoleonic tradition. You, I suppose, my poor dearie, are with the little man at trains. Would I were. Paris is to hand and the tug of war begins.

12.30

I write this in a French restaurant at the Gare de l'Est. I've got all the stores through, 'trois cents kilos', and have washed and shaved, and telegraphed to you and Bobby[3]. Now I have to get my permit at the other end of Paris, and then deliver a letter to a French official whose address I have still to discover. When all that is done, I fear it will be dark, so I shall not see much of Paris. The French tongue has few terrors in these generous days of fine feeling.

Love to you my dearie.
Kiss little Lew for me.

1. Lollingdon, Berks. See note, March 12, 1915.
2. Charles François Daubigny (1817–78), French landscape painter, frequently of rivers, member of 'the Barbizon School'.
3. Bobby and his wife Lion Phillimore, who lived at a house called Kendals, were great family friends of the Masefield's. Bobby served as a fellow volunteer with Masefield in the Red Cross. Bobby was to die in France in the course of the war.

[3]                                          In the train, going to Chaumont
                                                    8.30 a.m. March 3rd

I slept like a seaman last night from, 9.30–6.30 when I had to turn out. My hotel was exceedingly comfortable. h and c taps and an h and c footbath in my room (never tried pilgrim's limbs etc) and having wandered Paris on duty for 7 or 8 hours on end I was thankful. My waiter at dinner had been in London at a restaurant at Soho and hoped to go back after the war. I gathered that he was waiting to be called to the army but was not yet wanted. While I was at dinner one of Rob Holland's friends, to whom I had sent a letter earlier in the day, came in with a parcel of scalpels for me to take.

After dinner I walked to town awhile but poor Paris all very quiet much much quieter than London, and the lights rather few. At first one does not notice any lack of men, but after a time one sees that all the efficient men are gone.

I had a heap of formalities to go thro yesterday, and the charming French military authorities gave me a pass for all my stores, now to my horror they tell me that my stores, which I had to leave with them, are already despatched and will be there before me. I am praying they may be, but altho I am impressed by their general efficiency and wish to help, in this case I wish they'd been less eager.

A 'Kalli' is a rarity so far east as Paris and I get stared at by the universe and little boys come shyly to shake hands. Strange Turcos and Zonares, looking like Bedouins and Tartarins[1] and Mithridates[2], say 'Good afternoon, ow are you?'. One of the Brit Red X men, whom I met yesterday took me in his car to the Invalides where the German guns are kept. I did not go in to see them, but I saw a bit of broken Zeppelin, all tangled like a cobweb and a bit of smashed German aeroplane wing. I'm travelling now with a British Staff officer, a General grown grey in war, who is I suppose attached to the service de liaison. We've just read that a collier has sunk a German sous-marion. In the corridor there's a fine young French Captain with the Legion of Honour Cross and one arm gone. Further back there is a French General and his officers. The train is pretty fair so far, in fact amazing considering that only 70 miles away the war is raging. The Spring ploughing is pretty well forward, more so than with us I should say. They plough right up round the fruit trees, in the old English style (still used in Kent) and some of the farms are models, with magnificent ox teams in first class order.

I'll be glad to get to your letters and to work. I hope you'll get your letters safely. It takes 3 days or so, but is pretty regular. Love to the dear babes and to you dear heart.

Your
J.

12 noon Mar 3

My fellow traveller has gone to dejeuner wh I shan't do till I get to Chaumont, and perhaps not then if I am met there instead of at La Treq. We're passing the Aube country wh is of surpassing beauty, a kind of brown chalk hill bearing mainly pine, and the Aube a green blue river brimful.

At Troyes I saw my first of war; a red X train just in with last night's take; a lot of wounded (no serious cases) and a lot of men on leave from the trenches, mud to the eyes, some still cheery and well, but most of them white, with a look of horror in their eyes, yet horror isn't quite the word, horror, terror and anxiety mixed, which brought the war home to me more sharply than anything yet. Some men were sleeping on straw on the carriage floors, some were eating, the doctors in charge were a cheery competent lot, and there were many officers in their little snug dens evidently able to tackle the world. On the roads now one sees long processions of carts.

Arrived Chaumont where I've met Bobby and am sending this back by an envoy.

1. Tartarin, the boastful and lying Tarascon character created by Alphonse Daudet.
2. Mithradates, a first century King of Pontus, heading resistance to Rome, fighting

such generals as Sulla and Pompey, famous for his wealth, shrewdness and grand manner.

---

[4]                                                    Thursday, 4 March, 1915

My dearest Con,

I hear there is no Censorship, but they now delay letters instead, generally 3 or 4 days, sometimes longer.

I'd better begin with yesterday, much where I left off, with the old British General in the train. He was doing remount service for the French and had been along the whole front, principally in the East, & had seen & heard everything.

As to the duration of the war: everybody says a different thing, but it is much safer to expect a long long war, a year almost from now. None of the soldiers (I've talked with 3 French officers, too) expect a short war; it is a long way from peace still, but we are confident & cheery, & and know that the Bosches[1] are held.

We have 800,000 English troops in France. We have landed practically 400,000 this last month, & about 120,000 will land every month from now on. I hope that this will be news. The French gun 'soixante quinze' is the marvel of the war. It has a kind of oil buffer which checks all recoil, so that you do not have to aim afresh for each shot, but just plug away. What keeps us all back is simply mud and the difficulty of bringing up such an accumulation of shell and cartridge that a week's sustained attack can be possible. We are always short of ammunition & the factories are only just keeping pace with the expenditure. The French equipment (I've handled a lot of it already) is pretty bad, much worse than ours; the men good, the active officers first rate, but (I judge) a lot of slacking in the high ranks, too.

In some parts of the East here the trenches are 3 yards apart, in others there is only a wall between the two armies, in others, where the ground is hard, the dividing line is ragged, & depends on chance rocks & trees. The deep trenches are being abandoned, because they get filled with mud & because the men simply cannot get out of them quick enough to attack. The new fashion is a shallow pan in which you lie flat. All along the front the life is simply hellish. When a man is hit & screams, the men in the ranks call out, 'Taisey vois; vous avez la luxure d'une ʋiessure'. The men pray to get hit; but I don't think they would if they knew all it entails.

So much the old General, who smoked a briar pipe, loved horses very much, was a nice kind old soul who had been in Jamaica & through 20 odd campaigns, & whom I shall always remember, & often think of, for his charming friendly way.

At Chaumont I was met by Bobby with the Matron & Cloke, the latter going home with iritis. We saw them off, shopped in Chaumont for 3 or 4 hours, the centre of a huge crowd, crammed the car to the brim (I rode on the roof a good way) & so off to Arc En Barrois, which lies in a combe, much as Quenington does, & is an oolite place with many queer Cotswoldy roofs, winding streets, a deserted air, a lovely church & the chateau which is a well built foursquare place, very big & roomy, but badly built for our work, as the stairs wind, the kitchens are under-ground & there are no lifts.

The staff is not yet very distinct, but I gather that there are factions, gossip & tattle, some women who need the sack &c &c. God deliver me from faction. The men are a good lot. As soon as I came I had to help in taking off a man's arm at the shoulder. I did my part all right, & got a compliment from the chief. I felt too great pity & interest to feel queer. The man is doing well, such a nice fellow, one of the best here.

Today: I may begin by saying that we staff breakfast English fashion at about 8. Bobby contrives, God knows how, to be 3/4 of an hour late for every meal. 'We all offend in something'. After break we burnt foul old straw from mattresses (& stinking foul it was) & sent the canvas to fumigate. Then we carried wounded men into the open air, a hot & heavy job up & down these stairs, & then got the men's dinner along & drew their wine. Then we dined, & afterwards carpentered, making dodges for the wards, then got the wounded men back to bed, gulped tea, got the men's supper & fed them, & dined ourselves, & now I'm here. I like the men here. I don't mind one of the lady doctors, the rest I'm inclined to think make trouble; but this is mainly the supposition of one still ignorant. The work is hard & continuous but it simply has to be done or our 140 could not get on. I must get to bed, I'm tired. Bless you, dear heart. Love to you & the dear ones, all at Loll tomorrow.

Your old lover,
Jan

1. Masefield sometimes spells this 'Boche'. I quote *Soldiers' Songs and Slang*, edited by John Brophy and Eric Partridge, Scholartis Press, 1931.

'French slang for "German", taken into English . . . Practically never used by private soldiers, confined to officers. The word was first used in the phrase *tête de boche*, in which the great philologist, Albert Dauzat, believes "boche" to be simply an abbreviation of *caboche* – a head, such redundancies being frequent in the vulgar tongue. *Tête de boche* was used as early as 1870 of obstinant persons. In 1874 French typographers, it is recorded, applied it to German compositors. By 1883 (states Alfred Debrau's *Dictionnaire de la Langue Verte*) the phrase had come to have the meaning of *mauvais sujet* and was so used especially by prostitutes. The Germans, having among the French a reputation for obstinacy and perhaps as "bad lots", from *Allemands* became *Alleboches* and *Alboches*. About 1900 *Alboche* was shortened to *Boche* as a generic name for Germans. During the war propagandist posters revived the memory of *Alboche* by making it *Sale Boche*.'

My dearest,

No Censorship, only a delay of at least 3 days in *all* letters. I've just got your Tuesday's letter, so there's no delay in letters coming here; only in letters going there will be.

A cruel fate has happened. Cloke who was going home desperately ill with iritis, almost blind in fact, was stopped in Dieppe on suspicion that he was a deserter[1], & as he bore 2 letters from me & may have been locked up & anyhow was blindish, they may not have been posted & may have been opened & read. They were my Wednesday morning letters written in the train going to Chaumont. I hope you got them.

The main thing here is not the war but our own share in it. We have our own part of it to take by the throat each day & I think every soul in the hospital staff is sopped with sweat in doing some day in day out. The work is hard all through & 4 times a day excessively hard, carrying wounded in & out & carrying meals up & down, but I'm very well, & whenever I look at these poor fellows my soul boils. Nothing else in the world matters but to stop this atrocious thing. Blood & intellect & life are simply nothing. Let them go like water to end this crime. You've no idea of it, you can't even guess the stink of it, from the bloody old reeking stretchers to the fragments hopping on crutches, and half heads, & a leg gone at the thigh, & young boys blinded & grey headed old men with their backs broken. I never knew I loved men so much. They are a fine lot, a noble lot, I love them all. The man whose arm I saw cut off (I burned the arm afterwards, by the way, in the heating furnace) is a cultivateur in Brittany, the right arm gone, 3 little babes & a wife, 2d a day wound pension for each child, & perhaps 50 years life to come. He is about the best of them all, brave & good & fine, & we would all do anything for him.

Somebody told Bobby that I was a good orderly, so I feel very pleased. I'd feel more pleased if 5/6ths of the women were sacked. I like neither them nor their methods, but my job is mainly with men, and unless they come poaching all will be well.

There was a chasse du sanglier here today. Some of our lot went but saw nothing, being too late, but we heard that a boar was killed; there are many here. We're going to eat him if he can be bought.

I'm organising a fire brigade. Its about the vilest old death trap God ever permitted. Please God it lasts tonight; tomorrow I hope to have all possible precautions taken. The Germans were here (in the chateau) in 70. This time they only got to within 15 miles, & are now 75 (St. Michill the nearest) May God punish the Bosches for all they've done here.

I lodge at an inn (the Lion d'Or) and write this there, in my room, my only time being from about 8.45 to 10, so don't go thinking that I shall be in the death trap, for that is the chateau, 300 yards away. Jack Monsell's cousin is here, (a nurse I believe) and Wilfred Blunt's[2] cousin is one of the orderlys, but in charge of our convalescents in another house.

I must stop dear heart. Kiss the dear babes. I kiss you, too, in thought. I must get to bed. I believe that Bobby has done more here than any 20 others put together. We're not only needed dearie we're essential. This clock must stop without us. I'll try to be coherent in later letters; the thing is still too vast.

Your old lover

J

1. Desertion was common enough in the French armies in certain phases of the war, notably after Verdun and the disastrous Nivelle offensive. British desertions seem on a smaller scale, but could likewise entail execution. A poignant account of a British soldier shot for desertion is in *Rough Justice* (1926), a novel by Masefield's friend, C. E. Montague. Officially, two officers and 243 privates were executed for desertion in the British army during the Great War.

2. Actually Wilfrid. Wilfrid Scawen Blunt (1840–1922), poet, far eastern traveller, diplomat, critical of British rule in Egypt and Ireland, and son of a veteran of Corunna, in the Napoleonic wars, married to the grand-daughter of Lord Byron. His daughter married the Masefield's close friend, Neville Lytton. Blunt, who was also a clever artist, gave the Masefields some of his sketches of France, in particular of a bridge near Beauvais.

---

[6]

Chateau d'Arc

Sat. 6 March

My dearest,

I'm sorry the telegram was delayed. It was sent off at about 12 noon on Tuesday. It is the very devil telegraphing from here in war time. They change the system nearly every day so as to outwit the Bosches, but the system then took half an hour or more: thus:

1. go to post office & get your forms.

2. write your form.

3. Walk ¼ mile or so to the Agent de Police.

4. Produce every credential you have, & state the maiden name of your mother.

5. Walk back to post office & send in the form, provided the Agent has signed it.

6. The telegram is kept a day or two for safety & then sent.

They shot 45 German spies at the Ecole Militaire in Paris the other day, so I suppose these schemes are necessary. All my cases got to La Trecy before me, my authorities were splendid all through & I lost nothing at all.

The work here never ends. I never stop except for meals. I walk to the chateau in the morning & to the inn at night, & so far I know neither the village nor the country near it. We lie in a hollow, there is high ground, densely wooded, full of deer, boars & wild swans, all round us, & a river in the park, that is all I know. By rights it should be dense oak wood but they have planted too much pine & made it sombre. There is fine building here (it is Cotswold oolite) but they stucco the walls mostly. The chateau is grand enough in a slightly vulgar big way. The air of it is very seigneurish, the Duke's men, old trusty souls, who saw the Bosche here in 1870[1], & who must think us utter Barbarians, have a feudal sense of the house's importance. I broke their old hearts today laying fire hoses about. If we only had 30 more buckets we'd be pretty safe from fire. These careless devils have had 200 souls in that old death trap, & have trusted to 3 broken extincteurs & the grace of God. Tomorrow I'll rig up some further contraptions.

Our wounded go on pretty well. The late fine weather let a lot of them get out & get them on finely. The convalescents got drunk en masse & did a screamingly funny parody of the mass, in their night gowns, in the street, but I was too busy to go to see it. The convalescents are out of our charge you see, & no one has any authority over them. Worse came today, for one of our own wounded, who has half a shell in his thigh, hopped on a crutch to the village, with his mate, whose shoulder is half off, & there both got blind drunk & then came home & were sick, much to the disgust of our delicate nurses. We try to get a Prohibition Order, but, no, the Maire does not like the Military & will give none, so I suppose we shall have them drunk till one or two die. However, those who get drunk & are sick will in future have to mop up the latter themselves. I'm afraid I'm to be put on the Board here, having proved useful. Alack, alack, farewell kind peace if tis true. There are 4 people here whose ways I admire more than I can say.

Bobby, de Glehn[2] (another orderly) & his wife (an American) all three quite first rate for this kind of work, Sibbley another orderly, a rough kind of heavy worker, first rate for the hard part of

[portion of letter missing]

1. In that year, following Napoleon III's declaration of war on Bismarck's Prussia, the French suffered invasion, catastrophic defeat, revolution, occupation by German armies, and ruthless treatment of civilians and resisters.
2. Wilfrid de Glehn, a British artist, and his wife Jane, who later joined with Professor Henry Tonks in a plan to establish a convalescent centre for wounded soldiers, in the Vosges.

---

[7]                                                                      Arc
                                                                   7 March
My dearest Con,

It has snowed since 10 a.m. here, & given us an easy day (comparatively) as no wounded have had to be carried out. I had to be at two operations today, on fine young men. From one, we cut out great hunks of splintered bone with a piece of shrapnel & a wad of uniform, & from the other tiny splinters of all three, all over the inside of his foot. The second case was a magnificent lad of 22 or so, who had been hit in the foot, the thigh & the shoulder. He had been told when lying in the field that if he hurried up he might catch a hospital train that same day, so he *hopped* on his unwounded leg for three hours, & caught it. He was no easy man to chloroform, & made a great deal of noise going off.

Our convalescents got thinned out today. 18 of them in clean disinfected uniforms went off to their depots after touching adieux. Some will be in the trenches in 3 weeks from now: others perhaps will be exempt. The wards will be quieter tonight, but 25 new wounded come tomorrow, I suppose they are being maimed for us in the snow somewhere now, while I write. We shall have a bad time getting them in & washed and bandaged; they're like dazed mad animals the first few days, & rave of the last thing they heard: 'Mitrailleuse, tick, tick, tick; mitrailleuse, tick, tick, tick.' 'En avant. En avant.' 'Ne tirez pas; officer', then they realise where they are more or less. One gets very fond of some of them.

The matron is back from Paris. She ought not to be here; an insufferable woman who asks me to come in & read to her. Miss Strong the singer is here (very capable soul) & a host more women when God knows we have already too many. The really hard, trained nurse who knows her work, is a fine soul, but we have a lot of catty young minxes who have never worked in their lives, & they have catty society ways of wheedling, when it is a question of carrying stinking blood in a bucket. However they are all under capable nurses, a jolly good lot I should say, & they will be inured to handling filth in time. Don't mention these details to the Cross's, as they may come to the ears of friends of the minxes.

I got some rope given me & am making quoits for those who can walk a little. I make about 3 quoits in a day, time being scarce. I've made a lot of walking sticks for those who can pad about a little, a walking stick stand, and 3 buckets and a bottle carrier. If I could only get a lot more buckets made I could organise the Fire Brigade, which is on my mind night & day, for these women are the devil with lamps (imagine) & French oil at that. If only I had a dozen more biscuit tins. And tomorrow I shall have to fetch wounded somewhere. I've got the hoses up. One hears nothing of the war here. I think the French authorities accept us as competent, & the peasants as polite but wanting in sens commun.

Would I could see you & the little babes.

Dear love to you all
from
John

[8]                                                                        Arc.
                                                                   March 8th
Dearest Con,

One of your letters, the 4th of March one, supposing you wrote one then, has
not come. Probably the Censor is at work again. You might let me know,
without a fail, how long my letters are in reaching you, when you get them, &
whether they have been read. There is great delay, we know, but we are not
sure whether they have examinations now.

I could tell you a lot of Army gossip, some favourable, some less so, but if the
C is examining I won't, for it means that the letter won't reach you. You don't
say what letters have reached you, so I'm in the dark, but I fear that the letters
Cloke was carrying have been impounded.

It snowed hard for two days, & 25 wounded are due tomorrow; they'll come
half frozen, so harden your heart for horrors. At present, with the snow on the
ground, & a lot of the best cases gone to the Convalescents, the hospital wards
are quieter; but we have some awful cases still, men all smashed & maimed.
They are mostly cheerful, but there are a lot of anxious ones; one without a
right arm wondering how he can keep on his little farm, another wondering
what he will be able to do, whether a one-armed man can be a garde-chasse,
another with his left eye blown out wondering if he will have to go back to the
trenches, & most think he will since one shoots with the right eye. I gave my
Wingate mixture to one of the wards (Albert Ward). All the wards are named
after Generals. We have Joffre[1], French[2], Gallieni[3], Kitchener[4], Foch[5] and
Albert[6].

One of the men in Albert wanted to try the Wingate mixture but had no pipe,
so I got him one, & he was quite childishly excited & pleased, & today he called
me aside & said he had something to show me, which turned out to be an
inscription on the pipe, cut by himself:

Souvenir
d'Un
Anglais.

The hospital provides a lot of work to the neighbourhood, & I daresay a lot of
much needed food & money. We have a great many men & women helping
from the village, but the work is incessant nevertheless. The helpers have a
charming nice kind forethoughtful obligingness which amazes me. They
simply fly to open doors for one when one is laden, & today little Madeleine
held a lamp for me while I drew the 28 bottles of wine for dinner. We talked of
the war (her father is in barracks at Lanfres) & of how many relatives we have,
and whether she went to mass. She is one of the most beautiful children I have
ever seen, & by & by she gave me a sticky pink sweet from a paper. We wonder
very much what they think of us all. I feel that their opinion is: 'du bon coeur,
pas du sens commun', but the war has hit Arc hard, many killed from here,

many wounded (one of them in the wards here, where his old mother sends him a daily trout for dinner) & we sometimes feel that they look upon us as a shield from those devils the Bosches.

Goldy[7] & those other eunuchs with their messy points of view simply make me sick. This place is 2 counties breadth away from the war, but if they would stick their noses inside, not the walls here but the garden gate, they would smell the war, & realise that that stink comes from beautiful human flesh which is all mangled to death through the bloody damned lust of the Bosche. I guess they might get a point of view if they saw what I saw in Troyes station or hear a finer man than they or I will ever be calling for maman while we jab a probe into him. God deliver me from talkers. To get this damned misery & crime at an end is the only thing men can do & to do that is worth any sacrifice men can make.

Bless you, dear heart. It is lovely to have you & the babes to think of in this chamber of hell, but in the evenings in the inn is my only time for thought.

Bless you.

Your

John

1. Joseph Jacques Césaire Joffre (1852–1931), French Commander in Chief on the outbreak of the Great War, victor of the Battle of the Marne, but replaced after Verdun and the Somme by General Nivelle, 1916, who promised a break-out from the Western stalemate, through his huge, pre-doomed offensive. His rough, homely manner caused Joffre to be universally called 'Papa'. He was unenthusiastic about the Gallipoli venture.

2. John Denstone Pinkstone French (1852–1925), British Commander in Chief, 1914, but, after the Battle of Loos, 1915, superseded by Douglas Haig. He believed that the war could be won only by victory in the west.

3. Joseph Simon Galheni (1849–1916), he fought in the Franco-Prussian war, 1870: was military governor of Paris, 1914, and won fame by commandeering the Paris taxis, to rush troops to halt the Germans on the Marne. Minister of War, 1914–16.

4. Herbert Horatio Kitchener (1850–1916), Minister of War, 1914–16, who raised the volunteers for the British expeditionary force to France, and subsequently found 3 million men. Had some responsibility for the failures in planning and strategy at Gallipoli. Drowned, on his way to Russia.

5. Ferdinand Foch (1851–1929). He commanded the 9th French Army on the Marne, and replaced Nivelle as Commander in Chief, 1916, and, 1918, became Generalissimo of the Allied Armies in the West.

6. Albert, 1875–1934. King of the Belgians, who commanded his armies throughout the Great War, and was the symbol of Belgium's spirited resistance.

7. Goldsworthy Lowes Dickenson (1862–1932). Cambridge humanist and political philosopher, disciple of G. E. Moore, friend of many in the Bloomsbury Group and subject of a biography by E. M. Forster. His *The Greek View of Life* (1896), a somewhat idealised interpretation of Hellenism, had many readers, particularly amongst young men. A champion of internationalism he actively supported the establishment of the League of Nations – it seems just possible that it was he who first used this title. His reasonable, idealistic, many-sided tract, *The War and the Way Out*, infuriated his friend Masefield, who probably had not enthused over Dickenson's history, *The International Anarchy, 1904–1914*, commended by Marxists.

March 9th

My dearest heart,

I hate to think of your beastly time. It is easier for me, having unending work to do, of a dull hard kind, than for you alone, but we must look on this as a time that has to be won through, & can only be won through, by utter disinterested sacrifice; there's no other way of ending it for the world. I don't think that people in England can realise what this is; I know they do not. Words cannot describe it, except as a crime and infamy, and a stinking filth, & out of it all comes nothing but a kind of rapture of courage to do anything to end it, & it is that kind of show of courage that we & the French are living in, & I wish England could feel that, for it's unlike anything I've ever felt England feeling, with its foul press and dirt & drink & sport. It has made all the French here brother & sister to us. I never felt brotherhood before, for anybody, since I was a boy.

We had a operation today, probing a fearful lacerated wound, that had torn off a third of a man's thigh & heaped up the rest, in one of these recent night attacks. They got some bits of bullet out but no doubt a lot more remains in. It was the worst wound I've seen, & a nice man, too. That always makes it worse here. So many of the best men get the worst wounds. I'm going to bring him some cigarettes tomorrow.

I had to go up to the Convalescents Hospice today, with a box for the matron, & simply scored, for they were having coffee & cake (having a marvellous cook) which are foreign luxuries here, & then at tea old Tonks[1] had got some China tea & biscuits & Mrs de Glehn bagged us some cake, so Tonks & I had a glorious gorge, talking over our (my) Fire Service. I've got the hoses & water buckets rigged & a lot of wet sand boxes for burning lamps, & now I've only got to get a rope ladder rigged to defy the foul fiend. How these people can have had 100 odd wounded in this old death trap without once thinking of a fire service is a mystery to me. Tomorrow with a little luck I'll have a fire drill, & see how things work. If I catch any of these idle devils taking my water bucket water, instead of going to the tap, I'll get her the sack.

More poor blessees tomorrow, & 25 new beds coming.

One thing comes out very plainly here, 'the community feeling'. Just as at school or in a monastery, ones likes become devotions & dislikes loathings; and I am sure, now, of what I often felt, that men & women do not work well together at the same thing. Only one woman here really works with us (Mrs de Glehn) without putting our backs up. I don't think we like the rest, many we frankly loathe, & I know that they are responsible for the troubles here. I am not talking of the trained professional nurses. They stand apart. Any nation might be proud of them. I mean the imitations.

Dear. I've taken over an hour to write this & must stop now for bed, as I've a hard, perhaps fearfully hard day before me tomorrow. I'm very well (the rough work suits me physically) but sleepy, as you know, at this hour. It is snowing hard & freezing very hard indeed (ice in all the wards).

Love to you dear one & to the little ones.

Your<br>John

1. Henry Tonks (1862–1939). Painter and teacher, Slade Professor of Fine Arts, 1917–30. He was also a qualified doctor, which explains his presence in France.

---

[10]                                                                March 9th

Telegrams have just come to say that our new lot of blessees will be at La Treq at 2 tomorrow morning, so we are off in the snow soon after midnight to fetch them; three journeys, & in between the journeys I'm to be at the station to give the remainder drinks & soup & some attempt at cheering them up. This will fill up our numbers again to 140 odd, & make tomorrow a hard day for all hands. Today has been very hard indeed, for in a glimpse of sun we ran the wounded out into the open on brancards, & then it snowed & we had to run them in in a hurry, 18 big men, in 4 heavy blankets each, & then the brancards or beds, & many of them to go up 30 stairs or more, round all sorts of corners; It is really severe labour for so few men as we are; but I don't mind, it is such a pleasure to give these poor fellows the pleasure of being out of doors.

A very beautiful thing happened a few days ago. The curé here (who looks like a curé in a book) came to say that all the villages round 'wished to send', so might the cars go? The cars went & all the poor people for miles round, many with their sons & fathers killed, sent apples, milk, eggs, butter, salades, bread & cheeses to the blessees here (a great treat to many of them) till the cars were crammed.

Some of our wounded are natives of Laon & Reims, & have had no news of their families for half a year, do not know whether they are alive, & can only imagine them as slaves to the Boches. One man told me today that he was shot by a man whom he had spared, mistaking him for a friend, & the man shot him, & gave him the awful wound I wrote of yesterday, the lacerated thigh.

There is a great crowd of people talking in the room here, most of them sitting up for the blessées; the medicine chief & the other orderlies & two of the women.

Miss Strong has brought us 2 oranges each, noble soul; one does get so hungry here with all this hard work, one thinks a great deal of food. It is very like a school in many ways, one does see the people's characters so plainly, & then one is hungry, & gets strong attachments to the people who really do their job; Bobby is magnificent, in fact I feel that he (& I, too, perhaps) are really needed. The need is atrocious all over France, & will be worse when the fighting begins again; the equipment is shockingly bad & the results often unspeakable.

It is snowing & freezing & our poor wounded are ploughing along in the train from somewhere in the Argonne. For all we know they were put in the train 3 days ago.

The people here are a much travelled lot. Most of them have been half over the world. We travel more than any people in the world.

I'm worried to hear what you say of the Z's. I never liked him, & was puzzled by her look of suppression & pain.

Talk & smoke go on here. Its hard to write. I'll end & try to sleep. One gets mighty grieved when one thinks of home, but this work has to be done & the need gets greater. I can scarcely bear to think of the little ones & you.

Bless you dear heart.

Your old<br>John

---

[11]                                                                    10 March

Dearest Con,

I left off last night at about the time Miss Strong brought us oranges, about 10 p.m. I was then in an untidy little office heaped with old magazines; it had a little stove, & Sibbley the orderly was there, & the chauffeur; all of us sitting up to fetch blessees. I fell asleep for a few minutes, & woke to hear the chauffeur telling of a certain tall captain, who had recently committed adultery, & been rich & flashy & was now dead. Then they talked of cars & a night march of the Essex regiment, & I gave the chauffeur my orange, & he ate it and fell asleep & snored, & I sat up reading an old Matin, & at 1 o'clock they went to get the cars ready, & I looked at the night & wished myself at home; it was freezing very hard & snowing. I went out and sanded the castle steps lest we should slip with the brancards, & then Miss Strong had chocolate & bread & jam for us, & we ate, & got the cars loaded, taking hot soup & hot bottles, blankets &c, & then at 2.30 we set out in the snow, in a pitch black night freezing hard & got to La Trecy by three, & waited in the snow for the train. It came at last, & drew up & we could see inside. It had five hundred more or less wounded men in it (some had been there 2 days, & five were dead in it) & there they were, in every kind of filth, just as they had come from the trenches, in 3rd class carriages, & cattle trucks, with blood & vomit & the stink of death, & torn old rags & equipment, which they clung to pathetically, & bits of bread on the floor, & weary, but gentle soldiers looking after them. Everybody is weary & gentle among the blesses. There were lights (and that is strange at night here) & the trucks were hot, & they had a beastly invention in a good's van, an iron cage, four of them, each containing 3 brancards, & each an invention of hell, loaded down with atrociously wounded men. There were 23 for us, & the rest had to go to Dijon, in the dark & cold. God knows how many more have died by this. 3 of ours were at the point of death. One had been lying out for four days on the battlefield, without tending or food, one had a leg smashed into pieces, & another had been blown by a shell & had bits of rope in his face & no eyes & no nose, & his knee broken & his wrist, & another had been blown by a shell & then blown by a bomb & another had septic diorrhoea & is dying now. We got them out & into the cars, & gave them soup & hot bottles, & did what we could. Some were plastered with blood & mud, all were filthy, with mud caked on them & in their hair. Very few could remember when they were wounded; it was just a long blur of pain ago; many had been badly pansed [dressed] (all this side of the Army is rotten, rotten, rotten) & they were like poor tortured animals, with a sort of whimper of pain very weak & low going among them. We took the worst first, & got them into bed here, and then went back for the rest, & coming back the dawn began & we could see the rabbits & owls, & we got them all to bed, & I was allowed in the wards help, & held the poor fellows while they were cleaned. We are afraid we must lose three, for that strange stink of death has come back among us, and there they lie. The others ought to do, but one is paralysed, and all lie dazed, hardly moving, hardly speaking, except one, who was so like Cross I could hardly bear to look at him, yet he, shot in three places, was as jolly as a pig as soon as he had had a sleep. He ate a dinner, & got another man to eat some soup, & if only the sun will come: 'Soleil' as they cry, 'soleil de ma Jeunesse': that is the source of life here. Dear, I've had 2 hard days & no bed & must rest. I know my letters aren't tender. I've so much else to say that I think you may wish to hear.

Bless you & the dear little ones.

Yours loving
John

---

[12]                                        11 March 7 a.m.

My old dear Con,

I'm writing this just before getting up, because in last night's letter I had barely time to give an account of the going for the blessees. I know you're having a beastly time, we all are in this accursed war, the world is, & if one stops to think of this it is hell, & you are all alone with all the little worries & anxieties as well as the big. I've only got discomfort & hard work, & when I get homesick I take great draughts of these. There's no time for anything here but those. People in misery & fearful pain are needing things constantly instantly. You have the worst of it. Dear, I'm sorry if my letters don't seem tender. It's snowing hard again & freezing.

I've just bought a biggish tin that makes a lovely bath, as it holds nearly a big basinful, so now I disport like Leviathan & put perchloride in it too, to kill my parasites, germs being plenty here.

7 a.m.

Yes. Cash Lion's cheque by all means.

I cannot wire to Payne from here, without getting leave from the Commandant at Chaumont, which would take some days, & then the cable would be kept a week. So will you cable Request impossible. Mona's no good, & we know nothing at all of his cast, nor of the production.

My love to you, beloved.

Mrs Rendel's friend is the deaf man; a very good fellow, but a fearful man to carry delicate cases with, owing to his affliction. A new man named Waterfield has come to replace Sibbley, & he is a nice fellow, & a first rate worker, very clever at carpentring, so now our Works resound.

---

[13]                                                         Friday 12 March

My darling love,

I'm grieved to get your letter of the 9th (Ross's letter). This parting is hell enough. I wish you were in London. Will you not think of that? Judith at Mrs Moore's perhaps, & you at Isabel's[1], leaving the maids at Lollingdon[2] & Lewis with you? That would be less lonely for you. I can't get letters through quickly to you. They are stopped at Chaumont for four days, so I suppose you have only just begun to get my long ones; letters from you come direct, & I believe the English mail is not often opened. The work is very hard & continuous here, but not excessive, & I can do it, & am very well, or would be quite if I could think less of your brooding alone. I wish you would go to London. Don't worry about my being over worked, I'm broken in to it now; at first it was very hard. Its funny: I'm slight & slack-looking & not physically strong, but I can do the stretcher work better than any of the orderlies; perhaps I am younger, or perhaps it is that I learned to use my working muscles while they were strengthening their playing muscles.

As we feared, one of the newcomers died last night. He was wounded a week ago, & lay on the field four days & nights, & an ambulance came by & refused to take him in because he wasn't of the ambulance's regiment, & then at last he was found & dressed, & put into that hellish cage in a good's van, beside a stove, with 12 others, for a day or two, & came along in the night to us, with the stove red hot beside his face. He had rigged up a dirty towel to screen his face poor man, & had a wounded man just a foot above him, & another a foot below, & so came jolting to us. I tried to cheer him, but he moaned & said Non Non, & I helped get him to his bed, & we all did our best. He'd not been in a bed since the 17th August. He came from Dieppe, & his wife could not come in time, & he died at 8 o'clock, just as the ward was settling off. And all his marching & fighting & narrow escapes came to nothing, & all his letters that he wrote with a stub of pencil in the trenches will be all the poor woman has. She was screaming in the wards today. And I had to put aside his little bag of treasures (tobacco, & a bit of chocolate) for her to take, & he is to be buried tomorrow here, & we shall be the bearers. This is the damned hellish misery the Bosches are making all over Europe may God smite them with the sword.

The boy who is so like Cross is a dear fellow, & so happy to be out of the trenches. The relief of being with us acts like magic on most of them & alas they get well & go back. Many of our men have been wounded twice. 'It needs courage', they say, 'to go back the third time'. We have two brothers here, each with an arm gone. Many of the men are hit in the buttocks. The modern wound of honour is there, for in the trenches men are screened in front, & the shell bursts behind them & hits them in the buttocks. It is an odd sight to see the slightly hit sticking out their rumps to be pansed. One man with a leg gone at the knee, cocks up his stump & pretends that its a doll. The beautiful thing is to hear the cries of joy when the sun comes into the ward: 'Soleil. Beau Soleil. Ah, le Soleil': but not much soleil so far; mon dieu; bitter hard frost & snow & icy cold.

I try to organise a Fire Service, but one never has time. I either have to improvise, or to clean, or to carry something, & the Service de Fer never gets completed. I've not had any leisure of any kind since I came. I have at least made it easier to deal with a fire; before I came they trusted in God alone.

Dear heart, I'm lonely too for you & the babes. God bless you.

Your old lover

John

We have a case of typhoid from the Argonne. Like many fever people he is eager for fruit & not allowed it, but with a sick man's cunning he got a lot of pickled beetroot smuggled in, God knows how, & was caught in the act of privy supper. He got a pretty good dressing down. Then we have one awful man who is a chemist, & tells our shortcomings to all the newcomers, till they get temperatures from terror. We settled him yesterday by wheeling him into the darkest corner, out of speech, & the whole ward was overjoyed. He was a sergeant & they loved to see him squashed. The cook got some sour cream today; a feast for the Holy Ghost the comforter.

1. Isabel Fry, sister of Roger Fry, the painter and critic. Mrs Masefield's closest friend and confidante, once a colleague at Roedean. Later, they ran a small school together in the Marylebone Road, London. Isabel Fry later kept a school, in Hampstead, for artists' children. The Masefields came to Hampstead and lived near her. Later, in 1909, when her friends moved to Great Hampden, Buckinghamshire, she started a school near Aylesbury where Judith Masefield temporarily studied.

2. In 1914, the Masefields were living at the old Lollingdon Farm, near Wallingford, near the Berkshire Downs. John Masefield's *Lollingdon Downs and Other Poems* was published in 1917.

---

[14]                                                                    Arc.

                                                                    March 15

My beloved Con,

  In still weather here by day, & generally by night, if there is no rain, we can hear the guns at the front sixty or seventy miles away, making their roar. More wounded are to come to us tomorrow or on Wednesday. I suppose they are breaking them for us, & perhaps have even started them; we shall know tomorrow. Sometimes I hate this place with its stink of death and misery, & sombre pines round our cup-edge, more than I can say, & then comes work, or the sight of these poor fellows moaning, & I get a kind of reverence & a kind of joy; and the sense of France is always here, for the heart of the land laid raw, broadcast, & that is strange & deep to one, so one goes on.

  Today we had a lot of operations, following the X-ray men, & got out a lot of bullets, generally with chloroform. One man merely had a cocaine injection, & sat on the table being chaffed till the bullet dropped out of the hole they cut. It was a shrapnel bullet, as big as a small marble (the second we've had from him) & he was awfully pleased & proud with it; & especially pleased at a draught of brandy given him after the operation. Like all the other cases he ate a most hearty supper afterwards; a tumbler of wine, a tumbler of water, a pound of bread, 3 bowls of pea soup, a hunk of cheese, an orange, & a handful of biscuits. Dinner at mid-day is an even bigger business, & it is astounding to see what some of these blessees can eat. I suppose nature must be repaired.

  I don't think much happened today, except the usual host of jobs which prevent my doing my Fire Service work. I get up at 7 & go to the Chateau & fill the drinking water tanks & am punctual at breakfast at 8. The advantage of this is that the breakfast isn't all eaten, as it is if you are so foolish as to come late. Directly after break today I tried to get the pigstye of a hall, which would be fine & feudal, with antlers & sangliers' heads, tidied up; but drugs & stores arrived, 7 bales & cases, & they had to be unpacked & carried up to the store-rooms. Then some nurses were going to lodgings & others coming to the chateau, & their luggage had to be carried up & down & across to wherever they were going to be. Then it was time to carry the wounded out into the garden from the wards, & when that was done it was time to go & draw the wine from the cellar for the men's dinner, 28 bottles from the cask, & then carry the dinners to the wards, serve them out, & clear away again. Then about one I got my own dinner, a jolly hearty one after such a morning, & directly it was down I had to carry blessees to the operations & attend & be useful at the same. Then I had to mend the leg of a bed, & help carry in the wounded from the garden, & get my tea, & carry in more wounded, & draw the wine for supper, & carry, help serve, & wholly clear away the supper, & then, at 7.15, I was able to go on with the tidying of the hall which I had started at 8.30. When I had half done, a gendarme came for medicine, & then I had to fill a water tank, so I didn't get it done till 7.45, when I had to go to dinner, which, as we'd had a doe shot on the estate, was venison, cooked by a soldier who happens to be a chef, & he also made a kind of strange pudding to follow, the labourer being worthy of his hire. Tomorrow the hall will be a pigstye again & there'll be much the same kind of trouble to tidy it. Bless & keep you dear love & bless & keep the babes.

Your old lover<br>John

[15]                                            Arc.·
                                17 March, or 16th, I've lost count.
Beloved Con,

Only a card from you yesterday and nothing at all today. What has happened? Will you not arrange for someone to send me a card about you and the babes if you yourself cannot write? I've not had a line from Nana since I left home.

Here the usual round of exceedingly hard incessant work goes on, all the harder in this fine weather as practically everybody can be carried out now, to be made alive by the sun. I am certain that no hospital ought to have walls; I doubt if any house should. A pent house or open shed, with a sloping stone floor and a perfect drainage system, a big furnace and a south aspect, is the thing. The men in the south wards do twice as well as the men on the other side, and men who can stay out all day mend like different beings.

We had a strange case today. There is a lad who has lost his arm (he came in with the last lot) after a shattering time in the trenches and his nerves are gone to pieces. His wound had to be dressed today, with an anaesthetic to dull the pain, but the thought of being dressed made him mad, with rage and pain and terror, and he roared just like a wild animal, for something like an hour and a half, calling everybody butchers, toads, tigers, snakes and sodomites. Being weary of the noise and guessing it to be a case of nerves, the Doctor said, 'Come, you must have a little morphia'. The lad consented, the Doctor injected a drop of water, and the lad acted just as though it had been morphia. He bore the dressing with a smile, felt no pain whatever, and went to sleep like a lamb.

We have built a long open shed along our south front, and the blessees lie there in chairs to sun. The agent of the estate planned a surprise for them and during one night the men made flowerbeds along it, and when the blessees came down next day, there were the beds full of blossoming primulas, a great pleasure to them, for suffering makes people like children again, as so many deep things do.

We expect many more wounded tomorrow or next day.

I have got the fire arrangements pretty complete now, and I believe we shall do fairly well in case a fire should come; but if it should be a bad fire it will be no light task clearing our bad cases from the wards. We have some terrible cases, and one poor man, who came with the last lot, may die. He has a fearful wound high up in the leg, and he is very weak. If, by leaving him out all day, we can give him a little strength, he may begin to heal, if not, they will have to amputate high up, and he has not the strength for that.

Out blessees made a strange sight on the gravel today. Some 25 beds and stretchers of them side by side, with relatives and friends intermixed, and convalescents in pyjamas playing bowls beyond. I was carting sand or carrying blessees most of today, and tonight heard the guns at the front again, not continuously, but from time to time, and felt that rage against the Bosches which so many of our brave men (pace Napier[1]) feel, and with reason.

Dear heart, I'm sleepy. I can't write well tonight.

Your love,

1. Probably a reference to the anonymous 19th-century verse, *Bold Napier*, which refers to 'our brave old Admiral' and 'brave Napier, he leads the van'. In 1854 Admiral Sir Charles Napier (1786–1860) commanded the Baltic Fleet against Russia, in the Crimean War.

'Old England for ever!
With three times three,
We'll conquer, or we'll die.'

---

[16]                                            Arc.

Wed. 17 March

Beloved Con wife,

Two letters today, so I score. I was afraid the Censor had begun again.

. . . as to coming home. I hope to get away with Bobby either in the first or the second week in April, we can't tell yet which. It may be a day or two either way. This hospital won't be much good after the end of April; anybody who comes here after the flies begin will die; so we shall clear in good time we hope. No substitute need come, & A.P. would be waste at present, as we have 5 doctors, one having come on Monday. There is so much intrigue that it is really not very pleasant, except when one is helping the maimed, so I won't have any friend here. They have an impossible arrangement, a lady business manager who thinks that she can control the medical staff, & a medical staff who claim to control the manager in the interests of the wounded. Endless rows, endless complaints, & long telegrams to a business Committee in London, which claims to control both parties. All the telegrams are closely scrutinised at Chaumont, & the French Military Authorities must enjoy the game, much as Cushendall enjoys the evening post.

My dearest Con wife, this is not a question of being 'noble', or being 'spared', it is a question of going through a little hardship to save the lives of beautiful human beings. I do more hard work than any orderly here, & I can do it, & I was never better in my life, & I can stand any amount of it. France, as a nation, at this time, is heroic. I never thought to touch such a spirit in modern times. But heroic & beautiful as she is, much in her is unprepared, & though it sounds like boasting I do feel that every man here helpd daily to save poor broken men. Now, the fearful thing in this war is that the French hospitals are far from the front, & men die in hundreds & in thousands in torture & filth unspeakable from the want of men to carry them away from the awful clearing houses, ten or fifteen miles from the battles. Now, in May some time, Tonks, Bobby, the de Glehns, & a rich doctor friend who has got a house in the Vosges, want to start an open air hospital, which will save the men this horror, & they want me to come there. One must not say, 'O, one could do such work in England', one could not; the need does not exist; & one must not say 'O, it is waste, your doing such work, you ought to write'; it is not waste; the real waste is war & spilt life & poor beautiful men bled dead for want of a man to hold them. I could not write, thinking of what goes on in those long slow filthy trains, full of mad-eyed whimpering men. You must think of this & we'll talk of it when I come home, oh joyful lovely day, my sweet Con & pretty babes again, after these weeks of stink.

I don't want to crab Isabel's[1] coming to France, no doubt there is much she can do here, but do keep her out of a hospital, if that is her plan. She is unaccustomed to work of this kind, she isn't strong enough for it, & she will have to lie up from time to time and be a general nuisance. When I think of the un-necessary worry & labour the untrained amateur female 'helper' has given here, since I've been here, my blood boils. We've one or two faults among ourselves no doubt, but at least we come prepared to build a latrine one day & sleep in it the next. But, peace.

Another orderly has come. Deaf as a post, very big, yet not very strong, a hard worker, public school & Oxford, no initiative whatsoever, & follows me about like a mastiff dog to catch those crumbs of work which fall from the master's table.

Dear, I must stop.
Your old lover.
John

1. Isabel Fry.

---

[17]                              Arc,
                    March 18? Thursday? (Count quite lost now).
My beloved Con,

I've been very sad over your last letter, feeling that I've given you a harsh time, and not written very nicely or feelingly. The reason partly is that I've only this hour and a half before bed in which I can write, and I write slowly and have masses to say, which I know you want to hear, and by the time I have written some of that I'm asleep and many other things remain unsaid. I hope to get home early in April; I may be kept till mid-April; if any atrocious load of misery is suddenly flung at us I may stay till the third week in April, but I hope to get away before that. The Vosges hospital in May seems so much saner and more useful than this: but we'll talk of that when I'm at home. How wonderful for you to have the Spring. We have no sign of Spring, but there are a few primulas, snowdrops, and a few sprigs of Daphne. I'm going Daphne picking before break tomorrow, the blessees do love it so.

We had a sad scene here yesterday. All the local horses were mobilised and had to go off to the war, with their carts; poor old crocks which had escaped the earlier gleanings stood in the road and were sad, and one old man stood for a long time grooming his two farm horses and plaiting their tails and manes so that they might start in style. Arc itself is like a village of the dead. Half the houses are shut up and empty; the men are all gone to the war; the shops have nothing to sell, the ironmonger hasn't even a brad nor a turnscrew; and no-one moves in the street, but one or two lonely women and a widow or so, and a few little children and the Curé. I hardly ever see it by day and can't really describe it; I shan't ever think of it except as a town in a dream, as I see it at night going home, a pitch dark town with perhaps one distant light, and sometimes the diligence with a lamp waiting for the mails, and tonight a sort of hawker with a cart selling something to the very poor under a lantern. Hardly any one stirs after dark and those who have lights seem watching by the sick bed, and those in the road seem going for the priest, and there is always a noise of water, for there are many running taps, fed from the river, which dribble night and day and spatter and relent, and are slow, and sound as though the town were weeping.

Paysannes wash the hospital bedding in the river for two francs a day, and then the fair stream runs softly till it ends some of its song in the village taps, and I suppose they drink it and wash their houses with it at odd times, though there is beautiful pure water, too. Our head doctor used to bathe in it till he found some extra bloody old brancard which Bobby and I had put in to sweeten; now he says it doesn't agree with him. Our river gets into the Aube in time and so to the Seine, and I suppose every brook and river which mingles with it mingles life's blood, and runs blood to the sea, the blood of men.

Just before I came a man died in the Chateau. He'd been badly wounded in the Argonne and was dying when he came, so they telegraphed for his wife to come, but the Departments got muddled and the telegrams were delayed, and when the wife started she got into the wrong train and was three days getting here, and when she got to her husband's bedside he was in the act of death, and looked at her and said 'Maigre', which means excrement, and died.

Rob Holland and Lady Scott came yesterday, as there is some talk and war going on in the management. R.H. is a good fellow and gives a hand where wanted. They are going back to England tomorrow. My God, I wish I were. Lady S (According to Bobby) wants to do a bronze of me. The only time I've spoken to her was when I was sweeping out the hall; she gave me some snowdrops for the blessees.

Our nurses are a fine lot. I do admire them. I've been hard on the amateurs because they have been trying and troublesome, but after all they were bred in sloth and grew up in luxury and to come suddenly on blood and stink and filth by the bedpan and the bucketful and to have to wash men's rumps and to hold their poor fragments together, when one expected to be simply grande dame dispensing charity, must be a shock.

My gay man who had the bullet cut out of his back in Convalescent and goes to the Hospice tomorrow. I fed him at supper tonight and everybody who loves him brought him Dainties, and he ate 1 lb of bread or more, two large bowls of soup and bread, two heaped plates of salad, and five or six eggs, as well as an orange which I got for him and a quart of wine and water. He is an enchanting nice gentle fellow. It's sad when they go, even when they go hearty.

Dear heart, bless you and the babes,
Your old love,

The Etat Major of France inspected us today and were pleased with us. They said, that hardly any had been wounded lately in the Argonne, but that more would come to us soon.

---

[18]                                                      Arc.
                                                   21 March.

Darling Con,

It is so piercing cold here tonight in my little fireless room that I shan't be able to do much writing before hopping into bed. It freezes the water in my jug and the sponge in my saucer, with some 18 degrees of frost, though tomorrow probably a coat will be too hot, as it was today.

Many rumours run here about the war: that it will be over in 6 weeks, or in July, or in July if the harvest is bad, or in June, or very soon, each has his theory. Probably nine tenths of each country involved would be glad to end it now. I would, God knows, if there were any chance of its not springing up again; but my own feeling is, December, with awful fiendish slaughter, regularly twice a month, till then.

Not much has happened today, except that I made my fourth table (my third since yesterday) for use in the wards. I go in for a four leg type, while Bobby goes in for ⌁ legs, and I think the ⊓ type is better in hospital use. We make and use lots of tables in the wards for each blessee ought to have one, and the one I made today was for the fine young volunteer, with the grave face, who suffers so. I would love to sit and talk with these men, and I think with him especially (he is a little like Agnes Fry[1], perhaps) but the work is too pressing for that; I only get in a word now and then and sometimes an orange or some cigarettes. I'm glad he's not in a native hospital; for one of our doctors says that they are most fearful places, made anyhow, either not warmed or not ventilated, never cleaned, and heaped with the dying and the dead and smelling of death and neglect. I don't know what it is in this character which is so callous to suffering. It is partly due to poverty of mind in a state Department, and to unwise thrift, but mainly to some want in character. They have a disregard for others, and for life, which shocks us continually; not that we can blame them now, in this upheaval. I could weep all day for pity of these brave fellows here, but there it is, they're different. A woman brought some hens here the other day, alive hens, for use in the kitchens. She said she would kill them 'tout de suite' by snipping off their heads with a blunt pair of nail scissors. That is one side, I suppose. The other side I saw today when a paysanne brought in a poor plucked moorhen, as a little treat for 'un malade bien sage'.

The man whose life hangs by a hair sleeps out of doors now under a penthouse roof in clear air and improves and may just live. His old mother is with him all day and cuts up his food for him and cries and is a gentle kind old soul. He suffers a good deal and his wound oozes poison continually and last night his little pot of beer was frozen and he cried. These are the things that make one so hellish against the Bosche; it isn't only the killing and defiling, its the bringing down of life from her high place in the soul.

There are a lot of men badly hit, too badly hit to move, bad fractures of legs etc, whose minds are active and merry and to these men jigsaw puzzles and Chinese puzzles are unalloyed childish joy. Often, they don't suffer much (except from laying still) and you can see them working at their puzzles sometimes for hours, one yesterday from 1 till 6, and then when they've done them they wait for you to pass and shout out the glad tidings.

They have all sorts of explosives on them when they come in, in the way of French English and German unused cartridges which they have picked up as souvenirs. Some day the Disinfector, which bakes their clothes on arrival for them, will have its lid blown off, but so far we have escaped that. Another fear is that the nurses, in gouging the bullets out of the cartridges (for they have the belief that the bullet is the dangerous part and should come out) will have their eyes put out. I stopped a Nurse in the act only yesterday, with a fine new German cartridge, fresh from the Argonne.

Dear Con wife, I do long to be back with you and the babes.

I love and bless you, Darling,

Your old love,

1. Sister of Isabel Fry, naturalist and botanist. Judith Masefield comments that she was a very clever delightful woman who was deaf. She and Masefield managed to

communicate with sign language and written notes. In his letters to Agnes from France, he particularly mentioned flowers, and those gradually returning on the battle-riven earth and in the shell-holes. 'Most of the shell holes have dried up, and the grass has come, and is even shyly creeping back into the burnt and awful places, Thiepval and Beaumont Havel, and the black stumps of trees put out each a plant or two. I never saw so many dandelions; and there is a tall plant, like a cabbage run wild, with bright pale yellow flowers, the colour of a yellow poppy, it was too pretty to pick or I would have sent you some.'

[19]                                                                                   Arc.
                                                                              23. III 1915

My beloved Con wife,

Today has been a really bad day for us here, and I've again seen the results of low barometer. By the dead feel in the air the barometer must have been very low, and it was strange to see how it reacted on the bad cases, nearly all were worse, some markedly, and we've had another death, and another, if not two more, are pretty sure to die. I have hated today here, not for the work, nor for the death, for when one sees it here, death does not seem so evil as what precedes it, but because of all the fearful pain I've watched and been unable to help.

The death was the aneurism of which I wrote last night. He had been shot in the left shoulder, and been diagnosed here as a clean wound (serious enough) with an aneurism. The French x-ray man said there was no aneurism, but a bullet; a slight operation showed that there was an aneurism, but no trace of a bullet. As far as I can make out, an aneurism is an internal bleeding away into vessels which get distorted and destroyed by it.

The boy was not quite 21. I have not been much in his ward and did not know him particularly, but he was a great ally of Glehn's. He has been dreadfully ill here, poor boy, and very weak, but we all hoped he might pull round. Today they decided to operate, to find the bleeding artery and tie it, as there was no other chance of saving him, though not much chance in this. Glehn and I carried him in. He suffered a great deal in being lifted, and was very weak, and his hands were delicate and he did not quarrel with the chloroform: when they are lusty they do, and sometimes they hit and kick; but this man only muttered a little and so drowsed off. The operation was very long and very very delicate, for they were all about his heart, and I marvelled at the skill of it, and thought of all the skill that had gone to giving him the wound, to making the wound possible, and then of the skill which was trying to heal the wound, and wondered at the strange lapse which was somewhere in the chain, some lapse of folly or stupidity or crime. I did not see the end of the operation, as I had to get the men's dinners, but it was said to have been rather a triumph, for they found the bleeding artery and tied it; and then we left him in the theatre, as he was frightfully weak, and for my part I gave up all hope, though the Doctors hoped. About half past three, when I was disinfecting, after holding a poor stinking exuding fellow for about an hour, we had an alarm and I had to find the poor lad's father, who had gone to the garage, I think, to see the cars. I ran half over Arc in my shirt and trews to find him, but could not, though one of those whom I sent to hunt was luckier, so we got him in. The boy was lying with his eyes closed, gasping, and the poor old father (who was very like Hudson in the face) burst into tears, and I had to take him away to another room and talk to him and to say that we still had hope and that he must be calm. The poor old man was a farm labourer who worked in the fields, 'a hard life', he said, 'but pleasant', and his son was all he had, that he cared for, except the grand girl in service at Fontainebleau. He cried again in his chair, sobbing: 'Mon fils, mon fils', and 'C'est la faute de Guillaume[1]'. (I think this simply broke my heart, this last) and I could say nothing much, except that we hoped, and indeed we did, for his boy took a rally, and did better. I got the old man some cigarettes and wine and water and left him in Tonks' room, for I had to carry in wounded, and when I had finished that the boy was dead.

At the last parting the boy wanted his father to kiss him and made the noise of kissing with his lips, and the old man bent and kissed him. I tried to talk to the old man and he talked of his little house, and how he had four hens, and loved his garden, and how the English were good gardeners, for there was one at Melun who had jolis fleurs.

I laid the poor boy out in the mortuary and covered him with the pall and put the tricolor beside him, and he is to be buried tomorrow, and 'then', the old father says, 'I shall go back to se mer mes a voines'.

Your letter was very dear in all this grief.

Bless and keep you darling,

From your old love,

1. Kaiser Wilheim II, popularly identified as the instigator of the Great War, somewhat unfairly, though his bellicose posturings, disguising a nervy and erratic temperament, helped contribute to his role as arch-villain.

---

[20]　　　　　　　　　　　　　　　　　　　　　　　　　　　　　Arc.

　　　　　　　　　　　　　　　　　　　　　　　　　　　　　　　March 25

My beloved Con,

I'm sorry for the gap of two days. I have written regularly every night and can only blame the Censor. Perhaps they will turn up later. I reckon that if you have written every day five of yours have been stopped, so you must have done the more treason of the two. I don't remember saying anything likely to be censored, but one never knows in these times.

We went for blessees at midnight last night in muggy wet weather and the moon gone down and not much light in the lamps; we felt like conspirators, and not at all like the first time. One gets soon hardened here, and though the first meeting with a train of wounded is a thing no-one can ever forget, the second is no such matter. We found our station occupied by an empty line of hospital carriages a quarter of a mile long or more, and by and by, when we had been some minutes there in the dark we discovered that a male red X staff was living in them, so we knocked them up and talked through the windows and were very good friends. The two with whom I talked were in training there, and one of them had a cold, so I gave him an orange I had and he said 'No, no, you must keep it for one of the blessées', but as I had another, which afterwards got squashed in my pocket alas, so that I shall never suck its sweet juice alas, and as oranges are apt to give blessées very dangerous colic, I got him to take it and he was very glad of it. They liked my macker very much, 'un bon caoutchou'. They said 'not many wounded lately': they did not know why. The man with the cold was like L. Houseman[1] with his face in a bandage, the other was a beefy fat faced lad, like a lad whom I met in America: did not like him so much.

Our train came in rather quietly and we went in. I got again the impression of being in a very foul filthy ship's fo'c'sle in bad weather, the stretchers in tiers look so like bunks, and the dirty clothes and bad light and the grimy white faces peering at you, and the smell of sweat and bad food and oil and blood and wounds and the intolerable heat. I suppose the van measured 25 by 8 feet, and contained 12 wounded, two attendants, no visible window, and a stove which was bright red hot from the legs to half way up its chimney. I never saw a stove red hot before, this was; a blacksmith could have beaten it out into shoes, there and then. We could tell at a glance, almost by the smell, that the cases weren't very serious. Instinct will tell you that, I can't explain how, but it does. There was not that stillness nor the whimper, nor the way they lie. So we got them out, and it was 1 in the morning or so, in a desolate cold station and raining, yet before we had cleared one van the train was so filled with country people that we could hardly get by with the stretchers. Some little children were there and a lot of women. God knows how they got there.

We had to make 2 journeys, but they were all light cases, and they'll all be convalescent by Monday. One had had nothing to eat for three days, and another had been blown up in a trench he had just helped to take, and when he came to he found he was lying on a headless German corpse, and there was something on his chest which he thought was a cat, but it was some other German's hand and wrist which had been blown off. Their first day in the wards is generally quiet; they taste the luxury of leisure; tomorrow they will eat.

Dear one, I'm dropping with fatigue. Fond love,

1. Presumably Laurence Housman (1865–1959), art critic on the *Manchester Guardian*, on which Masefield himself worked, 1904. Also poet, novelist, playwright, a

feminist, pacifist, socialist. He edited the *Last Poems* and *More Poems* of his brother, A.E., whose biography he wrote.

---

[21]                                                              Arc.

                                                              26 March

My darling Con wife,

I do hate to think of you in London with all these worries on your hands. I wish I were back to share them with you on this Day of ours; but I'll be back soon I hope. And Judith's little letter to be gone astray, it is too cruel. I'm afraid they're been wrongly addressed. The address is

> Hopital Militaire
> Arc en Barrois
> Haute Marne

Not one of them has come to me and I've been desolated about it. If you put *British Expeditionary Force* at the top of your letters (envelopes) *very clearly* about 2/3rds of them will get through for a penny, the rest get taxed, but by bothering we can get the tax refunded here. This will be sent to Cholsey, because, allowing for the Chaumont delay, it ought to reach you about April 1, when you will be out of London.

The barometer has gone up and our stinking old barrack has seemed a different world. It is a foul hole in bad weather; down in a well, on a flat grass field, with low steep wooded hills all round, just as though it had once been a crater or the bed of a glacier. The air can't get to it and the smell can't blow from it, and the dogs defile it and the Duke avoids it- wise man, say I. The country round is rather like the Cotswolds about Stroud, but much more densely wooded, and infinitely wilder. A wild doe was in the Chateau grounds today (the blessees hunted her on crutches) and there are great hawks and owls. In the woods there are pink Daphne, and a yellow flowered shrub, and wood anemones, but no feel of spring anywhere at all. It might still be February here.

It has been a medium day today. Bobby and I represented the Hospital at the funeral of the man who died of tetanus. This was at 9 a.m. It was very like the other funerals, a beautiful little tribute from the whole village, everybody there in mourning, the gendarmes in full uniform, boys in white, and the priest, and pretty wreaths on the coffin. It was left to us English to do an infamy. Two men of our staff photographed the scene, and a woman took a snapshot of the procession leaving the grounds. It has made me almost weep with fury and shame.

The funeral was as sad as the others. The man's old mother crying aloud, and one of his tenants sobbing. He was a rich farmer, with five farms and all that heart could wish, and now he is dead and his old mother is left alone. 'C'est la fault de Guillaume.' After the funeral I began a ward table and worked hard at it till it was time to carry out blessees, and I finished it at about 3, and then got wood for another. Wood is very cheap in this forestland, and there is a lovely big sawmills just up the river, where they saw the wood for us and plane it smooth; and then in about an hour and a half I can tap up a 4 leg table with a shelf underneath it all complete.

As far as I can make out, only one of our men knows that he has killed a Bosche. He was in an attack on a trench and came on some unknown Bosche face to face, they lunged at each other and he killed the Bosche with his bayonet and the Bosche ran him through the leg and died.

Dear, I'll speak to Bobby about your coming.

I'm sodden with sleep, dear heart.

Fond love and blessings on this Day of ours.

God keep you and bless you,

From your old love,

---

[22]
Arc.
March 27.

My beloved Con,

I have been at the Hospice this evening, visiting Sergeant Gex, the pastoral poet 'who did not persevere'. The Hospice was a monastery before the suppression and it has a queer air of holiness about it still, though the Convalescents are apt to get drunk. A man was lying drunk on one of the beds in the Sergeant's room, but there were three others sober enough, and we had a long talk about the war; the first real talk I have had with the men, the work has been so unceasing. I expect Bobby's real phrase about me was 'too perfect to last' and perhaps my having the talk at all was a sign of having fallen.

The men had a picture on the wall: Crepuscule dans un champs de Bataille: a more or less conventional scene of corpses and broken equipment, and I asked if the reality were like that, and they said 'No, not at all, except for two things which are very characteristic, this, and this. . . .' a dead man's hand held upright, and a man sitting up, leaning forward. They began to get excited when they remembered their battles. They had been in the Marne fighting in the early part of the war and had seen the open war as well as the trench war, and they spoke with a clear passionate eloquence that they often burned into rage. A little man, whom I had thought to be quiet, began, 'Ah, an attack the first time is a fearful thing, especially at night when the brancards begin to come past, and you hear the cries, Mamman, Mamman, Ma Femme, ma femme, mes pauvres enfants, A moi, Secours, O, je meurs, O j'ai soif, O la la, O je souffre; but the terrible thing is when you hear them die singing. I've heard them die singing. Twice I heard that. He was shot quite through the head, the top of his head was blown clean off, and he was singing aloud in a clear voice "Mourir pour la patrie, c'est douce, c'est belle." The other was under a tree and he kept singing, what was it he kept singing, something unknown about a woman, how did it go, it went like this about a woman, to an air unknown. Ah, that is the most terrible of all. But ask that man over there (he was a great big slouching charming smiling fellow, just convalescent) he was a prisoner with the Bosche, and they put him in the trenches with ten others and made him fire at us, but he took advantage of an attack of tirailleurs and made his escape, the others they shot. And there was a Zouave, which I myself saw. He was prisoner with the Bosches, and the Bosches were attacking us and pushing him in front of them and the Prussian Officer said "Cry out that we are French or I'll shoot you", and when he came near us, the Zouave cried out "Shoot, shoot, these are the Bosches", so we shot and he was killed, that was a magnificent death, that was beautiful.'

I have been much struck, since I came here, with the strength and rightness of instinct among the wounded. They generally are right as to the exact site of the bullets inside them, they know, more or less, whether they can stand an operation, and tonight my theory of the sun was strangely verified by the sergeant, who said, 'Of course, we blessees go up and down with the weather'. I am much struck by the skill of modern surgery (I've seen heaps of operations now) but I think that it is not nearly imaginative enough, pays much too little heed to individual character, and is apt to lose life from the want of feeling: of care, of course they have more than enough, but 'feeling has no fellow'.

Oh, my Darling old Con how lovely it will be to be back. Bless you, my darling for all your lovely letters. I can't write more.

Your old love,

---

[23]                                                                          Arc.

                                                                    28th March.

My beloved dear Wife,

As usual, after a day with two letters, I have a day with none, which is sad enough, but on the whole you suffer more from the post's caprice than I. There is a great to do here over the coming visit of our chiefs to the Hospital Staff at the front; the future of the hospital rather hangs on it and it will be an excitement to all those who go, for they will see the Front hospitals and all the back of the firing line and some of the brain of the army, too. They will go perhaps this week and be away two days.

Perhaps you are weary of tales of what happened to somebody else, they seem to be the staple of talk in war time. We have a kind of French Count on our governing body, and he was on the battlefield of the Marne picking up wounded (in September I think) at night time with some bright motor lamps to aid him. He says that often he was knee deep in blood and a slough of bloody flesh all heaped together, and that all over the field, for perhaps miles, there was a sort of moan of Maman, Maman from hundreds and thousands of dying men.

When our blessées get a little well they like to rag the sisters, and you hear odd remarks like 'Seester, what is Will you kiss me, mean?' Tonight I heard one man pretending to have colic, which is an ailment very prevalent among them. He was moaning and writhing, with 'O, j'ai la colique, O j'ai de la peine, O, la colique, O, c'etait cet orange atroce, O, j'ai la colique' etc etc. Suddenly I heard a Sister's voice from the other end of the Ward 'Tasy vous toot sweet or je vous donnerai la colleek', and he was silent as the sucking dove.

I was sad at your mention of my old tools. O, to be using them after these French ones with which I knock up tables here. I am making a new one now, of a much more ambitious kind. I want it to be an ordinary bedside table, with a shelf below it for the man's books and slippers, and a top which he can eat his dinner from, but I want to have a double top, which will, if necessary, pull out, or fold over, so as to come across the bed, to let the man write in comfort propped up on his pillow.

The sergeant told me yesterday that the awful thing at the front in the confused Argonne is that you hardly ever know which is your front. The trenches zig zag about and the Bosche may be almost all round you, and then there is the mud and the cold (less than in Flanders but still pretty bad) and the food very harsh and chill and always the fear of death and the anxiety. One man here hasn't seen his wife and children since July, and they are all in a part of France over run by the Bosches, and he cannot hear of nor from them, and he has been badly hit and is now cured, and going back to fight, and still cannot tell them, and that is the sort of thing perhaps 10,000 have to face in this land, through the wild beast lust of the Bosches, whom may God smite. We literary men have been very evil, writing about war. To fight is bad enough, but it has its manly side, but to let the mind dwell on it and peck its carrion and write of it is a devilish, unmanly thing, and that's what we've been doing, ever since we had leisure, circa 1850.

I'm sleepy, dear heart, and its cold and snowing again, but I must just write to Nana. I hope the dancing was a success.

My love to you and them beloved,

Your old love,

We have three men here who have gone mad from the strain of the war.

---

[24]                                         29 March 1915.
                                             Arc.

My beloved Con,

Bobby is having a long colloque tonight with Tonks to discuss my idea, that we should start an Author's and Artists' Hospital in the Vosges and spend May in drumming up money for it. He is very keen indeed on having you on the staff and suggests that the dear babes should come, too. He is quite hopeless beyond his level, you see, like the rest of us. The result of the colloque won't be clear tomorrow, as Tonks has a toothache and is inclined to curse the world.

Whilst I was packing up some sackings in the Hall today, the lad who is so like Cross came in. He was only lightly hit in the arm and is now at the Hospice convalescent and about to go altogether for his forty days leave before returning to the war. He speaks a cruelly difficult patois, very rapidly, but, as in reading aloud to you sometimes, I often feel a kind of Holy Ghost coming down on me, when I listen to these people, and when that happens I can understand every word and they me. I got him to talk about the war and his own feelings. He is an orphan and has one brother a year younger than himself, and he himself is 18, and looks three years younger, a merry, cheery, honest, hard working, country boy with very warm affections and good hearty animal recreations, with much that country way which some of the lads in Hereford used to have when I was a boy, a sort of brisk emphasis. He said that his first coming under fire was in an attack with the bayonet, and that the fire confused him and all the other newcomers till they were like dazed people, but that one got used to it. He said that the trenches were not so bad; you had little shelters and you were under cover, and the shells could not get at you, and that the shells burst and when they burst they were done with, and that if a shell came into the trench you lay down and let it burst over you, or sometimes it sank into the mud and did not burst; anyway for his part he would lie down and go to sleep when there were only shells. Besides, ten metres away, there were the Bosches, who were very musical, and fluted and sang, and you could shout at them. But you were only in the trenches for ten days and then you had six days rest in a little village, and he did not like the six days rest, for there you had drill, and inspection of arms, sentinals to furnish, inspection of equipment, much worse than the trenches. The terrible thing in war was when you or the Bosche exploded a mine under a trench and blew people up into the air, for that was most terrible, for it is terrible to see men in the air an arm going one way and a leg another way and a heart another way and a head another way; ah, that is terrible. As to bayonet attacks, then you kill; 'pas des prisonniers', the officers cry that. He himself (aged 18, no trace of a beard) and killed two Bosche with the bayonet. He had been wounded on the 1st of his 2nd ten days in the trenches, so perhaps he had not yet lost the novelty of the experience. I was amused by him on Saturday, when he came to me for some wire. When I had found some for him, he explained that it was for lapins in the forest. However, he has caught none yet, and isn't likely to, with such wire.

I saw the operation of skin grafting today. We chloroformed a man and cut off the skin of a bit of his thigh and very delicately patted it down onto the wound in his shoulder, where it will grow in a day or two and make a neat patch. When he came to, he was very bitter with us. He said that he had had one wound and now we had made him another. It seems that wounds just on

the skin are much more painful than the deeper ones, and our light scrape with
the Razor stung intolerably.

Dear, I yearn for you and the babes.

Bless and keep you, beloved

Your old,

One of the doctors today said that Selah was what David said when he broke a
string.

Tonks, in his toothache humour, said that what our blessées would really
like would be a nice good wound that would keep them in bed for three months
and let them get drunk every day. (Our poor Hospice is in a sadly drunken state
again. Alas poor sinful man.)

I enclose a poem FGX wrote to me.

---

[25]                                            Arc.

29 March or 30

My beloved Con wife,

Two letters tonight, so I suppose none at all tomorrow, the usual way here.
And only a short one from me, I'm afraid, for its 10.15 p.m., & I'm only just
home, having been wanted for an operation on that poor man whose leg bone
(and life) hung by a hair. It wasn't a serious operation, only cleaning out the
wound, but it took a long time & was quite the most loathsome thing we have
done here, but one never thinks of that much when it is being done. It is
afterwards, when one feels the smell all about one like a garment, wrapping one
close, that one feels disgust, or not disgust, that isn't the word, one never feels
disgust for what comes from a poor brave gentle man's misfortune & suffering,
but loathing for the blasting crime of this accursed folly & wickedness. I'm
afraid the man will have to have another operation, to get out some broken
bone or other, & that will make him so weak that he will have to have his leg off,
& that will end him, that is the circle we move in. I'm not sure that the old
surgery was not the wiser way, that had the leg off at once, & killed at once or
got the misery over. His old mother is here. She's a widow & he's her only
child. She's very like Mrs Ward at the Post Office, & they come from Paris,
where they run a little jeweller's shop together; she sits with him all day & gives
him his meals, & sometimes cooks little messes for him & makes him sick. Its a
pitiful business.

The worst of our three lunatics got removed on Sunday. He was very mad,
but agreeably so, though he had a fearful spiritual effect on those men near him
in the ward. He had gone mad in the trenches, & used to tell a terrible tale of
how a drunken unarmed German came singing into their trench one night,
having missed his way, & how they all set on him & killed him. There is little
pity in this war.

You ask, when will it end? I now think, in about a year from now; not before.
They're too strong, & too well organised.

Since Bobby was forcibly kept from lifting stretchers he has come round
again & is well. He is a genius at carpentering. Tell Lion he is all right again, as
she is bothering him.

I'm very tired, dear heart, & must sleep. Dear love to you & the babes.

Your old lover

Jan

Its snowing hard again & freezing.

7 a.m.

Yes. Cash Lion's cheque – by all means.

I've just bought a biggish tin that makes a lovely bath, as it holds nearly a big
basinful, so now I disport like Leviathan & put perchloride in it too, to kill my
parasites, germs being plenty here.

---

[26]

Arc.

31 March.

My beloved Con,

No letter at all today, as I expected and feared.

Fighting has been slack in the Argonne & no more blessees have come in, &
none have gone along the line to Dijon, & the cannon have been quieter, so
speculation again, what does it mean? Some think negotiations for peace have
begun; but what peace is possible, with Germany in this frame of mind, with
Belgium & N France unpaid for, & Tsing tao to avenge: I see no hope nor
chance of peace, & put the slackness down to the falls of snow, the delayed
Spring, & a heaping up of more & more ammunition for the attempted advance
when the time comes. Our chiefs may go to the Front tomorrow to see the Etat
Major, & when they come back we may know more, if the Etat itself knows
more. The Chief, & Tonks, & I suppose De Glehn will go, & Bobby, I suppose,
will drive them. Its only 60 miles or less (Cholsey to London) to the centre &
brain of the war; and perhaps they will see Joffre himself, flying by on his 60
mile an hour car, wearing out one of his three daily chauffeurs. All the lot of
them are already swelling with vanity, & I believe they all secretly hope that
they may at least see a shell burst reasonably near, so that they may say, in after
years, 'Ah, it was no joke, being under fire in 1915. I had a narrow escape near
the French Headquarters once etc. etc.'

I hope the Moores'[1] visit went off well, & that they danced you the Pavane &
the Galliard. I can't help saying what I've always felt, that Isabel does not give
Judith enough fresh air, or in some way neglects to keep her out of draughts.

All her bronchial attacks for the last five years have begun when she was with Isabel. I'm sure I'm right: there is some failure or neglect there.

I'm writing this in the Lion, & a lot of Convalescents have just left the inn parlour below me and are now in the snow in the moonlight just under my window crying Adieu, either to me or to the landlady's girl, the latter probably. Then they will trace their wavering track to the Hospice & be exceedingly sick on the floor, for I'm afraid its not their wounds which give them their rolling gait; its the coeur tendre of the motherhood of Arc, with its 'Tenez. C'est pour l'indigestion; un p'tit peu de cassis, c'est bon pour les blessures au cuisse.' I do not envy Blunt his job. We, or the sisters, send him consignments of gentle loving lambs, such as a German Christ might consort with on a wall in Ledbury, & 2 days in that holy house of God, which still really smells of peace & happy quiet, as when the monks left it, makes them bold earthly carnal sons of Baal, who defy the night owl in a catch, & trawl the bowl till all sings.

Bobby's chauffeur here speaks no French, but seems to get on with the natives well enough. I was with him outside the chateau the other day, & 3 blessees came past & each grinned at him & said 'Good', 'Yes', he answered, 'Tres good'. Then we had a new cook the other day who was not tres good, but bad, & left next morning, & the chauffeur was heard explaining to the station master: 'Wee. Soon returny.'

Dear, I'm tired & must to bed. Would I were back with all my beloveds, thinking of John & Ada[2] coming to stay. Its strange but the 2 come into my heart very warmly always. I kiss you, dear love. Kiss my Lew & Jude.

Your old
Jan

1. Probably Mr & Mrs Thomas Sturge Moore, friends and neighbours of the Masefield's in Hampstead. Thomas (1870–1944), was poet, art critic, editor, well-known as an aesthete of the 90s. The Moores held a regular literary and artistic salon at their home in Well Walk, which George Orwell knew in the 30s. Masefield would have met many writers there, of which Ruth Pitter and Christopher Hassall now seem the most substantial.
2. The novelist, John Galsworthy (1867–1933), author of *The Forsyte Saga* and his wife. Another Hampstead couple. For the naval ambulance service which Masefield organised for the Gallipoli wounded, Galsworthy helped in financing the four boats, one of which was named 'John and Ada'. George Calderon was also a member of this circle.

---

[27]                                                      Arc.
                                                      Apl. 1st.

My beloved Con,

Two letters, & the Moores' enclosure, today, so for a few hours I'm rich, but I'm afraid there'll be nothing tomorrow. I'm glad the Moores were nice with you. They have got good hearts, & since this experience I doubt if anything else matters; intellect does not. I was touched by the Moores' writing to me.

It was strange, getting your letter about the boy who howls. He yelled again, fearfully, today, while a General was inspecting us, & lusty round French Tigres & Assassins came in the pauses between compliments. He yelled because his arm is in a bad way & had to be examined, so this time he got real morphia & then chloroform, & was examined, & was afterwards fairly quiet, but tomorrow they will have a fearful time when they renew the dressings. He is an unpleasant looking boy, a very cruel nervous face, & an unattractive way, but in this work one looks on appearance as simply a symptom, & he may, like so many others here, suddenly mend, & become, & look, a different being. It is odd. His nervousness gives him a kind of very fine stoicism. He will bear almost any pain to avoid being touched, and has a fine kind of pride in rolling himself in untold agony off the stretcher into bed by himself, while others, of ten times his stamina, are lifted or dragged.

We have a man here who has been wounded 4 times. He was mobilised in July & got wounded late in August. In October he was in the trenches for part of one day & was wounded again. In November he was in the trenches for a week & got another wound, & now in March after ten more days in the trenches he gets sent to us. All the rest of the time he has been in hospital, & we gather that this is the nicest hospital he has ever been in, not in equipment of course, for this ugly old wasteful house was never meant for a hospital, & our equipment is mainly makeshift, made by Bobby, but in our care & personal service, which is exceedingly good, especially now, with the wards rather empty & the nurses not too busy.

One thing one sees tragically here. It is a fearful thing to let anyone grow up without the habit of industry. There are a lot of lady probationers here who have lived idly & luxuriously, & who are now, in the main, useless nuisances. One of them, today, the 1st fine day for a week, when we four orderlies had to carry out every blessee who could stand carrying, & were hard at it, so as to get them out before lunch (12 noon) & give them a real day in the sun, actually asked me to leave the blessees & carry up from the basement for her an empty wooden packing case to put her clothes in. She did not get her desire, & I am sorry to have to tell the tale of her, but it shewed me to what depths of dependence idleness can sink a person. We must see to it that Judith never gets like that. Another fault they have, is that they pet the young good-looking patients & neglect the others, & so destroy both. This is a very human thing & I forgive it, having been like that myself; but I've learned now, here, that it is our duty to watch each human soul alike unceasingly & lovingly, or God knows what may happen.

As I rather feared last night our Convalescents did go home drunk, & were sick on the floor, & were then both noisy & rude, so two of them, in a very sick condition, were put into the car this morning & handed over to the depot at Chatillon, & very scared they were to go; and we have got a little pretty strict militaire, to settle the others, to the effect that any of them found in a home of ill fame or café after 8.30 p.m. will pay, the night in the cells & then go to the depot; so now behold us like sucking doves again, cooing love for Blunt & I daresay saluting him.

Bobby is an odd creature. The other day Holland was here & lost a new pair of beautiful motor gauntlets, worth I suppose a pound or more. We all searched high & low for them but could not find them, so he left without them, & the next day I said to Bobby 'Have you found Holland's gloves by any chance?' 'Oh', he said, 'I found them long ago, before he went, but as they were rather a nice pair I stuck to them.'

Dear love to you all, my darling. Keep well for me.

Fondest love
from
Jan

---

[28]

Arc.
2nd Apl.

My beloved Con,

No lett again; the post very jagged this week, & the papers empty, so perhaps a big movement preparing. More wounded are coming tomorrow night so perhaps it has already begun.

We have had a heavy day, for the days are fine just now, very hot & sunny, like May in England, though we get stinging frosts at night, with all the water frozen in one's room, & the sponge like a block. On every fine day we have to carry out the blessees who cannot walk, unless they are too ill, & it is very severe labour carrying these magnificent men up & down stairs, though it does not tire me now as it did. We put them in rows on the gravel below the steps of the south front, some on their mattresses, others on trestles or brancards, & there they lie all day (with enormous fivepenny straw hats on their heads) talking & smoking, with their ward mates beside them. Those who have relatives seem to share their relatives with those who have not, & people from the village come in, one or two, of the better kind, & those who can walk play bowls on the gravel for hours & hours, & then the nurses or the doctors photograph them, & sometimes dress a wound behind a screen, & the little pretty dogs of the village come up, as in the tale of Lazarus, & eat the dressing or the anointment, & go away a little & are sick, & then come back to get some more. I never saw so many mixed kind of dogs as here. Just up the hill there are the Duke's Kennels, with his wild-boar hounds, which seem to range from a kind of yellow dunghill dog, of a very evil ferocious kind, to a sort of dunghill louse which pecks with its little beak, but they all have the mange & make a noise, which seems the main thing.

There is a man upstairs here who comes from the Marne country, & his wife & four children are there, & the country there is ruined & the family were starving & the little children could only get food (in the time of the Marne battle) by begging for crusts from the soldiers. 'When my wife told me that in a letter', he said, 'I cried for two days'.

Your friend, the nerve case, howled again today, & this time was awful to see. He was being helped downstairs by the two female medical students, but there was a fool of woman with them who kept worrying him by trying to touch him, which he cannot abide, so after a little he let loose. He flung himself into the arms of the f.m.s., who are about as strong as oxes; I never saw such a couple. God deliver me from being treated by them; & lay in their arms limply, with his arms drooped, & his face like an idiot's, turned to the floor, with tears running from his eyes & slobber from his mouth, & yell upon yell pouring out with the slobber, all the Tigres & Assassins again. I got him into a chair, & by & by he was quiet. He is getting better, but as with so many it is fearfully slow.

I don't feel that I can ever think quietly of Germans again. They are guilty of this crime & folly & misery, & if there is such a thing as injustice there is such another thing as righteous anger, & it is that that one feels.

I'm a bit vexed with a lot of people here, because they are slack in their work, always knocking off for pipes (or asking leave for the afternoon, if female) & generally not buckling to. It seems to me that I am feeling the pulse of my country here, & I'm trying to reconcile the slackness, which is evident enough, with the excellence of the hospital, which is also evident: we are queer race, I do maintain. Bobby has just made an Altar for the Mortuary, with a pink wood cross on it & all, a fine piece. I'm still at tables for the wards: I've made about 8 or 9; & tomorrow must go on to crutches.

Dear love to you & the babes my Dearest Con,

Your old lover

Jan

---

[29]
Arc.

3rd Apl.

My own Beloved,

Less than 3 more weeks, I hope; some seventeen or eighteen days, only just a fortnight here. It seems a long eternity; yet there are seven or eight millions of fathers, now in Europe, longing, as I long, to be back at home, who have been away for months & may be away for years, & when I think of them I despise myself. It is no good thinking of these things; the crime has been done; mainly by a small body of intellect out of touch with any human feeling, and often, when I come back here in the night, I feel the rage come over me that I'm not killing these sales Bosches who have done this devilry. My God, they need some punishing. I hope that their type of brain may be blown from the world's skull forever, though I know it won't be.

It is Easter here, & the very beautiful little church bells have been ringing odd little carillons at odd times, such as I've never heard before; rather like the tunes for little children, without much range of note, but with gravity, & quirks & changes, to make the singer solemn & attentive, & perhaps as old as the church or older. It has made me feel almost more than the war, how puerile the Church now is. It has the women, & the bored little boys, & the fat old men with positions to consider, while all the rest are cutting each other's throats, & all that it has to offer is words repeated, and a few old tunes on the bells.

I have had a dull day in a way, since it poured with rain, & our promised new blessees are not to come. I cut up a sheep or two in the morning, & made 2 ward tables, one of them rather good, & started a third. Then I helped hold up a poor wounded man, & got all drenched in stinking pus, & before I could change there came an alarm of 'chimney on fire'. We have one Dangerous chimney, about which special instructions have been given, & this was the one selected by one of our lady amateurs for the burning of the contents of 2 straw pillows and some lint. A pleasant old blaze we had of it, & but for the chance that the local ironmonger, who made all our chimneys, was on the floor at the moment, & could shew us a quite unsuspected flue, from which we could get at the danger, I believe we should have caught, & if we had, we should have had to leave the place, for we could not put out such a web of dry rafters as these in there. However, one good thing; there was a lot of smoke, & they'll be more careful henceforth. As organiser of the Fire Service, I had a lot to do, tracing out the chimney's path across 4 floors, & patting it down to find out where it was hottest. I used to think that the French were an excitable gesticulatory people, but I do not find them so. I found them entirely calm, clearheaded sensible people, who went straight to the place & did the right thing, while our crowd, mainly young women, were simply romping hoydens who thought it a jolly good rag, & yelled 'O, do let me ring the fire bell, it will rouse up all the night nurses'. Tonks flung a bucket of sand over them, & thus do we help our Allies. I'm afraid they think us quite hopelessly mad, & yet in our way we impress them. Our kindness, our sympathy, our very real devotion to them, are all deeply felt in many different ways & responded to. What they are puzzled by are our manners, the want of care in our dealings.

Dear love I must stop. Bless & keep you & the dear ones.

Your lover
Jan

---

[30]
                                                                              Arc.
                                                                           April 4
My beloved Con,

The post continues to be erratic; no lett at all from you, though some of us got letters today which were posted in England on the 2nd. This is the 3rd day in one week with no lett, & I hate it when a day misses. I hope you don't miss many days in this way; but 'c'est la guerre'; that has to resign me to everything out here (& with you) in these days.

I was on duty in a car today, escorting convalescents from the Hospice to Chatillon, where they take train for their depots, 'discharged, cured', to get new equipment & their leave to go home for a time. There were 11 to go, the man who ate the 6 eggs after having the bullet cut out, the man, so like Spuge, who was shot in the throat, & 2 or 3 other old friends, among them. The Spuge man began to flutter about in the chateau, slightly drunk, at about 11 a.m. & when we finally started, in the midst of a crowd, from the Hospice gate, at 2 p.m., he was a little silly. 'Caroline', the man who ate the eggs, was not in my car, the others were. Nearly all had had a cup or two (or 3, or 4) before starting, & everybody in the village waved & cheered, & the dogs & hens ran out & nearly got run over, & our men stuck their heads out, shouted & hooted, & flung out orange peel & were especially gallant to ladies. I must say the ladies were not coy but did their best to inspire further efforts. We, as Anglais, rather rare in these dim wild lonely parts, were also much waved at: but I never saw so many dogs nearly killed, I think I'll remember the ride more by that than by the ladies. It was raining hard all the 30 miles to Chatillon so that the country did not much shine. It is very vast, gloomy & silent, with distant church towers & little villages, then great upland wolds, & sombre pine wood, then some-times a line with a train on it, and armed men slowly patrolling, then wold again, the half not ploughed, & all looking like January, & then far away the queer round Burgundy hills, the Cote d'Or hills, & when we got to them we were at Chatillon, which is a fine neat little town, with a beautiful old church dominating it from up above, & the Stripling Seine running through it, a broad shallow brook, clear as glass. We dropped our men at the station, & here the Spuge man was very excited & very sentimental, & smelt most horribly of all that had made him so, & of having been sick out of the window, en route, as well. During his stay with me I had brought him oranges for his throat poor little man, & now this made made an object of romance to him. He kept shewing me off to the crowd (which gathers in 3 seconds round an Anglais here) 'Il est mon sauveur. Il me protégeait. Vous êtes mon sauveur. Il m'a donné des oranges. Souvenez-vous l'orange que la soeur a defendu? Ah, j'avais la colique. Il m'avait donné la colique avec ses oranges. Il était mon sauveur.' He was nearly weeping & kept wringing my hand, & plainly wished to embrace me, which would have been, I suppose, a memory the more, but like other memories, not so pleasant at the time. An old Colonel, in faultless tenue, was receiving the men, & it was pleasant to see his fatherly familiarity with them. Both sides evidently recognised that there was an iron law to be maintained, but within that law there was room for a great deal of feeling which we seem to get only in the Navy. He told them that they would not get a train till midnight, & so dismissed them, & they all flocked round us then to say goodbye, & the Spuge man got another crowd about me, with his sauveur & his oranges, & this time I only just escaped being kissed by all the crowd. I was much touched to say goodbye to these men. Many of them I had helped out of the train, & stood by in operations & made tables for, & helped at meals, & Caroline I was really much attached to. He is a charming man & I'm afraid I'll never see him again. He was the only one who looked really smart, for he had a new blue coat, while the others wore their old tattered trench clothes cleaned up. Still, they were going home: that is the great thing. I hope to God they may all safely get there when this wicked war is at an end.

Bless & keep you dear love

from
Jan

---

[31]                                         Arc.
                                          5 Ap.

My beloved Con,

Unless another lot of wounded come in, to make my presence here essential till a new orderly can come out, Tonks, Bobby and I hope to leave here on Ap 15, Thursday week, about 6 days after you will get this letter. We shall have to be Thursday & Friday nights in Paris, as one has to get 3 or 4 different sets of permits, first to stay there, then to get away, but we hope to leave Paris on Saturday & reach England either that day or on Sunday, anyhow less than a fortnight from now. If the blessees should come I may be kept for some days longer. I don't know if any blessées will come. They rang us up from Headquarters today, to say that there were none in all this part of France, except a few slight cases of typhoid, & what this means we are all at our wits' ends to guess. It can only mean that (a) the bad weather has stopped the fighting, (b) that tremendous fighting is preparing, (c) that the war henceforth is not to be one of assault but of siege by rule, or (d) that the sales Bosches have at last learned that they cannot win, & never will be allowed to win by the general soul of the world, & are making an effort for peace. I myself, suppose either a or b, but it is certainly strange.

I wrote to you last night about Chatillon, but did not write very entertainingly, being sleepy from the fresh air. It is a pleasant town, full of the curious blues & greys & greens which French colour printers catch with such faithful skill. I had a strange feeling that I had seen it all before, perhaps because it is so like so many pictures of France. Very often here, I have realised that though my French is vile, I know France very well from her faithful literature & from her art. I can always tell a curé from a paysanne, and when I first heard sabots I felt that I had heard them all my life. I never realised before how curiously good French novels & stories are; ours very seldom come so close to the life; and I realise more & more what France has meant to modern civilisation. But all this is away from Chatillon. We weren't there more than a few minutes, after dropping our Convalescents. We bought 100 lettuces & 100 oranges & came away. Just as we started, we saw 'Caroline' walking about with his friend 'Birdy' to wile away his 8 hours wait: it was sad to see them go. A lot of little boys with fishing rods came round our car while we were waiting; they were most charming little boys & I talked with them about fishing; & then when we started, it went to my heart, they all took off their hats, & shouted 'Salut aux Anglais'. I don't know why it touched one so, except that suddenly one felt that a whole nation down to its children felt that England was a good friend. Yet I suppose 20 years ago it would have been 'Voila un godam qui passe.' One sees the folly of anything but love and courage.

Bless you, dear love,

Your old lover<br>Jan

---

[32]
Arc.<br>Ap 6. Tuesday

My beloved Con,

I got 3 letts today, by some freak, 2 taxed & 1 not, by another freak . . . I wish I could think that your colds were better; most of the staff have them here, but so far I've scraped & been well. I wish I were nearer to help look after you.

I ought to be home in 2 weeks from this. The journey home will take about 4 days, here to Paris 1 day, in Paris getting permission to leave, 1 day & a half, in Boulogne, or some other port, 1 day, & getting home half a day. Can you keep old Na at home for an extra week this time? I'd love to find her at Loll when I come. The mice will seem quite fragrant juicy little perfumes after what I've smelt here for the last 5 weeks. You must bear in mind that I'm probably soaked and drenched with dangerous germs from septic wounds, so when I come I'd better begin with a strong carbolic bath & have all my clothes washed in carbolic & then hung in the sun. My uniform is in a mess; it gets soaked with pus & blood & wine, men's dinner, water, sawdust, filth of all sorts, grease, sago, soup, jam, & worse things almost daily. Probably we all smell rather gamey, but then the crowning stink of the chateau rather saves me. On south westerly days like this we waft abroad half across the village. It is like nothing else, the smell of the power of death; please God Guillaume will have it in his nose from now till the blessed day he dies.

I've had a hard day today, making crutches. It takes about a day as yet to make a crutch, but with practice I'll be able to make a pair a day. There is no lathe here so we have to do it nearly all by hand. We get blocks of beech wood for the rests and long foursquare pieces of acacia for the handles, & then with a spokeshave, rasps & files we cut the blocks to shape & round out the handles, Bobby & I together, & when they're done the matron binds lint over the rests, & I screw rubber on to the tips, so that they will not slip, and then 'as proper men as ever went' go hopping along on them, & calling them voitures de bras. I made a fine pair yesterday, but then the handles were ready; today I only made one, doing it all myself; & I did a table too. Tables take an hour & a half. Only one more table is needed in the hospital: Bobby having made some 30 or 35 & I 15 or 16.

If we go to this new hospital, in the open, in the Vosges, I have made up my mind to have no one who is not used to rough manual work. Bobby is the only man here, except myself & a Colonial Doctor, who can be trusted to work without driving or beseeching. So don't talk of the scheme to people, my dear, & for God's sake let's have no seekers after experience nor lovers of men, but good hard workers only. I'm afraid the instinct for work is not common etc. etc.

We hear little of England here. I suppose the press is going on about drink in the usual way. I cannot help wishing that Kitchener would stop the two evils together once & for all, otherwise there will be endless talk & a compromise in the end, a sort of victory of the lukewarm, which English law so often is.

I'd a hair cut today in the village. The barber remembers the Germans here in 1870, & he saw some Uhlans[1] here in September again, on the day of the holy procession here, & the people all prayed to be delivered from the Germans, & the Saints heard, & that same day the Bosches retreated. He was an artist at his task & I enjoyed my talk with him.

We cut a poor lad's leg off this afternoon & afterwards cremated it, & unfortunately it put the furnace out, so when old Henri came to tend said furnace he had a surprise. These things are ghastly enough I know but they have a kind of hysterical comedy in them.

Dear, I must stop, Bless & keep you, dear love, & guard the babes,

Your old lover<br>Jan

Do you receive the picture cards I send? I must have sent 20 or 30, at least, to the babes, & you don't say if they reach you; so perhaps they have not come. Please answer this.

1. German cavalry, originally carrying lances.

---

[33]　　　　　　　　　　　　　　　　　　　　　　　Arc.
　　　　　　　　　　　　　　　　　　　　　　　　　7 Ap.

My beloved Con,

I think we are all counting the hours till we can get away from this hateful place. One loves helping the blessées, and the hard days of carrying brancards & beds pass bravely, for then one is giving health, really visibly giving it, to poor maimed men, & one cannot grudge a little personal ache in the arm, for that, but is glad of it; but the comparatively easy days, when there is no carrying, but only grinding away at tables & crutches in an ill-equipped carpenter's shop we have, drag & are damnable, & the place gets on the nerves, with its stink, & intrigue, & airless lifeless darkness. Next to Tranrossan & perhaps the Venice hotel, this chateau is the beastliest place I've lived in, in Europe. O God, I'll be glad to be back. No place could be much worse fitted for a hospital. It has rained hard for 5 days & its defects bulk big.

The new orderly, who lodged in this inn, has lumbago badly, (from going fishing on Sunday perhaps) & we had to carry him in a Porter's chair to the chateau, where we put him to bed & gave him a Sister to nurse him, & there he now is, in very great pain, poor man, & new orderlies will have to be wired for. I'll tell you who would make good orderlies, of the men we know: Clifford Philpot, very good indeed, David Strang, superb, Ian Strang, good; all the rough & ready souls do shine at this work, and with Bobby here going, a man who can tinker at machines is necessary, though don't think that I mean you to find a man, other men are coming. Bobby has kept this place going. I believe it will collapse when he has gone. We have put the new orderly into the Count's room in the Chateau. It is a rather fine room, decorated with 9 or ten engravings of dogs, surmounted by a huge framed print of old Victoria, in just such a frame as she herself would have chosen. The old Duke is the grandson of Louis Philippe & the son of the Prince de Joinville[1], who built this place as a hunting centre. One of the family, circa 1820, was a sailor, & there are good sea pictures of that date & a most beautiful, but broken, model, in ivory, of the ship he commanded. The castle library consists of about 100 volumes tastefully bound, as though for distribution at a Sunday school. There is a neat drawer for dinner napkins underneath them, & without the napkins the library would not seem complete, but with them it looks just right. One gets the impression of a rich and tasteless careless man, fond of outdoor sports, followed by a rich man whose tastes were purely political & instincts feudal.

The Local Service des Pompiers turned out today & gave us an exhibition of their craft, both with the pompe, which, from my doleful hours with it, I call the pompe funebre, and with the robinet. They flung jets d'eau for nearly 30 feet, & enjoyed themselves I think, though it poured with rain all the time & they got very wet. They are efficient at their work, & will no doubt save the situation when some other gentle lady pours oil into her fireplace or straw into her chimney. I'm afraid they meant it as a reminder that they were there, that we need have no fear, but might continue our mad ways with all confidence.

Bless you, dear love Con,

from your lover
Jan

1. (1818–1900), Louis Philippe's third son, who brought back to France Napoleon's body from St Helena in 1840. He fought for the French in 1870, under an assumed name.

[34]                                                       Arc.
                                                          Ap 8
My beloved Con,

This must be only a very short note, as there has been a sort of mad concert tonight, to amuse the nurses, & I've been attending that, but tho' it wasn't much in the way of work it was a cold & wet job so I've cut the latter half of it & have come to bed. The nurses & the doctors (some of them) dressed up, & made themselves into scarecrows of different kinds, one of them was a blessee & another an awfully good parody of the Matron, & they are making a hideous row, up at the Hospice, & playing the fool generally, rather vulgar, but they enjoy it, & the convalescents enjoy it even more. Macdonald is superb as a drunken coal heaver, & one of the sisters is a devil & another a nun & another a sort of John Baptist in locusts & wild honey. The cook has bagged an orderly's uniform & deceives most of them. She is the girl who knows Ivy Fox, or did I forget to tell you this? The head doctor went as a sister; a fearful sight.

                                                          Ap 9

It was not in good taste, perhaps, but the nurses did need a change.

I'm adding this bit before break, as I have a few minutes still. To my great joy, the nice volunteer has made a sudden incredible leap, & from lying in daily danger of death from secondary haemorrhage is now practically out of the pit & can stagger across the ward with his arms round 2 nurses' necks (a popular form of crutch here) & we have had him out in the shelter, & now I am making him a pair of special crutches. When I get back I must get people into the way of making crutches; they are really very easy, but take a long time, & scores are wanted. Some of the blessees joke in the midst of great pain. The other day your friend the howling man was lying suffering up in the ward. Next to him was a man with his arm in a bath, having his wound thoroughly soaked in a lotion. The ward was quiet except that the sufferer moaned from time to time, while the man with his arm in the bath puffed his cigarette & was stolid. Suddenly, as I entered the room, the sufferer sat up with a groan & asked the other 'Avez vous prit des poissons?'

                          Dear love, my Con,
                                from
                                 Jan

_____

[35]                                                       Arc.
                                                          Ap 10.
My beloved Con,

I'm afraid you've been hurt by my staying so long here. The time has been a cruel one for you I know, & you've been brave & good. I feel that I've been kept here the extra week by the failure of the promised visit to H.Q. Our chiefs were put off for a week, & are to go tomorrow instead of last Sunday. They'll be back on Monday or Tuesday, with a load of blessees. On Wednesday or Thursday I may be off, & if lucky should be at home at some dark hour in the night of Saturday or Sunday, I can't tell which, but I hope one or other. I may be kept 2 days in Paris getting leave to go, & then I may have another day in some French port; one never can tell now, but we'll hope for the best. O joy, I may be back in one week from now, almost as soon as this letter; joy, joy, if it can be so.

It has rained or snowed hard every day for a week, & the river is within a foot of the garden & almost all over the park. If it gets into the garden it will go into the kitchen, which is in the basement, & then there will be misery, but what will misery count when one is going home. I shall sing 'rolling home' all the way back, though Tonks have a million toothaches. It is a wonderful thing to be coming home: my God, some of these million fathers now out at the front all over Europe will almost go mad when they turn home. In a way I almost feel that a conclusively stalemate war will show men the criminal folly of war better than anything, & yet one longs for these sales Bosches & Guillaume to be driven like dogs out of this dear land they've harried. My God, I hope to see that done, & to be not too far off to join in the paean when its done.

Did I tell you of dismal Jimmy, who killed his Bosche at the moment the Bosche bayonetted him? His bayonet wound did not do at all well so we opened it up today, & it was not a bayonet wound at all, but a bullet wound, with a fine big bullet in the bone, which we got out, & now, though he still swears he was bayonetted, & indeed may have had the bayonet through his trousers just as he was shot, he is Smiling Jimmy, awfully proud of his bullet, & likely now to get well by force of faith. We have now only about 4 really very bad cases, but this bad weather sets everyone back rather.

I have to go again to Chatillon tomorrow, with Convalescents. Since our bad men left, the Hospice has 'got religion', & they all go to mass & confession & read improving books & butter wouldn't melt in their mouths. We have a privy fear that someone has started a bawdy house near the Church, yet it may be genuine enough. I hope that my Chatillon crew may be a little more holy than last Sunday's lot.

Bless & keep you, my darling Con, & 'send safe home'.

Your old lover<br>Jan

---

[36]　　　　　　　　　　　　　　　　　　　　　　　　　　　Arc.

　　　　　　　　　　　　　　　　　　　　　　　　　　　　　　Ap 11

My beloved Con,

Not more than a few lines tonight, for I reckon that with the normal delay at Chaumont this won't reach you till Friday or even Saturday, & with good fortune, avoiding delay at the port, whichever it may be, I may be back on Saturday some time, but of course with bad fortune may be delayed over the week-end & so not get to you till Monday. . . .

Bless & keep you all, & send safe home.

Your old lover,
Jan

# Part Two

## Letters from America, 1916

(Letters January to July 1916)

'I'm afraid my early years in America made me, in all sorts of ways, American. It is only now that I see how English I am in some ways.'

John Masefield owed much to America, to his early adventures there, and the impact of individual Americans and cosmopolitans. Returning there, as a famous man, to lecture on literature, read his poems, and dispense propaganda for the Allied cause, to a nation which contained a substantial number of Americans and 'a lot of damned disloyal Irishmen', he showed feelings that were by no means unalloyed affection or admiration.

This was not new. American rural beauties and urban tang and bustle had early quickened his imagination and enlarged his experiences; he was never to forget the vigour and generosity of people of many different backgrounds, yet, in 1900, he also mentioned his 'hatred of Americans'.

He undertook the tour only from duty. 'The trouble is,' he wrote to Florence Lamont in 1926, 'that I am not much of a lecturer, having little or no exact knowledge, small critical capacity, and little pleasure (as a rule) in lecturing. I am a storyteller, and all my knowledge, criticism and pleasure I put into stories.'

His delivery was often low-pitched, rather monotonous, coming to life only when he recited his poems. Audiences were unenthusiastic about Chaucer, Tragic Drama and general English literature: they wanted his poetry, which he was glad to give, though, at Milwaukee, 'a hard-mouthed terror of a female' demanded 'a good long story from you with plenty of pep'. Everywhere the young responded to him and he to them, particularly students and soldiers. At Yale, he found 'the young men enthusiastic about poetry, all the old arrogance seems changed to a kind of humble self-questioning and doubt.'

At Evanston he says, 'this land makes one love the young. I never realised before how wise youth is. Youth never asks fool questions nor bothers one, nor says any silly idiocy like "poetry ought not to be sad", nor asks me for autographs, nor drives one mad with half-baked praise. Youth is friendly & kind & responds to a word & will take me for a friend & companion so give me youth for my audience, say I, and O God, smite these women's clubs in their secret parts.'

He found, as John Cowper Powys had noted in 1914: 'Everybody seems to write poetry here. There is a poet on every bough & in every streetcar and what is worse in every postal delivery. I have seen the Chicago Chaucer and the St Louis Sappho & I am myself the Modern Chaucer, when I am not the Modern Burns or the Modern Shakespeare.'

Of New Yorkers Masefield says, 'I find them so strangely earnest that

I hardly recognise the race. Everywhere there is a deep love of poetry & an almost religious eagerness to talk about it.'

About Edgar Lee Masters, author of *Spoon River Anthology*, he heard a phrase everywhere quoted: 'He is not so good a poet as Masefield, but he has more sense.'

At Urbana, he watched college students drilling. 'It was plain that all the rank and file loathed the compulsion & took no interest in the drill, while the officers were too absurd for words . . . each officer had a glittering sword, which in action would give the range to every gun in sight, and each officer performed amazing twiddling antics with his sword, in a kind of negro cake-walk swagger, that was pretentious & vulgar & silly all in one . . . the slouch and unwilling boredom of the men was painful to watch: they plainly hated it, & the march was a slouch, & the fours were all over the place, & the men had on their faces a grim look of determination to let their officers die first, or kill them if there were any doubt of it.'

He hated Chicago, 'I never saw a town so hopeless nor so sad. Endless miles of degenerate mind, with more cans than in any city of the world.' Also Pittsburgh, from where he wrote, 'The Middle West is carnal, hard, rough, overbearing, false, crude, bumptious, empty, flat as their prairie land, and inflated as their natural gas.'

Elsewhere, 'It has a raw feel of east wind always, & it is dirty & flat & cold, & badly built, & it is noisy & vulgar & very haphazard, & it is still very much what New York used to be.'

He liked the south and enjoyed Boston, and Niagara Falls induced some vivid letters.

What makes it specially fearful is the dead wan colour and the thick slush of ice on the top which makes it almost semi-solid, and to see a semi-solid acting like this makes you marvel. Sometimes you see a big heap of water thrust its snout out of the rush and swim back and bite some big wave coming at it and burst it all to bits, & then it jumps aloft & laughs & smashes itself on a rock with a kind of devilish glee . . . It has force enough to light the world & grind the world's bread beside.

He made, of course, many warm personal contacts. One of these was with John Quin, a lawyer, financier, collector of books and paintings, remembered today as the friend and patron of W. B. Yeats, and also of Ezra Pound and T. S. Eliot, who gave him the original draft of *The Waste Land*. Masefield wrote, 'He tired me to death, but he impressed me enormously; a really wise man with fine instincts & a big mind & fun; a really fine achievement of a man.'

The most important personal event on this visit must have been meeting Florence Lamont and her husband, Thomas W. Lamont, a wealthy banker. Florence was a tireless hostess to artists, poets, dons, politicians, journalists, diplomats, and her friendship with the future Laureate lasted until her death in 1953. Corliss, the Lamonts' son, studying at Oxford, became a close friend of the Masefields, assisting with the Boar's Hill theatre. He edited a selection of Masefield's letters to Florence (1972).

Masefield had lugubrious experiences of journalists, giggling college girls, pompous academics, mens' clubs. At Milwaukee, 'they had a story at the club, that a visitor looking out of the windows had said, "you have a fine view here of the Reservoir". The Reservoir being Lake Michigan.'

Women in groups seem to have been his worst experience, particularly the womens' clubs. Of these he was not the last British writer to comment unfavourably.

At Chicago he wrote, 'I lectured yesterday to a Club of Jewish Women, a fair audience, but a fearful room to speak in, quite the worst acoustically that I have ever known, it was in a way like shouting into felt, and all the macaws down below somehow gave me the grue. Speaking generally, these afternoon audiences are the devil, and the women who run them are the devil's dams.' From Cincinnati: 'The most deadly audiences are the women's clubs in the suburban towns: they are truly awful; never again I trust. They do not want to listen & God alone knows why they ever come.' Everywhere he was besieged by 'slabs of awful women'. Back at Chicago: 'Four slimy female reporters, all dirty and evil looking like retired whores, if I may say so, and the dodge was that 3 should question me while the 4th hid behind their backs & took notes. However, a mirror revealed their design to me & I got away unscathed.'

Nevertheless, at a women's college at Dedham, he found 'a singularly earnest staff, of very very fine spirited women. Earnest even for this country where everybody is passionate for perfection.'

His old-style courtesy, even gallantry towards women took severe beatings, though it had more of a chance in smaller, informal occasions. In Chicago, he went to tea 'with a lady whose forbears had all fought for the South, & whose mind was very full of , & close to, that heroic time, and at her house, in the crowd of guests, they wept on my bosom with emotion for England & I felt queerly near to that old mood of 50 years ago, when the fathers of all that company had marched out to fight for the South as one man. It was strange to have the heart of the race laid bare like that, a heart of blind generous impulse. It made me realise that when this nation does face something big it will do it with a sacrifice utterly beyond all telling & all precedent.' The next day he added, 'They are a bold kind friendly capable people, seeking a way of salvation & a ready prey to anyone who will show them. With all their shrewdness they do succumb to the charlatan, though never for long.'

His good humour swiftly faltered. 'I never saw the sights of Chicago. Never saw the 700 hogs killed in an hour, nor the 10,000 cows butchered in a day, nor the men brooming the blood into the pans and having their fingers sliced off into the sausage-meat, & no time to stop and pick them out, so perhaps I ought not to judge the place: I never saw its art. I saw its soul, though, at that Paderewski concert, *et je m'en fiche*, say I, and as the train goes South I sing, "I'm going away from Chicago, I'm going away from Chicago. I may perhaps never be in Chicago again". My God, I did hate the place; in spite of people's kindness.'

The reference to the pianist, Paderewski, who became the first prime minister in 1919, of independent Poland, needs reference to an earlier letter from Minneapolis, which again shows Masefield's tarter side.

I was in Chicago on the 6th, and went to a Paderewski concert in aid of the Poles, and there had a real chance of seeing the want of style which commerce brings with it. The 4000 audience entered like a mob as though they were going to wreck the building. I never saw an audience enter a building more like a mob, with so complete a want of order, quiet decorum & consideration. After some unlovely hustling & barging we got into our places, & presently a mob came upon the stage & jammed the stage full, again without any order, except that they all wore red rosettes, & presently the mob sang the Polish anthem & that parody of God Save the King with which the American makes himself feel the elect of heaven. Then Paderewski came on & made a speech which was on the whole a very good and tactful appeal. He spoke for ½ an hour & then went off to rest, as he was to play Chopin later on to us. As soon as he had gone, an eminent banker came on the stage, with a draughtsman & an enormous blackboard. Money & promises of money were then received, & the draughts-man kept chalking and rechalking the total received, while the banker shouted aloud the amount of each gift or promise. It was a very good way to get a big subscription but I cannot tell you what a revelation it was of the commercial mind. This was what they really liked, to hear a sum of money growing bigger under their eyes, & the way they cheered the word dollars, & the sort of loving roll the banker gave the word in his mouth, 'Mrs James P. Lewvinski, one hundred dollars,' was beyond belief oily with Mammon. That was the music the audience came for. One felt them going home muttering in a kind of dream: dollars, a hundred dollars, a thousand dollars, a thousand five hundred dollars, & so climbing slowly to a kind of pinnacle of dollars, above a list of greenbacks, upon a pathway paved with cents. This went on for an hour or so, and as there was no chance of any music until God knows when I came away & did not hear the great man after all.'

He noted the grey hair of many American women, even young ones, and found many of them small, due, he thought, to their parents' early marriages. He heard of a 17-year-old hanged for witnessing two men firing a hayrick, and in extra heavy chains to facilitate his death, the chains later made into paperweights, for sale. At St Louis he had to dine with a German family 'who played old French & Scottish music to me afterwards, & none of their own. This I thought fine tact in a Bosche, & we parted the best of friends.'

St Louis itself pleased him less.

It is dim and smoky here, not black and foul like Chicago & in a way, but for the incredible badness of the streets, it is like London; the same beggars, the same haze & floating smuts, the same roar, the same absence of a civic sense. I never felt it much before, but since I've been in these big commercial cities I have said to myself almost all day long, 'What shall it profit a man?' and a kind of pitying wonder takes me, & I ask myself what in God's name do these people get by it? They keep chaste & temperate & rise early & slave like factory hands all to make a city as like hell as it may be, & they die young & their children have no love for them; their children despise poppa for not living longer & making more dollars; and momma takes to christian science & flounces out of the room at the mention of death. It is a land all false teeth & spectacles, the most tragical hollowness I know, the elaborate shell of a coffin, without the humanity of a corpse inside.

Masefield's poetry got small chance to spread itself, though his descriptions are brisk and vivid.

I don't know why one goes to Italy when there is a place like Memphis on the globe. I do wish you could have seen it. I can't describe it, as it is all flavour, but it is a wonderful living town, full of negroes who ride about on mules, & all the whites fly about in cars, & then there are dogs, & dirty negro shanties, & the houses look exactly as if they chewed tobacco, all very lean & knowing, & rather hard in the mouth, & then I expect you could get killed for 5 cents almost anywhere there, and little negro boys and girls go around on roller skates, & whenever 2 negresses pass you you see that one has a green turban, & purple skirt & an orange parcel, & the other a scarlet parcel, a green skirt & a black turban, & the men wear purple & bright blue, & spit through their teeth, *a merveille*, & just as you think it all worth ten of the East, you see the river. It's nothing of a river in a way, it is flat, it isn't angry, & the land is feeble on both banks, it has no setting, but if you look at it, you see that it is a mile and a half across, & full of the most devilish current wherever it will float a ship, you can see the ships barely moving against it, & trees wallowing down, & trees on the further shore half-drowned.

His general comments are mostly unexceptional. 'America is producing an architecture which is already great, & is alive and growing, & we have no intellectual achievement at all comparable, I'm afraid; though of course we write them simply off the map in every kind of writing. They are as kind as we are, their hospitality is biblical but they don't produce such fine individuals, they live in company & grow up with communal minds.' He added later, '"Self-expression" is a great cry here.'

He never forgot the most momentous issues of all, in that grim year 1916: the year of Verdun and the Somme, Kitchener's death, the bloody failure of the last major Russian offensive. 'The Verdun business is occupying me very much, but I feel that the French have it in hand now. The Bosche seems a kind of heroic sheep officered by a kind of cross between a goat & a weasel. How like the Kronprinz is to a weasel.'

On arrival at New York, he had written:

I suppose people's generous kindness & the amazing beauty of the buildings are the things that strike one most. What I feel most dreadfully is England's *apparent* apathy before so much warmly expressed friendship. Why, in God's name, aren't we stretching out our hands to meet them half way & more, giving travelling scholarships in England, India and Egypt, exchanging professors & sending our young men over? Americans are won by warmth and feeling . . .

They are a great-hearted people & plainly on the brink of a great utterance. And I am deeply impressed with the need of linking such a race to ourselves now, while the iron is hot. So far, nearly everyone is hotly pro-Ally but one has to be careful, the Boshe taint goes deep.

Elsewhere, less amiably, he adds, 'Americans respond to a little kindness, exactly like well-beaten dogs; they come round whimpering and lick my hand.' To counter 'the Boshe taint' was Masefield's real mission behind the lectures and readings, and the chief theme of his letters, his spirits rising and falling according to the reception, not of himself as poet, but as delegate for the Allies.

Immediately upon arrival, he wrote from New York:

I have had various opinions about the war. There is a rather angry feeling that the solid, well-organised German element should have such power here & a still angrier feeling that it should have taken American citizenship & yet talk of a Fatherland. This no doubt will lead to a good deal of talk & legislation in the future. As a whole, the place is strongly pro-Ally, & I notice in all sorts of ways among the nicer people a fear that Europe (the Allied Europe) despises America, for not having done something for Belgium, humanity, or even for herself. There is a fear too, that America has lost spiritually, & will miss the great spiritual awakening which perhaps all people expect from the Allied nations after the Victory. I have only been here 20 hours yet I have the feeling that America expects an internal struggle of some strength and intensity over this question of half-hearted alien citizenship, owing allegiance to other lands.

The great spiritual awakening that Masefield awaited might be said to have occurred, in contrasting forms, for, from different angles, it could be related to the League of Nations, the abolition of the German, Turkish, Austro-Hungarian and Russian monarchies, the rise of the secular religions of communism and fascism. Only perhaps the first would have gratified him, and that not for long, as America refused to join it.

He was soon writing further:

So far I have been only in the Eastern cities, New York, Boston, Philadelphia . . . & everywhere I meet with the strongest expression of pro-Ally feeling . . . I find everywhere the same uneasiness that America must be despised in the Allied countries . . . They want to be our friends, to have a common culture . . . now is the time, & any overture from us would be tremendously welcomed . . . There is intense admiration for France and for the English soldier and a great deal of criticism of Italy, who is looked upon as selfish and rather base. One great reason for their friendliness towards us is the feeling that we are taking & and are going to take great steps in the way of State socialism, and that the English of after the war will be a truly great democracy. They expect us to rise to the reconstruction as nobly as we rose to the war, & they want to reconstruct themselves side by side with us.

At Nashville there was admiration for Britain's 'reception of the Belgians; several have mentioned that to me almost with bated breath, as a generosity unparalleled.'

However, with America subjected to propaganda from the Allies, Germans, Turks, and Irish and Indian nationalists, he found some hostility and much ignorance of what was occurring in Europe. 'The Press here is apathetic, and I hear wild ideas.' He found German propaganda telling Americans of Allied contempt for their neutrality, particularly in Milwaukee, where German brewers controlled most of the saloons. The Germans were making special propaganda efforts at Harvard, exchanging professors, and sending Prince Henry of Prussia, on a special visit. Britain, Masefield felt, should despatch one of King George's sons.

At Memphis he wrote:

I can feel that as far as America is real it is pro-Ally, but that large sections of the land are not real, but only fictitious America; the Germans & the Jews seem bent on a society of their own here, & in this town the Germans & the Jews do both contrive a kind of anti-Ally propaganda. The Germans are much ostracised here (I am told) in the Clubs, since the swine sank the Lusitania, & the Jews are only listened to as men with intellects which demand a hearing. The Jew mind here rather leans to the Bosche view of a State. No doubt in a Germanised America the Jew would be happier than he is now.

At Illinois University he found Indian students 'seeking popularity by screeching anti-British sentiments, & are avowed revolutionaries.' Swedes were mostly pro-German. In Minnesota, a Swedish woman lectured on her visits to hospitals in France, announcing that American generosity in sending medical supplies were quite unnecessary. She was, he discovered, in German pay, and had never been to France.

Then, 'On the fringe of this Bosche wedge in parts of New York & Pennsylvania, & in the East of Illinois, I found the papers sitting on the rail. The headlines would be strongly pro-German, & the editorials would be, in the main, pro-Ally.' He read articles by a pro-German journalist 'in which an attempt was made to turn the Puritan conscience against us. This is the artful insinuation that in Germany all the men in the army (pretty nearly) are married, & that Germany with its old love of purity (see Tacitus) sends her men home to their wives periodically but that of course in France, there are brothels, where the men contract loathesome diseases while the English follow their natural leanings, as shown in the Wilde case, & refresh themselves with sodomy. This has been circulated & repeated & believed.'

This New York State is, of course, a centre of anti-British feeling which existed before the war, & it is based partly on the old antipathy, partly on a very real jealousy, & here & there I feel it still here, though much diminished owing to the methods of the Bosche. There were also some fears in New York that, after the war, the German navy would land some five million Germans and take over the country.

Travelling from Illinois to St Louis, he wrote (February 15), seemingly not to his wife, but more officially:

As elsewhere in the Middle West I found cultivated people on the whole pro-Ally, & a very strong strain of people of German extraction, wielding some power against us. Some of the professors of English told me that for 4 or 5 years before the war the Bosche had made systematic attempts to cow and coerce the Middle West press into being anti-British. Men who wrote signed reviews of English books, praising them, or who praised English public men or institutions were systematically attacked & vilified by men with Bosche names, while the owners of the papers would receive letters saying 'Are you aware that such sentiments will alienate from you the 2 or 3 millions of educated Germans in this State?' It seems to have been a campaign of clumsy malice, directed from above, in the usual Bosche way, with some success of course. Bosche emissaries go all through the Middle West daily now & are very clever. Their chief occupation just now is to preach the impossibility of any German being involved in the explosions which take place daily in the Munitions factories. Their attitude is: 'There haf always been explosions. Der powder explode of itself' & so on to the same tune, with airs of injured innocence, 'what, a German blow up a powder magazine, it is der strikers, we are educated peoples.'

Besides this work, traces of which I find in all the Middle West, I find them hard at work preaching everywhere, insidiously, daily, in the press, in the cars, & in talk that the English & the French despise & hate the Americans & that 'somewhere in Paris' or 'at a big concert in London' or 'at some great meeting' somewhere, only last week, the name 'America' was mentioned & received with hisses & hooting. They squirm under this, & the Bosche see their advantage & spread the suggestion everywhere & it strengthens the hands of the very many who are against all sending of munitions. 'Look,' say these, 'how our generosity is received. The holy name of America received with hisses. This is the reward of being the accomplices of murderers.'

Of course, most of the press is pro-Bosche, & is so dirtily, in the true Bosche way. A paper loudly proclaims its utter neutrality, &, in fact, prints no item of news which could possibly hint at any possible success of the allies. There is always present the suggestions that the Germans are winning. Not much is said, not much war news is printed, but the headline is always: 'German Gain. French Defeat. British Cruiser Sunk. Blow to British Prestige. Egypt Must Fall, say Germans.'

Of course the German organisation cannot fail to succeed in a nation so lack & apathetic & prone to believe what it is told. The Bosche have their task made easy for them here, it is handed to them, as they say here, with parsley round it.

I hope to reach St Louis in this dirty car somewhere at midday, & I'll be glad to watch the Bosche at work there. It is one of his headquarters, & there are 125,000 of them there. They have been welcoming lately the woman who played Mary Magdalen in the Ober Amergau play. Her role is to preach the sanctity of a people who could produce such a play, & as she is a trained player she impresses people with her holy fervour. Germany in the role of penitent whore is rather funny.

The pace and strain of the work was considerable, and, on March 1st, he wrote:

Today I can say with the Conway boys '3 cheers for going home this month'. Hurray, not much longer. I don't even now know what I think of America. I suppose that in the big Eastern cities, N.Y., Boston, & of course in Yale, I have felt in the presence of the English mind set free, & going to be immense and generous & beautiful beyond all modern idea. Then outside that (which has been happy & inspiring) there is a crudeness & a baldness & a self-satisfied mechanical achievement which is the very devil in hell, & some of these ghastly mushroom makeshift towns like Chicago, which I shall always regard as hell on earth, & Pittsburgh, which is where the devil was born, these rough Middle West cities like Columbus are among the beastliest places I've ever seen . . . Madras is a gentleman to any of them.

Three days later he was continuing, 'My God, I am weary of American hospitality. My God, I loathe myself every time I get up to speak.'

Masefield was returned to England in March, having incorporated the substance of his experiences into an official memorandum for Sir Gilbert Parker and his colleagues, but crossed again to France in August, busy in following up many of his own hopes of Allied-American co-operation, preparing a report on the American contribution to Britain and France, in medical supplies, volunteer doctors and nurses, finance.

In 1918, he did a second lecture tour, of four months, in America, and again felt at his best not on the platform but amongst the young, in freer or impromptu circumstances.

I have had some wonderful talks with the soldiers here. I do really think that the *average* American man is a nice fellow, good tempered and easy to get on with, and when you meet men above the average as in the O.T.C. & G.H.Q. you meet a very splendid type, brave, self-reliant, cheery, friendly, generous without stint, & very highly and quickly intelligent. They told me all sorts of interesting things; & I met the 2 finest American fliers, & I heard of the American daredevil who goes up in a 'plane 6 or 7000 feet, & then says goodbye to his pilot and jumps down in a parachute. I went up in a plane 5000 feet with *the* finest American flier and I looked down, & thought of this man getting up from his seat with his parachute, & then jumping down. It is a daredevil thing to do; yet if one could do it once I suppose, that like morphia, it would become a habit. 6000 is twice the height of Snowdon. Well, to every man his taste and talent, & would we all had leisure for them.

My flier was the most wonderful looking man, about 27 years, with wild long brown hair, as long as Willy's [W. B. Yeats] with one of the wildest & most beautiful faces I've ever seen. Big fine eyes, wide apart, full of intelligence & daring, a quite splendid broad-based nose, & a mobile, firm mouth, & a great look of courage & swift decision, & an indescribable look of a restlessness to discover something better. He chewed a cold cigar all the time, & grinned.

He said he had never lost the wonder of flying, & that every flight was as great a marvel & pleasure to him as the first.

# Part Three

## Letters from France, 1916
(Letters 37 to 97, 29 August to 23 October)

These letters were written to Mrs Masefield while inspecting the American medical services in France, and in doing research for his book *The Old Front Line*.

[37]                                                          29 Aug, 1916

My darling,

I begin this as usual in the train at Reading, with the feeling that as I have now begun to go I am already, in a way, on my way back, though it seems a long way round.

I am so grieved the last days were so dull: the arm rather took it out of me, and there were such lots of things to get done and people to see. We'll have a great colloque when I get back, to make up.

Things look so much likelier now, that our beautiful time in the happy lodge may come true in less than a year. I've just passed a pub with the sign 'The Rising Sun' and I take it as a splendid omen.

I hope that you will be met at P.R. I do hope that. It will be too dreadful. I can't bear the thought of you trudging in this rain.

My darling dear wife I hope Hampden[1] won't be sad and tiresome to you. Kiss both the dear Jude and the dear Lewis for me, and tell Jude how proud I am. Mind you send Nevi[2] a copy of the pamphlet[3].

Bless you my sweet Con.
Always your old lover
John

1. With Isabel Fry, the Masefields had the Rectory Farm in the village of Great Hampden, Bucks in 1909. There John wrote *The Everlasting Mercy, Dauber*, and finished *The Widow in the Bye Street*. They also retained a home in Hampstead, London. In 1914, they moved to Lollingdon Farm, Berks. Great Hampden must have had many poignant memories for the family. Constance here seems on a visit, perhaps to Isabel.

2. Henry Woodd Nevinson (1856–1941). Journalist and war-correspondent, humanitarian, essayist, autobiographer. Covered wars in Greece, South Africa and at Gallipoli, writing *The Dardanelles Campaign* (1918). He had the leading part in the campaign for Macedonian famine relief (1903) and against slavery in Portuguese Africa, and for female suffrage. He opposed the atrocities resulting from the British post-war military activities in Ireland before the establishment of the Free State, 1922. His son, C.R.W. Nevinson (1889–1946), mentioned in a subsequent letter, was an official war artist in the two world wars, mingling elements of cubism with those more traditional. Masefield had small liking of the former.

3. Masefield periodically issued pamphlets on literary or topical matters. I cannot trace this one, but infer that it discussed Anglo-American relations, or the needs for further efforts to improve the medical facilities for the men in France.

[38]
Hotel Meurice,
Rue de Rivoli, Paris.
30 August.
10 p.m.

M.O.D.C.

I have just arrived here and am sitting in my room before going to bed. My passes worked like charms and I had a very easy time till I got aboard the ship, and then I lay in a bunk for 3 hours trying to sleep while people worked a winch some ten yards away. I heard a sort of symphony every 2 minutes. 'Click rattle. Hoist. Rattle rattle rattle. High enough. Lower. Rattle. Rattle. Lower. Rattle. Lower another link. Rattle. That's got her. Another bloody half inch your end. Rattle rattle rattle.' and so on and so on till sleep was far away. Then at about 5 we started, and soon found that we were in for it, for it was blowing fresh, there was a dirty sea, and a belt of cold rain. I kept on deck and slept a little on the deck, in a nook in which I slept over a year ago, but it was wet and cold, and the sea got up and there was universal spuage and groanage down below, and when we came to port we weren't allowed in, so had to flounder about outside, which collapsed a lot of bold souls who till then had only looked green, but I held out and had another sleep, and at last got in to Havre, where again the passes were charms.

At the station I had a row with the cocher, who was a knave, but I routed him finely, being in the mood for a row, and he went off cursing under his breath, and then I launched (3 p.m.) and jolly glad I was to have some food and so on to Paris, where now I am writing this. This place is a fine hotel 'avec reductions pour la croix rouge', and I shall be here tomorrow and probably the next day, so that if you write to me here the letter will be forwarded, though I hope to have letters sent on from the Embassy, but this latter way I shan't know of till tomorrow.

Tomorrow I hope to present all my credentials.

Dear love to you my darling. Kiss the children from me.
Your old love,
John

I hope that you were met yesterday and so avoided the drenching walk. Mind you send me full news of Gt. H'den.

---

[39]
Hotel Meurice,
Rue de Rivoli, Paris.
31 Aug, 1916

M.O.D.C.

I have begun my task today by presenting credentials. First of all I got rid of my bag of office at 10 a.m., at the Chancellerie, and then crossed the river to present my letter to Lt. Col. Bigham. He is rather like Cazenove[1] to look at and to speak to, and was at Imbros for most of the Gallipoli time, so that we had a subject in common, and I am to see him again this evening. Then I went to the American Embassy and presented my letter there, and was kindly received, and may have something fixed up for me by tomorrow at mid-day. I also had a sort of resume or sketch given to me of the organisation of the American work. It is mainly in and near Paris, but there are other places scattered about, one with the Belgians somewhere, one with the English, and one towards the East somewhere, all rather vague, but I shall soon know more. One great Deport of their's is next door to Bourgeois, on whom I called, but he was not in.

Paris does not seem to have changed at all. It is a very beautiful, rather formal expensive city. In 1000 years New York will be rather like it. The spirit of the place is unchanged, a sort of careless gaiety overlying something formally granite and critical. Most of the poilus wear steel casquettes now, which are rather becoming.

On my way back from the Embassy I looked in to see some tapestries from Reims Cathedral, some of them rather noble; and with them was some wood-work from Ypres all smashed and bulleted by the Bosches. . . .

I wonder what you are all doing at Hampden. I hope that it is fine enough for the place to be pleasant and that you are having picnics and divertissements. The storm here was pretty bad. I hope that it hasn't ruined any of our crops.

Mind you let me know if the post cards reach the children. I am told here that they can go from here, and so I send them and I hope that they will arrive.

Tonight Bigham is going to show me the big Somme offensive films, which will be very interesting. I cannot tell you how deeply the efficiency of our men here strikes me. All now seems working admirably towards victory; no more muddle, no more ignorance, no more pigheadedness, but all in avant avec les drapeaux.

Dear love to you my darling. Send me full news.

Your old lover,<br>
John

1. G. F. Cazenove was Masefield's literary agent before the war, and encouraged him to write fiction, beginning successfully with *Captain Margaret* (1908). He died during the war.

---

[40]

Hotel Meurice,<br>
Rue de Rivoli, Paris.<br>
1st Sept. 1916

M.O.D.C

I am hanging about here till the Americans send me word one way or the other, as I expect they will during the afternoon.

I went last night to see a private view of the Somme offensive films, but I don't think they are much more interesting than other films, except that in their general dusty darkish colour they looked like Gallipoli again, and in their general ruin and waste they were like the real thing. It was not easy to get from them any sense of the Somme country except that of a big expanse, something of the nature of the Berkshire downland but with gentle contours.

Before I was taken to the films, there was a dinner, where there were some friends of the Ponsonbys, and also an old French general, whom I recognized at once as one of those who had stayed at the Tours hotel when I was there. He was a charming old man, much such as one as Ian will be in 20 years, and had just come from Verdun, where things are quieting down now, though by no means quiet. The Bosche admit the loss of 200,000 in July alone from all causes, so that their real losses are probably half as much again at the least, since they generally understate by a third. Still, even so, they are full of tricks and I've no doubt they will fight like wild cats to save Hungary from the new offensive.

A telephone message has just called me up to say that I am to go to see the Medecin Chef at Neuilly at 4.30 this afternoon, and I suppose when that is over I shall know more than I do now; so I will write again this evening. Tomorrow (Saturday) if I am not at Neuilly I shall be lunching again with Bigham; discoursing concerning the Dards[1].

Will you send me presently some 3 or 4 copies of sonnets[2], as pourboires, shall we say, and also, when they are ready, some Gallipolis[3]? If you will tell W.H.[4] he will send the Gallipolis and so save you the trouble. I want one for the fine old French general, and one for Bigham and one for the Charge d'Affaires (the Ambassador being absent).

This letter is not very precise, because I am writing of the great, and as Proverbs says 'a bird of the air may tell the matter'. The city is not too hot, and not too sad; quieter than London and not so much under the cloud of war as it was long ago when I first came out. Would my French were better and quicker: it is dreadful to have an accent as gross as a Boche's.

Dear love to you and to the babes. Let me hear all about Hampden.

Your old lover,
John

You are too beautiful for mortal eyes,
You the divine unapprehended soul,
The red worm in the marrow of the wise,
Stirs as you pass but never sees you whole.

Even as the watcher in the midnight tower
Proves, from a change in heaven, an unseen star,
So, from your beauty, so, from the summer flower,
So, from the light, one guesses what you are.

So, in the darkness, does the traveller come
To some lit chink through which he cannot see
More than a light, nor hear, more than a hum,
Of the great hall where kings in council be.

So, in the grave, the red & mouthless worm
Thinks of the soul that held his porridge firm.[5]


1. The Dardanelles.
2. Masefield's *Sonnets and Poems* were published 1916.
3. Masefield's *Gallipoli* was published in 1916.
4. The publisher, William Heinemann. Heinemann published virtually all Masefield's work after 1910.
5. Published in *Lollingdon Downs*.

---

[41]                                                           Sept 2nd. 1916

M.O.D.C.

I was so glad to have your first letter today and to hear from Jude. . . .

Yesterday I began my tour by going out to Neuilly in the late afternoon, so here begins my first report.

Neuilly.
Sept 1st 1916

Neuilly is a piece of flat river-bank land between the Seine and the fortifications to the north-west of Paris. It is about 2½ miles from this place. It is all built over of course, in fairly goodlooking but not very prosperous suburban homes and streets, with a good many trees in the avenues and Defense d'Uriner in pretty nearly every available corner, as though Neuilly kidneys were specially frail. The Ambulance is in a rather spacious avenue, on the left or western side, and I should say that the wards must be dark, as the main building runs, like the avenue, mainly north and south. It is a big place, designed, just before the war, as the Lycée Pasteur, or medical school, but was never finished and never opened; the war broke out, the Americans took it and now it is the Ambulance. It is a long building, about 150 yards long, with about 3 storeys, and a gravel patch, full of ranked motor-ambulances, in front of it. It is this sort of thing and at the back of it is a western wing of the same kind, & between the wings are traverses and a quad, so that the whole is thus:

It is built of red & yellow brick with leaden facings and roofings.

I went in at the central door & met the Medecin Chef, who is (I should say) an American of French descent. He was practising in Paris at the time war broke out. He came down in uniform (a khaki modelled on the English pattern but not so smart) & we had a talk. He is a fairly big fellow, with an attractive face, something of the Warry & something of the Duse type, easy to get on with, and he thinks that it will be possible for me to see everything in France, though it will be a big order & will take me into many different parts. As to working in the hospital, he seemed to think that that would be impossible, but he felt that I could spend practically all day at Neuilly for some weeks together, & that then I should see everything without wearing myself to pieces. A very special thing at Neuilly is face-repairing, & if they will only take me in hand, who knows but I may come back an Adonis. Then a man whom they called the Commandant came in. He is a Benet[1], the uncle of all that family of poets of whom I have told you, & I should say a good deal shrewder, being as it were a very competent child of this world. He is going to run me through the hospital tomorrow, Sunday, at 2 p.m. so I must dejeuner early & gird up my loins.

When this was arranged, I came back to the hotel & dined, & then went for a walk, meaning to come back to write to you; but I had only walked a quarter mile when I saw the theatre, with *Polyeucte*[2] as the attraction, & I thought 'I may never have the chance again', so I went in & saw the tragedy, with the alexandrines & all, Polyeucte behaving as a perfect lady all through. The house was packed. There were many poilus en casque there, & for the first time in my life I saw a real audience, & that was as big a pleasure as the play. I came away after the tragedy (they finished the 5th act at 10.15, & then gaily embarked on Moliere) murmuring jolly good alexandrines.

Dans cette cité de luxe, cette ville de tours sublimes,
Il faut beaucoup de francs et beaucoup de centimes.
Plus fatal que serpents, plus dangereux qu'un ours
Le Parisien poursuit ma malheureuse bourse, etc.

You should hear me spout alexandrines now. Polyeucte is nothing to me.

I went into Notre Dame this morning, having nothing to do, & heard an amazing boy singing Kyries. I do wish you could have heard him.

Dear love to all
Your old lover,
Jan

1. The most considerable poet of this family was Stephen Vincent Benét (1898–1943), author of *John Brown's Body* and *Western Star*, also of the prose narrative *The Devil and Daniel Webster*. His brother, William Rose Benét, published *The Dust which is God*, a novel in verse.

2. Pierre Corneille's play, 1640.

----

[42]                                        Hotel Meurice,
                                            Rue de Rivoli, Paris.
                                            3rd Sept

M.O.D.C.

Yesterday passed sans evenement. I presented a letter to an American doctor who was away from home, and lunched with that officer to whom I had the letter from the F.O. (It is always nice to be discreet thus.) He attracts me and interests me a great deal, but I'm not likely to see him more than once or twice before I finish. Without ever ceasing to be the man of action type he has the adornment of letters, much as Wolfe or Sir John Moore had, and this combination commands respect more than any I know.

After the lunch, there was nothing to do, so I wrote & read and wished it were time for dinner, and then after dinner I went to the Theatre Francais again, to see the play *Les Affaires sont les affaires*, which you may have seen the State Society do, some years ago. It is a rotten play of course; the business man who makes money, the unhappy wife, dissolute son and neglected daughter, the daughter has nerves and runs away, the son has a motor car and gets killed, and so all comes to grief. It is of that type of modern play of which Brieux[1] has done so many, and from which the English stage has caught a sad infection. But when we do that kind of thing we do it with a Puritan whine, and pause after every moral sentiment, and rub in every mean little bit of social satire, and the result is hideous. Done as this strange people do it, it becomes a work of art, that is, a thing which makes one understand what life is, and the result is a living memory. We have not got this power of acting. There was a man who played the business man. He made one realise every little shade and light in the commercial character. He was vulgar unspeakably in his triumph, his cunning, his affection, even in his grief, and yet he left me with a profound sense of the nature of the greed of life, the extraordinary power of a low and swift vitality, and the ruin that hangs like rags on every resolute intellect. It was an extraordinary study. He made it more affecting and terrible than I can describe, and did it with a vulgar wit which was irresistible. There was another business man in the play; a most perfect bit of acting. A bounder, in a red tie, with very white teeth. I never saw such a study. He might have stepped straight off the Clacton Belle. It seems very heartless going to a theatre here; but it is difficult not to do so. I know no-one yet, and the only alternative is to go to bed, as if one reads in the hotel one must have the window shut and curtained 'a cause des Zepps'. Still, after today perhaps my evenings will be occupied with work. I shall begin real work this afternoon.

I peeped in at mass at Not'Dame this morning, but it was a dull mass and I came away.

It is said that the Germans have a good deal of sickness of a minor, travelling kind, but nothing to be of much account. If it could become general, a Herodian, on both their fronts, it would be a blessed dew of Heaven.

Dear love to you, my dearest Con.

Bless and keep you.

Your old lover

John

1. Eugène Brieux (1852–1932). His plays, harshly satirical, have the social realism of Zola and the early plays of Bernard Shaw. *Maternity* (1903) was first translated by Mrs Shaw, and included in a volume of three plays, introduced by Shaw himself. His work has outspoken discussions of class, hypocrisy, feminism, adultery, slum housing, murder, syphilis, the effect of divorce on children, the tempting but misleading implications of 'free love' which itself can be as tyrannical and complicated as marriage. In England, his most celebrated play, often attacked for alleged immorality, was *Les Avariés*, (*Damaged Goods*), 1901.

---

[43]                                                                    II

3rd Sept

M.O.D.C.

As tomorrow is likely to be a full day I had better write my letter tonight.

I went out to Neuilly at 2 p.m. this afternoon. I must modify my past impressions rather. The front elevation is indeed of red brick, rather pale red, with whitish or pale yellow stone facings, something after this style (French chateau style, with poivrieres at the ends and an attic story in the rather abrupt leads.

and then a high pitched lead coloured roof) but the main scheme of the building is this shape.

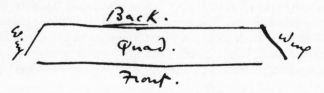

the whole making a rather splendid public building.

It used to be said that the Japanese hospital was the best in the war, but the Japanese have given that up, I dont know why, and the English and French run it together, and I've been in it but not over it, and I didn't like its arrangements, as it was built for an hotel, and is not very convenient as a hospital. Probably Neuilly is the best all round hospital now, though as a little, small, special jewel the little place at Tours is still ahead of it.

Of course, they were lucky to get Neuilly. It is a brand new fine French lycee, with all the splendid big windows and lighting and great salles, with external well-lit sheltered corridors and flat roofs, that those splendid public buildings have. All the good hospitals I've ever seen, with the exception at Tours, which was built as a hospital, have been lycees of this stamp, and it occurs to me that the French meant them to be used as hospitals. All that the Americans have had to do is to put in stretcher lifts and the usual laundry and sterilizing plant. But apart from all the luck, they have made the place a very beautiful thing. I never saw such charming wards, nor such nice and neat arrangement. Their special pride is face-making. You go out to the front and have both your jaws and your nose blown away and everybody else says 'O Lord, Billy, you are settled as a lady's man'; but not a bit of it, you go to the Neuilly people, and they cut out one of your ribs and make you a new pair of jaws, with excellent teeth and palate, then they cut out a calf's tongue and tie it on to the roots of your old one and water it till it sprouts; then they find an old nose somewhere or other, or make a new one out of the calf of your leg, and they solder up the gaps and rouge over the white parts and there you are, able to talk and eat and much more lovely than ever. I am not joking. They really do these things. They shewed me some 50 casts of Before and After treatment and really they make human heads out of things that have no single feature left, not even a swelling.

After I had seen the hospital, there came a call for ambulances to go to the station for wounded, so off I went in an ambulance, and by and by the train came in, and the Americans unloaded it very ably and swiftly and the men were sorted out to the different hospitals and taken away at once. My car went to a fearful hospital that looked like a prison. It made my heart sink to see men taken into it. You see, when a nation has only 600 men to care for, as at Neuilly, it can pamper them all. When it has 600,000, as in France, or at home, c'est autre chose. I had no letter today from you.

Dear love to you and all.

Your old lover

John

---

[44]                                                    III
                                                   Sept IV 1916.
M.O.D.C.

Before I forget it all, I had better set down what I saw at Neuilly this
morning.

I went to see the dental clinic, which is the place where the face-making
begins. The actual room is small, with windows all down one side, and facing
the window are about half a dozen dental chairs, with the usual fixings. On the
walls are rows of numbered plaster casts of the jawless and faceless wrecks
which have been mended since the war began, and in chairs behind the dental
chairs are the patients awaiting treatment. Today they were the usual type of
wounded Frenchmen each walking with a stick, and dressed in pyjamas, with
swathes of bandages everywhere.

The first case I saw was that of a man whose face had been divided
diagonally, comme ca: – and at the same time shred round to one side.
All the lower half of the face was 3 inches lower than it should have been and 2
inches too far to the left. They were engaged in hoisting the lower part back
into position and propping it back to the right, with some most ingenious pads
and props which were made next door. Then there was a man who had come in
with neither nose nor jaw of any kind, and was now quite perfect but for a chin,
which was going to be added immediately. They get hold of the man, and clean
up the infection of the wound first, and then lay the sort of foundation of his
future face by moulding new jaws for him; the jaws they make out of his spare
ribs or out of bits of his leg, and when they have got the framework laid the
surgeons set to work to put on a new covering of flesh, which they cut from the
patients cheeks or elsewhere, and in some cases they make quite good new lips
and noses. Of course, as this is a special thing at Neuilly they have a good many
cases to see to, some of them very terrible to look at. Some of them were done
by rifle bullets at 15 metres, evidently with dum dum bullets, and these are
frightful in the early stages, but the recovery is very swift and the remaking
wonderful. I saw men with new noses, just setting, so to speak, but not yet in a
condition to stand a blow. Then there were men with no mouths, and men with
mouths between the ear and the throat somewhere, and men with nothing but
mouth between the throat and the chest and men with little round orifices
instead of mouths, and other men with already one lip set and a second
beginning to grow, and all as perky as could be. Then there was one man who
had been 'finished' by certain surgeons in a condition of such awful ugliness as
would have wrecked the poor fellow's life; but he was being taken in hand, and
they were going to make him a nose, and straighten out his eyes, and give him a
mouth; and they thought he would finish as a beau. The whole scheme is really
an adaptation of dentistry to surgery. The dentists, who are jaw specialists and
jaw artists make the frame and the surgeons cover it over. The man who was
perfect but for a chin has been under treatment for a year and is now likely to

have a few months more of treatment, and may then, for all I know, be recalled to the war. 13 months more of actual war is the popular cry here, I know not why.

I do not find the Americans as helpful as I could wish. They seem not centrally organised, but working in independent, unrelated groups, and it is difficult to get into touch with the different groups, but I am beginning to get the hang of them now. One of the drivers is a young man whom I met at Yale in March. He has been of use. No letter from you today, nor yesterday.

> Bless you, my dearie, my love to you all.
> Your old lover
> John

---

[45]                                                        Sept 5, 1916

M.O.D.C.

Only one letter from you since I left, and today comes the rumour that the mails are discontinued, owing to submarines, and that they will not be running for a week; so, alas, you will not be getting my letters either and there will be general gloom in both camps. Still, let us hope for the best; it is better than a year ago when I was in Malta.

Not much to tell you today, for I have no further inspections till this afternoon, when I go to see the Neuilly annexes, of which there are, I believe, eleven. God help us if I am to see the eleven at one go, but no doubt the wind will be tempered a little, if not by the American mind, by a puncture or some shortage of petrol. Tomorrow I hope to see the Neuilly pathological laboratory which has done very good work, in the action and palliation of gaseous gangrene; and if I can be left alone with the surgical reports for some hours I shall be fairly happy. In the afternoon of tomorrow I hope to see some skin and bone grafting in the afternoon clinic there.

Am much worried and bothered at not having Sir G's[1] report on the pink paper. Not knowing that result, I can arrange nothing.

Being free for most of yesterday afternoon I wandered into the quartier to see the rue d'Assas where Synge used to live. It is as gloomy a street as a rider to the sea could choose, Gower St would be genial to it, but no doubt a young writer would find quality in it, and get a pleasure by trying to describe, and see it all through the haze of ambition and excitement and sadness of which youth is made. 'none lives there now but the peewit only', and a variety of pale, hard, unwholesome, fattish hideous women, young and old. You cannot guess what a grue[sic] the place gives, there is no sort of joy there.

I used to call this city the city of franc chasseurs; for they hunt the franc with singular skill and pertinacity pretty nearly everywhere; but, close to the rue d'Assas I found a cafe where one can eat almost as cheaply as at Roche's. So I dined there 5 courses for 2 francs 50c, and do purpose to feed nowhere else henceforth. Everywhere else I have found alas that in buying a slice of meat one has to pay for the joint. They have sometimes a noisome way of appearing very humble but putting no prices on the bills. Then, when one has fed, in one's humble way, they set what prices they choose on la note and there one is, stuck. But on apprend. I have learned a lot of dodges already and one must pay as much for savoir vivre as for wisdom.

The sole of one of my shoes has begin to come off, qu'il soit damne. Why the devil didn't it give some sign before I started; it will cost me a small fortune to have it cobbled here. Je pousse des jurements epouvantables.

A good many English here. We stare and are silent, following the manners of our race. Don Quixote and walking are my only friends. I cannot imagine this city gay. London is a joy ride to it.

So far, I have made one friend, the pleasant young man from Yale. He goes back this week to America.

So you will be back at Lollingdon by this. I wish I were.

Dear love to all.

Your old lover
John

1. Sir Gilbert Parker, at whose suggestion Masefield was now in France. Gilbert Parker must have had more than professional interest in Masefield, for he was a prolific, if slapdash author. His thirty-six books included many novels, mostly set in Canada, on which the Dictionary of National Biography comments, 'although sensational, unconvincing, inaccurate, and turgidly written, they appealed to conservative tastes'. Like his fellow Canadian, Lord Beaverbrook, Parker believed in Imperial unity. He was MP for Gravesend, 1900–1918.

---

[46]                                                                6 Sept.

M.O.D.C.

Still no letter from you, alas, so I suppose the beasts are still lurking. I do hope they will be caught and settled soon for I am afraid you will be fretting. My only consolation is that there is a wire and that it is better than it was a year ago.

As soon as you get this, will you please at once open me a credit with the Paris agents of the Lon Cty Bank? I shall be at the M. hotel for a while longer because it is a good place to give as an address when one is speaking to an Ambassador; it corresponds probably to a good but not very smart London hotel. But I mean to leave as soon as I can feel that I have met all the smartness likely to be necessary.

My general impression is much what it was a year ago, that nothing but direct duty will ever drag me here again. The women seem to me to be continual repetitions of the bucket, with I suppose the very worst manners in the world. The poilus still strike me as wonderful, with quite charming gentle simple manners, and the most touching appreciation of every word and deed. The place or city I dislike intensely, but wild little queer hilly suburbs like St Cloud and Renil and Mendon are pleasant and even fresh.

It is a fearful nuisance not knowing what G.P.[1] has settled for me; I can arrange nothing till I know.

I went out to see the annexes today in the care of a very attractive Philadelphian surgeon. I found him splicing a man's nerve (in the forearm) and passed about an hour seeing him do that while another man gouged chunks of stuff out of an adjacent throat. The surgery seemed excellent, but the methods and drill of the place had that air the A things have, of depending on goodwill always rather than on discipline. After a while we went off and saw the annexes, where soldiers who are recovering are, as it were, 'potted out', so as to leave their beds at Neuilly vacant while keeping themselves within reach of visits and final treatment. Here again, as last year, I saw the Fr system at work. The A's pay for the maintenance of the hospital annexes, but the French women run them, and once again the Sisters were miles and miles ahead of the V de F de F.[2] I cannot tell you how charming and beautiful some of the Soeurs de Charité were, really holy and wonderful souls, whose wards were spotless, and patients gay, merry and happy. As you may remember, I do not love the F de F but, prejudice apart, they cannot compare with the Soeurs in any way; and the poilus know it and ask to go to a Soeur's house whenever they know that there is any choice. My surgeon knows the Jasper gang very well and also the Jayne people, so we had a happy talk, and I asked him to dine, but he could only stay for a cocktail (me a lemon squash) and tomorrow I am to see his early morning clinic.

I may at the end of this week go for a night or two to Verdun or to some place behind it, or between Bar le Duc and it, or somewhere there, Dieu sait, to see a unit which will be around there if it hasn't been moved. It won't be under fire, so do not worry, and we don't even know where it is yet.

Dear love my darling Con to you and the dear children. My fond love to you all. Kiss Jude and give Lewis a hug for me.

John

1. Sir Gilbert Parker.
2. Probably a volunteer force of French women.

---

[47]                                                                    6 Sept.

M.O.D.C.

Still this stoppage of mails, & so no news of you, nor much likelihood of any for some days probably. Well, c'est la guerre, & must be endured.

I am to go to the East on either Saturday or Monday to visit the different sections of the Field Service. As far as I can tell, I shall be away for from ten to 15 days, and during all that time shall have perhaps little or no chance of writing to you and probably none of hearing from you, but this is the pessimistic view one has to take in war-time in order to get agreeable surprises. If there is any chance of getting letters from you I will find out, and wire an address; if not, you must go on to writing to the Meurice and I will get the letters on my return. The Field Service is a different thing from the Neuilly place. Its quarters are at Passy, & it holds a very jolly lot of young men, whom I look forward to knowing.

I passed this morning from 9–1 going round the Neuilly wards, seeing the surgeon's clinic; some 200 cases I suppose. It is a great treat to get among people pretty much of one's own race, and to see women who are clean and in low heeled shoes, and men who are not Etatismed and regled out of all [illegible word]. Some of the wards are too small, but otherwise it is a jolly good hospital, & after stinking old poisonous Arc, where you could scent the death from outside the building, it looks like a miracle. The appliances (tell Bobby) are made by two real carpenters, & jolly good men at their job they are, & all their dodges for lengthening limbs which would otherwise be contracted, are excellently neat and clever. Then they have a real artists to do the plaster of Paris work, which keeps limbs rigid, and each man (patient) has an excellent little table of 3 trays at his bedside, to hold his books and tobacco.

 It was dejeuner before I had finished, so that I saw the men dining. Each had a neat little tablekin on leglets to stand on his bed, and then had soup, meat & succotash, and then fruit, all served by the sisters but brought up by the French assistant helpers. After that I went up and bore a hand in the operating room, where a man had his knee drained and another man had his elbow mopped up. I do not know how it is with their best operators, but their juniors are certainly less stylish artists than our men. Tomorrow or the next day however I may see one of their stars at work.

I got to know another of the surgeons this morning a nice, elderly man who knew my books, & I also met the matron, a refined lady, less terrible than matrons I have met, but with an augustness which one meets in matrons. I then went on to Passy, & just saw the city quarters of the Field Service, very jolly, bachelory, & free & easy, with a wonderful view from a sort of cime or plateau, over the Eiffel Tower, & a kind of gorge, the latter much built over, but impressive.

I talked with a young Rhodes scholar there, who knows Parker, & came to the conclusion that the Passy people know more of the American organisations in France than the other lot.

Well, my dear, how are you, & how is pleasant Loll? I wish I were back with you, but that cannot be, my dear.

Bless you and the two dear children.

Your old lover

John

---

[48]
Hotel Meurice,
Rue de Rivoli, Paris
Sept 7, 1916

M.O.D.C.

Your letter of 2nd has just come (the first news for a week) and I was jolly glad of it. It means probably that the beastly sousmarins sont coules; hurray & hurray, and now we shall have regular mails again.

I'm worried about Na & the school; as I have found it so very hard to get at Na's real feeling about it, and some of it she seems really so fond of. I agree with you that she had better come away.

This is only a snip, as I must off now, but I'll write again tonight. Send *all* letters, & especially G.P.'s report. I can do nothing without that.

Dear love to all.

from

John

---

[49]
Sept 7, 1916

M.O.D.C.

It has been hot today, & as I have padded some 9 or 10 miles on the roads, gadding from place to place, I am weary, & shall write a poor letter.

I have passed much of the day in the pathological laboratory looking at germs through the microscope, & had the pleasure of seeing my old friends, the 'stifling cockums', being eaten by phagocytes. The staphilococci are just little dots, ⠶ comme ca, and the phagocytes simply *eat* them up, & then, it is thought, die themselves, but in the act of dying liberate some essence of being fatal to staphilococci. So that I felt awfully cock-a-hoop, feeling my whole theory of life justified, at any rate in this instance. The junior pathologist is a charming man; the senior, not like. I saw the germ of gaseous gangrene. He is more of a man; than that dot. He is something like this ⠕ , and he has the nasty way of generating gas in himself & in some way breaking down the carbo-hydrates in muscular tissue. He works and breeds with fearful speed. A few of them in a broth in a test tube will make enough gas to blow out the cork in twelve hours. I saw some guinea pigs that he had killed, & I saw some men who were having him washed out of their wounds with a neat arrangement of drains. Some lotions wash him out & kill him, so the treatment is to open the patient wide & then rinse him. The surgeon who does this at N is a splendid man, very like Harry[1], with much the same really great ability & swiftness. I haven't seen him operate, but his way of summing up cases is excellent. I found that I was right in diagnosing conditions & treatment in about 3 cases out of 4, & this skill I owe, I suppose, to Ave.

I don't find the people very forthcoming. They are all very busy & they have with very few exceptions never heard of me, so tis uphill work, & I still haven't the remotest notion how long the job will be. I can see hospital work till the end of this month, but after that there will be the other work, & I don't know how long that will take.

I send you my dear love. Kiss the two dear children for me.

Your old lover<br>John

1. Probably Masefield's brother George Henry Masefield who was always known as Harry in the family.

---

[50]                                                                Paris.

                                                                 8 Sept, 1916.

M.O.D.C.

No letters come through, & so I suppose the submarines are still holding up the mailboats, but it may be that your directions are not sufficiently clear, so will you, in future, be sure to address your envelopes unmistakeably

Hotel Meurice<br>Rue de Rivoli,<br>Paris,<br>France.

for, remember, our postmen, & possibly France's, are mainly in the service of the armies now, & civil mails are of less account.

I go to Verdun tomorrow to be with the Field Service for a few days, & I'm afraid there will be no chance of a letter reaching me till my return, & as I've had only 2, & may not be back till the 20th, I am sad enough. Mind, please, my dear, in every letter you send, to say what Parker said about the paper, & *please stablish me a credit.*

If I get back on the 20th, as I may, I shall have next to arrange to go a trip in the American hospital train, which will bring me to about the 25th or 26th. Then I shall have the local hospitals to do, & the local charitable work, which should take 3 weeks more or so; after that, I don't think there will be very much more to do, except the outlying hospitals, some of them far in the south, but it is so difficult to be precise, when so much of the work is not centralised.

I called on Bourgeois today & found him in, & we had a long talk, & he gave me lunch. He asked very nicely after you and the babes.

He is much stouter & much more of a person. He was wounded in the Vosges, & has been decore, & now he is rather a dog. We talked about the Whites a good deal. Apparently Jack lived a very rakish life here, & was considered rather an authority on what he called 'the metaphysics of love'. As far as we can find out, Willy & Augusta are not in Paris; but they may be in Normandy with Mrs MacB. If GP[1] has saved me, as I hope, I think this journey will supply me with work enough for months, as I see offshoots.

But I see no reason to change my opinion about the end of the war. From 14 to 18 more months before any army demobilizes.

Dear love, I do hope this will reach you. Bless & keep you & kiss the dear children from me.

Your old lover,
John

1. Sir Gilbert Parker.

---

[51]                                          Sept 13, 1916 Not far from Verdun

M.O.D.C.

Letters have been difficult to manage these last few days; for I've been living in motorcars, flying from post to post, often all day long, & then at night going out many miles to the postes de secours, & coming home at 1, 3, 4 or 5 in the morning. I am very well, & hope to be in Paris again in 10 days from now, after going further east.

This is written in a sort of Cotswold country, in the heart of a wood, with the big guns going off, far away, on both sides, as though men were blasting in a quarry. Down below in the valleys, there is a continual noise of hammers, as though there were a shipyard there. There are camps everywhere, of all kinds, & building & roadmaking, & cavalry going to the water, & waggons going up, & motors coming down; endless ordered activity, with aeroplanes up above superintending.

I hesitate to say much of what I have seen, for possibly this will never reach you, posts being what they are.

I have seen Verdun twice, & been all over it. It is a town of the dead now, a little, little town, about as big as Troy, not so long as Ledbury, with a cathedral Louis Quinze, & the very look of France about it. It must have been a stronghold always. It stands on a rising ground above the Meuse, which is as big there as the Thames at Lechlade, only deeper & swifter; & it's biggest height must be 125 feet, I should guess. Probably the Gauls, the Romans, & all who have followed, have used it as a fort. Of the old formal fortifications, of the Louis Quatorze & Napoleonic types, one need not speak. They are very fast, dark, stern & cold. 1,000 years hence, when they are even as the Palatine, they will possess similar interest. The modern fortifications are the hills outside, a sort of ring of low downland, of semi-detached hills about as big as the Hurst, with gaps between them. All these hills were once covered with trees, & green & pleasant. Now they are ploughed with shells, pock-marked with shells, lepered with shells, on a sort of livid & earthy scab of shell holes which looks like a disease. They look like sick hills, & all the blasted splintered rampikes of the trees stick up like bristles on them, & the shells drop on the hills, & blast them up a little more, at odd times, all day and all night. For all the miles of the half ring of Verdun, say an arc of 30 miles by seven miles, every field has its shell hole, & every vital field its similar tether, as though the earth had had a pox which had destroyed its life.

Verdun itself is a town of the dead; much of it, especially the higher part, is in ruins, & the civil population has gone. It is like a town sick of the plague, or some city after the sack, or what Pompeii was, after the earthquake. The cathedral clock had stopped at twelve minutes past three, & other clocks at odd hours, just as the shells fell, but there *were* clocks, & there were streets, & you could say that it was a city & find your way about in it. But in the half ring outside, there are villages, big villages, places as big as Missenden & Risboro, which are nothing at all, but heaps of broken brick & plaster & half burnt floor, with a pock of craters in every little garden & alley, & nothing unsmashed in all their extent. I was in one yesterday which had suffered a rain of big shells for the month of the big attack, & every day since till 10 days ago. It was a place rather like Mitcheldean, if you remember that, & I should say that there was a crater 7 feet deep by 10 ft wide in every ten yards of it. Quite lately they took to shelling the graveyard. I never saw such a sight as that. They had dug up the dead of the past 200 years & flung them broadcast, & had laid bare the corpses of the soldiers who had died in the field hospitals during the attack. The place was littered with broken crosses, broken wreaths, bones of men, rotting bodies & mildewed rags.

Down in the town I found a letter dated 1869. It was about a denied debt of 1100 francs, & the right, also denied, of somebody to take Aline to St Petersburg. I did not read it through, but I felt that the writer was in the right, & at the end there were notes in a crabbed sour hand by the man who received the letter and was probably in the wrong, & I wondered who Aline was, & whether she was still alive, & why the letter had been kept so carefully.

Dear love to every one of you, to you & to the dear children.

From your old lover
John

[52]                                                                    15 Sept

M.O.D.C.

I'm hoping to finish up in the East tomorrow, in Alsace – so get to Paris on Sunday or Monday. This will end all my visiting the Field Sections, as I don't expect to get leave to come out again. I'm so looking forward to having letters & news of you. Dear love, this is only a note, but I've been up all night since 1 o'clock & up all night the night before, & must now go off on a very busy day. Dear love to all.

A sonnet on being shelled out of bed.

Quand guillaume sonne son clocher
Il faut descendre vite
Dans puits ou cave ou rocher
Où tout le monde s'abrite

Dans puits ou cave ou rocher
Dans rocher, cave ou puit
On mange des oeufs bien pochés,
Vêtus dans robes de nuit.

---

[53]                                                      at Nancy for tonight.
                                                                      Sept 15

M.O.D.C.

I start off, to see the last of the sections, early tomorrow morning, & may be back in Paris, to find your letters, O joy, on Monday night. Hooray for the thought of a fortnight's letters & news, & possible leisure for jotting down what I have seen. I've had a wonderful time, & being in the air night & day for a week has done me good. I haven't felt so well since I first left home for France.

But you, my dear heart, I wish I had news of your being well, & poor little Jude back at school tonight, my heart bleeds for her.

                              Dear dear love
                              from John

---

[54]                                                                  In Alsace
                                                                      Sept 17

Dearest heart,

It seems long ages (& is really a fortnight) since I had any word from you, &, alas, my letters to you have not been very long nor very frequent since I came to the east. I get up early (if I go to bed at all) & go untold miles to various places, & then go to some more, & then, when it is dark, go to some others. When I get back to Paris and hear the news of Lollingdon, & whether you even get my letters, I'll try to tell you what I have seen.

Here I am in the Vosges, among hills which are pretty big and lumpy, not unlike Wales, only vaster, & sometimes just a bit like Ireland, which I can hardly bear. Here & there, at the top, one can see into the Promised Land, the Rhine, & the Hartz Forest even, & they say that with a glass one can see German citizens walking German streets. All this place is conquered territory, won back from the Germans, I hope forever, & it is wonderful to see how charming, tactful, thoughtful & wise the French are & have been in their treatment of the re-conquered province. After seeing so much of the stern side of the French, in their heroic fight, it is wonderful to see the other side too, on so great a scale. Now I must stop, my dear heart. My dear dear love to you & the babes.

Your old lover,<br>John

---

[55]                                                              Meurice.
                                                                 Paris.
                                                             20.IX.1916

M.O.D.C.

I got back this morning at 9.30 or so & found all your letters, & was jolly glad to have them. At least, in looking over them I find I have letters for about half of the days, & the others haven't turned up, but may later. . . .

It is distressing about poor Jude, but I'm afraid we did send her too young, & then she has, for some reason, not been very forthcoming about it, & has not helped us at all to her real feelings. In some ways it has done her good, quand meme, & if she could only have a friend there, gog or crony, it would make all the difference to her, & be a big thing in her life.

You have not had much news of me since I left Paris, so it would be best to begin at the beginning & put you au courant with my adventures. Please be very careful to acknowledge the receipt of all these documents of my experiences: this is the first.

I left Paris somewhere about the 8th or 9th, in a train all crowded with soldiers, & had to stand for the first two hours, watching the battlefield of the Marne. At Bar-le-Duc I got off & was met by the Americans, who had come in with an ambulance to meet me. They were a very nice friendly set, mostly Harvard men, & after lunch we did the Section shopping, which was mostly sweets, pies & tarts for those in camp & vegetables for the mess. In the saddlers shop I saw a whole heap of marten skins gathered in the forests of the Argonne & the great woods thereabouts. Bar is a pale coloured French town, with trees, a little river, a formal Place, & the old town or stronghold up above it. It was badly bombed by aeroplanes some time back, & one of the young men said the aeroplanes cruised slowly up & down, low down, dropping bombs at leisure, while the crying of the hurt & frightened went up in a long & awful wail.

By & by we got into the ambulance & started out & up into a sort of open rolling country, like the Downs above Lollingdon, only on a bigger scale. It was a fine hot day, & the road was dusty, & presently we got into the Verdun road, which runs up & down on this chalky roll through a very fine country, often densely wooded on the hills, & with the Meuse, like the Thames at Lechlade, only swift, on the right. Now the Verdun road is the most wonderful thing in this war, for the salvation of Verdun came along it, & was still going along it when I saw it. You must not think that Verdun was saved by anything special, but by an endless procession of 5 ton motor waggons, carrying up shells. All along the road, going to Verdun, there were sections of these enormous covered waggons, moving fast, head to tail, all painted gray & all covered with dust. There was a cloud of dust miles long along the road, & as we whirled by in the ambulance I could see dimly waggon after lumering waggon, with a dusty old man gripping the wheel in front, & usually a hopeless patient face fixed on the tail of the car in front & a never-ending roaring bumping rattle & the taste of dust, & continual shouts of A droit, to make them leave the middle of the road. Then when we would get past a section we would pass a similar section coming down, & then overtake a section of horse waggons or mule waggons, with mounted men guiding & chains clanking, & then there would be more shouts of A droit, & the horses would be shoved to one side, & the dust would go in clouds, & then we would get past & hear them clinking on behind us; & then we would come on a company of poilus walking like old men under their packs towards the trenches, & all white with dust & dried mud, going in a kind of slow stagger, just as labourers come back from harvest, & then we would pass a battery, all the same grey colour & dim blue & dust colour, with boots tied on the wheels for brakes and the men's gear heaped on the caissons, & the horses trotting on in a mounting cloud of dust, & then there would come a kind of scream & we would swing to one side to let a staff car go by, & we would just see a general, all dim in the dust, disappearing in the dust, & then there would be more poilus, more batteries, more waggons, more sections, arrays of dusty men breaking piles of dusty stones, & dusty camps, & dusty villages, & placards on the fountains to say Eau a Boire or Eau non Potable, & messengers galloping on the turf of the downland by the road, and flowers of the autumn, hardhead, & yellow rod & scabias all coated with dust like rhyme, & then at a turning a dusty group with a dog, or men halted in a village, all so gray with the dust that all looked haggard & weary but patient & unconquerable like old age.

Presently we came to the Meuse, which runs in a flat valley about half a mile across & probably fills the valley in the winter, but is now a small swift clear rather shallow but still swimmable river of bright & pleasant water. Many men were swimming in it, & many more were washing their clothes & many were fishing. There are no fish to be caught, as they were all killed long ago by hand grenades, but you know what fishers the French are. Just beyond the river was a brook with a solitary horse standing in it as though he were thinking & always when I passed that way he was standing in the same place, as though the dust & the passing of the world were nothing, & some grouping of the cells in his brain a recompense for the madness of life.

Soon after this, we reached the camp of No. 8 Section. A section is a fleet of 20 motor ambulances, with their drivers, cook, handy man, lieutenent & mechanic. This section was housed in the out buildings of a sawmills. The mill was at work, making plank for the trenches, part of it was a hospital, part of it was the section's machine shop, kitchen & office. The grounds made a park for the cars, & in a flat field, near a brook, beyond, were 2 big tents, one a sleeping tent, the other a map tent. I dumped my things in the sleeping tent, where I was given a bed, & then washed some of the dust off myself at a basin in the field; after that we all had supper in the map tent, soup, meat, bread & jam & coffee, with wasps & flies galore. After supper, the cars got ready for duty. The system is this. The French stretcher bearers take the wounded from the trench to what is called a Poste de Secours, where they are dressed & sometimes amputated. Then the ambulance cars call at the postes & take the wounded to hospitals from 5 to 20 miles from the front. Nearly all the postes are under fire, but strongly built, with perhaps 8 thicknesses, of timber balks, earth, sand-bags, rock etc. on the top of them, & they may be fully 10 feet under ground, so that shells do not often reach them. I asked to go to the very interesting post of what I will call Corpse Village. They gave me a steel helmet & a gas mask, & a good thick coat, & away we went, a Harvard man of about 40 & myself.

> Dear love to you, my dearie, & to Lew.
> Your old lover,
> John

---

[56]
Meurice. Paris<br>Sept 20.<br>II nd letter

M.O.D.C.

I left off this morning at the starting out for Corpse Village.

I should say that Corpse Village is some way from Verdun, & a rather important point in the defence, like many others. The fighting there, in attack & counter-attack was bloody, even for Verdun, though it is quite there now. It lies very much as Knocknacarry lies, though instead of the steep hill behind Knock (the rd to C'dall) imagine a gentle hill, with woods on it, & to the left, instead of the Dun river, a valley with gentle hills beyond it half the size of the

C'dun[1] hills. I am imagining that you look on Knocknacarry as coming by the inland road from C'dall.;

Well, we started, & it happened to be the night of the releve, when the men in the trenches were to be relieved, after 8 days in the trenches. The relief was falling in, in companies, in the village, & some of it was already on the way, and the moon, almost full, was up, & the night was as quiet as June, except for the cannon away over the hill from time to time. Our road was uphill all the way, through woodland, & we went without lights of any kind, & all the way up the hill we passed companies of poilus going wearily to the releve, with their great packs on their backs & their rifles slung, & a kind of tired plodding stagger in their gait, & bent over sticks like old men, shambling up the hill in column of twos, with many stragglers, & all often halting & looking round, & shambling to one side to let us pass in the dust & the moonlight; & ammunition carts trotting past them, and empty carts shaking down the road on the other side & more coming round the bend. Some asked me for a lift, but it was defendu & we could not.

Presently in the heart of the wood we came to a cross roads with huts & a little sort of office, & there the ambulances had to pull up, & we got out to walk. Corpse Village has no particular road to it, but a rough sort of track, very like the road over the hill to C'dun. From the post in the wood you go on foot down a high road for half a mile, & then you turn across a field of downland into this track, & then you follow the track 2 miles or so to the ruins of the village. All the way is pitted & pocked with shell holes & well under mitrailleuse fire from the German lines & most of it under rifle fire, too; but the enemy is quite there now. I stood on the downland for a moment looking at the rolling gentle country so beautiful in that light, and all along the downs star-shells were rising & burning white & drooping & fading, & others following; & on the distant downs was a swift glimmer, like summer lightning, from bursting shells & the flash of guns. All along the track groups of men were going to the releve, & carts of munitions were passing, making such a noise, in that still night, that the enemy must have heard & known. In Gallipoli, the whole track would have been arrose with a machine gun, & the carts & horses & men made quiet forever, but nothing like that happens there, the carts jolted on, & the men talked, & one man pointed out 'The Gully of Death' in the downland to my left, & said that it was terrible there, during the attack. There were little brooks near the track & men gathered at the springs & shallows to drink & rest & talk, & there were owls crying in the wood up & down & about.

Dear love to you,
From your old lover
John

1. This would be Cushendun, in Constance Masefield's home country, Antrim.

                                         Meurice's
21.IX.1916
III

M.O.D.C.

To go on with the Corpse Village story.

Of course, all the time, there was a noise of cannon, but most of it distant, where the French were attacking (with success). Near at hand it came about once a minute, or less, generally a bomb, sometimes a torpille or trench-sweeper, a ghastly thing, which makes a ghastly noise; but there was none of that crack of rifles & rattle of machine-guns and pipe of bullets which went on all the time at Anzac[1]. Between the bangs there was peace, & moonlight, & the crying of the owls, & the quiet noise of water.

When we were drawing near to the point of wood below which Corpse Village stands we went down a rough bit of hill where the track was rough with dried mud, stones, & shell holes. Then from behind us a battery of soixante quinze opened up, with a shattering sharp bang, & the shells went screaming overhead, till one felt that one could see them, & after a few seconds they burst in the haze of moonlight beyond & made a secondary glimmer & were gone. The another round came, making the hell of a noise, & then a torpedo burst in the trenches, & one big German gun fired & the shell came over but did not explode, but even so there was no rifle fire & none of that rattle-rattle-rattle, as though there were rattlesnakes everywhere just going to bite.

We turned sharp left in a sort of trodden field where there were groups of poilus, and mules & horses, & carts being unloaded, & men in the saddle holding the led horses, & a sort of beauty of moonlight on it all unspeakably strange. Just beyond, the road was like the dried bed of a brook, & it went up a few yards over pebbles, & there we were in Corpse Village, one of the famous places of this war.

Many years ago in Galway I went to the ruins of Ballylee, where most of the cabins have fallen; and in the moonlight, in that rolling downland, with the wood & the brook, Corpse Village reminded me of Ballylee. It stood once on a tiny rise above a brook, with a wood above it, & there were the ruins standing still. They had not the look of houses; they were not houses; there was no roof in the place. Sometimes there was an end wall, sometimes a bit of side wall, sometimes a sort of square of wall as big as a pig stye, sometimes a kind of column of ruin like a Druidical stone, & all a tas of rubbish, half burnt wood, broken tiles, stones, sandbags etc. inside them & in the lanes.

I looked at this place. There was a lane to the trenches just beside me, & soldiers were going down the lane, following the sign posts, and then I realised that I was on a path beside a graveyard which must once have been a little garden. It was about as big as our garden at Hampstead, only level, & it was filled full with ranks of graves, lying as close as they could lie, & all with crosses, some of them with wreaths. The inscriptions varied. Generally they were:–

'Foutaine, Marcel, 27 ans – <sup>me</sup> Chasseurs à Pied.

Mort pour la Patrie (ou Tué à l'ennemi) 15 Oct, 1915.'

Sometimes they were

'Un Français. Inconnu.'

Sometimes simply – 'Un Allemand'

for in the heavy fighting often the bodies were not found, but heads & parts of bodies, sometimes only rags of flesh, which they had to gather up in bags. By the German graves were bottles buried neck downwards in the earth, & the bottles contained whatever photographs, letters & objects of identification were found upon the dead. After the war, perhaps some of these bottles may tell relations in Germany where their men are lying.

The wreaths were the touching things. They were all the gifts of the companies in which the men or officers had served. The men subscribed for them out of their cinq sous par jour, & made the inscriptions, & then sent down, by ambulance, or revictualling car, or man going on leave, for the wreaths & tickets they had decided on, & after a time they came back & were placed upon the graves.

Just beyond the graveyard was a ruined house, & above the ground, backed against the ruin, was a heap of timber balks, stones, sandbags & corrugated iron, making a mound. There was a hole in the mound, covered by a sack, & inside the hole was a narrow stair leading into the poste de secours, 7 or 8 feet below. We went down into a lit cellar as big as our sitting room in Lollingdon, only partitioned off. There was an operating table in the centre, with an acetylene light above it (not lit at the time) & stands for brancards, & a few benches. Further in, was a sort of stand of bunks for the traucerdiers, & on one side a passage, floored & pannelled with plank, leading to the cabin of the medecin chef. The ceiling of the place was so low that we had to stoop. It was supported upon great boles of trees. There were shelves on the walls for operating instruments, sterilisers, saline-injection-bottles etc. & on one side were two tables, covered with red & white toile cire, one, far in, for the traucardiers, who sat there at a lamp, reading or writing, the other, near the floor, for a party playing cards.

This party consisted of the medecin chef (who looked like a chef, in his overalls) a cure with strangely bright black eyes, & two officers. They had dined there together & were now playing bridge, under a lamp, with a good deal of life & gesture. On a bench against the wall were two slightly wounded men, one hit in the head, much scared, the other an arm case. By them were two malades, rather weak from dysentery, & all four were waiting for the midnight horse voiture to take them by the jolting track to the ambulances.

A brandardier offered me wine & coffee, & I drank a mug of coffee with him, & then sat on a bench for hours & hours, while the cards flicked about on the table, & the players laughed & said Tiens & sometimes turned to stare at us. The curé was opposite to me, & whenever I looked up I found him staring at me, a pale man, with strangely bright eyes & a beard, evidently a saint – a devoué. They talked about a famous supper that the curé was going to give them in his little cave the next night. I wished that they were not there, for I wanted to talk with the wounded.

Now I must stop this once more.

Dear love to you all.

From your old lover,
John

J'ai touché mon credit, merci bien. J'ai un joli petit carnet de cheques, et peut être dans quelques jours j'aurai un joli petit traitement de 'deux cent cinquante' par semaine de Sir G[2].

1. Probably a reference to Gallipoli.
2. Sir Gilbert Parker.

---

[58]                                                                      Sept 21
                                                                              IV
M.O.D.C.

To go on with the Corpse Village story.

After a long time, the card players stopped their game, got up to go. The curé said that the marmite would be on the table precisely at six the next evening, & they parted with laughter & good cheer. The curé stared hard at me again, as though he wanted to speak, or would have wanted to speak, had he been able to ask someone about me first, & then saluted & went out. I saw then that he wore the medaille militaire, for something very markedly brave. It corresponds to our V.C. or D.S.O.

The medecin chef said something or other, that the voiture might start, so the wounded and sick men went up to the open, & we followed.

There were still some delays, for the horses had not been put to, but the men got into the cart, & I stood about looking at the night. It was brighter now, for the moon was higher, and you know how that dim downland suits the moon. The ruins near me were mostly whitish oolite stone, almost the colour of the moon, & all the crosses of the graves were casting shadows. Someone said something that made me look down, & there, just at my feet, lying on stretchers on the graves, where they had been laid but a minute before, were two dead French soldiers, whose flesh was still warm. One lay on his back, one on his side, as though asleep, & their dignity in death broke my heart. One had been shot through the heart, one through the head, & both must have died at once. I think the one on his back was a city dweller but the other was a countryman, very big and strong and grave, older than the other, & a finer character. There was no mud on their clothes, so that I knew that they were men of the releve who had marched up the road that night, & that very likely they had seen me passing only a few hours before & had stood aside with their comrades to let me pass.

The star shells were still rising & falling & giving light along the lines. The French star shells are lovely pausing globes of white fire, the German are much like rockets. The soixante quinze still fired at intervals, with a very sharp terrific bang, & other guns answered, not often. We set out up the broken road by which the carts were going, & passed stray groups of weary men, staggering slowly home, stiff with mud & labour & want of sleep, after their 8 days turn in the trenches. Some were eating by the springs, & some had fallen down to sleep, & looked like the dead-weary, but not at all like the dead; life never looks like death.

All of that downland had been sown with shells. The shell holes were in regular lines, evenly spaced, like the holes for an avenue of trees, & then in amidst the regular spaces o o o o were irregular splashes & splotches, due to hurried fire & tirs de barrage. Presently I was back in the forest, & the carts came up & the wounded & sick were put into one of the ambulances & sent away to hospital, while I stayed with the second ambulance in case more wounded should come before dawn. You see, in all that country, the wounded are only moved between sunset & sunrise, & the rough road is too bad for the motor ambulance. The first stage has to be done in a horse cart.

I talked with the American driver, a Harvard man of about 45, & then we got into our ambulance & lay down on the floor of it, with our heads in our helmets (the steel helmet is the only hat comfortable for sleeping in) & slept very heavily for 3 or 4 hours. When we woke up, there was a French soldier at the tail-board begging for a ride down. He was a young man, but dog-weary & covered with mud, & I suppose he had been 4 or 5 hours dragging up the hill to us, but we could not grant his request, & it cut me to the quick to see him turn away & go dragging on along the road.

I should have said, that when we got back to the ambulances, we found an Englishman talking to one of the drivers. He was (I was told) half French, & born in India, & had tossed up a coin to decide which army he should join, & it had come down French, & there he was. He was talking about some attack in Champagne, where the Germans ran up in lines, so out of breath that they fell against the bayonets, while their officers stood behind to shoot any man who wavered, and the pistol used by these officers was 'the hell of a gun'. 'God, eh', he said, 'I couldn't help laughing to see these fat old fellows puffing up, running like hell to have a bloody bayonet stuck into them. God.' He went off with the first ambulance, as they always give him a ride down on account of his nationality.

After our first waking up, we went to sleep again, & did not wake till the carts brought up the second batch, except once, when there was a big explosion down in the lines. It was a long drawn out explosion, as though a succession of mines had been fired along a long line of trench. We do not know what it could have been.

The second batch were two stretchers, & a sitting case, none of them very seriously hurt. The sitting case had dysentery, & had 'been' (I think he said) 96 times that day, & surely deserved a rest in hospital, as well as his relief. He said that the two men had been killed by accident. 'Ils etaient tues par notre regiment.' We turned out of the clearing, into the road & drove home in the dark (the moon was gone) a little while bfore the dawn. All the way down, we passed groups of dog tired men dragging their half mile an hour in a sort of rocking stagger, & my heart bled to see them.

Presently we were in camp, eating a meal of bread & coffee before going to bed.

Dear love to you.

I loved your letter to G.P. Thank you, my dear.

---

[59]                                                            Meurice's
                                                          Sept 21. 1916.
M.O.D.C.

This must begin partly as an answer to your letter & as a business letter.

To begin with: was not Ian's[1] letter quite beautiful, in style & feeling? It seemed to be a part of a man who had style, both in action & in thought, & struck me like a page from Cervantes. No wonder you did not trust it to the post. If Brett sends the 6 copies of the Am edn, as he should, soon, please send one to me and one to Ian. I was most deeply pleased to receive such a letter. . . .

Next, as to my probable movements. As far as I can make out, I have to go to Pau, in the Basses Pyrenees, to Lyon, Compiegne, Avignon, and a place called Passy in the Yonne, to visit hospitals.

Then, either before or after this, I shall have to go somewhere in the Verdun sector, to see some more American Ambulances. These two journeys will probably each take a week.

Probably the charitable work near Paris will take a fortnight or 3 weeks to do; & then there are schools & refugié work. If lucky, I may be done by the end of Oct., if not, by mid Nov; if unlucky, by 1st Dec.

It is rather a crow, the McLennans staying on.

Dear love to you and the babes.

Your old lover
John

Will you find out, if parcels can be sent to Paris? If so, I shall *presently* be wanting you to send me some things.

Greetings to Bobby if you see him.

1. Sir Ian Standish Monteith Hamilton (1853–1947), one of Masefield's heroes, to whom he dedicated *Gallipoli*, together with all officers and men, 'with the deepest admiration and respect'. Hamilton had served in the Afghan war (1878–80), commanded successfully in the Boer War and showed much personal courage. He commanded the Anglo-French forces at Gallipoli, with diplomatic skills and military decisiveness which were yet insufficient to achieve final victories. Perhaps the personal qualities which so appealed to Masefield – an intellectual, all-round approach to problems, feeling for words (he wrote many books), human sympathies – prevented him from exercising the absolute vigour, ruthlessness, even brutality, less in the field than within his own staff. Whatever the truth, Masefield remained his admirer and defender for the rest of his life, comparing him to Roland at Roncevaux, defending Christendom from Islam. Hamilton's letter would be in appreciation for his copy, and dedication, of *Gallipoli*.

---

[60]                                                    Meurice's
                                                  Sept 22nd, 1916.

M.O.D.C.

. . . I had an interesting talk last night with a Colonel here, who was at Gallipoli & saw the landings from a battleship. He said that he saw, mainly, X beach and W beach, but did not, as he watched, realise that anything very heroic was being attempted. He said that all that could be seen was a collection of little dots moving up, or stopping, or seeming to be doing nothing, while the battleship's shells burst beyond them & seemed to achieve nothing at all. He had been at the front here within the last day or two – had seen the now famous tank guns, which seem to be horrible things, like ante-diluvian animals, all speckled & mottled, 'and without eyes: that makes them more horrible still'. They walk over a trench & into a trench & inside forts and up trees (almost) & scare everybody into fits. More power to them, I say.

I've had a very wearing day, gadding about Paris, mainly on foot, seeing people, but had better go on about my time in the East or will never get that done – So: – the day after Corpse Village.

I got up at 7, after an hour in bed, & had a cold shower bath in the middle of a field, pumping my own water & pulling my own string. Then I breakfasted on bread & jam & coffee, & found a snug place in the sun & slept till dinner, at noon. Then I went away up into the woods to the 'barrier' beyond which the enemy lay, & there they shewed me a big church bell which they ring when there's a gas attack. The trenches were beautifully made & kept, for up there in the woods they have plenty of timber & stone, & dress them themselves & apply them with art. The little gratings at the bottom of every trench were excellent. After that, we took some wounded to an evacuation hospital up the river, & there we watched some poilus swimming, or trying to swim, for only one man did it, against the rush of the Meuse round a corner. After supper, we sat on benches outside the tent while the men of the section sang. Most of the songs were southern songs, one or two were war songs, like 'My Maryland', & some were comic, but among them, sung to a strangely beautiful tune, was a sort of country ballad which moved me very much, it was so real, & so plainly a voice out of common life. It was low enough, but it was real, & it went more or less like this.

My name is John & I live in the town
I'm a weaver to my trade
And the only only time that I done wrong
Was courting a fair pretty maid.

I courted her all of the sunny summer time
And part of the winter, too.
And the only only thing that I done wrong
Was to shield her from the foggy foggy dew.

She came to my bed one cold cold night
With tears in her eyes of blue
She sobbed & she cried & she nearly died
To be shielded from the foggy foggy dew.

Then, of course, he took her in, and then at once it goes on.

I have a little son with eyes of blue
He works with me in my trade
And whenever I look in his eyes of blue
I think of the fair pretty maid.

There was another stanza, & some of the words I know I have set down wrongly & I cannot give the tune, but it made a deep impression on all of us.

Next morning, I bade adieu to the Section & went off to another section nearer Verdun, but found it gone away only half an hour before. . . .

> Dear love
> From your old lover
> John

---

[61]                                                            Meurice's
                                                              Sept 23 1916
M.O.D.C.

After a dusty half hour in the road, staring at the abimé wheel, another ambulance came up & took us into Verdun, where we saw & heard a big

German shell come over the wall & dub into a garden without bursting (rather a sell for William[1]), & after that we went up into the town & watched the photographer take photographs. In one of the chief streets, which was a double tas of rubbish between two lines of broken wall & ruin, a painter sat at his easel; making an official record, in the right way, of truth, with neither sentiment nor judgment added.

When we reached camp, we supped on rude plenty, on meat, cheese & bread & jam, with coffee to follow, & then, having watched the harvest moon rise, we got into our ambulance to go to the postes de secours. As this was rather a special ride, and as I am sleepy tonight from a hard hot day of gadding on enquiry I will wish you goodnight & put it off till tomorrow. Dear love to you.

Sept 24

After a letterless day, I receive yours of the 20th, which makes my heart bleed for poor Na, & makes me long to be back & to hear all the news.

To continue the visit to the postes.

X All that Verdun land is camp, though perhaps no one camp is very big. The early part of our ride lay through a land of little camps, & at first, before it grew too dark, we could pick them out, rest-camps, Senegalese, cavalry, hospitals, genie, & then camps preparing and picketed horses & parked carts & lines of huts & tents & graves.

We were going to two postes just behind the two most important forts outside the city. You will know their names, but I wont mention them, because I might conceivably give some secret away, though it is hardly possible. Anyway, in the days of the attack, those two hills were heaped feet deep in flesh; they were very terrible places.

Of course, all the shells & food & reinforcements, both of men & material, go to the front lines at night, for most of the roads can be seen by daylight, & can be shelled. So on both sides, at night, for miles behind the front, the roads are thronged with the ravitaillement, going up or coming down, at the same jingling sort of trot, in charge of men who seem never quite awake, though they are never quite out of the peril of death, for at any moment the shells might fall at a venture, &, nearer up, the machine gun or the rifle.

When we were not out of the camps, we climbed a hill on to a moor which was as lonely as a wilderness. We could see all the Verdun front, or tell where it was, by the roar of big cannon & the rolling rapid blast of tirs de barrage. It was a good long way away from us, but all that part of the hazy distance was one swift glimmer of flashes, & at every minute a green or red signal went up, & two or three of these lovely white star shells, which impress me more always than shells. The French were pushing these that night, very successfully.

We were without lights of course, but up on the moor we could see by the moonlight, which was as fair as june, and when we had run along the moor a good way we came to a cross road & ran fairly into the stream of ravitaillement. We ran down hill a long way, among trees which made the road dark & at every instant had to peer ahead to avoid running into a horse or cart. The riders & drivers go up half asleep & get into the middle of the road & jog along at a trot there, & in darkness under trees they are almost invisible, & motor horns are not allowed. Every 20 yards we had our brakes on, & then had to whistle & shout 'A droit', often a plusieurs reprises till the cart would shog to one side & the led horse would side-shy away from us or whicker back to kick us, or (if it was a mule) try to get up the bank. Often as we passed one of these carts we almost ran into a cart coming down, for on a dark road in darkness a dark object is as dark as necessary. But we never really hit, though I shall never hear a sort of slow dog tired trotting tittup, with a jingle of chain sounding in it, without wanting to blow a whistle & shout 'A droit'. After a while, the night & the jingling carts became unreal & ghostly, and I wondered if it could be, that all this multitude of men & horses & guns were going up to the war, and whether we ourselves were not, but were only cells in a blood-stream, going we did not know why in a brain which did not concern us.

We stopped in a village at a secondary hospital, where some of the ambulances parked themselves, ready for a call. The village was half destroyed & no lights were burning in it, but the moonlight, & the ravitaillement passing through it, in its never-ending jingle, gave the place a kind of life. We went into the hospital, which was in a cellar, and pitch dark, & empty. Presently some traucardiers came, with a candle in a lantern, & lit us along, past two corpses on stretchers & a man asleep at a table, to a room where there was a lamp & a telephone, & a big tin can full of coffee. We had some coffee, & some formalities were gone through, God knows what, & then we went out to the ambulance again & shogged along towards the outermost posts behind the famous forts.

In the big attack, it was not so much a question of destroying the forts as of preventing the ravitaillement from reaching them, and the roads which led to them became the strategic points, and the weary men in the carts became the defenders. I cannot give you any faintest conception of what the shelling of the roads was like in the weeks of the big attack, but every bit of ground near the roads was bedevilled & lepered & dug into great pits with shells, & the hills beside them were pale with furrowed and hollowed earth.

Engineers were working on the roads in the moonlight, & here & there prisoners were getting in the harvest, piling stooks in waggons, & harvest carts were going down.

All the time, as we drew nearer, we saw the starshells leaping white, & pausing, & floating down, & heard the shattering bang of guns & the flutter & the bursts of shells, but there was no machine-gun & rifle firing, & very little bombing. It is these little personal attacks which discourage me.

We went through what had been a village, but was now a few columns of wall

standing white in the moonlight, & rather famous in its way, for one of the
outhouses was supposed still to have a roof. It was full of rats, & one or two
deserted cats, which have gone wild there, like on the rats, and make their lairs
in the ruins. Soon after this we passed the wreck of a big house near the road, &
my driver said, 'Gee, that's a peach of a ruin. Golly, you can't beat it' and he
pretty well summed it up. Then we came to a cross road, or rather a fork in the
road, & each branch led to one of the two forts, & this fork-road had been the
scene of as much blood & death & slaughter as any place in the war, for it had
been shelled night & day for weeks together; but in spite of the shelling, the
wayside crop still stood, though pretty well scarred with flying iron.

We turned to the left down an avenue of trees which had been cut off at the
tops by shells & left in a bedevilled state, like telegraph posts than trees. My
driver turned to me and said 'That Turnong which we've just tournonged is
called the Tournong de la Mort', and indeed I can imagine nothing fitter as a
cemetery approach. At the end of the avenue of trees we passed a little troop of
pack donkeys going down. I suppose there were 20 of them, all over the road, &
all very little, much smaller than Joey. They shogged out of the way for us & we
went on, & presently came upon a brook with part of a dead horse in it, the rats
scampered right & left as we came by, for no doubt dead horse is good pasture,
so we splashed through the soup, & soon came to a couple of shell holes full of
more dead horse, and then to the village where our Poste lay.

Now I must stop. Dear love to you.

Yours old lover,
John

1. The Kaiser.

---

[62]

Meurice's
23 Sept. 1916.

M.O.D.C.

To go on with my tour.

We came to the rather big, deserted country house which had served as
billets to the section which had gone. It was about the size & shape of the
Moon's house, but it had the real look of war about it, weeds all over the garden
& shell holes in the drive, one big one only a few hours old, & a broken cannon
lying against the wall just as it had been flung there by a shell. Close to the
cannon was a child's toy horse, also broken, & fragments of glass from every
window in the house. There was a fountain in front of the house, & the
departed section had somehow made it work & had used it as a bath. In a flower
bed near it, they had put up a little cross for us, with the inscription

Gone, but not forgotten

We went into the house, which was sadder than a house to let. There were children's toys here & there, & broken furniture & traces of habitation, sauce bottles & things like that, & on a shelf was a torn copy of Victor Hugo's *Last Days of a Condemned*, & that exactly suited the house. It too, seemed condemned.

From outside of the house one had a fair view of rolling land, the valley of the Meuse, Verdun & the rolling low hills which guard it. The big guns were firing, & one could see the glimmers of guns and shells, and the burst of shrapnel in the sky round some invisible aeroplane. I don't know what landscape it is like, but if anything, it is like the Salisbury Plain country, that is, a big expanse, and rolls of hill never quite big enough or abrupt enough to block the view of the expanse.

Verdun itself seemed (from there) to be built on a kind of long low green island. Afterwards I decided that it was perhaps once an island, in marshy weather, but generally a presqu'ile, like so many old strongholds. The guarding hills, higher than it, are about 4 miles from it, & lie round it, not in a ring, but in an expanse of rolling downland, often wooded, on each side of the Meuse. It is difficult to explain, but in going from Verdun towards the enemy you climb up onto this downland & find the forts on the higher parts of it.

The official photographer was in our car & we went into Verdun, that unconquerable city of the dead, & passed through silent, deserted streets of shut up, shuttered & ruined houses, & the Meuse with its sunken barge, and the heaps of its ruin. Inside it, one sees that it was a strong place even in pre-historic times; it goes up high and steep to the cathedral. It is not so much destroyed, nor anything like so much destroyed, as may of the towns I saw later, but it gave one more of a grue from being more of a place. It is pretty big, & was very densely populated for its size, & held always a good many troops, & now it is without inhabitants except soldiers, & to see the signs of life, without life itself, is a grim thing. What impressed me most were the stopped clocks, pointing to all hours of the day & night, as the shell took them or as they ran down. Many of the windows were left open, & one could see the curtains blowing about, & sometimes a sewing-machine with a bit of work on it, or an open book on a table, or a little of clothes or toys. The silence of the streets was painful, & every now & then one came on the notice.

Attention. Vu à l'ennemi.

which was hard to bear, for one could see no enemy oneself.

Outside, one saw, close at hand, the leprous & battered & blasted hills of the nearer forts. The feeling they raised was strange. It was as though a friend had become scabby.

We went along towards the next section & saw some enemy prisoners working in the fields, sad-looking men, for whom one was sorry, & then, in the door of a cottage, looking out into the road, we saw an enemy officer, just as he shews up in the French comic papers, a little cad in an eyeglass, a little raffish rat-faced cad, posing as a soldier, with the insolence of office & the efficiency of the city, and the Belgian crime as his record. He made one understand the Germany of this war like nothing else.

Presently we came to the Section, who were camped in huts in a wood, & we went in to dinner, & then away to take photographs in Verdun. On the way a wheel fell off the car, & the photographer promptly took us 'en panne', & probably we shall appear soon in the press as 'Abimé par un obus. Incident du front.'

Dear love to all, & to you, my dearier.

Your old lover<br>John

[63]                                                     Meurice's
                                                        Sept 24. 1916
M.O.D.C.

To go on with my tale.

This second village had better be called Skeleton Village. but it was not a skeleton, not even a recognizable heap of bones, it was a waste so utter that even the ruin was ruined. One could only say that the moonlit fields were white with plaster, and that the ruin had blocked the brooks, so that the putrid washings from the ruin lay stagnant across the way. In the moonlight it was very strange & very beautiful, & beyond the ruin was a gradual rise of hill, a world-famous lump of earth, or roll of earth, smaller than Lollingdon, smaller than Tivera, a little rise or heap, & beyond it was the enemy.

In one part of the village was a flat piece covered with shellholes rudely filled with ruin. On the enemy side of it was the wreck of a wall, the one standing wall in the village. Even it had shell holes through it, but it stood, & someone had daubed on the plaster, in mud or blood or smoke:–

Chateau de Skeleton Village

& it was called the chateau, may, perhaps, have once been the chateau. Going to the chateau, something twisted under my foot, & looking down I found a filthy old candle stick, which I gave to my driver, who seemed glad to have a souvenir so filthy with the real look of war on it.

Up against the Chateau was that pile of balks, stones, sandbags and corrugated iron which marks the entrance to a Poste. They had been clever there & had altered the cellar steps to a gradual slanting entrance, so that traucards could easily be carried down. All over the flat expanse, rats were flitting to & fro in the moonlight, all fat & big & happy from many a good meal of dead horse. It was a most marvellously lovely night of moonlight, & there was all this ruin & corruption & beauty & infancy & energy all muddled up together.

We were hardly out of our cars when the enemy started shelling the village behind us, with shell after shell, which went right over our heads. God knows what they thought to hit there, except empty carts going down, but they sent over a lot of shells, which went wailing past & fell & burst. Perhaps they had heard of the outhouse with the roof remaining & felt touched in their tender pride. Some of the shells did not burst, for I expect they use old shells on these quiet sectors & keep their best for the Somme.

Some traucardiers came out of the cellar, & I began to talk with them, of the old topic, how long will the war last? They thought 3 months & I thought 13, & they agreed that my estimate was the likelier. They asked me to come down into the Poste; so I went.

On the operating table a French soldier lay dying, & was even then in the article of death. His legs had been shattered by a torpedo, & they had amputated them, but he had lost too much blood to live. A little company stood about him, one man to fan him, a doctor holding his pulse & watching his face, one or two others standing by, ready to do anything, all very alert, efficient, & full of feeling. They had a saline injection going. 'We did what we could', one of the men said, in good English, 'but he was too far gone', in fact the man died half a minute after I reached him. He was a tall, thin man of about 27, a man of some refinement, by his hands.

The ride back was very like the ride out, with a great noise of cannon, & much shouting of 'A droit', & some anxiety lest they should still be shelling the village as we passed through, but they were not. We reached camp in the early morning, ate some bread & porridge & went to bed.

Next day, another very beautiful day, we went through the Argonne to Ste Menehould, through a variety of ruined villages, some of them big places all blown to pieces, with shell-holes 7 feet deep by 10 across every few yards. I think I wrote some account of this ride to you. The Argonne is simply the forest of Deau, & Clermont in the Argonne, the famous place, with a view for miles & miles of plain to the north & east, is Symonds Yat without the river. Ste Menehould is exactly like very other French town, it is pale, & it has a place, & the houses have sunshutters, & the bread is in two kinds, pain long & pain boule; when we had eaten some dinner there & laid in food for the Section we returned to camp. After moonrise, we went again to Skeleton Village & to another Poste behind another of the famous hills. This time we had to park our ambulances & wait in the road for a long while, and a battery of soixante quinze opened up about 200 yards behind us, & fired right over our heads for half an hour, but the enemy did not reply. For noise, give me a British naval gun, but for a shattering blast to make you jump give me a sudden rafale from a battery of soixante quinze. The row the brutes make must quake the dead.

Next day it rained & I had a chance to write to you.

G.P. has arranged the medical business & it is to stand over till my return.

What is Nevi doing? I wrote to him from here, but have had no reply: perhaps he has gone again to the Salonika front.

Here there is some anxiety lest the enemy forestall us in making a generous & workable arrangement with Poland. I fancy that Russia is not as wise as she might be in her Polish policy, & if the enemy win Poland, they will have 400,000 extra men at a stroke.

Dear love to you, my dear & to little Lew.

Your old lover,
John.

---

[64]

Hotel Meurice
25.IX.1916

M.O.D.C.

I had better go on with the story where it left off.

The evening was very wet, with cold wind. We set out through the mud for a drive of many miles, past camps & graves, till we reached another section. This section was hutted in an orchard, which was trampled into a slough. The rain was pouring. The village beyond was half destroyed & the steeple had a canted peak as though it might fall at any minute. The section leader took me for a walk in the rain. The Germans had been there & had systematically burned half of it in the days of their pride before the Marne. Then the battle of the Marne came, & they herded all the villagers into the church, put a machine gun in the steeple, & held the village; but were driven out, & plenty of their corpses lie buried in the orchards there. The machine gun men were bayoneted on the steeple stairs, & the church was knocked about, mainly by bullets, but one shell had burst inside it, & the pock-marks of the eclats were all over the chancel.

We supped in a tent which had no side to it, nothing but a fringe of dripping (again rude plenty, or, rather, civilised plenty, for this section had a caterer who insisted on style & a cook who had been a chef) and we talked of pleasant topics, such as how long the war will last, and again decide 18 months, or two years, or until the German empire breaks. After supper we found a breaking sky, but bitterly cold, so I borrowed a sweater, & set off on a long & lonely ride to the outermost post of all. For a long way we ploughed through the mud alone, & were glad of it, for although there was a full moon, the sky was clouded, & wherever there were trees in the hedges the road was pitch dark. Presently we ran into the train of ravitaillement, & were like a ship in a tideway in a fog, groping our way among barges. A little rain was falling & it was very difficult to see. I peered ahead, & would see a dark shape & shout 'A droit', & sometimes it would be coming towards us & it was for us to 'A droit'. It was just as it always had been, half asleep men jogging with a jingling dreary tittup, horses, mules, carts, batteries, camp kitchens, camions, sometimes solitary riders, sometimes poilus alone, once or twice a company of releve plodding along in the mud.

After a long long time, we reached a long straggling village at a cross roads, where there was an underground post said to be very big, with a bathroom & electric light. We stopped at the village & got down & walked up & down in the mud, & saw the door of the famous post, but could not go in, & had a drink at an 'Eau Potable' & watched the rats & the cats. At the cross-roads, the ravitaillement went past with its dreary jingling tittup, with sometimes a horse swerving & the man beside him snatching him back, & the mud splashing on the walls. The village was only partly in ruins, but nobody lived there, except soldiers, & A.M.C. & they only in postes, in cellars & sousterrains, in little snug vaults with sandbags on them.

When we went on again, we came out into open rolling plains, with the glimmer of flashes, & the rising & falling of starshells, just as before. The moon came out now, & the night cleared up, & we could see the whole great battlefield, for miles & miles. We had to go very slowly, for all the road, being whitish oolite or crayey, makes a good target, & the enemy had been shelling it all day, & now, under cover of the night, the engineers were filling up the holes, and we had either to dodge the holes or the engineers. All that debateable land lives a strange life at midnight. The harvesters (mostly German prisoners) were gathering harvest on both sides of the road; carts were bringing up cracked stones for the shell holes, & engineers were filling the shell holes, & the ravitaillement went on & on, going up to the famous forts. They went on just the same, in the days of the attack, night after night, & the wreck of their carts & the bones of their horses lay in heaps all along the road on both sides. I don't think any soldiering comes up to the ravitaillement. In a trench, you have comrades, & bombs to fling & a gun to fire, & a parapet to hide you; but out on these open roads the drivers were alone on their horses, & the roads were like rivers of fire, & they had to go on & on, as though they were carrying the host; and they saved Verdun; nobody else.

At a cross-roads we passed a marvel, a big white house, apparently untouched. Probably it was a wreck inside, but we could not see any wreck. 'The cure lives there', they said, probably in the cellar.

We were soon in flatland, for we were near the river, & the road got worse & worse, so cratered with unmended shell-holes that driving was difficult. Then, after splashing into a gully of mud right across the road, where several shell-holes had combined, we came into the Place of a destroyed town, where the road ceased all pretence & became shell hole, partly filled with rubbish. We were close to the outermost fort now, & could see the fury of the first attacks, which had spent itself on that poor fort in a rain of all the fire of hell. The town was in wreck all round the Place.

We turned out of the Place into a street, which had plainly been battered early in the war, for some of the ruin was covered with weed & plants, though the rest dated from the attack. We were close to the Germans here, & were told not to laugh, not to talk loud, nor to make more noise with the car than we could help. The enemies' spies sometimes appeared just there; I do not know how; one had been there a day or two before & had talked with a traucardier.

We left the car outside the post, with the shell of a good big house between it and the enemy. There were no wounded for us, but we were to wait till about 4 or 5, in case there should be some. We had all those hours to wait, with nothing to do. We went across the road & climbed a ruined wall & got into a garden & down into a huge big dirty cellar full of flies, and as hot as a kitchen. It had a kitchen range in it, & was, in fact, the kitchen of the traucardiers, but it was a filthy place, & everything in it was filthy, & the flies were like Gallipoli. Some traucardiers were playing cards for counters, & a fat & very dirty man, who seemed to be the cook of the kitchen, was playing with them. The cards were the dirtiest I have ever seen, but the men played with spirit & laughed & joked, & the man who won was as happy as a child. When the game ended, they gave us coffee, & we talked for a while, till the men went off to bed, & then we went out into the fresh air again, & walked up & down in the moonlight.

It was a sad little stretch of street, about 300 yards long, with a ruined mill at one end, & a ruined place at the other & lots of barbed wire at both, & ruined houses in between. We walked up & down, talking of all manner of things, while the guns & bombs banged up & down, without any apparent system, & not very near. We had passed about a dozen times across a space open to the enemy, when the man said:– 'the Germans have got a mitrailleuse trained on this space'. 'In that case', I said, 'we'll walk at the other end of the village.' We did, for a bit, but not for long, because when we had taken about a dozen turns, there came a shattering bang, & the battery of soixante quinze on a hill above us fired a sudden round. The bang or the sudden affront angered the enemy. It was just as though a battery captain had been roused from sleep, for instantly three enemy shells came over, pointing towards the battery, but all bursting in the village, & then two more followed & burst just across the road, & the sixth burst down by the mill. The soixante quinze took up the challenge & fired another round, & then another French battery joined in, & there was the devil's own roar, & we expected a vigorous enemy reply, and went downstairs into the Poste.

Down below there, it was strangely quiet; a man writing, a man reading, a man smoking; the day's papers on the table & the comfortable feeling that is in a dry forecastle at sea in heavy weather. They gave us the papers & coffee, & presently the cure came in & colloqued with us, in a simple merry way, & presently he left & we fell asleep.

Dear love to you, my dear
From your old lover,
Jan

M.O.D.C.

I am going on with my tale of the night at the advanced post.

Towards 3 or 4 in the morning, word came that there were some sick to go down, but no wounded, so we left the poste (the traucardiers always go to bed as soon as this final word comes) & walked up & down in the street till the sick men turned up. All firing seemed over for the night, & the place was quite enough, except for passing rats & a cat making love. We waited & waited, till there was some sort of a feel of dawn in things, and my driver said, 'if it is light when we start, we shall both get the croix de guerre, for everybody gets the croix de guerre for going down that road in daylight'. However, as a visitor, I should not have got the croix, so had no inducement.

By & by, we lost our chance of crosses, for the sick man turned up. As a matter of fact they were not sick, but the doctor said they were so that he and they might have a joy-ride, instead of trudging 15 miles in the mud. They overloaded the ambulance, & I had to hold one man in all the time, & when we started, in the setting of the moon, over that broken road, on which new shells had fallen since we came, we went at a snail's pace for fear of a smash. The enemy must have heard us start, & I cannot think why he didn't fire his mitrailleuse at us; but all this fighting is unlike Gallipoli; and he didn't fire; & we crawled past the open space, & then, very gingerly, began to pick our way in & out among the shell holes, till we were out of the village. Loaded as we were we could only crawl, at five miles an hour, so long before we were at home it was dawn & all the camps were up and the prisoners were marching to their work, & men were at breakfast or cracking stones by the road. We reached camp at 7 and breakfasted & went to bed.

Last night a shell came into that very village, just at the Poste, & struck one of the cars of that section & killed the driver & wounded his mate, so I suppose another spy has been through & has told them what to do.

That afternoon, I started for the next section which is at Pont a Mousson, or was. I was motored to Bar-le-Duc, across a good big patch of the battlefield of the Marne, & saw the graves of the French advance, & a famous farm, called Vaux Marie, where the enemy tide turned, & where the Kronprinz[1], so the story goes, saw the battle lost. You had better not believe the fact, for a good many farms are mentioned as *the* farm from which the K.p.z. saw his defeat, & probably he watched it, first & last, from a good many farms, but anyway the French line came over & along the rolling hill there & beat the enemy back, & the colours of the French graves lie here & there in the open, & their battery emplacements can still be followed.

I went to Toul, got there after dark, dined there, & saw nothing of the town except a bit of Vauban[2] wall, & then motored out under a moon of heaven to the banks of the Moselle. The town had somehow an air of being mainly safe, & the big house where I was to sleep seemed undamaged. It was sandbagged up of course, but the electric light still worked & one went upstairs to bed, instead of down into the cellar, & the windows were intact. I went up to bed in real sheets, washed in real running water from a tap, & settled off to sleep. I had been up all the night before & was weary.

Dear love from

Jan

1. The Crown Prince Wilhelm, 'Little Willy', eldest son of Wilhelm II, in nominal command at Verdun. After the German defeat, and the revolution which deposed the Hohenzollerns as Kings of Prussia, and German Emperors, he lived for some years in exile. Later he joined the Nazis. Known for his conceit, womanising and lack of humour, he inherited his father's faults and few, if any, of his better qualities.
2. Sebastian le Preste de Vauban (1633–1707), foremost French military engineer and general. He fortified the French fortresses, notably along the frontier with what is now Belgium.

---

[66]                                                                    Sept 25, 1916

M.O.D.C.

Il faut-en-finis, weary as you must be.

I went to bed between sheets, after a jolly good wash, expecting not to wake till breakfast. It was freezing cold, which made bed all the snugger; it was the first autumn frost. About one o'clock, in my mid sleep, there came the bong of a big gun & the roar of a shell bursting somewhere not far off. I cursed William, but hoped that that would be all, & resigned myself to sleep again. Instantly there came another & another, all good big fellows, of about 105, that is, one size bigger than the ordinary enemy field-gun. 'We're in for it', I thought, 'Goodbye, sweet sleep', and then they really settled down to it and shelled us hard, & now the shells were going over me & knocking down buildings beyond, somewhere in the town; so I cursed William again, and dressed & went down into the cellar. Everybody was in the cellar, all half awake, very cold & cross at William. Someone said that it was a reprisal for an air-raid, that ten aeroplanes had gone over, some hours before, to bomb an enemy fortress, & that now we were paying for it. By & by they slackened up, sent in one extra big one, and knocked off for the night. Probably, like us, they wanted to be done with it & to clean their guns & go to bed, but it shows how they want imagination. The thing to have done, would have been, to knock off for 53 minutes or so, & then give another few rounds, & so on till dawn. That would have got on people's nerves & produced an effect. But I feel that in these lone parts of the front they do not wish to produce effects, but to fire off their ammunition & get what rest they can or go back to their dominos in their dug-outs. Next day we heard the 'official' account, that William had fired 200 heavy shells into the town. I should have said it was 40 or 50 medium shells, & to make 200 of it he must have counted in the bang, the burst, the echoes of both, & the noise of falling buildings. Still, who am I to judge?

So back to bed and to sleep & to try to get warm again, & up at 7 to breakfast & then out to see the town. We did not hear of any damage done, but we saw some green sprays of chestnut on the ground & a few new shell holes already filled with gravel. The town is hardened to bombardment now, & there are open doors, every few yards, by which, at a second's notice, one can leap into a neat safe cave & defy all the shells of Essen. One goes shopping behind a wall of sandbags, & when an aeroplane goes over one goes below & waits till the banging stops. There is no rifle firing, no machine gun firing, it is all shells & bombs & hand grenades. One could dance on the top of a bus on the middle of the bridge there & perhaps not draw a rifle shot. The town is a pleasant place enough, & the lovely September weather, with the mist, made it beautiful, & the Moselle is a stately stream & the woods beyond are noble. About half the town shews signs of war (the Germans were in it once) & if the enemy chose he could knock the rest to pieces within a day, and he does not because he has not got the shells to spare, but needs them all for the Somme.

After wandering about the town for some hours, I went up to the Postes. All the lines in this part of the front, on this side of the Moselle, are in a great wood or forest, called the Bois le Pretre, which consists chiefly of a kind of beech, not quite the same as our own perhaps, for it seems a taller and a sterner tree, though this may be due to some chance of soil or stone. It is an oolite country, rather woldy, with many springs, & a stone that is easily worked. Where the beech has not taken, the woods are like English small wood, dumpish oak, big hazel, & the usual coppice trees.

Our first Poste lay through the wood, & beyond it, about a thousand yards away, was a part of the enemy line on a rise of ground. This rise had once been wooded with big trees, but they were all shot to stumps, & the top of the hill looked like a chin that had not been properly shaved. The Poste was the usual sousterrain; so we left it and went on to the next, going for a long way on a soldier's road into the very heart of the splendid forest. We wound in & out among the trees, past abris, camp kitchens, dugouts, shelters etc, all splendidly built in a kind of forest village, & came upon a part where the soldiers had cast aside wood as vieux jen and had taken to build with stone, Further up towards the front, we went into the trenches, & found them most beautifully made, with gratings to walk on, & running water with taps, & real electric light, 'replete with every modern convenience'. The poste had an operating room in every way like that of a hospital; far better than the room at Arc, & the doctors had cabins decorated charmingly, with (improper) pictures of ladies stuck upon a background painted black. They had cut the pictures from illustrated papers, & the effect was really pretty. 'C'est digne', said one of them, 'C'est Français'.

Coming out of the Poste we found a wounded man on a stretcher. He was just going down to the base after his dressing. He was horribly wounded, both legs broken, his left hand blown off & one of his eyes torn out, by one of these trench torpedoes. He was crying, & nothing much could be done for him, except a little morphia, which I'm glad to think they gave him.

We visited one other Poste, which was very famous in that part of the line, for its fountain, or succession of jets of water, from the spring in the side of the hill to one stone trough after another. As all the work had been done by the soldiers, & will probably last for centuries it was worth seeing. The daily papers were just being delivered in the camp as we came away.

After a dinner (very luxurious, for one grows in luxury as one nears the front, as the front gets everything) we walked over to Mousson. Pont a Mousson was once simply the bridge to Mousson a ruin, which it still is, only more than usual, owing to the enemy. Mousson looks very noble from a distance, like an Italian hill city. They have a big Vierge on a tower on the top, & though the enemy has fired tons of shells at her they haven't got her down. The hill from a distance looks like a big cone, 700 feet or so.

When we got across the bridge we passed a splendid Gothic church, in a fair state of preservation, not badly smashed, & full of most noble power. Then we came on a soldier playing catch with an enemy helmet. 'Look', he said, 'what I got this morning. I got the head inside it, too, but I left that behind.' These casques are much sought after as spoils of war, & happy is the man that has his quiver full of them.

A little up the hill is the city cemetery; a big graveyard measuring a quarter of a mile by 200 yards. The enemy had taken full toll of the dead, & had shot the tombs to pieces, partly in an effort to knock out a battery very cleverly hidden near by, but partly wantonly, for any aeroplane must have seen where the battery lay, & the graveyard could not have served any military use. I sent you a picture of the graveyard. I hope you got it.

I must stop now, for the time, but will write again later today, for if I do not get my letters finished before I go off we shall be shent [sic].

Dear love to you.

From your old lover,

Jan

---

[67]                                                  26 Sept. 1916

M.O.D.C.

I left off, going up the hill to Mousson, by a little track or road, sown with shrapnel bullets, which reminded me of that track, half the bed of a brook, leading down, & then up, from the gate leading to Layde churchyard past the house we thought of buying, to the Cushenden hill-road. At the top of the hill there was a ruined castle, & rather battered village, & the battered but triumphant Vierge. But the best thing was a wonderful view over miles of the front & away into Germany. We could see the valley of the Moselle, & Metz[1] itself, all spread out in a coloured picture, & the thought was, 'How soon?'

On getting down the hill, we started off for Nancy, a rather dull ride, but Nancy an attractive, beautifully built little old city, spacious & clean, & though a little shelled by no means defaced. We had tea with M le Prefect, who seems to be something between the head of a college and the 1st citizen in a play. Then to bed in a hotel, half expecting a shell or so, or perhaps a little bombing from an avion. Next morning I rose early to catch a train, but the train was delayed for hours, & I had to spend 5 hours at Epinal. It was very cold, very wet, I had caught cold, & I didn't enjoy it. Presently a very slow train took me into Alsace, & I got out upon a piece of conquered territory, which was the enemy's at the beginning of the war.

I was taken up into the hills in the dark, & reached the section very late, in cold wet misty weather. There was a noise of water rushing, & a stink of sauerkraut in the making, which is something between vinegar & a tanyard. I was taken to a room, which was very like an English lodging house bed-room; enlarged photographs of wooden faces, male & female, china ornaments, open work mats big blue glass vases filled with dyed grass, yet some warmth & solidarity & a bed not likely to be lousy. There was no chance whatever of being shelled, that was another thing.

Next morning, I found the brooks full from the rain, & the Vosges hills (3000 feet or so, & wooded, & much like hills than mountains) all grey with mist & looking evil. We went down the valley as far as we could, to the places called Thann & Alt Thann, & all the way I had the feeling that I was at last among a people whom I could understand. The houses were not unlike ours, & the gardens were full of flowers, & the people had the look of our own people & were friendly in the same way. The men were all serving in the enemy army, & many of their little children looked ill-fed, having been shelled out of home long ago & placed on an allowance, which, though sufficient, is not that little more which makes all the difference to little bodies. Thann had a fine church, not much damaged, & was a pleasant place as far as a town so near the front can be pleasant. It is shelled a bit still now & then, & has been fought through, & most of the inhabitants had to sit in their cellars listening to the fight, & hearing the orders given first in German, afterwards in French.

Coming back, we stopped at the Cercle, or military club, where they had rigged up a theatre. Some artists in the regiments there had done the decorations, really very well, but in a very male fashion. There was a huge panel of Kronprinz sitting in a box, with his legs over the edge, & a female figure, nearly naked, farded scarlet, sitting beside him. As we were coming out of this, some young officers came in, & one of them, a lad of about 20, whom I will call Vermouth, asked if we would 'have some grog or flip. I will make a jollee flip or cocktail.' However, we could not stay for jollee flip, but went on.

In the afternoon we visited two of the Postes. We turned out of the village & began to climb, & snaked in & out of the hills, going up & up, till we were in a forest-road, which climbed up & up between montrous columns of firs about which mist was wreathing like smoke. Sometimes we had a gleam of the valley down below us, but more often we were shut in by the firs, which were noble trees, well-planted & well-cared, by one of the big enemy departments. After a long ride, we crossed the watershed, & ran level into the enemy's side for a good way, then tilted up again & stopped at the Poste.

Pretty nearly all the forest is lived in, in the underground way of this war, & as the fir is easy to work, the building is all very good, & the dug outs even luxurious. Then, in most places, there are springs, & the men have plenty of water for baths & washing & drinking, & of course ample wood for firing. But the winter up there, after the snow has fallen, must be hard service, & about the loneliest on all the front. Even then, they were often lost in clouds, & sometimes they are shelled.

We went up the hill a few yards & came out on a sort of upper spur, shot clear of trees, & saw, on the one hand, the land of the enemy, with Mulhouse only a few miles away, down in the valley, & a great whitish streak that was the Rhine. On the other hand, about 600 yards away, exceedingly clear & plain, like the skull of a monk, because the trees had been shot from the top, was the top of the Hartmansweilerkopf, one of the famous places of this war.

I suppose it is about 4000 feet above the plain, & (at the top) about as big as Lollingdon; the peak is just a little cone, & looks just nothing, & yet it was the scene of the most fearful fighting in the war, & taking both sides together some 70,000 men were killed in the struggle for it, & perhaps a quarter of a million wounded. The French have the top of it, & the enemy are just beneath, & we heard them flinging bombs at each other.

We went through the wood & had a look at it from the other side, & then came down through the forest, along a road which bore many marks of the fight. There were trees cut down or uprooted, great scars on the road, & shell holes beside the road, & in one place a little cross to mark where one of the Americans had been killed. He & his ambulance were blown clean off the road into the trees, where part of his ambulance still hangs. Further on was a little pretty hill village, shelled to pieces, & inhabited only by a few rats, & then, below that, a few graves of soldiers & deserted vines.

In the village, as we passed, we were hailed by Vermouth, who had had his jollee flip, more than once, since the forenoon. We gave him a lift to his club, & on the way he explained that what he wanted now was a nice pretty girl. So when we reached the club he promptly embraced the maid, with the words 'Tu coucheras avec moi ce soir, toute la nuit, n'est ce pas?' She patted him away, with a 'Vous etes mechant', & he made the same proposal to the maid's mother, without much success, for he soon came to tell us that 'she said he was awful'.

He talked a fair English & was rather drunk, but very gay & merry. He was in hospital for a wound still, & expected soon to be court-martialled, & he had been a private before & could be one again. He got his rank at Verdun for taking an enemy lieutenent prisoner, but the lieutenent was killed by his side just as he brought him in. 'What I want now' he said, 'is a nice pretty girl & some jollee flip or cocktail.'

'A French soldier', he said, 'is always gay, but when he has some jollee flip he is very gay.' Then he speculated, would the maid's grandmother consent to his proposals, or would it be unwise to try? I expect he tried.

Alas, alas, here is my tale still not finished, & no word from you yet to say if any of it has reached you. I have no news of you later than the 20th, & this is the 26th.

> Dear love to you,
> Your old lover,
> Jan

Kisses & greetings to LEWIS

1. The scene of a siege by the Prussians, and the surrender of Marshal Bazaine and the last army of Imperial France, in the Franco-Prussian war.

---

[68]                                                            Hotel Meurice
                                                               Sept. 27, 1916
M.O.D.C.

Since clearing off the story of my journey, one or two things stay in my mind, in connection with the famous siege[1].

It was mainly a struggle of revitaillement, for apart from the battle & the attack the great chance the enemy had was to prevent supplies reaching the forts. It should have been fairly easy for him to do this, for he knew the roads & the railways, & having ranged them, he shelled them continuously for weeks together, & God alone knows the slaughter he made, among ambulance men, waggon-drivers, ammunition carriers, & soldiers going up or down in all those weeks.

In the outer forts & in the outer enemy works men died of hunger & thirst, for the tirs de barrage made it impossible for either side to approach. In some outer works, attackers & attacked would be lying down together for hours or even days, shut off by tirs de barrage from going on or back. When the tirs de barrage stopped, they used to count heads, & if there were more French than enemy, the enemy would be prisoners, if the other way, the French would be.

All who were there knew that it was the enemy's big effort, & I suppose, like all other efforts in war, it very very nearly succeeded. Men used to kill themselves or fling themselves under cars when going up to those forts. It was a terrible defense.

While I was there, the staff went there, to decorate the town, & I saw their cars, parked during the function, & supposed that the generals had come to plan a big offensive.

During the siege, one of the young Americans was waiting near a poste with his ambulance when he saw shells searching the road towards him, flash after flash, coming nearer & nearer. He jumped down from his seat & flung himself under the car & just as he touched the ground a shell burst right on the car & blew a big chunk of the radiator into his back. His friends got him to hospital & they gave him back the chunk, & he said 'I always had trouble with that radiator'.

One of the sections, the Pont a Mousson one, is off to Salonika, & I've been seeing one or two of the men, to wish them farewell.

By the way, do you remember Mrs Richards who ran away? She is married to a Mr Tiler or Tyler here, & is rather a power, a great pillar of the American colony. I have not yet seen her, as she has lost her son, & is in England, in great grief.

I got an old French poem, Vie de St Alexis, the other day; a rubbishy tale, but it begins like the very finest Chaucer.

My journey wont be so very long after all, for I can do it in 2 bits, & perhaps the trains will not be so bad. I have to go to Aix les Bains, where Charlemagne went after beating Marsilies[2] 'To Aix, where God has given you baths'.

Dear love to you, my dearie, & to little Lew, & the creatures of Lollingdon.

Your old lover,

Jan.

1. Verdun
2. The Saracen King, Marsilian, in the 11th-century romantic epic, *The Song of Roland*.

'Marsilian sat in Saragossa Town,
He sought an orchard where shade was to be found,
On a bright dais of marble he lies down;
By twenty thousand his vassals stand around.'

The poem, in its romantic simplicity and tragedy, had lifelong appeal to Masefield, who saw in it some evidence for his own justification, not of war in general, but for Britain's support for Belgium in 1914.

---

[69]

Hotel Meurice.
Sept 28, 1916

M.O.D.C.

I have your letter of the 23rd. I seem to get a letter every other day from you. The gaps in my letter are mainly due to field-posts, but in that continual whirl there were 2 days in which it was not possible to write. However, since my return I've written never less than 2 & sometimes 3 or 4 letters to you in a day.

I am so grieved that I led you to think I should soon be home. I myself thought so till a few days ago, when some Americans who are helping me brought me their list of places run by Americans, 29 hospitals, & 54 other works, which is of course ten times the number I'd been led to expect. However I am buckling to on them, & go off in a few minutes to see Juilly, which is on the battlefield of the Marne, not far from the Ourcq river. On Sunday I go to Limoges, & on Tuesday probably down to Nice, but may not have to go quite so far. When I finish this distant visiting, the work will go more quickly, for then I shall be in Paris. Nearly all the charitable works, schools, refuges, homes, canteens etc., are in Paris.

I must not write more now, as it is time to start, but I'll write again tonight if I am back in time.

Dear love to you,
from Jan

---

[70]                                                                 Sept 28. 1916

M.O.D.C.

I'm very grieved and sad to be leaving you alone like this. I lie awake & curse William, not that that does any good, for here are the best years of our marriage passing, with us miles apart, & you with the children and the household. Sometimes I feel that nothing good comes out of war, except perhaps the destruction of the tyranny which is presumptuous. There is a kind of spirit which it destroys, & it is best destroyed.

Today I went to see the hospital at Juilly. I was motored out eastward to Paris, on that very paved road on which Blucher hastened to his defeat at Montmirail. A paved road has a very Roman feel about it, & it runs straight away to Metz, under a double line of trees, aspens, planes, balsam poplars & sometimes apples, with rolling plain-like cultivated land stretching away on both sides.

Juilly is a little village, probably of exceedingly rich farmers, & the hospital is in a part of a wonderful monastery and school built in 1638 at a great cost. It is not so beautiful as a big English building of that time, but in its immensity a variety is impressive. It goes on for about a quarter of a mile, big block & chapel, & big block & school, & big block & grange, the big dovecot, the big pond, & then garden, bowling green, wilderness & park, the whole immense, & at one time one community.

The hospital has rather more than 200 beds, & most of the wounded come from the Somme. The big dortoirs in one of the blocks make very good wards, with a southern aspect on one side of them. There is a sort of column of arches down the middle of the wards, as in a church, & this column makes the northern half of each ward rather dark. Most of the wounded were out in the grounds, but a few were in bed still, & one of them, a grizzled, old looking man of 44, was wounded in that Ravine de la Mort, near Corpse Village, & had been in bed for four months. I hate going round a ward without stopping to talk to each man, but he was the only man I had a chance of talking with. The place was clean, & the work, I should say, well done, the lighting, plumbing & feeding excellently done, & yet there was a want of style. There is genial goodheartedness, and yet that is so little. Gammer Gurton has genial goodheartedness, but put it beside Twelfth Night.

After we had seen the hospital, as Plutarch puts it (speaking of Pompey's corpse) our bellies full, we walked in the grounds & saw the huge pond, full of huge carp, &, judging by the smell, of drainage also. The wounded catch the carp, which are said to be 3 feet long & 300 years old, & eat them, though the Staff say they are quite unfit for food. The pond is yellow, green & semi-solid, & on a warm day you can tell of it at some distance.

Jerome Bonaparte[1] was at school in the monastery there, & Napoleon wrote to him, while he was at school, & perhaps came to see him there, & walked up & down with him; & afterwards must have thought of Juilly as he drew near to it before Montmirail. Somehow this seems a fact, & the Americans being there an accident.

After our smell of the pond we went off to a kind of aviation camp, where there is a good big stretch of ground for the aeroplanes to land on. The French types of plane are very rakish & smart, & they are brightly turned out, & the men are wonderful in them. How I longed for Lewis to see them. The men would get in, & the starter would start them, & they would run along the ground for perhaps 4 seconds, & then they would be up & away, & then they would poise & curve & be hawklike & mothlike & rook-like in half a dozen successive seconds, & then go ringing up like a heron, & then be two tiny scratches on the sky & disappear. We watched them for over an hour, & then came away to the battlefield of the Marne, to that part of it, rather, where the Armie cachee fell upon the German right & caused the retreat. It is big open cultivated plain or plateau there, & all that one could see was the plain, with cultivation, & harvest, & people at work, & countless graves of the dead, with little French flags, sometimes, a cluster of French flags, & wreathes & crosses over them, & (for the enemy dead) small black crosses, with numbers. In a wreck of a church, the bell had fallen from the tower & lay uncracked on the wreck; & in one place there was a great ring, which was all grave, for most of three battalions lay buried there, where they had been killed. It was one of the saddest things to see the lonelier graves, for in some places there would be only one grave in a mile, & quite the loneliest grave of all was that of an unknown Englishman, who I think, must have fallen wounded in the retreat & died by the road or on the road.

Dear love to you, my dear dear Con, Kiss little Lew for me.

1. Jerome Bonaparte (1784–1860) was the youngest brother of Napoleon I, whom he created King of Westphalia. He served briefly in the 1812 campaign and, at Waterloo, led some of the left wing, with considerable courage. In exile until 1848, he joined in the coup d'état in 1851, by which his nephew, President Louis Napoleon, took the imperial throne as Napoleon III. His daughter, Princess Matilde, was important in French artistic, literary and intellectual life, her salon attended by Flaubert, Saint-Beuve, the Concourts and others. His son, usually known as 'Plon-Plon', as Prince Napoleon, had a considerable though erratic part in Second Empire politics and beyond.

---

[71]  Meurice.
29 Sept.

M.O.D.C.

About my coming journey, as far as I can see it.

Starting (probably) on Monday the 2nd, I go to Limoges. On the 3rd, if trains are good, I hope to go to Lyons, on the 4th, to Aix les Bains. On the 4th, if very lucky, but more probably on the 5th, I may get back to Lyon, & from there to a village nearby, & on the 6th (perhaps) to Avignon. On the 7th, I may have to go to Nice, a fearful journey, & on the 9th (perhaps) get back to Paris. Then on the 9th or 10th, to Sens, & back to Paris. On the 11th, 12th, 13th, 14th & 15th I shall hope to be doing hospitals within 30 miles of Paris.

Trains & posts are so uncertain that all this scheme may come to grief & there may have to be modifications, & it is really not worth your while trying to send me letters to the postes restantes. Last year, when things were working fairly well, I only got one letter out of about a dozen; this year, going further afield, I should probably get none; so write here, & I will get them when I return. I may quite easily have to come back to Paris on the 7th, or even on the 6th, as the Nice-Avignon journey may be cut.

This afternoon I went to 5 hospitals, not American, but French, to see the American Distribution system pouring forth necessaries. There must be a multitude of wounded men in France, & they have had to utilise some buildings very ill designed to serve as hospitals (old Arc chateau was one) but on the whole their hospitals are good, & the Sisters of Mercy hospitals are really beautiful, and the Sisters themselves are beautiful human souls, with that best of politeness which comes with holiness. I have seen now the courtly in Sir M de Bunsen, & the knightly, in Ian, & the Spanish, in Graham, but the holy, in Father Russell & in these obscure & gentle Sisters, is a more wonderful thing, & I wish that I might myself be a little holy & perhaps have some of it myself. You, too, my dear, whom all love & honour & yearn for have that kind, & it is the rarest thing in this sad world.

Thinking over this so great book of Cervantes, it seems too profound a thing. It is all that we have been saying together these last ten years, that 'the heart of man is upright always continually, but has sought out many inventions'. It is a study of an upright heart, that man has, with the honest sense that man has, & his passion & his fineness & his commonsense, all led astray by his intellect, that ingenious thing, which is so blind. It is a wonderful work.

Dear love to you & to little Lew

Your old lover

Jan

It is strange: this great barrack of a place is full, & I believe all the other hotels are, & the city is without crime & practically without vice, & all because of occupation.

---

[72]                                                                                   Sept 29. 1916

M.O.D.C.

Your packet letter, post-marked 25th, has just reached me safely; but it contained no letter from Lew, as you said, & I have still had no letters of acknowledgment from any of those to whom copies of Sonnets were, or should have been, sent by the Press. Will you please let me know if any of these letters come to you, for I can't help thinking that the Press has ignored all my instructions. I take hope from the one exception, Ian certainly received his.

I agree with your & Lion's reading of the events. I fancy that things are going well here, even very well, & that elsewhere there is trouble, or at any rate pressure. The Dobindjka[1] is the quarter which worries me. These Balkan peoples[2], one after the other, seem to play for their own hand and imperil the general situation by doing so. No news from there at all today, so one expects a bad blow tomorrow. One gets very clever at reading this barometer.

There is a rather angry feeling here, among our people, against the Ams, & an indignation that their press interests have been so well watched. Some of them arranged very good cinema films, which are shewn all over France, so that the general feeling in France is that the Ams have done more charitable work here than we have, whereas they have perhaps done not quite a tenth as much. One big official asked me yesterday whether I would not undertake similar work for our own people when I have finished this. Probably it will not be possible, but you may as well turn it over in your mind, & let me know what you think. The idea would be, to write for the instruction of the French people & to shew them what we have done for the cause.

I get little time here for anything, but I read a page or two of Cervantes before going to bed each night. He seems to be the greatest man of his time, though Shakespeare got further in pure poetry. I haven't yet got at his meaning, as perhaps I have at Shakespeare, but turning over a Spanish essay yesterday I came on this, which is interesting.

'Change the battle-field of Don Quixote to his own soul; put him fighting in that soul to save the Middle Ages from the Renaissance, so as not to lose the treasure of his childhood; make of him a Don Quixote of the mind, with his Sancho, a Sancho also of the mind, & also heroic, at his side, & tell me of the comic tragedy.'

I dont see it so, but it is strikingly put.

I've met an American, of the Berenson[3] type, who is an architect, & wealthy, & knows all knowledge, & has seen all the world, & speaks all tongues, who tells me of all the new thought in all the old universe. He is taking me to see some more hospitals this afternoon. Tomorrow I lunch with some American diplomatists & (I hope) visit 2 more hospitals, & on Sunday I go to Limoges for one night. No-one says a good word for Limoges.

Dear love to you, dear heart, & to dear little Lew. I hope that the variance soit rien de chose.

Greetings to Bobby & Lion.

1. Masefield must refer to Dobrudja, in Romania, the scene of much fighting between Romania against the Austro-Hungarians and Germans. During this September, Romania was suffering defeat and retreat at Dobrudja, from Field-Marshal Mackensen.

2. The perennial 'trouble in the Balkans' precipitated the Great War, by the Sarajavo murders, and at first the outbreak could have been construed as 'the Fourth Balkan War'.

3. Bernard Berenson (1865–1959), art historian, critic and collector, whose probity on the valuation and identification of certain works has recently been questioned. Author of *Italian Painters of the Renaissance* (1932).

---

[73]                                               Meurice
                                              Sept 30, 1916.
M.O.D.C.

I was so glad to have your letter of 25th, with Lewis's . . .

Today has been rather a racketing empty day, arranging things. I went out first thing to the ends of Paris to arrange about going to a hospital near the English lines, & have a sort of doubtful promise of being taken, or at least of going, on the 2nd, which will put back my start for the south till the 3rd. Then I hurried back to tidy for a lunch with the American Charge people, who are very nice, & at the lunch were some other Americans, who were just back from Corsica, where they have been inspecting prison-camps. The talk was about the war, & I felt that the Americans here learn strangely little of what is going on, though of course this may be diplomatic innocence, designed to draw out the unwary. Otherwise, they were nice cultivated Boston people, genuinely pro-Ally.

The Americans over here have no language fierce enough for their own country. All those who have been in England or France since the war began speak out straight, & call their country despicable, & today I heard one say that the only Americans who did not deserve to be shot were those who are now working in France. This is understandable, but it is also understandable that a people 3000 miles away should feel the war to be a distant thing & no concern of theirs. One of them today, rather a hot headed lady, rather Italian looking, seemed afraid that the war would end with friction between the States & England, & that the enemy propaganda would in the end triumph. They work their propaganda insidiously; they say how nice peace would be, until some journalist asks a minister whether we will not consider peace, then the minister either thumps a little drum, or says something which can be misconstrued, & then the enemy has a text. Still, this war gives the lie to prophets; let us prophesy nothing, but say, with the poet, who alone knows the uncertainty of life:–

'The end men look for cometh not,
And a path is there where no man sought.'

for that is what the end of this war will be.

After this, I had to go to the private view of some war photographs given by the British. There I came upon Eric Maclagan, who was in charge of the photographs & had been helping to arrange them, so I had him out to tea, & had a little talk with him. He has not changed at all, he is still the same, & his task is Wellington House[1] under Sir G, doing various propaganda.

Tomorrow is like to be a day manque unless I can get out to Versailles to see an Ambulance there. I've just had a telephone to say that I cannot see the hospital near the English lines until Monday.

Dear love to you, my dear heart,
                    Your old love,
                    Jan

Dear love to Lew.

1. The nickname for the Propaganda and Intelligence unit installed at Buckingham Gate, where Sir Gilbert Parker and others directed their operations.

---

[74]                                              Oct 1st 1916

M.O.D.C.

I have been cursing my fate all day, an envelope from you containing several worthless notes, but not a word from you. O cursed spite.

Last night, after seeing Maclagan, I had to go to see Moore of the American Institution. He gave me dinner in his little flat, which is in the old Palais Royal, built by Philippe Egalité[1] & let out by him, in order to make a little money, to card sharpers & birds of the night. It is quiet enough now & rather like Gray's

Inn, with a fountain & pigeons, & people meeting. Moore is a Yale man & knows some of my friends there, Edward Reed etc.

After dinner he took me to the Comedie to see *L'Avare*, which was well acted, but left me with the feeling 'Ben Jonson is Molière's master in every way; for wit, wisdom, style & knowledge of the stage our man is the better'. The man who played L'Avare was full of tragic power; we have no man so good; but the purely comic acting was not so good (it seemed to me) as the comic acting we can see at home. The performance was much less brilliant than *Les Affaires*, perhaps because the traditions of the House weigh upon the actors. One good thing they had: a swiftness that carried you with them.

Today, having risen an hour early, owing to the new time, I went by train to Versailles, 25 or so, in a carriage to seat 8, & all the windows shut. At Versailles, having seen the seats of the mighty, all the great palace deserted, a habitation for bitterns, where the cockatrice doth build her nest (& probably charges a franc admission) I went to a little cheap cafe & had a beastly lunch. I then sought out an American Convalescent Home, & after calling at the Police Station I found it, miles from anywhere, in a distant country road. I went in from the road to a very trim secluded garden, with a walk of trees to the door. Then, after due delay, I was received by a tiny elegante, aged about 65, & strongly ressembling Mme Santer, only very frail, very white, & I should say rehausse with a little carmine, still, exceedingly trim. The house was about as big as Battler's Green, only white & quite modern, & the garden was well done, but a little common in its formality, except that there was a fountain, & in a little garden beyond it a big jet of water falling in a big oblong stone pond fenced with fine turf, this very beautiful indeed, with a music pavilion beyond, most pretty.

The house was owned by 3 American ladies, all very wealthy & all with excellent taste & a sort of passion for house-making. They had taken the adjacent cottages, some time before the war & had made them very pleasant houses, then, when the war broke out they made these into convalescent homes for 20 officers & men, & have been having not less than 20 (& now have 30) ever since Oct, 1914. The convalescents are looked after by Sisters of the Assumption (which is a black habited order) & the ladies have fitted out a chapel & had it consecrated, so that the Sisters can keep their rule. Then on weekdays, the ladies work as nurses in some regular hospital & on Sundays have regular nurses down for a rest in the country. The lady whom I met (the only 1 (of the 3) whom I saw) is a Miss de Wolff. She is at a hospital near Paris where they are trying a new stuff for burns called Ambrine. Apparently you have your face burnt off with a flame projector, or blown off with a shell, or get skinned alive by a hand grenade. They take you to this hospital, & they warm a little sort of wax in a fire & pop it on hot, so as to cover the whole burn (like New Skin) & then they cover it with cotton & next day renew it.

In about 3 weeks or a month you are healed, without a scar, & so there is some excitement about the treatment, & there is to be an exposition of the method, & I am to be asked to see it. It is rather miraculous stuff, it keeps out germs & stimulates the cells, & I mean to try it on my brain when I grow old.

These ladies pay all their expenses themselves & receive no grant of any kind, & as the cost must be nearly £5 a day, or more, they deserve well of France. . . .

One of the wounded officers was very very melancholy & so was his poor wife. His right arm was gone & he was an architect, & all his art and his power & all the thought of his brain & all the dream of his imagination are without a hand. What is one to say to such? What can one say?

Well, dear heart, I must stop. I am written out. Dear love to you and to Lew.

Your old lover,

Jan

1. Louis Philippe Joseph, Duke of Orleans (1747–1793), cousin of Louis XVI. He supported the French Revolution, perhaps with hopes for the throne, calling himself 'Egalité', following a fashion for taking names synonomous with classical and revolutionary democratic virtue. He voted for the King's execution, but was himself guillotined shortly afterwards, for alleged treason to the Republic. His son became King Louis-Philippe of the French in the revolution of 1830, abdicating in the revolution of 1848.

[75]
Meurice's
Oct 2nd, 1916.

M.O.D.C.

I went today to a place near the lines to see a hospital of 76 beds. It was opened in the first days of the war, then evacuated, then re-opened for the battle of the Marne, & has been open ever since, though with one or two presqu' evacuations, when the enemy threatened. It is a private chateau, charmingly placed in woodland, & with a jolly annexe run by a genius of an old French soldier, who is cook, comforter & cleaner up, in a sort of Holy Trinity way. They take officers & men, & do it very nicely, though some of the rooms are small & troublesome to attend at night. There were some English officers, very nice people. They had some nice installments.

Afterwards I went to another place, where the personnel were French & Swiss. This was a place of research, magnificently equipped, and the special research made is in a new treatment of wounds by continual irrigation with a certain liquid. This liquid trickles into the wound continually & keeps it clean. As soon as it is clean, that is, free from infection, it heals, & they have discovered

a. that the healing process is in the body itself & cannot be quickened by any known agent.

b. that it depends on the age of the patient, the size of the wound, & the keeping of the wound free from infection.

c. that, given the cleanliness of the wound, guaranteed by this process, the doctor who knows the age of the patient & the size of the wound can tell to a day the date of the wound's healing.

The process is the discovery of an English chemist named Dakin. The liquid is colourless, but is supplied pink to prevent people drinking it instead of water. It heals a ghastly wound in 3 weeks & anything else in from 4 to 15 days. It reduces the process of woundhealing by 5/6ths at the very least, & is not difficult nor expensive. The only difficulty is the arrangement of the irrigation tubes.

The people say that it is ever so much better than Ambrine for a deep burn. Ambrine is only good for a surface burn, but this cures you if you are burned away down into the marrow. They had a magic lantern, & shewed us coloured pictures of the wounds they cured. Men with their lungs hanging out and their bellies exploding through gaps in their thighs, owing to gaseous gangrene, were normal & cicatrised in less than 3 weeks. There is no doubt it is a good liquid.

> Bless you my dear love,
> Your old lover,
> Jan.

---

[76]

Meurice's<br>Oct 3, 1916

M.O.D.C.

Just a year today since I got back from the Dards. I wish I were getting back in the same way now, but no such luck. I'm just starting for Limoges.

I went yesterday to see the little town of Senlis, where the enemy behaved as badly as they behaved anywhere. They marched in, early in Sept, 1914, & captured the Maire. They asked him if any French soldiers were in the town, & he answered 'no, as far as he knew, there were none'. Just as he spoke some Zovaves crossed the bottom of the street (I do not know if they fired or not, perhaps they did) & so the enemy said, 'You have lied to us, we shall shoot you tomorrow & burn the town.' The poor man's wife asked, that she might see her husband, & they told her 'Yes, you may see him tomorrow'. Early next morning they took the Maire out, stood him up against a wall, close to a little pit they had dug, & shot him. They then put him in the pit & raked some earth over him, but left his feet sticking out. They then took his wife to the grave & said 'There, you can see your husband'. Then they sent out their gang with flame projectors & burned half the houses in the town, & spared only those good ones where they had pleasant quarters. About 3 days later they fled, owing to the battle of the Marne, & the town lies in ruins just as they left it, with the good houses still standing.

I can't write a letter now as I must catch my train.

Dear love to you & Lew.

> from your old lover,
> Jan.

I'm very glad Na has told us that she wants to leave.

---

[77]
Meurices.<br>Oct 4.

M.O.D.C.

I am just back for one night from the gritty & stinking city of Limoges, where I spent last night.

There are several cities which I dislike very much. They are Larne, Dublin, Carrigart, Chicago, Columbus, Epinal, & to these I now add Limoges. Going there in the train wasn't so bad, as one crossed the Loire at Orleans on pretty much the site of the bridge by which the brave Jeanne[1] crossed it; then later on there was Issodum, supposed by some to be the place which Caesar besieged, by an immense ring of trenches with pointed stakes in them, & afterwards took & sacked. I was a little doubtful of the point, but there was a hill, all heaped with relics of a wall, & I concluded that that was the old Gaul stronghold. Caesar had a great job with it, according to his account, but from the train it looked as though it should not have been hard. Stoffel worked over that ground in the sixties, & traced out Caesar's lines, & found his stakes still in situ.

Limoges was, & is, a pottery city. It stands on a hill, which seems never to end, & at the bottom of the hill there is dust, & in the middle there is stink & at the top there is both dust & stink. If you can imagine Camden Town without the London gaiety, stuck on a hill & calling itself a city you will have seen Limoges. But up at the top there is an hospital Anglais where I had to call with a message & there, in that god forgotten dusty hell, are 19 of our country people working like the good souls they are, & oh what beautiful fine courtly gentle ladies those humble working women seemed after these others, & oh what happiness & cleanliness & niceness of merry health they had brought to the poor wounded there. I simply bowed down before them with praise & admiration.

There are 2 American hospitals there.

1. The Haviland Hosp. is run by an American pottery maker long established in Limoges, & by his 2 daughters who are married to Frenchmen. They have 70 beds in a disused part of the factory. They opened at the beginning of the war & have no American nurses.

2. Hop Benevole run by one of the Haviland daughters (M de Luze) & an

American nurse, contains 20 beds, & is designed to give special nursing to grievously wounded men. It was being cleaned & repapered, & was rather in a mess, but probably does creditable work. It opened Aug 6, 1914.

I am beginning to open my eyes, & to say to myself, that America, as a nation, has done Nothing, & that all that is being done is done by people who live & make their living in France, & by a few generous young men in search of adventure.

The enemy fire a good many duds, or shells that don't burst, & these the soldiers call 'Yanks' (or too proud to fight[2]). There is a story of an American talking about Verdun & saying 'Some fight!' & an Englishman looking up & saying 'Some don't'.

Dear love to you, my dear, I'm too dog tired to write more.

Your old lover,<br>Jan

Dear love & a kiss to Lew.

1. Joan of Arc captured Orleans, April 1429.
2. This refers to the celebrated announcement by President Woodrow Wilson, after the sinking of the Lusitania, 7 May 1915.

'The example of America must be a special example. The example of America must be the example not merely of peace because it will not fight, but of peace because peace is the healing and elevating influence of the world and strife is not. There is such a thing as a man being too proud to fight. There is such a thing as a nation being so right that it does not need to convince others by force that it is right.'

---

[78]                          Hotel D'Aix et Grand Hotel – Aix-les-Bains.
Oct 6

M.O.D.C.

I could only write a card yesterday for I was in the train almost all day, from 7 till nearly 7, going to the beastly town of Lyon, from which I escaped very early this morning to come here. Late tonight I purpose to take the train for Paris, & shall then use my best endeavours to finish up quickly & come home, but when I say finish quickly, expect nothing, for it is still difficult to say how long the work will take, & then I have been practically ordered to go to the Somme before I leave, & all this will take weeks.

Aix is a sort of superior Malvern, with better hotels & a more rapacious kind of citizen. I never saw anything like the expensiveness of this kind of life. I often feel that a franc is worth, at the very most, 2½d or 2d; and with my utmost thrift, going to out of the way little humble places for meals, I can't avoid expense, I have to go a long journey, eat in the train, take trains, & taxis, & sleep in hotels, & you will probably have to send another credit of £20. Of course, I expect to get all this out of G.P. who has practically promised me £10 a week for my expenses, & I have spent about £13.10 of the American money on things for the wounded, chocolates, books, cigarettes etc. Let me know *by return* if Wallingford can stand a cheque for £30 I want to spend some American money on an arm for a poor man at Juilly & an arm costs that if it is to be a serviceable one.

When I get back, I shall tell Sir G.P. that the Am have really done very little. A lot of generous young men have served in the Ambulance, & the hospital is very well done, & a lot of bold & brave young souls have come to serve in the French & English armies, but apart from that, at present my feeling is that the nation at large has done nothing. I shall know more in another week. The individuals (always rather numerous) who live in France, did their best, & started a lot of things, & ran them as long as they could, & then had to stop them. I come upon the bones of these things fairly often & a fearful pest they are, giving me a lot of trouble for nothing. I have had my journey here for nothing, as the hospital I came to see has petered out for want of funds, & the casual A way in Paris has kept no record of the fact, but is probably still allowing people in A to print that it is established in the beautiful scenery of Aix etc.

You will judge that I am not very pleased with the A's. No, I am not. I like a lot of them, but having seen them & my own countrypeople at work together they have not any place at all, and so everybody with any eye would say.

Still, there is something very fine in the young men.

As soon as my report is done, if I am not wanted by G.P. & I don't think I shall be, I must just harden my heart & take the plunge.

Dear love to you my dear & to Lew.

Your old lover,<br>Jan

x x x for Lew

---

[79] 7 Oct.

M.O.D.C.

I am so dog tired from a night in the train & a very hard day in Paris that I can't write you more than a scrap. I've been charmed with a little note from Na, shewing an interest in surgery, & saying that she would like rather to be a surgeon, & now I wonder what easy preliminary books there are which would turn a child's mind that way & treat the problems of surgery in an intelligible & interesting manner. Probably none, yet it is a thing which would interest most children.

G.P. sends a note to say I'm to have cent pug [*sic*]. C'est tres bien pour le F.O. n'est ce pas? It will just about just cover.

I've been to 2 hospitals at the ends of Paris today. I got back from Aix at 8.30,

& found an elderly English nurse lost with a pile of luggage at the terminus. There were no porters, no taxis, no anything, so I offered to help, & lugged her things about ½ a panting mile till we found a broken down fiacre with a cast-off army horse, & in this I saw the poor woman through Paris. She was very like Miss Christy & kept saying that Paris was an interesting town with very interesting associations. After that I came here & had a bath & got some breakfast (& also a nice read of all your nice letters) & then wrote my business letters & went off to see hospitals.

1 Hospital Stillman is a convalescent home for 26 officers in a banker's private house. It is in a quiet street overlooking the park Mouceau & is a rich man's house, with a lot of bath rooms, & is entirely supported by the banker. The nurses & medical officer are French. Founded Aug 1914.

2 Hospital Hyde, is a convalescent home for men, 20 beds, 3 French nurses, beds on ground floor opening into big garden, with summer house; excellent tone & cleanliness & spirit, entirely supported by Mr. Hyde, a rich A who lives in France. Founded Sept. 1914.

Then I came back & have been writing letters to hospitals to find out if they are still closed, & now I am simply deadbeat.

Dear love to you from your old lover, Jan.

Aix is a whitened sepulchre of a place, my golly.
I'd better see Jasper & Amory but *not* Louise
John & Ada are going to Valence, nearly down to Avignon, on the Avignon line.

---

[80]                                                                    Meurice.
                                                                        Oct 8
My dearest heart Con,
    Thank you so much for the two nice letters & for sending Jude's letter. Harley's[1], by the way, you did not send. . . .
    Late last night, I was called downstairs to a Certain who lives here. I went down, expecting a Court Martial & military execution, & wondering what I had done. I'd had a row over my pass at Lyon & wondered if this had been reported, though it had been a bit of a triumph for me. But when I got down, lo, GHQ, if you know what that is, were asking me to go to the English front, would I go, to do something for them, & if so, when could I start? This rather flummoxed me, for it is not our wont to go out of our way thus, so I asked, what do they want me to do? This had not come through, but the Certain said that he would ask, & I, on my part, said that I could start at once, if necessary. There the matter rests at present, and thinking it over, I think it only amounts to this. There is a very spangled Certain who lives here & has read *Gallipoli*. He is rather of the I.H.[2] faction, & he said that he would ask if I might be allowed to

see the Somme, as that is so much more important than Gallipoli. Probably at lunch or somewhere he has asked this, & being very spangled, his asking made rather a flutter, & some telephonist has made the matter seem urgent. For a moment, but only for a moment, for one must never expect, ever, I thought that an historical section was being organised, in which case (I thought) Newbolt[3] & Kipling will be there, but perhaps an adroit soul could work in Harley. I put aside the notion at once, knowing the way of things; I am quite sure that all that has happened is as I say. Still, the idea remains, and your letter about H came this morning to confirm it. Perhaps the wisest course would be this. If I go to the Somme, I may see the heads of things, & they may be forthcoming. If they are, I might be able to suggest some such section. The French of course have a 'record section', & employ civilians in it, & have uniform & decorations for it, & you see it at work in the ruins, doing excellent work. But it seems to me that the suggestion had better be made to the army & then by the army to the politicians, if the army approve, & not to the politicians, & by the politicians to the army if the politicians approve. Anyway H is treading dangerous ground in applying to Eddie[4], for Eddie is, so to speak, A, & A (as we know) is furious with H for his breach with L (who lets A hold her hand) and my instinct, which I never yet knew to be wrong, tells me that A dislikes myself, & that V encourages this feeling. Still, Eddie is adroit. Eddie is very clever.

There is a sort of maitre d'hotel here who is exactly Eddie. The same age, voice, & manner. 'A wonderful room, looking out onto the square, you can see the gardens, only forty francs, wonderful. Let me know your name, will you sign this paper, the lift is working, will you come this way?' He is Eddie to the very life. 'Wonderful, wonderful.'

As to dear old Na leaving. I'm much struck by the power & clearness of her little mind. I gather that what she wants is an intimacy with someone, & that if she could have that, nothing else would matter to her. The school is nothing much to her. She only wants to learn the 'cello & to have a friend & to be able to play games. It seems as though Moya had come on towards her, & then perhaps A.V.J. who was a nice child, has also a little chummed up. But the school system is probably quite rotten & absurd, designed, really, to look well in a prospectus, & to give an appearance of Education to those parents anxious to be rid of their children at their awkward age, & Judith is much too much alive & wise to be taken in by any such system. She knows what work is, from the farm, what life is, from the Dolmetsches, what romance & fun is, from us, and she asks nothing from school except just those things which we & the farm & the Dolmetsches can't give. This is probably the whole explanation.

She can have another term as she thinks fit. We shall know more & she, too, as this term progresses. Much will depend on Moya & A.V.J. Moya, I should judge, might be a handful.

I've succumbed to the French breakfast. It is the only way out here. I eat a little bread & honey with some cafe au lait, & then have a 12 o'clock dejeuner, & I cannot think now of going back to gross bacon & coarse eggs at 8 a.m. I don't yet tuck my napkin in my collar, but that will come, & someday I may be able to tackle the whole of a French dejeuner.

I send Ada's little purr. Valence is on the main line to Marseilles, about ½ way between Lyon & Avignon.

Dear love to you my dear heart. Kiss Lew from me.

Your old lover,

Jan

1. Harley Granville-Barker, a very important figure in Masefield's life, at the time married to the actress Lillah McCarthy, the original Nan in Masefield's *The Tragedy of Nan* produced by Granville-Barker, 1908. Granville-Barker, as actor, producer, dramatist, had profound importance in taking the British Theatre into the 20th century. His famous seasons at the Court Theatre introduced London to serious contemporary plays: his productions of Shakespeare gave almost wholly new insights into Shakespeare to those accustomed to the spectacular presentations and drastically edited versions from the self-centred actor managers, Tree, Irving, and lesser men. Barker's own plays, concerned with social and moral problems of his day, included *Waste, The Madras House, The Voysey Inheritance*. His Prefaces to Shakespeare's plays put into print his own notions of Shakespeare's meanings, problems, stagecraft, giving exceptional standards for producers, critics and audiences. As an actor he was the first Eugene Marchbanks, in Shaw's *Candida*, and the first Cusins, in *Major Barbara*. Lillah McCarthy created Anne Whitfield in *Man and Superman*, with Granville-Barker as Tanner: Jennifer Dubedat, with Barker as Louis Dubedat, in *The Doctor's Dilemma*, Lavinia, in *Androcles and the Lion*, and Margaret in *Fanny's First Play*. She was an enthusiastic supporter of Masefield's Hill Players, and his theatre at Boar's Hill. Masefield, earlier in the year, had had a pleasant time at Valley Forge, and wrote to Constance, from America: 'It was like a really good Harley and Lillah day in Kent.' But the marriage was now failing, and he had written from New York some weeks earlier: 'Get hold of Lillah, & find out from the Red Cross where Harly (sic) is, & oh write to Harly & try to get in touch with him. I'm so distressed about these two. I dearly love them both. They are woven right into our lives and I can't do anything from here.' Barker was with the Red Cross in France. Uneasy references to the marriage occur in future letters. Divorce was granted, 1918.

2. Gallipoli still aroused much discussion, often angry. Ian Hamilton had his supporters and detractors, as had the chief inspirer of the venture, Winston Churchill, who had resigned his post as First Lord of the Admiralty, with a seat in Cabinet, after its failure.

3. Sir Henry Newbolt (1862–1938), barrister, romantic novelist, patriotic poet and naval historian with special reference to the War at Sea, 1914–18. *Admirals All* (1897) sold widely, and several of his poems still appear in anthologies. He had supporters who claimed him for the Laureateship, though it went first to Robert Bridges, then to Masefield.

4. Sir Edward Howard Marsh (1872–1953), Civil Servant, private secretary to Winston Churchill, translator, art collector and patron, friend and helper of many poets, he edited *Georgian Poetry* (1912–22), whose contributors included Masefield. He collected and had published the *Collected Poems* of his friend, Rupert Brooke, and

published translations of La Fontaine and Horace. The reference refers to a further breach in the Granville-Barker marriage.

---

[81]                                                        Meurice
                                                           Oct 9 1916

Darling heart Con,

Look here, my dear.

Lord Esher[1], who is a friend of Ian's & of Haig's & of most of the Staff, called me to him this evening, & said, that I am wanted on the Somme, to write the Chronicle of the big attack from the very beginning, & that, if I will go there next week, & look round, I shall have every facility, shall be allowed to see everything, & shall then be able to decide about it. He said, that he & Haig are very eager for me to do it, that if necessary an honorary Commission shall be given to me, that a car shall be at my disposal, & a guide, & maps, & everything else.

So, what of this?

Of course, nothing can be decided till I have had a look at it, & I am to have a look at it from about the 16th–20th.

Of course, too, I must finish up the American business before I settle down to anything, & there is still some amount of work to be seen, let alone the writing, not that the writing would take very long.

If I undertook the Somme, & had an hon Com & the rest of it, I should be lodged in a mess at Amiens, with other odds & ends of staff & semi staff. There is loneliness for you in it, my poor dearie, but anyway there will be that, for I shall have to serve, & I cannot appeal as some do. I could get back from time to time.

There is no alternative job to suggest that would keep me in England, except home defence, & I might not be given that.

I don't know what is the fine thing to do. Perhaps to say, No, to it all, finish the American work & then come back & serve. But there is no immediate need to decide. Think it over & let me hear what you think, & ask Bobby & Lion, if they are there, & ask some other good soul, Mrs Bridges[2] or John & Ada.

> Dear love to you,
> from your old lover,
> Jan

1. Reginal Baliol Brett, Second Viscount Esher (1852–1930), Member of Parliament, 1880–85, organised Queen Victoria's Diamond Jubilee, 1897 – which in part enticed Masefield to return from America – friend of royalty, military reformer and much else. During the Great War he was on confidential missions to France. When he met Masefield he was head of British Military Intelligence in France. Masefield knew of his support for Gallipoli and his friendship with Ian Hamilton. Rather surprisingly, Esher appreciated Siegfried Sassoon's bitter and sardonic war poems, and, presumably

for their seering vitality, compared them to El Greco. Arnold Bennett had met him in Paris, in 1915, 'wearing a fancy military costume – perhaps that of Constable of Windsor Castle. A star was depending from his neck. As soon as he saw my eye on it he tucked it inside his double-breasted khaki coat.' Masefield had long been brooding on the battle, and, in January, wrote to Florence Lamont: 'It has been in my mind for many months, that this is the biggest thing that England has ever been engaged in, & that it must be a possession of the English mind forever, faults & splendour & all, & that we now living have a chance of beginning its tradition. I hope to make something of the battle. I cannot write what I feel about it, but I went over the field in the autumn, just after the most bloody & terrible fighting, when the ground was not ground at all, but the flesh and bones of men, all mixed with wreck & little, half-burnt scraps of their letters, & the photographs of their mothers & wives, & bits of the weapons they were carrying, & it gave me a feeling for this race deeper than any I have had . . . a very feeble kind of service for one's country, though all I can do, for I am not up to much now.' Different conclusions were reached by another poet, Siegfried Sassoon. Decorated for gallantry on the Somme, he returned to England, issued a public protest against the continuation of the War, before returning to France and fighting with reckless courage.

2. Wife of the poet Laureate, Robert Bridges. The Bridges and Masefields were good friends, and became neighbours at Boar's Hill.

---

[82]                                                                        Meurice
                                                                             Oct 9

My dear heart Con,

. . . As to J. There are only 2 courses to pursue. Take J away from school *now*, till the war is over, & keep her at Lollingdon, or leave her as she is. It is no good taking her from Southwold, going up to London, & letting her go to classes. She will be in more danger there than at Southwold. I don't believe she likes Isabel, & I doubt very much if she would like her school. What J wants is an asylum for her affections, plenty of games & a little music; but a friend first & foremost. I wish that it might be possible to have Jude with a friend at Loll, & let them have my study, & go in together to 'cello lessons in Reading. If Irene were only eager for the 'cello'.

If J finds her friend, in Moya or A.V.J. she won't want to leave, & it might be best to let her stay. If she wants to leave & is eager to go to Isabel's, she had better leave right now at once & go to Isabel's for the ½ term. If she stays on, she will be in danger, but not really in more danger than a full half of England. There will be many raids this autumn, & perhaps the safest plan is to have her away at once from S'wold & keep her at Lollingdon. If however you mean to go into H'stead this winter, you had better leave her at S'wold, for H'stead will be a good deal more of a danger spot than S.

No-one can make a safe decision in war time. Even Loll is not safe. The Zeps are sure to try to come to Did, & probably will come, & as for London they'll be there twice a week all through the winter. Germany is probably by no means 'crazy' for peace. American journalists are not the shrewdest of judges, nor do I believe for a moment that the populace is more than short of a few things. But they are 'crazy' for a stirring headline, & it is becoming more difficult for their

Command to give it to them, & you may be quite sure that the Zeppelin & submarine efforts will be quintupled within the next few weeks. American ships will be sunk & America will be intimidated, you will see; that is the next thing. Both Wilson & Hughes[1] are peace men, eager for the German vote. The submarines will simply sink A ships on sight & the 2 candidates will slur it over, & America will say 'Thank God, we are not to go to war. What are we to do with our German citizens?'

I've had a dreadful day marching to & fro in Paris getting information. I've walked at least 11 miles & had little to shew for it. This is the sort of thing.

Responsible As give me a list of American Paris hospitals in the nearer suburbs. I go to one, say at Swiss Cottage, & find it closed. I go to the next, say at Clapham, & find that it is not American, but a French military establishment in a house left by an American, a very different thing. I go to a third, say at Greenwich, & find it closed 18 months ago. I go to a fourth, say at Lewisham, & find that it is not a hospital at all, but a big office of the French Government in which the accounts of all Foreign hospitals are kept & audited.

Now this is literally an account of my day's work during yesterday & today; though I have had other things to do, too.

Yesterday I went to tea at the A diplomats. He is an old sailing ship sailor, so we had a great colloque. She is a Boston lady, a little like Mrs Daffarn, if you could imagine Mrs D in the body of Dorothy Scott. This was the only social & unofficial hour I've had since I left home. My poor old dear heart, we must steel our hearts for this coming year.

Dear love to you.<br>Your old lover,<br>Jan

1. Charles Evans Hughes (1862–1948), American politician and lawyer, Governor of New York, 1906–10, fought Woodrow Wilson in the Presidential Election of 1916, but lost. He was later Secretary of State, Judge of Permanent Court of International Justice, at the Hague, and, 1930–41, Chief Justice of the United States, finding unconstitutional much of F. D. Roosevelt's New Deal.

---

[83]                                                          Hotel Meurice
                                                             11 Oct.

M.O.D.C.

I could not write to you at all yesterday. Up at 5.30, catch a train, & off to Sens, then a long hot walk in the valley of the Yonne, which is as big a valley as ours at Wall, & the river bigger, & the walk was rather like that from Lulham to Goring. The day was hot & beautiful & the country lovely but deserted; it seemed without life, except sometimes an old man with a dog or an old woman with a cow. Even in the villages half the houses were closed, & hardly anyone, except a child or two, about them, & no games & no noise in any. After going through 3 villages which might have been sick of the plague, I came to a bigger village, where 4 infirm souls watched me pass & a boy came by on a bicycle.

Presently I came to a place called Passy par Veron, where there is a big chateau used as a hospital.

A very rich American woman, married to an English soldier, gave the funds for the hospital & the arrangements were made through the Fr Hosp in New York. The Fr Govt gave the chateau.

But I can't write now I must run to catch a train.

Dear Love,

---

[84]                                                                    11 Oct

M.O.D.C.

. . . To go on with my report, or I shall get all behindhand. 10 Oct I crossed the Yonne at Etigny & was soon across the valley in sight of the Chateau. An immense wall, 500 yards by 200 yards, & 12 feet high & 3 thick *shut in the estate*,

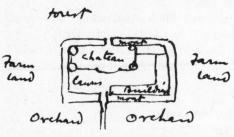

& within these was the following arrangement. A very deep, broad, but drained moat shut in the chateau, which was of all dates from the 11th century to the revolution, but it had evidently been grandest under Louis Quinze. It was then perhaps very grand, & still had an air of the lord in power, with stables, vinepress, colombier, granaries, cider mill, & no doubt prisons & gallows in case of need.

It is financed by this lady married to the Englishman, & has a staff of Am & Fr doctors & Fr, Canadian, & English & Swiss sisters. It holds 157 wounded, & the work of keeping it going is done by the Medecin Chef, a very able Am, who has made it pay as a farm while running it as a hospital.

In the Revolution it was attacked by the mob, who sent all the family to Paris to be guillotined, except one girl who was very ill, & they flung her out to die in the fields. She lay in the fields 4 days, without help from anyone, & then someone took her in & nursed her. All the family were guillotined, except another girl. As they were being sentenced, someone cried out that this particular girl was going to have a child, & that it would be wrong to guillotine her. It was a lie, but they sent her to a hospital & forgot about her, & by & by, when Robespierre fell, she was let out, & presently rejoined her sister.

Their descendants (or they) got back the property under the Empire & their last descendants went to the dogs, the man shot himself, the wife ran away with a priest, the daughter with a Belgian, & the son, after a dissolute career, lives in a cottage in the village. The house was sold to speculators, who cut the timber & then sold the estate to the State, who made it into a House for Convertites. The Convertites did not like it, & they broke out, & corrupted the males of those parts; the scandals are still the talk of the countryside, & indeed 50 light ladies might do a good deal. The State rounded them up in time, & sent them elsewhere, & the village more or less got over it. When the war began, the State gave the place as a hosp.

The Ams put in electric light, broke up the cells of the Convertites, to make wards, cleaned & set going the well, improved the drains, put in a big engine for light & pumping, put up a tent for lung cases in the field, ceiled, floored a ventilated the stables, so as to make 2 more big wards, put in a big X ray plant, & got the whole thing going, with a dentist, a laboratory, & running water. Then the young Medecin Chef, who is a genius for thrift, made the most minute tables, found out exactly what was being paid per day per person per item, & resolved to reduce it. He ploughed up & planted the cornland, bought pigs, & fed them on the waste of the kitchen (he makes £15 profit on each pig. They are all about as big as donkeys), & then started a big rabbity of 2 or 300 rabbits, which would have won Nana's little heart. Then he started a hennery & duckery, & now produces nearly as much white meat as the hospital can use. He raises nearly enough vegetables & quite enough potatoes for the 200 people for all the year round; but has to buy fruit, & has not been able to manage cows. He has a few sheep & may have more next year. Pigeons he keeps in a run with the ducks. He put in a cement pond for the ducks & they are doing very well in a small run, the pigeons were as big as owls, but did not look very wholesome. Cruising round in the yard was a pet hawk who eyed the pigeons from afar.

After seeing all these delights I came back to Sens, & had a slow 4 hours journey doing 60 miles, in fact it took almost 5 hours, & I got back to Paris dead beat. As soon as I got back I was caught by his Lordship & had to sit up talking till 11. O, I was weary.

Today, still weary, I've been to Ris Orangis up the Seine, 15 miles away, where there is a hospital, run partly by the Am wife of the Br Ambass, but mainly by Reckitts' Blue. All the surgeons are Am, but all the personnel Fr, English & Canadian. It is really a Franco British hosp.

Now I must stop, or this will miss the post.

Dear love to you my dear
from your old lover,
Jan

I'm to start for the Somme on Monday or Tuesday, 16 or 17th.

xxx for Lewis

                                             Oct 12. 1916

M.O.D.C.

. . . I hate to think of your loneliness, my dear heart, but this is like to be a lonely year for everybody in Europe, & one can only say, that the one who gives in to the loneliness soonest, will be beaten, & that one must just harden one's heart. Of course, one must not write, but there is no possibility of anything decisive for many months yet, I fear, if then, but one can only hope.

'The end men look for cometh not
And a path is there where no man sought.'

Yesterday, as I said, I was at Ris Orangis, seeing this English hosp with Am surgeons. They have done a good deal of work there with gaseous gangrene (not asphyxiating gas, this, but a gas made by a bacillus who lives in cultivated soil) & have had some good results, sluicing the wound with weak quinine. There was a clever young surgeon there who is working on some antiseptic treatments for uniforms; & he has found one cheap compound into which uniforms can be dipped, & this stuff not only makes the cloth antiseptic for months, but makes it deadly for lice of all kinds, so that the soldier can put on his antiseptic clothes, & defy the little galloping graybacks & go out & get wounded with a light heart. If he gets, as he will, some chunks of cloth blown into his wound, they will not infect the wound, & he will make a quicker recovery.

It is strange, that this is being thought of now, in the 3rd year of the war. 'Figures-toi.'

Today I was up betimes, to see the early clinic at the Ambrene Treatment for Burns in a big Mil Hosp outside Paris, at Issy. An Am lady, a Miss de Wolfe, whose hosp at Versailles I've told you of, took me (she is learning it) & I saw the whole thing.

As you know, I've seen pretty nearly every kind of wound, including some which took a stout heart to look at, but the burns easily surpassed anything I've ever seen. There were people with the tops of their heads burnt off & stinking like frizzled meat, & the top all red & dripping with pus, & their faces all gone, & their arms just covered with a kind of gauntlet of raw meat, & perhaps their whole bodies, from their knees to their shoulders, without any semblance of skin. One can't describe such wounds, they have to be seen to be believed. Perhaps you could kill Bobby by just reading the little I have written here. Still, it is not so terrible to watch as a bad haemorrhage, & I was glad to be able to bear a hand with the poor fellows.

The Ambrene looks like a mongrel between a cake of glue & a piece of chocolate, it is semi transparent & has the feel of chocolate. It is a waxy stuff, made partly of wax, partly (I believe) of resin or amber. The wound is washed very lightly, then dried very lightly, then thoroughly dried with those electric driers or 'sechoirs' which women have their hair dried with in superior coiffeur's shops. Then the Ambrene is boiled up till it is a-septic, & liquid, & then it is painted on with a brush, pretty hot, & it forms over the wound like a skin of wax. Then this coat is covered with gauze, & a new coat of A is painted over the gauze, & then wool is put over the whole. A stops all pain directly it is put on. Men who have not slept for a fortnight, or known an instant's ease for months, lose all pain on the instant, & recover, literally grow a new skin, in 2 weeks or three, a lot too soon, often, for their own liking. One poor man was brought in whose hand was burnt pretty nearly all off his bones, & his fingers were dropping off in the room before us (this I actually saw. I could have had one of his fingers as a souvenir). But directly they put the Ambrene on him his pain ceased. He moved his hand & plainly felt no pain at all in it, while before, he was in agony.

While I was looking, in came Millicent S, the grande dame, if you remember her. She had 2 little baggages with her, & she was made up to look the youngest & most innocent of the three. I expect you will remember the lady I mean. She came up & talked to me of her writings, much as Victoria must have talked to Tennyson about hers (if this may be permitted me) & she was really rather nice, but I could see that the Fr Infirmieres saw what she was.

It was a little embarrassing, for the doctor insisted on shewing us all a poor man whose genitals had been scorched, (luckily not destroyed) & the doctor was so proud of this case that he had him all laid bare for us; and there was the poor emaciated man, with legs like stalks, lying exposed, with his poor little red genitals up in the air, & the duchess & the baggages & myself all saying 'Tiens', & the doctor waving his arms & getting so hot & proud, & saying 'On prend un couteau de palette. On decrotte la pomade. On verse un peu d'éther, etc. etc.'

The English nurse whom I helped thro' Paris had said that French nurses are clever with their hands. These certainly were, very, & very gentle, & very quick. I had not seen Fr nurses really at their work before. Of course, it was a mil hosp, which is as much as to say very dirty, smelly, & full of flies. It was revolting in that way, & to see the flies settling on the wounds & then having a nice little sip of ambrene, & then a drink of pus, & then a quiet pounce down on where one had cut himself in shaving, filled me with fury. All of that could have been prevented & should have been.

As soon as I got home I had a good hot boracic scrub.

Dear love to you my dear heart.

Your old lover,<br>Jan

xxx for Lewis

M.O.D.C.

I am just about weary this evening, having padded up & down Paris streets for eight hours on end, to no very great purpose.

This morning I set out to see some charities, following a list compiled by the best authorities, & expecting, as usual, to find the list inexact & misleading. My first address was a huge sort of bureau of the charities of many nations, Appni Parthe, Restoration du Foyer Elamite etc, but the American people weren't there, so I had to go on. My next address was (when I found it) a closed church. God alone knows what was done there when it was open, & after pounding on the door, remembering the text, 'Knock & it shall be opened unto you', & proving it to be misleading, I went on to 3, which had moved elsewhere, &, when I reached elsewhere, had gone somewhere else. Cursing 3, I went to 4, which was another closed church, but rather remarkable, in being painted yellow. I called it the church of Laodicea & did as the apostle said he would, & went on to 5, where 9 modest young women were making clothes for the hospitals. At 6, I found a rather big institution for providing what they call Marraines to lonely soldiers. The American Marraines write to the lonely Fillends & send them little presents. I shall go to 6 again to find out more about it. 7 was a room full of modest seamstresses, the same as 5. 8 was very much the same as 6, only smaller. It had provided 4,000 soldiers with extra socks, mitts, shirts, etc since the autumn of 1914. It also provided many women with the work of making these things. 9 was a big place for giving clothes to refugees from Belgium & N of France. It had supplied clothes to 16,000 people since the war began. I shall go to 9 again. 10 was a smart young lady in a palace, providing delicatessen to the hospitals near the front, wine, game, beef tea, etc. 11 a small room full of seamstresses. After 11 I had to lunch.

After lunch I went to 12, but seeing that it was a French Mil Hosp I went to 13, where a half-naked old concierge referred me back to 12. I then found that 12 was in American premises, nothing more.

Rather weary, but still hopeful, I went on to 14, where there was a newly opened Atelier for the making of splints, rests, extensions & supports. Going in to the gard, I met an elderly lady wearing Purle & smoking a cigarette. She turned out to be a Miss Gafsette, an American painter, who came over from New York in August, 1914, & worked in the hospitals. Presently, she began to experiment on the making of splints & supports in a more intelligent & more comfortable way than those in use, & she found that she could do it jolly well. She says, and she may be right, though others claim it, that she made all the very remarkable equipment at Neuilly. Anyhow, she is a trained craftswoman, & I saw her adapting rests to a wounded hand with skill & imagination. She is about 50, rather like Mrs Flinders P.[1] in the face, though a coarser & rather liver sort of face, & she is certainly doing remarkable work.

After this I went to 15, which is a workshop of 55 women from the poorer parts of Paris; an ordinary charity for the destitute.

16, I thanked God, is amalgamated with 15.

17 & 18, after a long search in the wilderness of the Louvre, I could not find at all; they may be there, but very likely aren't. After a search, I had some coffee & a bun & came back dead beat. I fell asleep in a chair directly I got back, for there is nothing like a long walk in a city to exhaust one. O golly golly, I said, what is this atom, etc.

Now I have to spruce up, as I have to dine with the people of the Am Embassy, & I must shine all my beastly buttons.

So glad the G/B tragedy is settled.

Dear love to you my dear heart & to Lew.

Your old lover<br>Jan

1. Mrs Flinders Petrie, wife of the archaeologist who opened up much of ancient Egypt and Sumeria using new scientific methods enabling accurate measurements of time, cultural deductions and more general conclusions.

---

[87]                                              Oct 14 1916

Dearest heart Con,

There is not much to say about the dinner last night, except that my buttons were probably the brightest things there. There were present, the host & hostess of whom I have told you, he, the old sailor, she, I have decided, like Mrs Hammond[1], then there were 2 Under Secs from the Am' Emb, one of them a petit maitre of the Beerbohm[2] stamp, an old friend of Wilde's, the other nothing much, but nice. Then there was a Sir something somebody, one time officer of health for Egypt, & now doing charities here, a Mrs C, an old & affected lady, a Miss something, & a girl from Boston just over to do nursing. I did not talk with any of these, except the host & hostess & the petit maitre. It was a dull conventional dinner. Sir something S told a funny tale in cockney rather well, but he had found it in Punch & everybody knew it; still, poor man, he did his best. I don't think anybody did better than he, but the Boston girl seemed a merry soul. At 10.30 we broke up.

Today I have fagged up & down again at charities, seeing what is called The Clearing House, where most of the American Charities & goods received in charity, are collected & dispersed. From their figures, I have estimated, that at the most, taking a liberal view of things, the Americans have spent in charity throughout France, since the beginning of the war, some sevenpence a head, or 3½d per year, more, that is, than the price of a glass of beer, and less than the price of a glass of whiskey. Of course, with this, has been given a lot of personal service. I cannot even guess how many young Americans are in the English, French & Canadian armies; there may be many; & there are, besides, the (say) 1000 young men who are, or have been, in the Ambulance & the Field Service. Still, the other helpers are few in number, & when one sizes it all up, one says:–

Perhaps it is much. They aren't in the war, & are at least 3000 miles from any front of it. It may be a vast charity. It is probably bigger than any charity ever sent to any country. But is it? Is it bigger than our American charities, or our Indian & Russian Famine Relief Funds, & our gifts to Messina & the Congested Districts? It is probably not one half of what we have given *in charity alone* to France, but then of course, we are in the war. Still, we have not made our fortunes ten times over in the war, & we are not the traditional allies of France, far from it.

What do you think?

Tonight, I rather dread, as I have to dine with some very spangled officers. The secrets of the Staff will fly about, & the spies will be obsequious at the changing of the courses.

Dear love to you my dear & to good little Lew.

I'm so glad of the truce you speak of.

> Your old lover,
> Jan

I hear nothing of Ireland[3] here. Here it seems a dirty little distant island, & Am a contemptible big continent: the only thought here is just the Somme.

1. Mr & Mrs J. L. Hammond collaborated in a trilogy of late 18th- and early 19th-century social history.

2. Max Beerbohm, drama critic, essayist, novella writer, dandy: not his half-brother, the actor Sir Herbert Beerbohm Tree.

3. The Irish Rising of Easter 1916 had attempted to establish an Irish Republic, with German help. The subsequent court-martials and executions laid a trail of hatred, anger, grief fermenting through the years.

---

[88]                                                        Oct 15 Sunday

My dearest heart,

I have just seen Lord E. who says I am to start for the Somme on Tuesday, so 'ça-y-est'.

I have your letter post-marked the 11th, with Judith's little letter inside it. Jude's letters are much improved lately, & one gets much more of herself in them. I think the 'cello was a good stroke, my dear; it has added a lot to her little life.

In my letter yesterday I was unjust to the Americans. The way to look at their contribution is as follows.

There are 70 millions in America, of whom 50 millions are adults & 40 millions in a position to give something. Of these 40 millions, at least 20 care nothing for the war one way or the other, & so give nothing. Of the remaining 20, fully 10 are Germans, or ultra-American, or anti-European, & so give nothing. The contribution comes therefore from, at most, ten millions, & this being so, it works out at four or five shillings a head, which is (perhaps) a creditable gift. What do you think? Their total gift may be as little as a million & a half, & may conceivably, since much (even of American) charity is given in the dark, be as great as these millions, though, if so, it has been mainly private, & I myself don't think that the figure can possibly exceed two & a half millions & is probably less than two. Do you think that this is much or little? There are no standards & no precedents & one knows not what to think, except that in war time one feels with Christ, he that is not for me is against me, & that, if that is so, they have simply played the base part of a shopkeeper who abuses his customers.

Dining last night, there were present, young Hartington, son of some Duke, Westminster or Devonshire I forget which, but a very attractive clever lad who had been at Suvla & is now in the Intelligence, a Mr Phipps[1] & his wife, diplomatists from Madrid, & a Mrs Baring, also from Madrid. Phipps (if that was his name) was an amusing, clever, well-informed man, rather of the general trend of Eddie, but with much more fun in him, though of course with an eyeglass, & what is called a Lip Eyebrow (i.e. a toothbrush moustache). His wife was of the general make of the Lady Lytton who we met at Ian's, though smaller. She was rather amusing. She wore a sort of a black hat which I shall try to remember for you. Mrs B. was short & potelee, & in mind exactly Mrs Lindsay, without the interest in letters.

Talking to P. I learned that 'opinion' in Spain, in Madrid & the Basque Provinces, that is, is pro-German; especially in Madrid. The Spanish hate the French anyhow, remembering 1808–1815, & they hate us, because we have Gibraltar & are friends with the Portuguese. The Germans have taken care to work these hates against us, & have succeeded very well 'Gibraltar' is their main war-cry. They said that the Italian diplomatists in Madrid cut the Austrians long before the Italians declared war.

I talked with P a good while about America, & came on the whole to the conclusion that during the next 20 years the States would become Germanised, & that the culture & perhaps the speech of a large part of the States would be German, & that the rest of the country would be either independent, or perhaps subservient to, a strong German nation running down the line of the Mississipi. This may seem a wild opinion & time may disprove it (I hope it may) but one cannot avoid the feeling that there is something in the climate there which takes the iron out of the blood, & that the English & French stocks have lost their iron in 4 generations & are going to succumb to the German stock which has been there less than 2. A knit body of men with a purpose must triumph over a disorganised body without one. It remains to be seen whether the young men now at the Universities or serving in France will pull the land together on any question.

I had a note from Florence Lamont a day or two ago, enclosing a snapshot of herself, which I send. The lady to the left of the picture (full face, rather like Lucy) is a Mrs Tildesley. The sort of die-away duck to the right is Florence Lamont, though she is only just recognisable. Mind you let me know if she is at all like the person in your dream. Of course, I never saw her look wilted like that, nor indeed look anything but a most competent, resolute, driving energy, of 100 lbs to the square centimetre. Still, if she is like your dream it will be one to you.

I also have today this nice note from Ronny.

In a spare hour last week I wrote a sonnet, which I send. It isn't up to much.

In Amiens, there is a chance that I may meet Nevi. According to the papers, his son's picture-show has made some stir (it is all drawings of the war) but I still cannot see things in cubes & vortices, & I withheld judgment. Perhaps the cube revolt was the only possible one. Something violent had to be done to destroy the sick convention of the curve, which was as languid & as lifeless as it could well be. Anything hard & square & box-ended was preferable to that, & apparently the war has tempered Nevi down to doing something box-ended which may still be recognized. I have no theory of painting. If I were a painter, I should probably try to be as like a 14th century portrait painter as I could be, in the doing of portraits, & in general scenes as like missal-illustration as I could be, though with a far greater dramatic movement, if that could be. Latterly I've been trying to get at what I really see when I see a thing; but no analysis yet.

This is getting to be bulky for a letter, so shall send Ronny's letter & some of Nevi's pictures in a sep env.

Bless you, my dear heart & give my love to little Lew.

> Your old lover,
> Jan

1. Eric Clare Edmund Phipps (1875–1945), diplomat. He was later British Minister in Vienna, ambassador to Germany, then to France. His fears for French morale and the danger from Nazi Germany, though appreciated by his immediate superior, Robert Vansittart, were largely disregarded in government circles, and amply justified.

---

[89]                                                                          Oct 16

My dear heart Con,

If my pass comes, I am to start for the Somme tomorrow, & to be there on & off, gadding about, for perhaps a week. It will probably break the even flow of letters, but I will write when I can & post when I can, though you must not expect news from the front, only the baldest general statements.

No letter has come from you today, so I suppose the mail boat is hung up again.

There are some articles coming out, by an American journalist who has been in Germany, which seem to me to be almost the limit of news-papers baseness; and this kind of thing is approved & allowed to pass; while the man who writes it would probably treat us in the same way with one little turn of the cards. Perhaps you have seen the things, too. My general impression of the A's now is, that by all means they want to keep out of the war, that they will keep neutral by making money out of either party & by being always ready to betray either, & by criticising both. Some little sop of conscience money they will dribble out here & there; and for the rest, they want to spare themselves a little unpleasantness & so yield to any pressure applied. I really have very little enthusiasm left for them, & the thought that I am to praise them & to let their dirty vanity be swelled by what I say is exceedingly repugnant. I can praise the young men & (to a less extent) the big hospital & a little of the individual effort, but glorify them I will not, & so I shall tell G.P.

Dining last night with Lord Esher, I heard that Cannan[1] had been writing letters to *The Nation*[2], to say that his work was of national importance & that he etc etc should be exempt etc. Thinking over that young man I am not sure that he had not just a streak of unbalancedness, like Guillaume.

One hears a lot of strange things about the early part of the war. It all seems a marvellous kind of nightmare which happened to work out luckily for us. The general feeling one gets is that Tolstoi was right, in war & peace, & that no man can conduct either a war or a battle, but that Providence works through a sort of blindness and welter to a kind of justice.

I've been trying to determine what I see when I see a thing, but have not got very far, except that in no circumstances can I see things like cubes or whirlpools, and that, in general, what I see is a pattern of moving colour against a pattern of stationary colour.

No more ink.

Goodbye my dear heart

Dear love to you & Lew

Your old lover

Jan

A little ink has yielded to the squeeze, & I go on to say, what I ought to have urged on you before, to be very very discreet about my proposed appt. It will mean no pay, but a lot of work in London as well as here, & I shall know more about it later. Do not speak of it, for if it were to get abroad God knows what would happen.

1. Gilbert Cannan (1884–1955), novelist and playwright. A very long article in *The Times Literary Supplement*, by Henry James in 1914, entitled *The Younger Generation*, placed the future of the English novel with H. G. Wells, Arnold Bennett, Gilbert Cannan, Joseph Conrad, Edith Wharton, Compton Mackenzie, Hugh Walpole, and, perhaps, 'hanging in the dusty rear', D. H. Lawrence. Masefield's reservation about Cannan was later justified. Ill-health and instability restricted his output and reputation.

2. A weekly political journal evolving from J. L. Hammond's *The Speaker*, edited by H. W. Massingham, and later incorporated into the *New Statesman*. H. W. Nevinson was a regular contributor.

[90]                                                         Oct 16

M.O.D.C.

Your letter came a few posts late. Thank you.

I am to start off tomorrow a.m. for the Somme, but expect to be away only two days or three itself, & afterwards we shall be able to have some Eclaircissements as to the future. I do hate the thought of your loneliness in these shortening evenings, but I should hate to think of you in London worse.

This American journalist who has been in Germany is filling me with fury daily. He has by his own confession dirtily betrayed his hosts and those who trusted him, & now influential English papers are printing his dirty inuendoes, suggesting that we should adopt reprisals in bloodiness & dirtiness. It makes my blood to blish & to boil.

Do you by any chance hear or see anything about the Dards Comm[1]? Is it all secret, or does anything come out? Today, for just a second, I had the privilege of meeting General Gourand, a very strange & rather noble looking fine man who commanded the Fr at Helles till his arm was blown off (I think in June). He impressed me more than any of the soldiers I have met. He was like a portrait by Velasquez.

Dear love to you my dear heart love.

Your old lover,<br>Jan

1. The commemoration of the Dardanelles effort at Gallipoli.

[91]                                                         Oct 17

Dearest Con,

I have only a few minutes before I start, as all these beastly trains are early.

I was dining yesterday with some Ams, who seemed to have the general impression that we should all have been lost but for America, & that France especially would have suffered , but for American sympathy. At the same time, they felt that France was not in the least grateful & that the French thoroughly despised the lot of them, & that the English (though they did not say so in my presence) probably despised them more. It was an interesting evening of confession. They seemed to think that it was 'their' munitions which had saved us, & from the way they talked one might have concluded that they were healing half the French wounded and housing half the French destitute. As a matter of fact, I reckon that they are healing, at the most, 1000 wounded, out of the million or more now in France.

The seemed to think that Hughes would just be elected, & they thought that he would have some backbone. Personally, I believe that Hughes is simply Wilson over again, though not yet elected, which makes some difference.

Dear love to you my dear heart.

Kiss little Lew for me.

> Your old lover
> Jan

---

[92]                                                                    Oct 19

Dear heart,

This is not a letter, but a line to say that I am well, & that I hope to reach Paris tomorrow & find letters from you. It is horrid to have to miss one or 2 posts from you, but it has this advantage, that one finds a fine batch at the end.

The Paris work is near and end now, & I should think I could soon get back, but it is no good making plans till I have seen some more people in Paris.

Dear love to you, dear heart

> from
> Jan

---

[93]                                                                    Oct 21

Dearest heart,

I don't know that anything is at all settled yet, & everything may very well fall to the ground, but the way things stand is as follows:–

Sir D. H.[1] says that I may go to the front, stay there as long as I like & do the story of the battle.

One of his staff says that I may have a car & a guide, whenever one of each kind may be to spare, & that I may go about with Muirhead Bone[2].

Lord Esher kindly says that he will represent these things to those in power & will try to get me given a commission or whatever it may be that Bone has, so that I may be on a perfect equality with Bone.

If these things come to pass, my time will be passed partly in London, partly in France, in the Record Office or on the battlefield, till the story of the battle is finished, & when that happens, please God, it will be time to begin the battle of the Sambre et Meuse, or the battle of the Rhine itself, or, let us hope, the battle of the Spree.

But nothing is decided, nothing sure, and it is best to look on the whole thing as a pleasant event which may be & may not be, & to say nothing & expect nothing, & to think, that if it comes off, it will, in a way, much lighten our anxieties, & if not, we did not expect it, and ainsi soit. I do not know how soon I shall know.

I write this, not as a letter but simply to keep you posted, as far as I can, in what to expect & not to expect.

I hope that cold is better.

Dear love to you.<br>
From your old lover<br>
Jan.

No, Nevi isn't out here. If he were, he wd be in the Press mess just down the street from Montague's[3].

1. Douglas Haig, the British Commander in Chief in France.
2. Sir Muirhead Bone (1876–1953), painter and etcher, an official war artist in France. He and C. E. Montague collaborated in the illustrated *The Western Front*. The establishment of the Imperial War Museum owed much to Bone's proposals and enthusiasm.
3. Charles Edward Montague (1867–1928), journalist, drama critic, novelist. Worked on the *Manchester Guardian*, 1890–1925, with a gap for war service in the Great War, on which he wrote one of the most powerful war-novels, *Rough Justice* (1928) and an effective, sombre work of autobiographical journalism, *Disenchantment* (1922). Masefield knew him from his Manchester days.

---

[94]                                                                    Oct 21

Dear heart,

My 2nd day began with the terror of an invitation (or royal command) to lunch with Sir Douglas.

I polished myself till I shone & then went out to Mesnil, above the right bank of the Ancre, & peeped from a ruin across to Thiepval, taking great care not to shew myself. Going on to GHQ we stuck in the mud, & had to get soldiers to pull us out, so that we arrived 40 mins late & covered with filth. Owing to this, I barely saw Sir Douglas, but he was like Ian & Lord Methuen & these other wonderful men, rolled into one. No enemy could stand against such a man. He took away my breath.

I don't know what it is in such men. It is partly a very fine delicate gentleness & generosity, & then partly a pervading power & partly a height of resolve. He made me understand Sidney & Fairfax & Falkland & all these others, Moore & the rest. He is a rather tall man, with grey hair, a moustache, & a delicate fine resolved face, & a manner at once gentle & eager. I don't think anybody could have been nicer, & I don't think any race but the Scotch could have produced just such an one. Perhaps when I come home I'll be able to make a more definite picture: this is as far as I can go tonight.

Dear love<br>
from Jan

---

[95] Oct 21

M.O.D.C.

I got back late last night & found a jolly batch of letters from you, & 1 from Lewis, & this morning yours with Na's came, so I feel very rich.

I do hope your cold is better, my dear heart. I wish I had been back to see that you kept in bed for it; because as like as not you went weeding in the rain with it. Take care of yourself, dear heart, for you are all we have.

Thank you so much for the credit. Now I can finish off in style & come home. Paris is not so frightfully dear when you have learned the ropes. One can dine on about 11 courses for 4 francs, & on 6 for 2½, when one knows where to go, & I am beginning to be cunning in the underground, which is very good here, & cheaper than ours.

As to coming home: with decent luck I may be free to start in a week or ten days, only its no good planning a meeting, because sometimes the boats are held up for 3 or 4 days when subs are in the Channel, on the principle that 'its better to be sure than sorry'. So you might have to wait the inside of a week for me. So you'd better stay at Loll, & next week I ought to be able to let you know about what day to expect me, round the 1st, 2nd, or 3rd. . . .

. . . Now about the visit. I went to a place on Tuesday & was met at the station by Basil Williams & Montague. It was awfully nice meeting Montague again. He has gone very white, but looks twice the man he was, & has been much improved by the war. They took me to lunch in an inn (very crowded) & then we went off to Albert in a car. Albert has a very noble brick church with a huge brick spire. Of course both are shot to pieces, & look pretty ruined, but the notable thing is the Virgin & child, a colossal gilded piece, once the the spire top, which has been so shot that Virgin & child are hanging down, as though the V were diving. You expect to see her dive each second, but she never does, as the French engineers have secured her (so they say), but no doubt a shell will send her down sooner or later. When you go under her & look up you hope that the engineers really knew their job.

After leaving A, which is on the Ancre, you are on the battlefield.

I don't know quite how to describe it. Of course the country from Amiens to

Corbie (the junction of Ancre & Somme) is simply Didcot & Lollingdon, big open chalk valley with gentle chalk downland, but up the Ancre you are on ground which is only chalky near the river; to the right, or east, where the battlefield is, in fact the whole body of the battlefield, you are on rolls of rather fat light marl, good big lolloping rolls, many miles long, trending east & west, with little valleys between them, running towards the Ancre. They are easy long swells of ground, going up 3 or 400 feet in gentle waves, & until recently they were wooded, with good big clumps of wood, (oak & elm) & dotted with villages, compact, as the French village is, round the central church, & having their byres in the street, & stabling their beasts there. In the battlefield of 13 miles by 9 miles there were about 22 of these villages, & I daresay each was as big as Cholsey, reckoning from the church to half way to the asylum. All the land which was not woodland was under cultivation or grass, & no doubt was prosperous.

I cannot give you any dim conception of what the battlefield is now. But if you will imagine any 13 miles × 9 miles known to you, say from Goring to Abingdon, raking in Dorchester, Wallingford, Nettlebed & the Chilterns above Goring, you will get a hint of its extent. Then imagine in all that expanse no single tree left intact, but either dismembered or cut off short, & burnt quite black. Then imagine that in all that expanse no single house is left, nor any large part of a house, except one iron gate & half a little red chapel, & that all the other building is literally blasted into little bits, so that no man can tell where villages were, nor how they ran, nor what they were like. Here & there are cellars, in one place there is a well, in several places there are mangles, farm implements, & bundles of burnt plank, but the rest is gone. Then imagine that in all that expanse there is no patch of ground ten feet square that has not got its shell hole. To say that the ground is 'ploughed up' with shells is to talk like a child. It is gouged & blasted & bedevilled with pox of war, & at every step you are on the wreck of war, & up at the top of the ridge there is no ground, there is nothing but a waste of big grassless holes ten feet deep & ten feet broad, with defilement & corpses & hands & feet & old burnt uniforms & tattered leather all flung about & dug in & dug out again, like nothing else on God's earth.

We went up to Pozieres, where the fighting was terrific, for the windmill which marks the top of the peak, & we stood by the sort of mound on which the windmill once stood, & we could see the hollow beyond in which Bapaume lies. There was a good deal of noise. This front is quite unlike Gallipoli. Here it is all cannon, there it was all rifles, or at most field guns; but still no gun we have makes such a racket as the soixante quinze; & the Verdun noise was perhaps intenser. Later, I stood behind a cannon & saw the projectile go up into the sky, comme ça.

Later, we went back to tea in Montague's mess, & Neville Lytton came in, &

then we dined at the Press mess, where were Palmer, Beach Thomas, Percival Gibbon & some other men & officers (the officers cleverer & better bred than the writer perhaps) & so to bed in the inn.

But now I must stop my dear heart.

Dear love to you

> from your old lover
> Jan

---

[96]                                                                          Oct 22

My dear heart Con,

There is just a chance that I may be home at the end of this week or beginning of next, but do not count upon it, as I may have to go to the East again. Now that I have seen the A things, I realize that they amount to perhaps 1 fifteenth of our own charities (not to speak of our war effot) & that with it all they are slipshod and haphazard, however well meant, & what the devil I am to say about them, God knows.

> 'Come, Holy Ghost, & re-inspire'

as the hymn sayd. What a row I shall have with G.P.

I think that chronicler business will fall through, somehow. I've asked to be on exactly the same footing as B, & as B touche cinq cent livres d'appointements, c'est bien possible que les spangles hesiter out. However, il faut stand out for the honour of letters. What is literature that it should be less than art, & what is a poet that he should be less than a painter (& him Glasgow Scotch)? The business must be on a proper footing or not at all.

There is a lot to tell you about my visit, but fear of mentioning names deters me. It rained very hard one day, & the mud was worth a visit for itself alone. It was necessary to travel on new roads, less than a month old, & all made under fire, with wood & brush & stone & whatever came handy. Imagine an army traffic on such roads, all day & all night, with shells from time to time, blowing big holes in them, & at last a steady hard 16 hours rain. To call it mud would be misleading. It was not like any mud I've ever seen. It was a kind of stagnant river, too thick to flow, yet too wet to stand, & it had a kind of a glisten or shine on it like reddish cheese, & it looked as solid as cheese, but it was not solid at all & you left not racks on it, they all closed over, & you went in over your boots at every step & sometimes up to your calves. Down below it there was a solid footing, & as you went slopping along the army went slopping along by your side, & splashed you from head to foot. It was very jolly as soon as you had realised that 'even so if life', and though I would not have liked to lie down in it I could have brought myself to it, & perhaps slept in it, remembering the poet:–

They sleep as well within that purple tide
As others . . . .'

We went into a wood, which we will call Chunk-of-Corpse-Wood, for its main features were chunks of corpse, partly human, partly trees. There was a cat eating a man's brain, & such a wreck of war as I never did see, & the wounded coming by, dripping blood on the track, & one walked on blood or rotten flesh, & saw bags of man being carried to the grave. They were shovelling parts of men into blankets.

C.E.M. lent me some dry slacks, & a bonne dried & cleaned my things, & we had a pleasant evening at the mess. C.E.M. overheard the following after one of the attacks.

| | |
|---|---|
| A German officer, surrendering. | 'Kamerad. Kamerad.' |
| An English officer. | 'Not so much bloody Kamerad, but hand over your ticker.' |
| The German officer | 'Here is my watch.' |
| The soldier, beaming | 'Now 'ow much shall we say for this mate?' |

He also saw an English sergeant bringing in a Prussian guard; both were wounded, & the guard looked extremely sick, even for a prisoner. The sergeant said. 'we had quite a little trouble at first; he stuck me through the leg and I stuck him through the cheeks; but now we're the best of friends.'

The next day was beautifully fine, clear & cold, with a brisk wind to dry the mud, & we went along a river & then to a certain place to see some old enemy dugouts, which were very elaborate, 20 or 30 feet down, with bolt holes everywhere to escape by, and electric light laid on. But they had none of the grace & finish & sense of style that the French good dugouts have. They were, rather, strong & sensible, without any delicacy; with self-indulgence rather than delicacy! Now good-bye my darling Con.

Bless you. Kiss Lew for me.

Your old lover
Jan

---

[97]                                                                    Paris
                                                                      23 Oct
Darling Con,

If I am very lucky, I shall be able to get away from this place in a day or two, if not, in about a week or ten days. I've been finishing up, in a frightful whirl of visits, & have been worn off my legs today, going right across Paris twice, & half way across four times.

You mentioned a letter from Peter Warren. It never came, nor another charming letter you mentioned. I have your letter about *Gallipoli* (W.H. has evidently been caught unprepared) & I hasten to say that the things behind the aeroplane in Nevi's picture are partly cloudy, partly searchlights.

I won't write more, as I may perhaps be able to get away.

Dear love to you.

Your old lover
Jan

# Part Four

# Letters from France, 1917
(Letters 98 to 167, 26 February to 23 May)

In February 1917, Masefield began ranging the Somme lands, where the battle was now expiring, slowly, though sometimes noisily and brutally. Neville Lytton, with his staff contacts, gave much useful help. I must borrow from Constance Babington Smith:

'It is incredible that after producing such a masterpiece as *Gallipoli* his unique gifts should have been wasted.' So, after the war, wrote Neville Lytton – artist, Francophile, aristocrat turned Bohemian – whose admiration for Masefield's narrative poems was such that he called him 'a second Homer'. In early 1917 Lytton was a major attached to the General Staff Headquarters in France, with special responsibility for the French war correspondents, and when Masefield returned to the Somme at the end of February, a humble and somewhat bewildered honorary second lieutenant without pay, eager to make a start on the research for his new book, Lytton met him by chance and thenceforth helped and befriended him. But he was amazed when he heard that the book was to be confined to the Battle of the Somme, which was by now virtually over. If only, he felt, this great poet could have been attached to the armies that would soon be going into the heat of new battles, and given a free hand! Then perhaps there might be another long narrative poem of the calibre of *The Everlasting Mercy* or *Dauber*. In Lytton's view, a commissioned book on the Battle of the Somme savoured of official history, and was doomed to failure.

Masefield himself, however, saw things in a different light. He regarded the assignment he had received from Esher and Haig as a supreme opportunity . . . he intended to become as familiar as possible with the topography of the battlefield – this was an essential beginning – and he also hoped to talk with men who had taken part in the fighting. Then when he returned to England he would combine this with all the factual material contained in the brigade and battalion diaries.

Soon after Lytton met Masefield he asked to have him attached to his mission. The request was granted, and Masefield found himself surrounded by French correspondents to whom at first he was a great puzzle. As Lytton later wrote, 'They could not understand his shy, unassuming manners. "*Mais voyons, c'est une jeune fille*," they said, until gradually they found out that he knew considerably more about most things, including French literature, than themselves, and that

his remarks, uttered with a voice no louder than that of a mouse in a
cheese, were full of point and wit.'

The Hon. Neville Lytton (1879–1951), later 3rd Earl of Lytton, was a
considerable artist, praised as a boy by Bonnard, though developing in
the tradition of the English water-colourists, in his youth somewhat
forgotten. A deep admirer of Gainsborough, he instigated Eddie
Marsh's collection of classical paintings, and remained unenthusiastic
about most of his contemporaries. An early work by Duncan Grant he
judged 'atrocious . . . incompetent beyond measure . . . a disgrace . . .
not art at all.' His portraits included ones of Wilfrid Scawen Blunt,
Francis Thompson, and Bernard Shaw robed as a pope.

He married Judith Blunt, daughter of Wilfrid Scawen Blunt, great
granddaughter of Byron. This marriage was not a success: Judith had
said of her future husband, 'There is something about his face that
repels me.' She did not reciprocate his love. Her father had virtually arranged the marriage which she felt 'false' and it ended in divorce.

Lytton was later wounded in France, but survived intact.

[98]                                                     1. (d)
                                                       E.H.Q.
                                                       B.E.F.
                                                      26 Feb.
Dear heart,
   I am sending you this note to say that I arrived safely, after a very quiet
crossing, & was motored here, arriving after dark. It is a rather beautiful place,
not unlike the Wilfrid Blunt country in Sussex. I shall write about it later.
   As post does not go until the evening I can write this forenoon . . .
   . . . As far as I can tell at present, I shall be here, & shall visit the lines from
here, starting tomorrow. My billet is in a sort of a house like the store at
Cushendun. I have a big room, facing south, & if I had a saw, some wood, a lb
of nails & a hammer, I would make it to blossom like the rose. Still, it has 3
chairs, a handsome bed, a wobbly table & a wash-hand table. It commands the
village, which is scattered, almost in the English style, & the chateau, which
stands beside a swift clear chalk stream, about 7 yards broad & 2 feet deep, very
beautiful, & green with weed. There are troops about of course, & they practise
with guns, in the way they have; otherwise it is a quiet place, all cocks & cows,
& one church bell, too near my billet, which rings at 7 a.m.
   Montague is here, billeted in another house. He is now promoted to be a
Captain. Dodd,[1] the painter, whom you met years ago at Aitken's in Church
Row, is also here, grown to some 3 or 4 times the size he used to be, & doing
portraits.

My landlady here is about the size of Yvette Guilbert[1], only not so clever nor so handsome. She is like a fat Kate McNeill, only she has 2 teeth, one at each corner, instead of one in each middle jaw.

I suppose by this time Tim knows about this afternoon & is in a fine flutter to be off. I hope that you are having this kind of weather so that the expedition may be a complete success. How did the performance go, & how loudly was it booed? I keep thinking how good a play could have been made of it with another 6 months work, scrapping all the first half of it, & making it a complete Greek structure, as of course it is, the death of Dionysus, after a contest, the messenger, & then the transcendence or reawakening. As it is, the whole early half of the thing is without life, though no doubt Jean & Nevvi dissembled & were gracious. Mind you tell me the people whom you saw there, & those with whom you had any talk. How did the Fiammetta drama go?

Tomorrow you will see sandpits. I look forward to hearing your verdict. Make sure that the pits are as I think they are, 200 yards south of the house. How is the cut healing over?

There is not much to say today, as I have neither seen nor explored anything. I mess in a quaint little hut with Dodd & others. Tomorrow I shall hope to have more to tell you. Dear love to you & Tim.

Jan

I think it is rather white than chalk here; like Arc-en-Barrois, flat, with a steep scarp above.

1. Francis Dodd (1874–1949), an official war artist.
2. French actress and diseuse whom Masefield saw perform, perhaps in New York. Toulouse Lautrec's portrait of her 'shows the famous yellow costume, with black shoulder-knots and long black gloves, coming well above the elbows; she was then at the height of her glory, where she remained, without a rival, a peerless wonder.' In another letter to Audrey Napier-Smith (1964), Masefield wrote: 'There has been no-one so great in her particular work, no-one with such a range, such power, such perfection. She could do wonderful things, religious things, and then uproarious & merry & terrible things, & could become a child or a maenad at a moment's notice.'

---

[99]                                                    1st March

Dear heart,

I am writing this in the mess, waiting for my car which is to take me to A.

I had nothing to do but click my heels yesterday, & curse the system, but in the evening I was asked to dine with Montague's mess which was not bad. Russell, a press man, very like Nev, is the president of it, & one or 2 other good souls are members, so the evening atoned for the day. Tilson Y, who took the whore to Aston, & scandalized Dorothy, is also here, writing for the Mail, but he goes out of an evening, for bridge with some cavalry officers, so I did not see him.

Montague is a 1st rate chap & has lent me some blankets to take into the wilderness. Greater love hath no man than this, to lay down his blankets in possibly chatty places for a chance acquaintance. Probably I shall see Neville Lytton today at A.

Things are in very strange & perplexing ways here.

Dear love
Here's my car

---

[100]                                                                 3rd March, 1917.

Dearest heart,

I am very doubtful about the posts going from here, but I've written every day, & trust in God that you get them. The work is very interesting, but hard, for I am walking all day long from directly after breakfast until tea. Today, my second day of full walking, I went 15 miles, which was pretty fair on unknown roads, with the roads as they are here. Not that all are bad. Whole stretches are very good; that is, we shouldn't think them quite impossible in England; but the most are difficult for walking on, & every now & then one comes on a morass. But I went today over ground I crossed in October. (It is very different going over the ground on foot, one sees much more, gets a picture of the country, & really appreciates the rises & slopes.) The difference is very great. Then a great part of the country was filled with battle. Our guns were in action everywhere, there was a roaring & a crashing from half the roadsides, & enemy shells were falling. Today, all the battle has moved on, & the old battlefield, except that it looks that it has been skinned then ploughed & then bedevilled, is the home of countless squatters and gipsies, who have destroyed nearly every vestige of the original lines, & built themselves huts upon the graves of heroes. It was a glum, overcast, fine-weather day with no sort of view, & I hoped to get as far as Captain Denis Browne; but I heard on the way that he was moved in from the line, & may be at a rest camp near here. I shall try to see him tomorrow.

This place is often fairly full of Australians. One sat next to me at dinner last night. He had been at the taking of the Bismarck Archipelago & he knew those two nice fellows, Howe & Trevor, whom I met at Anzac. Trevor is now a Major, & Howe a General, so that virtue has been rewarded. My informant said that the Bismarck natives[1] are still cannibals, & ate two policemen while he was there. He says they eat men, not because they are short of meat, but because they like the taste. 'Kai Kai, man.'

After that I slept in my Dormi, with 3 other Australians, one of them an Anzac, wounded on the 17th Aug, & very nice to get on with. He said that the A battalions aren't what they were (indeed, how could they be) but they are certainly a fine lot of men. It is wonderful to see these overseas men cantering down a road, they ride as though they were parts of the horse, & they box the horse's ears when he shies just as though he were a cheeky younger brother. How differently does the Mary & the Caroline take the air on horseback –

Out of ink –

Dear love to you my Darling & to Tim cat[2] & Nana. I hope all goes well. I'll be glad to get back to the mess to find your letters next week.

Dear love to you

Jan

1. Not Prussian officers, but inhabitants of the Bismarck Islands, in the southern seas, discovered in 1699 by Dampier, whose works were edited and introduced by Masefield as *Dampier's Voyages* (1906).
2. Pet name for Lewis.

---

[101]                                                                   March 4th 1917

Dear heart,

I am writing this before setting out for the day, as I am up rather earlier than usual. I hope to get out today to a place near the Somme where I believe Denis Browne now is. It is cold & bright, so it should be a jolly walk.

I left off here, in order to make the most of a chance of a lift. I found out exactly where Browne's ambulance is, right out of the line in a peaceful village in the country, & found an Australian friend just setting out with some comrades in a lorry. There is a rule here that a lorry will always hold one more, so they emptied a petroleum tin & inverted it for me to sit on, & away we went, & I must say that a ride on a lorry on a war time road is not such fun as walking. After some 5 kiloms of jolt I had to jump off, which I did (with great skill luckily) before an admiring road gang of prisoners, who saluted me. After that I had to walk a boggy lane to the village, through strings of mules going to water. There is no doubt that a mule is a great beast & an army mule a great devil, the worst of all army animal life is that the masters are continually changing, & this plays havoc with the nerves of both mules & horses. I see a good many jumpy beasts everywhere.

I found Denis Browne quite easily. He was out near the line through all the frost; and he said that in those days there were dead horses on the road, frozen so hard that the wagons used to go over them just as though they were parts of the metalling. I only saw one horse out there yesterday, but he was pretty well thawed; & so one fetched a compass about him.

Dennis is to have tea & then dinner with me this evening, which will be a change & society for both of us.

There is a devilish war of battle going on on the line, so I suppose the enemy is not finding his withdrawal so easy.

It is almost impossible to say what the battlefield looked like before the battle began. The slopes are long & rather gentle, & the place must have been pleasant but very monotonous. It is not morne, like so much French landscape, but a little like chalk downland. There are hilly bits to the east of the G.W.R. line just before you come to Cholsey station (from Reading) which give you a very fair idea of it. Before the fight it had a lot of wood on it. Mametz Delville & Contalmaison woods are all really pretty big, but Lord to see the poor wood now; after 4 months winter & 3 months battle. They are one with Babylon & Tyre, with not one 20th part of their trees standing, & all that are, all pollarded & splayed & pruned. I saw the stub of one shell stuck in one tree. It had gone in, burst, & skinned some bark off, & there the rest of it remained.

One gets a very interesting, but very strange view of the war here. Every night I talk with men who were fighting 4 hours before, & who know (intimately) the geography of the whole of north west France, and (vividly) how the war is going on a quarter mile of the front, where they have been, yet nothing whatever of the general question. In a way, you know nothing of the war, in England, & we know nothing of it here in France. I'm afraid Fritz is full of buck still, but let us hope for the best. He may get his pains, the old cock may get the axe, and so an end; but not soon.

Dear love to you, my dear heart, & to little Tim & to Nana.

Your old love

Jan

---

[102]                                                        March 6th 1917.

Dear heart,

I left off my yesterday's letter (as far as I recollect) at the river bank, wondering at the beauty of the water, which is extreme. The river itself rises only 4 miles or so from where I then was, & it curves round from west to south & so into the Somme. Its valley is strange, for it is broad & flat, say 200 yards across, & though the actual river cannot be broad, it is deep, & swift, too, & it has spread into lakes, which are all fairly deep, & yet reeds have got into them, & trees grow in them, so that you have river, lake, lagoon, marsh, reedbed, osierbed, & river coppice all in one, & all this when the sun shines, is most beautiful, especially now, when the lakes are all overfull, & there are rushes of water under each causeway which the troops have made.

Roughly speaking, the enemy held the east bank, which is steepish, or even very steep, from the lip of the main stream. We held the west bank which is sloping, & trends back a long way from the river; & of all the daredevil feats, our going across, in fog, & up the steep, to tackle the great works on the top, is nearly the finest. Of course, when you look at it all from the western bank, it seems a trivial bank to climb, but when you cross the river, & are actually under or on it, you are amazed at its strength. Attacking from the river you have this steep & difficult approach, through marsh & across rushing water; & attacking from the shore you have to go up a sort of long easy gradual glacis; so that you get withered & plugged from people you can neither see nor reach, for the greater part of the way.

I was at the windmill yesterday (where Basil was so tappy[1]) but Lord, the difference. Then there was a whirl of shell fire coming across all the time, & flying iron all round, wherever we went, but now, nothing at all of all that, no single enemy shell came anywhere onto that ground while I was on it: not that there was anything there to be hit if one had come over.

Roughly speaking, the battlefield is now a more safe place for visitors.

Talking to some gunners yesterday, I heard that a dead German woman had been found & buried in one of the redoubts, & that another had been seen walking outside one of the others, though they thought that this second woman may have been a man in disguise, doing it out of bravado or for a bet.

So probably the Fricourt story[2] may be believed in.

I expect to go to Am for the night about Saturday, & then to G.H.Q. for some nights, & then back here.

Dear love to you my Darling. Kiss little Tim from me & give him my love. I hope the buns are being good. Love to Nana.

Your old love<br>Jan

1. Perhaps a variant of 'tapped', defined by Brophy and Partridge as 'slightly mad, below the normal in sanity; of eccentric behaviour.'
2. Clearly some sort of spy story, but I have been unable to trace it.

---

[103]                                                                    March 6, 1917.

Dear heart,

Today, after I had dressed & breakfasted, I found an officer sitting up, breakfasting in bed. He was a cheery soul, & began a conversation. He said that it was his battalion, not the S Africans who took Delville Wood, & as a proof, told me that when his battalion reached the heart of the wood, he found a wounded S African who had been living there for 10 days, eating the rations of the dead & drinking from the shellholes.

He said, that when they first came to the edge of the wood, he & his company were in a bit of trench about 20 yards long. It was night, there was a hell of fire everywhere, & no one had any hope of food. Presently, in the darkness, a little thin voice called out 'Is Captain — there? I'm the cook with dinner.' He had brought up the officers' dinner over a mile & a half of road simply ablaze with shells, & had provided soup (in a Thermos) fish (from the tin) hot meat with 2 vegetables, cheese, port, whiskey & soda, & bread. They took the dinner & began to eat, & then the company commander said 'Where's the salt?' 'O, sir,' said the cook, 'I forgot to bring the salt.' 'Then why the bloody hell,' said the Commander, 'did you forget?'

My man also told me that the enemy dead, outside Delville, were 3 deep, piled up & heaped. He went out for a stroll to see this sight, which was one of the awful things of this war, & a sentry said 'Who are you? Where are you going? Put up your bloody hands. Put them up quick.' So he put them up, & was marched past some men of his own company, on the way to authorities. One of his men called to the sentry 'Who've you got there?'

The sentry said, 'I don't know; some bleeder or other.'

One of the men called out: 'You bloody fool, you've got our bloody platoon commander'; so they released him & the matter ended.

I asked the man, if he enjoyed the push. He said, 'I enjoyed the Delville Wood stunt, every bit of it; it was top hole. When shells are coming across like machine gun bullets the mind can't take it in; you can't think of it; so you go to sleep. I lay down & went to sleep & slept for 12 hours & when I woke up I was buried up to the neck by a barrage that was just outside our trench. I know one thing. If I come through this war, I'm not going to do a stroke of work for six months. I'm just going to enjoy myself tophole, & then I'm going to emigrate to somewhere where there is sun. I've got no capital. I've lost all my money, but I'm going where there is sun. I'm fed up with mud & cold; but I'm on here to see this stunt through. I couldn't miss this stunt for anything.'

After this, I walked a fearful walk to T from the land side, & took in the Leipzig salient & Wonder Work on my way. I never saw such mud, or such a sight, in all my days. Other places are bad & full of death, but this was deep in mud as well, a kind of chaos of deep running holes & broken ground & filthy chasms, and pools & stands & marshes of iron-coloured water, & yellow snow & bedevilment. Old wet rags of uniform were everywhere, & bones & legs & feet & heads were sticking out of the ground, & in one place were all the tools of a squad just as they had laid them down; in order, & then all the squad, where they had been killed, & the skull of one of them in a pool, &, near by, the grave of half a German, & then a German overcoat with ribs inside it, & rifles & bombs & shells literally in heaps. Then there was a kind of quarry, with a fine iron bedstead in it & a heap of enemy, all mashed up in a pulp with the rags of their kit on top of them, & such a hell of a desolation all round as no words can describe. Can you imagine a landscape in the moon, made of filth instead of beauty.

Dear love to you, my Darling & my dear love to Timcat & darling Nana. Kiss them both from me.

Your old love
Jan

[104]                                                        At the Club still.
                                                            March 7, 1917.

Dearest heart love,

I am still here away from letters, but I must go back in a day or two, & oh how good it will be to get them. I long to have news of you & to see your hand & to think of all our times together, & to hear about the dear babes again.

I went to bed early last night, being weary from the mud, which is bad again, from the snow, though drying, under this bitter easter. At about midnight some officers came in to the dormi, & went to bed. One of them was my friend of the salt & sentry stories, so we talked for a long time about the battle. One of the officers said that up at Montauban the dugouts were far finer than the great one at Fricourt; for they had splendid hand painted panels on the walls, h & c bathrooms, suites de luxe, & black & white china services (all these delights being for an artillery brigade headquarters, comparatively feeble people) the whole costing many pounds, except that the labour was forced & the furniture probably looted. They were all positive that the enemy had occasional women there, though it seems to me possible that what they have are sodomites who dress as women. Either way, it is ugly.

My friend said that a friend of his rode across country the other day, a frightfully dangerous thing to do, on account of the scattered explosives. The horse kicked a bomb a good lusty kick, & was blown up, & the rider 'got a blighty touch, the lucky devil.'

I got a compliment yesterday from a Colonel. We both came in here filthy to the eyes, & he had no servant to clean him up. He was not exactly butler bred, but he seemed very lost & hopeless; while I set about a cleaning up. When we came to dinner I had clean boots & gaiters & a bright set of buttons, and he was still 'foul with sluttish slime.' He said 'You are a clean man, sir.'

Lots of Australians here; jolly good fellows; though I fear they all think that we let them down at Suvla. The truth is, I'm afraid we did. It is heartbreaking to say it, but we did. We sold them a pup as they put it, that is, did not deliver a full sized dog.

Cervantes says somewhere (& he had ample means of knowing) that war intensifies a man's natural bent. What I notice here so much is the kindness of man to man. Yesterday an officer, after nearly running me over, offered me a lift in to A. He said he was being given a lift himself, so he felt 'like doing the Samaritan touch.' Then today a red cross (RAMC) man, gave me a lift in his ambulance for 5 miles. People can't understand what lifts mean in this mud.

Then today a Colonel's servant gave me a most lovely dip of 'saddle soap' for my gaiters, which was fine of him. Of course, all these gifts were, in a way, not theirs to give, but the thought was beautiful in each case. 'Here's a poor old bleeder, lets do the Samaritan touch.'

I'm writing this by firelight in a billiard room.

And had to stop, because Denis Browne came in to dinner.

He said that when he was going out of Mudros to Anzac for the first time his ship passed a big ship load of wounded coming in.

All the Australians raised the yell 'Are we downhearted? No.' A big rough voice came back from the wounded.

'Well, if you're not now you damn soon will be.' He also said that at an inspection he asked one of the men the regulation question 'Who is your next of kin?' The man thought he was referring to an article of clothing, so he said, 'I had only one issued to me, sir.'

Dear love to you, my darling Coneen. Kiss little Tim from me & send my love to Nana.

Your old love<br>
Jan

---

[105]                                                    March 7th, 1917.

Dearest heart Con,

I expect to move back to A, & thence (by degrees) to GHQ, tomorrow, & though I long to have your letters the journey to them is likely to be tedious.

Today I walked in all about 14 or 15 miles, & did not get tired, for there was a brisk & violent northerly wind which made the roads clean & the ground hard. I started along the Bapaume road, & then struck inland, so as to be on the ground over which the Anzacs advanced to the attack on Pozieres, which was some of the toughest fighting of the war. The old enemy front line was certainly wonderfully strong, & as far as I can see wherever they withdrew they had glorious gentle slopes, with no cover on them, from which to plug the attackers. So that, until they lost Pozieres, which is the top of a sort of plateau, as flat, as, say, Prestwood, but infinitely bigger, they had all the advantage. From Pozieres, a man in a tree could see all the attack & telephone the guns to get onto it, but after they lost that vantage they felt something of the same themselves, & their lines after (that is, north of Pozieres) were not long held, for they got plugged out of them. From Poz, I went across to High Wood, which is about the limit in woods. The first thing I saw there were two German legs sticking out of the ground, the boots half buried, & the socks flapping round the bones. Just inside the wood, there was a skull high up in a tree, & helmets with bits of heads in them, & legs galore & several pairs of boots with feet in them, and the wood simply ripped & blown to tatters. It snowed hard while I was there, so I took shelter behind an abime Tank & when it cleared I had a wonderful view, over flattish rolls of infinite down, to Bapaume & the promised land, & I saw far off the enemy barrage bursting beyond Le Sars. From there, I walked on to near Flers, & then to Delville Wood, which is nothing to High Wood, it has been so nicely tidied. Still, the nw corner of Delville must have had more shells onto it & just over it than any part of the ground, & all the earth there must be mainly enemy flesh. They lay there three & four deep, & the bluebottles made their faces black there.

As Delville is about as far as I can compass, I walked home through Contalmaison into the old English lines, & Lord, it is like passing into spring to get into a wood which has been shot by the Germans after being in woods shot by ourselves. The enemy fire cannot have been one fifth part of the fire developed by us in the Somme battle. Verdun can only have been child's play to it.

Denis Browne is very wise about the war. I think that most of the officers get a kind of enjoyment out of it, & most of them admire the enemy as a brave & very cunning able kind of soldier, & most of them wonder when mankind will learn a little sense, & most of them seem to expect two or three more years of it.

I must now stop. My dear love to you, to Nana, & to dear little Tim. I send kisses to you all

Your old love
Jan

[106]　　　　　　　　　　　　　　　　　l.d.
　　　　　　　　　　　　　　　　　　　G.H.Q.
　　　　　　　　　　　　　　　　　　　B.E.F.
　　　　　　　　　　　　　　　　　March 8, 1917.

My darling heart,

I am writing this up in the Dormi out of the noise of tea & gramophone. I have had a pleasant time with Denis Browne, who came out to tea yesterday & stayed dinner. He is a very clever, shrewd & well read young man & may come to something if this accursed war spares him. He is out of the line for a while in a pleasant bit of country. I took him up the road to see the big crater, which is one of the show sights, & as he had not seen it, it made an impression on him. It really looks like a volcano's crater, or, as he said, like one of the craters on the moon. As it is deep down into chalk, which is probably porous stuff, it is dry, & one can see to the bottom of it, & trace where the dugouts were, before it went into the air. He said that quite accidentally he met an Australian, who began telling him of a young fellow in his platoon, who went out to Anzac. He was a nice young fellow, a good boxer & a keen sport, & well liked. Early in the Anzac campaign, this lad & a corporal went out on patrol, & the Turks turned on a machine gun & killed the lad at once. They buried him in a hurry, & left his feet sticking out, & by & by they won more ground, & used to pass the grave going up to the line. The men used to reach over & give his boots a shake & say 'Good old Brownie; you weren't half a bad sort.' Browne said, 'I realised, when he said Brownie, that this was my younger brother.'

Today I've been out to the November line, past some seven or eight Abimés tanks, one of them labelled 'the Bing Boys are here[1]' & another 'Tonight's the

Night', & all of them done in by shells; & I'm afraid the poor Bing boys as well. After that I went to a hell of a place. Sodom & Gomorrah were April to what I had seen before, but the next show passed anything I ever conceived as a picture of smash & horror. It snowed last night & thawed today, so nature gave it a setting worthy of it. Its name begins with a T (if that is not sedition & burglary to say so) & my golly after such a tea may the Lord make us wiser. All the slope below it was a litter beyond conception of half & quarter buried men, with broken gear & dud shells & old bombs & smashed clothes, helmets torn into spirals, gas masks, rotten sandbags, bones, backbones, legs, boots, old wheels, miles of bedevilled wire, packsacks, straps, rifles, bayonets, bits of spines, tins, canteens, socks, gloves, & a litter of burst shells & a pox of shell holes.

Curiously, within 200 yards of this, was an exquisitely clear swift chalk river, at which I gazed & gazed, it was so wonderful as an afterpiece.

Dear love to you my Darling.

> Dear love & a kiss to Tim.
> Your old love
> Jan

1. A London revue, *The Bing Boys are Here* (1916), starring George Robey, Violet Loraine and Alfred Lester, which introduced such songs as 'Another little drink wouldn't do us any harm' and 'If You Were the Only Girl in the World'. The words 'The Bing Boys' caught the soldiers' imagination, and were common in graffitti and jocular expressions and inscriptions.

---

[107]                                                          March 11, 1917.

Dear heart,

I could not send you much yesterday, but I have now more or less settled down, & may be able to write more fully. My address is to be the same still, though I have left that part of France, & am now quartered in the town where we supposed I should be, & perhaps I shall not go back to the old place at all.

Coming along in the car this morning, it was really like a Spring day, & one had a few hours of hope that it was going to be hot & sunny & dry up the mud, but as Shakespeare puts it, 'the region cloud hath masked him' & it is wet again. Mud is the real enemy: mud & war. So call upon thy God, that it may please Him, so to dry etc. that we may bash that German part of His creation.

Did I tell you how I left the front for this place? There were trains available, but very slow; so I resolved to lift & carry. I walked about 1 Kilom, & then a lorry full of stores gave me a lift for 6 Kiloms more, as my lorry had to turn off the road, & it was jolly cold walking. Then a car came along at 90 miles an hour,

& stopped, & took me on for 5 Kiloms more, carrying some famous men of war, who, although great, had not lost those bowels of mercy which some great are said to lack, which is why Christ told them to go to, weep & howl. (By the way, they would look odd doing it.) When I say that the car went 90 miles an hour, I put it mildly. We went gunwale under & were all under water forward, besides having to put preventers on our braces; and if it had been cold walking, it was truly bitter in the car, except that the kindness of these unknown soldiers kept one warm. When they had to turn off, I walked for several Kiloms more, till an empty lorry offered me a lift, & I sat with a soldier, inside, on some spare wheels, & was joggled. So after that I had but one Kilom more, which I did in company with a French civilian, who had been 9 months a prisoner of the enemy at Lunéville, which these blackguards pillaged, under a scoundrelly Ordre de Reclamation.

By the way, dear heart, you should at once order from Hodder & Stoughton, their book called *Scraps of Paper* (1/-). It is a reprint of some of the proclamations issued by these ruffians in France & Belgium, & it is pretty terrible.

I still do not see things in cubes & lozenges & whirlpools; but the problem of what one does see, as compared with what is there, is still with me. A company on the march, a mile away on these straight roads, is like an obstruction, say, perhaps, a broken down lorry, or a group of men round a dead horse; not more than that. Then as one comes nearer, it looks like one of those 'plumps of spears' in Dürer's etching of war, but still a form, rather than anything human. Then it becomes a big wobbling humping caterpillar, with men in front, pumphandles swinging down the sides, as the arms swing, & round, rather shiny knobs on the top, which gradually become helmets covering marching fours.

I wish that I could describe these things, so as to make people see them.

I've written a tale for Walpole[1]. Montague will send it direct. It was told me by a Major of the battalion involved. 12 of our men went out on patrol one night last week, & a machine gun killed half of them & drove the rest into a shell hole. The Germans came out 40 strong, & took their rifles, helmets & gas masks, & then went on to raid the English line disguised as the patrol returning. The 6 men left in the patrol remembered that they still had their bombs; so they suddenly set upon their guard, broke free, & charged the 40 Germans in the rear, flinging their bombs & yelling. They killed 20 Germans & took the other 20; so it was rather a fine feat of arms.

Dear love to you, & to Tim & to Nana.

Your old love

Jan

1. Sir Hugh Seymour Walpole (1884–1941), novelist and critic. His novels, notably *Mr Perrin and Mr Traill* (1911), *The Dark Forest* (1916), *The Cathedral* (1922) and the Herries Series, 1930–32, achieved huge popularity, though little of his large output remains in print. He served with the Red Cross in Russia in 1914–15, and was now in

Petrograd, supervising an Anglo-Russian office of information. His biography, by Sir Rupert Hart-Davis (1952) won great acclaim.

---

[108]　　　　　　　　　　　　　　　　　　　　　　　March 12. 1917.

Dearest heart,

It is 10 p.m., & we have just finished dinner, & I have missed the post through being in late. The rain has made the road worse by far than anything I have ever seen. I have been ploughing along over the ankles, in a sort of lovely creamy mud, sometimes fluid sometimes thick, but always the very devil.

We set out, Lytton, a French writer, & myself, to go out beyond Beaumont Hamel, to see the ground of the battle of the Ancre. We got out to Mesnil, which was a good deal more smashed than when I was there in October, & then across the bedevilled battlefield. It is no good trying to describe the land. It is roll upon roll of rather gentle downland, much as you see from the high point of the Fair Mile; but mile after mile of it, wherever you look, is blown into holes, mostly very big deep holes, half full of water, & running into each other, & without any grass, but all raw & filthy, & littered with bits of man & bits of weapons, & old ragged sandbags, helmets, skulls, barbed wire, boots with feet in them, bombs, shells, eclats, till it looked like an ash heap put as a dressing on a kind of putrid pox that was cankering the whole earth. You can perhaps imagine what walking on such mud means. There is no skin nor grass nor twig nor shrub nor building nor anything left alive upon it. It is bedevilled mud, with a few broken bricks where the village stood, & a swill of mud where the road was, & we wandered in that kind of land for hours & hours.

Presently we came to a god forgotten valley, with 3 blasted trees in it like the witches in Macbeth, & a foul brook swishing mud through mud. We crossed this, & came out on a roll, & had a wonderful view of the Promised Land, with a hell of battle raging like blazes all along it, & the enemy line far away being crumped to hell. However big a beast the enemy has been, I felt sorry for him then. He must have been suffering every known agony of awful terror, & the fire fell upon him all the time spout on spout & crash on crash, often coming in a salvo, then dropping singly, then simply blotting the line in blackness. If that was 'according to plan' he has strange views of war. He must have been having a hell of a time. I picked up a poor enemy postcard, from a poor fellow's mother, who will never see her son again, nor know where he lies, for there were no graves up there. The dead were in the shell holes, or blown to bits.

When we got back to M, we found our car stuck in the mud, so had to get four gun horses to pull it out, & then we came home in the dark.

I cannot tell you what a charming person N L is. It is wonderful to be in this accursed kind of life with one of one's own kind. He is a most winning attractive person, & if you can, without trouble, send me a Sonnets, I should like to give it to him. Sonnets are in the book case in my study, a largeish, solitary key in the left hand drawer in the bedroom.

I am too dog tired to write more, my dear heart. Bless you, & my love to you & a kiss to dear Mr Tim.

Your old love
Jan

---

[109] March 13.

M.D.O.C.

Today I received safely your letters of 3rd, 7th, & 9th of March. I am concerned that you have had a gap between Feb 27 & March 3rd. The cause of the gap is probably some miscreant orderly who forgot to post; but one will never know. Out there in the wilderness the thing happens or doesn't happen; alas, we are far from happy peacetime when letters never failed.

It has been fairly cold since I landed, but is now warmer, & today in the valley of the A, I saw green grass, new & vivid, & the beginning of a green sprout in the reed, & any number of fine fat water hens. I was up at T again, & up there in the bedevilled wreck, the weeds were certainly thrusting, so that perhaps spring will cover even that horror, the chateau, & the Tank that attacked it, & the ruin of the awful wood. We walked on what are called duck boards, or gratings, for 1 mile & a ½ from T, inside an old Boche trench, & came out above a mile from Grand court, in a place littered with old dead, English & Boche, very well preserved. I don't know why, but one seldom finds heads about, though legs with the boots on seem to be everywhere. Perhaps men bury the heads, & do not bother so much about the legs.

Coming back, we saw the Boche trying to strafe our aeroplanes, but quite without success. He fires a black smoke shrapnel, whereas our shrapnel has white smoke, & after sullying heaven with his impurities for an hour or so he seemed to give it up.

On our way up the hill we heard someone with a shot gun, which seemed very odd up there. Probably some brisk young officer had borrowed a shot gun & was having a quiet go at a rabbit or a moorhen. There are lots of partridges up there. Probably they do very well on the stuff spilled at the horse lines in the camps by the roads & elsewhere. They seem to like roosting just inside shell holes.

The Ancre battle was a much finer feat of arms than the Somme. The Somme was partly a surprise, & the enemy was overwhelmed before he was ready, & the awful fighting was his effort to get back; but on the Ancre he was expecting an attack, & had every conceivable advantage, & positions of terrible strength, with good observation, & guns by the hundred. At St Pierre he had a great tunnel, which held 400 men, & these 400 used to lie quiet with machine guns

until our attack had gone past; then they used to come out & shoot it in the back
& destroy it. They did this with huge success; but at last the dodge was
discovered, & then, at the next attack, all our guns centred on the mouth of the
tunnel, & the 400 had a thin chance; for a more hellish thing than a British
barrage you cannot imagine. . . .

It is now time for post. Bless you my dear heart & my dear love to the little
ones. Kiss Tim from me.

Your old love
Jan

[110]                                                      March 14. 1917

M.O.D.C.

I have this day been out to T & beyond, motoring to Poz & then walking. It
had rained all night & was raining hard when we left the car, going tinkle tinkle
on our helmets, & the road, bad even for the Somme, as I knew from of old, was
at its limit. Its limit was not a sticky one, but a soft receptive one at the sides (up
to the shins or calves about) & in the middle a hard one, varied with pools
where old shell holes had been partially filled & then rained on. You could not
tell where the shell holes were, for all was under water, so we went slop slop,
plunge; an old captain & a Portuguese visitor & myself, till we came to a
bottomless bog in a hollow, where a poor old lorry had stuck. Generally a lorry
can get out of anything, but this one was bet [sic], so we left the road then &
walked over graves & shell holes, dodging the bombs with great circumspec-
tion, & pausing now & then to look at the old smashed tanks. The poor old
tanks made a glorious advance in September, & these are their poor old bones,
all camoufle all the colours of the rainbow, & rather heroic-looking, but very
derelict & hic jacety.

T was unchanged; but muddier than usual, & looking very foul & evil in the
rain. We looked at a Tank, & then ploughed over the mud till we came to duck
boards, or gratings pour promener, in the direction of the enemy. We walked
about ½ a mile on filthy duckboards, with filthy shell holes, all full of filthy
water, on both sides of us, & then came to a filthy trench, labelled 'officer's
latrine', with a dead German officer's legs sticking out of the wall, wearing a
rather fine pair of boots. Just beyond the latrine there was a shelter, where
some of our men had once had a fire, & had used old bayonets as pokers. It was
pretty filthy & wet, but we went inside, & sat on some old tins & ate our lunch
& listened to the battle of Bapaume.

By & by we shogged on along the duckboards, past corpses & pieces of the
same, & the usual filthy muck-coloured beastliness of rotten destruction,
which makes the landscape here, till we came to Lucky Way, as it is called,
where we could see a skyline being strafed to hell, & made out a little of the

battle. After we had seen enough of this (& it had no comeliness that we should desire it) we turned home, over a soft muck that broke the Portuguese's heart, & so over the river to our car, which got in for tea, by way of a change. It was the muddiest day I have seen here; but it is certain that spring is coming; the catkins are out, there are snowdrops on the graves at Maricourt, & grass & weeds & buttercups & cow parsley are already green all over parts of the blasted battleground. God knows, if they grow high & cover the bombs & grenades the field will have wary walking, like the adder.

One very touching thing there was. Away up in the squalor, miles from anywhere, there was a rough wooden cross, made of packing case tied together & pencilled To an Unknown British soldier. Someone, perhaps the man who put up the cross, had brought up some imitation violets & put them on the grave. The violets could not have come from anywhere nearer than 20 miles away, so that it was an act of charity, whoever did it.

Dear love to you, my darling. Kiss little Tim & get old Na to write to me.

Your old love

Jan

---

[111]                                                   March 15. 1917.

My dearest heart Con,

Today I had your letter of the 11th & the Macmillan letter. My address is changed; it is

1. (d)

c/o R.T.O.

B.E.F.

Amiens,

France.

& I hope will remain that for some time. Je ne veux pas l'autre.

Today, after backing & filling for an hour, I was taken out to Delville & then to a strange place in a hole, from which I could see a marvellous panorama & (for the first time) the Butte of Warlencourt, which is a white Butte, like a very big chalk tumulus, very plainly visible. The rest of the panorama is big, like the campagna, or like the Salisbury plain country, only not so bold as this last. The skyline of it is mainly trees, the Bois de Loupart, the trees about Bapaume, & (to the east) the trees (or what is left of them) about Le Transloy. Bapaume was plainly visible; houses & ruins, with smoke rising from them, for I fear the Boches have fired them; even if our shells have not; and by the time we get it, it will probably be like Contalmaison or La Boisselle. All the ground up to Bapaume is dark brown desert, just blasted battlefield like these other places, but on the crest you see places not yet blasted, & trees still alive. Looking through a strong telescope I saw into Transloy, where a German squad was marching down a road. However, from what one can see, they will not march in Le Transloy very much longer.

All that bedevilled land was littered with dead Boches in various attitudes of agony. War is certainly the vilest form of crime; & these poor fellows have paid for their rulers thinking otherwise. One man, cut in half, seemed to be drinking at a shell hole. One very common attitude was on the back, with the chest raised, as though gasping for breath. They had been dead for months, & I suppose each of them meant the end of the world for somebody. War is truly hell on earth.

Coming back I noticed how our soldiers had got hold of derelict dogs & made mascots of them. The French dog is a mild beast as a rule & very much a mongrel, but once or twice I have seen a savage one here, which has gone wild on the battlefield & eaten dead men. I saw one pulling at a man's ribs only a few days ago. Our soldiers are wonderfully kind gentle men. I think the dirty misery of the mud makes them look on the horses, mules & dogs as they would look on women. I've seen them cheering up weary horses just as one would cheer a tired child. I don't know what the brains of our officers are like, but the hearts of our men are beautiful & wonderful. There is a dwarf shrub (one single shrub) at Hamel, the only green thing there. One of them has labelled it 'Kew Gardens. Please do not touch.'

Dear love to you my darling, & to Tim & Nana. Kiss them from me.

Your J–

[112]

1. (d).
c/o R.T.O.
B.E.F
Amiens, France.
16-III-1917.

Dearest heart,

Today was something of a day manqué, for we could see nothing in the fog, though we went out to see.

We started out (mighty cold driving) to see the western flank, on the Ancre side, towards Hebuterne, where Edward was, & we got to the place called Serre (for the only indication of the town is that brickdust is mixed with the mud there) & tried (at least I did) to make out the lie of the land. In the push on July 1st our men got right across from about Hamel to Serre, & then had to fight their way back, & had hellish losses poor fellows, for the Boche position there is incredibly strong, as strong as the Turk lines at Anzac, low, sloping hills, parted by gullies, & commanded by other hills on the flanks & in the rear: so it is no wonder that he said Tush, Go to; but all the same he has now gone from there & I don't think will come back, willingly, in our lifetimes. He has been blown & blasted out till his heart failed him.

The ground on these strong positions is infinitely more awful than in the happy vallies near Albert. There he was rushed, & the lines are intact, except where they have been camped on since the push; but all these hills are skinned, gouged, flayed & slaughtered, & the villages smashed to powder, so that no man on earth could ever say that there had been a village there within the memory of man. It is mud, full of holes half full of water, with a few black tree stumps sticking up, & an old tank or two, & any quantity of Boche wire; tons & tons of wire, enough to fence London, & a few of our dugout-chimneys smoking here & there from the ground. The word 'bloody' is on every lip there, & the beastly shellholes for some reason stain the water in them a sort of irony blood colour, like bloody wine; perhaps the explosive affects the ground near the bursts & gives it this power of staining the water. Anyway, you take colour from your surroundings & call it a bloody country, a bloody awful country, & you call your bloody little dog, if you have one, to keep clear of the bloody mules, lest their bloody heels hit him in the eye & rob you of your only solace.

I don't think the Boche will be much longer on the Somme battlefield. He is going back a bit (probably not very far) & even if he goes, as he says, 'according to plan', it cannot be cheerful going for his men. I suppose since July we have booted him 9 or 10 miles. It isn't much. One could walk it in a day, & back again, but to be booted even 9 miles is no joke. Our men would feel it acutely, & they must feel it, too. They fix up all sorts of contrivances for us, spiked helmets with mines beneath them, & corked rum jars with mines inside them, but that is nothing to what he gets as he goes: and the thought, *that he is going back* is one that thrills; the filthy tide recedes. The Boche War game craft is aus ge bloody spielt as they say. Another 18 months & there will be peace on earth (that is, comparative peace).

Dear love to you, my darling. I hope the move isn't an endless anxiety to you. Kiss little Tim from me & send Nana my dear love

Your old love
Jan

---

[113]                                                      March 17.

M.O.D.C.

A year ago tonight I was having dinner (I believe) with Florence[1], & then rushing off to hear Harley's confessions. Now, they, for all I know, are having dinner & confessions together, & I am here wondering when the mails are going to be straight again. I've had nothing from you for two days. A year ago tonight I was getting ready to start home on the morrow. Alas, there is no chance of that yet from here.

Well, today has been good. The Boches are gone from Buèquoy, Achist, Loupart, Bapaume & Le Transloy; from all the long crest where I saw him being shelled, & where I saw a squad of him & from which his shells used to come. He has gone back, leaving his filthy ruins behind him. He is burning & devastating just as if he were marching in as a conqueror. Alas, I don't think he means to go far; but he has now been booted one whole long cannon shot from his original roost on the Somme. Probably we may look to his big offensive being launched within the next few days. I don't know where it will fall, but should say it would be Champagne, where his line is nearest Paris. It can hardly succeed now, for the French must have more guns & stuff than he has, but no doubt it will be sincerely meant on Fritz's part. On the other hand, he may have another go at Ypres.

I still cannot see why he didn't break through at Ypres in Nov, 1914. He had our men beaten dead, & yet whenever he sent in his massed attack, our poor old dismounted cavalry stood-to & gave him rapid rifle fire & withered him. Then he had the whole line open there when he started gas; but he either didn't know, or couldn't make use of his victory. So let us not speak of the Boche as a military genius. As a hard worker & a brave man; & a very ingenious painstaking nasty devil at all kinds of soldier dodges, & as a good preparer & equipper; but as an 'efficient' man; no. He is in the business of soldiery & pays a big staff to write his ads for him: that is how he gets his name.

My dear heart I must stop for post.

Dear love to all.

Your old love

Jan

I've been today to a tragical & terrible gully running into the Ancre. It is called the Boom Ravine. It is between Miramont & Grandcourt, this side of the river. It is a real chalk gully with steep sides 40 feet high & such a scene of smash, ruin, death, wreck, waste & mutilation as you never saw. The Boche are lying dead all over the place & it is Sodom & Gomorrah & Gehenna, & the valley of Acheron all rolled into one. I don't think anything can top the Boom Ravine; though 'Le Barque' is said to.

1. Mrs Florence Lamont.

---

[114]                                        1 (d).
                                     c/o R.T.O.
                                        B.E.F.
                                       Amiens.
                                       France.
                                 March 18, 1917.

Dearest heart,

It is very interesting to be here when things are happening. The Boches have gone back a good step, & there is some chance of their going further, though slowly, bit by bit. Their main stand will be made a good deal further back, after various surrenders of ground. They talk of a new strong line of theirs, 'the Hindenburg Line', all made of concrete, with baths, h & c, & indoor sanitation etc, the usual plumber's paradise that goes into their American propaganda. But however strong it may be, it cannot be stronger than Thiepval, the Leipzig, the Schwaben, & the Stuff Redoubts. Concrete is nothing compared with earth, & with enough guns one can blow them out of anything. It is mainly a question of dry weather that will let the destroyed roads bear our heavy guns & the traffic of munitions. With dry weather, guns & shells can pass. With the roads in mud Julius Caesar himself would be no more than a subaltern, & little can be done.

Some of the men here were in Bapaume itself yesterday, the day the Boches left it, & they got some spoils of war there, casques, a rifle or two, & a packet of Boche Field Dressing, made of treated paper instead of lint; the Boche having run short of the same a year ago. They said that the Boches had set fire to the town & that it was on fire in many places, & that they were registering their guns on it. Today & the subsequent days they will shell it, & probably knock it into the likeness of Pozieres; though at present there is as much of it left as there is of Albert. Their policy will be to smash, burn & destroy everything they leave, from the palace to the cottage, & what they do not wantonly destroy they will probably defend, so that we shall have to destroy it. It is a sad prospect for the poor people of Northern France & Belgium; though one still believes a little in justice, & feels that they will be paid. The Boche cannot triumph being what they are. In their advance, when they were proud, they used wantonly to use the beds of France & Belgium as latrines. They thought that they showed their superiority so. Now they are so short of bed linen that they have to dress their wounds with chiffons de papier; so justice is already at work on them. Ca commence.

One rather neat thing happened at Bapaume. Before they left, they mined the roads & blew them up, so as to check our advance. One big mine, which was to have made a hole 30 feet deep & 50 feet across, in the middle of the road, missed the road altogether, & will now serve as a neat drainage tank to take the mud from the road. Deo solis gloria, as Drake used to say, when he had a lucky stroke at piratery.

I saw a gun yesterday going back to Hospital after being in action daily since the middle of last September. In the 6 months, it had sent practically 200 tons of iron & high explosive into the enemy lines. When you consider the multitude of such guns firing all along our front at this rate you get some idea of the mass of metal being flung at the Boches. The normal human being needs, I suppose, about 3 tons of food, drink & fuel per year, to do himself well, so the one gun ate in the half year the keep of 70 or 80 for one year.

I told you that I saw a German squad in Le Transloy. Well, the squad is gone & Le Transloy is ours; the Moor has taken his last look over the ridge, & now cannot see any part of the Somme battlefield. The trees will grow green over us, & not over him, in the Bois de Loupart & on the ridge by Bapaume; and all our maps of the field, which began at Albert & ended at Bapaume, may be put aside, & new ones, beginning at Bapaume, may be begun. We begin a new geography.

This is the 3rd day with no lett, alas, alas.

Dear love to you my dear heart. I hope things go well.

Kiss the little Timcat from me & send my love to Na.

Your old love<br>Jan

---

[115]                                                     19 March.

My dearest heart,

I got 4 letts from you tonight & two last night, one of the 14th & 2 of the 15th. Thank you so much. . . .

Yesterday was probably Sunday. Neville L took me to lunch at a mess near here, & then we went to see some prisoners' camps. I have passed many hundreds of prisoners on roads, but this was really my first sight of them near by. They live in very nice huts, very clean, dry, warm & snug, & though it may be a tightish fit, they have more room than sailors have in a ship of war, & after the trenches & the fear of death the huts must seem like little paradises to them. They have rigged up little lockers for themselves & all sorts of hooks for hanging their clothes, & shelves for their pots & pans.

But the interesting thing was to see the Boche war machine still at work. Directly we came into the camp with the Commandant a Boche corporal ran up, halted, advanced, gave himself a clockwork jerk, & saluted. He was a shifty looking card, who reminded me of Uriah Heep, & partly of some of those butlers in fiction, who are scrupulously correct, & at last cut their masters' throats. The Commandant, to rag him, said 'We've taken Bapaume & Peronne today', & he answered in good English, exactly like a butler, 'Yes, sir? Have you indeed, sir?' What he thought behind his butler mask I could not tell, & I got from his face the idea that these people are the Japanese of Europe, a race of patient industrious homicidal Jesuits with an appalling power of hand & no power of mind. Presently the Corporal cracked his voice at some men, just as you would crack a whip, & the poor devils did clockwork jerks, like a jointed doll suddenly hit in the middle, & jerked themselves stiff & saluted. Then the Corporal cracked his voice again & they unjerked themselves, & squirmed & looked like very nice fellows. One of them had an interesting face but was evidently in consumption, being ghastly thin. He was an artist, not a very good one, but rather like Dauber. He painted British soldiers attacking, & I think officers buy them from him.

We then went to another, much larger camp, in a charming chalk valley near a forest, where they run a saw mill. This was much like the Boche chez lui, for they had toiled like the good workers they are to make everything as neat as new pins. Each hut had a garden neatly fenced with white chalk & then with wicker. Each garden, instead of being planted with plants, was stuck about with bits of white chalk, in patterns of hearts & doves & cupids, so that each looked like a little cemetery. There were more corporals & butlers & jesuits & homicides & a lot more clicking & jerking, & a great many big slow kindly stupid sheep who grinned & kept working all the time. I know Germany now & shall never go there I hope. I have been there, & I hope not to have to go again. Good God, they are the devil.

Today I went out nearly to Bapaume to see the Butte of Werlencourt, which (I suppose) is a chalk tumulus about as big as Kendals house, only I think taller. It must be artificial, & I suppose it must be a tumulus. Only last week, I saw shells falling like rain all round & over it & now the Boche can't range it, & it is about as safe as Lambourne Downs. I walked on to Le Barque, which must once have been a pretty village, but is now a fearful ruin of smashed houses & torn trees. There was a poor starved cat there, but it had had enough of men & I could not catch her. Outside there were a lot of enemy dead, torn in two & across & generally bedevilled, poor men, & a lot of rats, who probably live upon them, as they were rather gnawed. After that I walked on to Delville, & so to Albert where the car met me.

It is said that an Australian patrol first found that Bapaume was empty. The officer in charge of it came back to his Colonel & said

'They've hopped the bloody twig. They're out of it.'

Col. 'Who? The Boche? Out of Bapaume?'

Officer. 'Yes. The bloody place is empty.'

Col. 'You're a bloody liar.'

Officer. 'Bloody liar be damned. You give me the bloody battalion & I'll take the bloody place, right now.'

Alas, alas, the word bloody is on every lip & in every speech.

Dear love to you & to Tim & to Nana.

I'm so proud of Tim's letter.

Your old love

Jan

---

[116]                                           20 March, 1917

M.D.O.C.

I hope so much that your cold is better & that it has not gone again to Tim. Take care of your poor throat.

Today, being rather wet & there being no cars, is so far an off day, & I expect to lunch indoors for the first time since I came here. I am not sorry, for I had a gruelling day yesterday, walking from Le Sars to Le Barque, from there to Bois de Delville, across the battlefield, & from the Bois to Albert, some 25 or 30 Kiloms all told, with the necessary divagations; for there is no walking direct. One comes to a trench half full of water & has to walk 30 yards to find a crossing place. Then the ground, where there are no trenches, consists mainly of big holes & wire entanglements, & again one has to wander to find a crossing, & then, when one is through, one finds a row of duck-boards or claies de trottoir, gratings in other words, zigzagging anywhere, & one walks along them bien content d'étre off the mud, & not much minding where they go as long as they provide a path. As they always zigzag to avoid shellholes you do not go direct along them, & as the battlefield is shaven & burnt quite clean of landmarks you cannot see how you are heading. The battlefield beyond the woods is simply burnt monotonous moor now. Can you imagine Elstree & Radlett burnt (trees & all) level with the ground for ten miles by eight miles, & then try to find your way across, from one place to another, each looking exactly alike, & each burnt roll like the last, & each lynchet (of which there are many, generally much longer than with us) dug into in the same way, for dug-outs, stores or batteries, in one blank muddy monotony.

It is all pretty evil, but when you get up on a height & look down, you see all the shellholes which hold water blinking like eyes with a blear on them & that is horrid. You look over the beastly waste, & see a greyish heap, which is a dead enemy, & a yellowish heap with some dark leather near it which shows where one of our men went down. If you go near to the greyish heap you will see the enemy, & if you go near to the yellowish heap you will see our own man's grave, with the man's feet sticking out & his hands showing & his shrapnel helmet on his chest, & perhaps his rifle jammed into the mud as his gravestone. All over the battlefield there are crows, starlings, hawks & partridges, pies and larks, in great numbers, & many rats, more than you ever saw at Hampden. They will follow the army & eat the dead & be a plague & a pestilence for years.

I don't see how the land can be cultivated, for apart from the vast holes made by the shells & the monstrous holes made by the mines, & the unending holes of the trenches, the place is sown with tons & tons of unexploded explosives all ready to go off if hit hard enough. Perhaps they will get steam ploughs & drag them across from safe distances, & then, when the ploughs blow up, no one will be killed. They say that a British general is already starting a corps of agriculture with some theory of his own about it. It will be rather a score for him if he brings it off.

They tell a story here of a Br staff captain 'telling off' an Australian private for not saluting. The Australian patted him on the shoulder, & said 'Young man, when you go home, you tell your mother that today you've seen a real live bloody soldier.'

There is another tale of a Br gunner, who was weary & hot during the terrific firing on the Somme in July. He was heard to say, 'If God hears this bloody noise he'll drop a bloody meteor on us & put an end to the bloody war.'

I've had no time for Icelandic; none whatever; nor for any other reading.

Dear love to you & to Tim & to Nana (whom you will soon be having home again, hurray)

Your lover

Jan

---

[117]                                                        21 March.

Today I expect to go back to Albert for a time, to live at the Club there, though how different it will be there now; it will be a town of the dead, with the guns almost or quite out of earshot and the movement of the campaign already many miles away. My job will seem like an archaeology, moving there in the mud of forgotten events. The advance has made last week last century.

As usual, the old enemy god played up & sent rain, to make the roads bad, but not enough to hurt. Now he sends cold, with snow, of a regular March type; so no spring here yet, though one sees snowdrops here & there, on graves & in shops. Still, in three weeks time there must be some kind of a spring.

You would have thought, that the enemy would have learned a little, & been perhaps humble, & eager to win the sympathy of neutrals now, as a brave people about to endure disaster; but all through this retreat he has been repeating Belgium. He has systematically destroyed what he could not carry away. Everything easily moveable has been pillaged & sent back to their dirty nest the Vaterland, & everything not easily moveable has been fouled & broken. Bureaus, mirrors, tables, sofas, have been smashed with axes, fruit trees have been cut, lopped or ringed. Beds have been used as latrines, so have baths & basins, & the officers who used them thus have left their cards on the mess. Houses, churches, cottages, farms, barns & calvaries have been burnt, blown up, pulled down or gutted. Every dirty wanton devilry of rape, defilement & degradation has been committed on the inhabitants. In Peronne, the books of the library were taken down, defiled with human excrement, & then put back upon the shelves. In the same town a poor cat was found crucified by these devils, & they had put a cap on its head & a cigar in its mouth. I can understand mental degenerates doing these things, but not men. They are not the acts of men. They are not the acts of beasts.

I think they will be punished. I think they are beginning to give, though I don't think they will break this year; but I don't think that anyone ought to dream of making truce with such a spirit until they are broken. They are not civilised human beings. They will bloodily suffer for what they have done during this retreat.

The worst of this job is, that if I stay in Amiens I cannot always get a car to the battlefield, nor ever be sure of getting one once in 3 days, while if I go to Albert I cannot have a room to myself, nor any privacy of any kind, nor any letters, while most of the letters I write get lost or not delivered. Still, I must go to Albert, for at least while I am there I can see the battlefield, which is what I came out for to see.

Thanks to N.L. who has been extraordinarily helpful & nice, I have had 9 or 10 days here, with almost daily visits to the field; but now that so much country has been abandoned to us out Noyon way the cars go there & I am left darkling; there being a grand manque of cars, owing to the awful roads which crock them. Any sort of a ploughed field is better than one of these roads to a walker.

I suppose the Boche will begin his offensive as soon as he has got his new line arranged. The chief gorilla Hindenburg[1] is in the West now, where I hope he'll get his ugly mug kapouté[2]. From what one can gather, the Boche is glum, & feels himself kapouté already.

This letter ought just about to reach you on our day, with my blessings on it & you.

Dear love to you & to Tim & Nana.

Your old love

Jan

1. Field Marshal Hindenburg, together with his nominal subordinate, General Ludendorff, had been in charge of the Eastern Fronts, effectively withstanding, then crushing the Russian armies. This March saw the outbreak of the Russian revolution, the abdication of the Tsar, and the end of any serious Russian military effort against Germany and Austria-Hungary. This enabled the celebrated Hindenburg-Ludendorff partnership to assume command on the Western Front, restoring much of the German morale, and very nearly defeating the Allied armies, March–July, 1918.

2. A French variation of 'Kapout', a German rendering of the Latin 'Caput', a head. Germans anxious to surrender might cry 'Kamarade, pas kapout', roughly, 'don't finish me'.

---

[118]　　　　　　　　　　　　　　　　　　　　　The Club.

　　　　　　　　　　　　　　　　　　　　　　　　March 22.

M.D.O.C.

This has missed the post, owing to Denis Browne coming in to tea. His brother has just been hit in the leg with a bit of bomb & has gone back to Blighty, & he & his set are moving up to the line again, starting tomorrow; so unless he is put in to camp, in or near Bapaume, I shall not see him again for some time; and I'm sorry, because the person whom one has known at home, even slightly, like that, has a special value out here. I can tell you, one longs for a familiar face. There is a line in the Wanderings of Usheen[1].

'O sweet to me even were now bald Conan's slanderous tongue.'

Today I've been over a lot of the line as it was on the 1st July, between La Boisselle & Carnoy. It is all a gradual slope towards the Boche line, & the Boche had certainly the easier task of the two. He had only to sit still & shoot.

If you will look at the map, you will see a place called Becourt, which is on a hill just behind our old front line. Of course, it is knocked about a bit, but it is in the midst of trees & there are real habitable houses in it, & it looks pretty & quiet & peaceful. So does Carnoy, further along, in our old line. But directly you leave these places you come to woods which are razed & villages which are obliterated; Mametz & Fricourt, with a broad valley or ravine between them & the Fricourt & Mametz woods.

Yet the ground shows you plainly that these places were taken (in the main, & comparatively speaking) by surprise. Fricourt, a place as strong as Gibraltar in its way, was surrounded, rather than assaulted, & after these places & Montauban on the right hand had fallen, the whole of the first position was ours. But there is a valley running n.e. from between Mametz & Fricourt, & about a mile from Mametz it has steep banks, on the top of one of which, the east, is Montauban. On the top of the west bank, a slope begins, & runs gradually, very very gradually, backwards & upwards to a small wood called Bazentin the Grand wood, which is the highest point. This sloping hill has a valley on either side of it

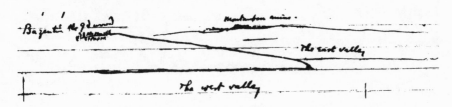

& here the Boche had a citadel after his own heart, & here, for the first time, the real typical Somme shellfire began. From the Bazentin time till the end, the fighters had to destroy the whole surface of the earth at each advance.

The queer thing is that many moles survived (they are everywhere) & today I found a dead weasel, killed (apparently) by the stroke of a hawk or owl.

This place is closing down, alas, as the house is wanted for a G.H.Q. of sorts, or else a hospital; so I shall have to find new quarters.

Will you please arrange me a credit of £30 in Paris?

Dear love to you. Kiss little Tim for me & Nana too.

Your old love

Jan

1. A poem by W. B. Yeats, who actually wrote, 'Ah, sweet to me now were even bald Conan's slanderous tongue.'

The Club.
                                                             March 23rd.
M.O.D.C.

I am away from all letters & the chance of letters; unless some eminent man comes to N.L. & asks to see the battlefield; then N.L. will send letters out with him, which will be muy bonito. But the battlefield is vieu jeu & passée. Eminent men don't want to see it now; they want to see Bapaume & Peronne & Nerle & these places, where they can still hear the guns; the war has passed on.

I'm afraid the English are a very 'bagging' lot. One of the officers stole the telephone here last night, cut it loose & pocketed it, comme butin de guerre. This was about tea time. I suppose he was an R E officer & liked these things & knew about them, & thought the little bell would remind him of home.

Today, after break, I walked to Ovillers, along the old English line, as far as it remains unbuilt on, or undestroyed by roads, railways & cavalry. I get from these walks a far more vivid sense of what the Boche fortifications were. They seem to have been immensely deep & strong wherever there was any chance of a direct attack; and the ground runs down to the English line in a series of tongues. The Boche had enormous trenches across the ends of these tongues, & enormous redoubts on their highest ground, & for the flanks they trusted to machine guns: thus.

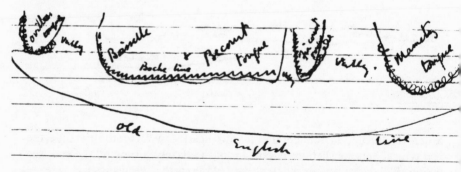

This may give you very roughly the idea of it. Directly they were turned out of these positions they were almost on tableland & had to go back a mile or so, to the positions Thiepval, Pozieres, Contalmaison, Bazentin; & these places, naturally strong, were most desperately held, & were only won by a concentrated & awful gunfire. The Boche did not know what gunfire is till he tried to hold that new line; I am quite sure that the early fighting on the right of our line succeeded by audacity; it was a surprise, & the bombardment there was nothing.

Ovillers is entirely destroyed, hardly a brick left whole in it, & just beyond it is a field littered with broken skulls & bones. I think dogs have been at work there.

This afternoon I went to see the 2nd big crater at Boisselle. It is a terrible place, as big as Piccadilly Circus & 90 feet deep. It is much more awful than the other. . . .

I've had 1 bath since I left home & may get another next week.

Dear love to you my darling & to Tim & to Nana. I pray God little Na won't be heart-broken to be leaving.

Your old love

Jan

I don't think your letters are censored. Mine may be, but then over here that has to be done, or secrets might get thro.

---

[120]                                                          The Club.
                                                          March 24. 1917.
M.O.D.C.

Today no lets, so I suppose the cars weren't out this way, but I can't grumble as I had 4 yesterday.

My constant solace here is the Y.M.C.A. You must never let anyone attack this excellent body. They are doing quite first rate work here, & without them I could not even live here. They run this Club, 18 miles from a store, at 15 francs a day (4 meals & a bed) which is just 5 francs a day less than the mess at Amiens. When they close next week I don't know quite how I can manage to do my work. I'm afraid I shall have to give up living out here, live in A, & 'work the lorries'.

You have never worked the lorries, so I will tell you how it is done. You go out onto the road & stop the first likely looking lorry & ask for a lift in her. Then you climb up near the driver, if there is room, or onto the load behind, if there isn't, & then away you go at a good 10 miles an hour. Generally there is an Australian officer on the sacks behind, & by watching him you learn how to spit, & so combine instruction with pleasure. Then generally there are several others, men or officers, having a lift at the same time, & they are a jolly nice lot, either kind, & so you travel happily; though unless fully loaded these lorries bump like the devil. When this place closes on the 31st, I shall have to go to Amiens & work the lorries out to the battlefield & back every day; or perhaps vary them with the ambulances, which are much quicker.

Today in the forenoon I walked out to the Leipzig salient, which is just south of Thiepval, & from there traced out the line of the British attack in July. It is a very very strong place, & all smashed to ruin, for it was very important to the Boche. As soon as he was out of it he lost sight of half our positions, so he fought very hard to hold it. I can't describe it very well except by saying that the ground looks like this:–

A very gentle slope up, with enormous trenches at the top, & also a sort of quarry, which makes the top look almost like a crater. Then linked up with the fort at the top, & level with it, is another awful place called the Wonder Work, with a big German trench-mortar still in place on it, & then just beyond is the broken bell of Thiepval. Looking down from this beastly smash of old rags & filth & skulls & legs & old tins & broken weapons, you see the lovely Ancre valley, with big blobs of blue water in the copses & woods of its swamps. My dear, I can hardly tear myself away from the Ancre valley after seeing these battle places. The water comes out of the chalk all along the valley as clear & lovely as at Lollingdon & I long to gaze & gaze on it. Coming back to lunch I got a lift in a lorry.

After lunch I went out to Fricourt again, & all over the Boche positions, which are the very limit for strength. You never saw such places; & they are everywhere, wherever the Boche came. But we weren't quite such fools as he thought. Instead of butting our heads against the iron point we cut off the spear at the handle, & caught all

the Boche who happened to be in the point. . . .

Dear love to you my Darling. I do hope all this worrying week will straighten out.

Kiss Tim from me. My fond love to Na.

> Your old love
> Jan

---

[121]                                                           Aim.

                                                      26 March, 1917.

M.O.D.C.

Today being our day I am glad to have a few minutes to myself to write to you my dear heart & to say bless you.

Your letter of the 23rd reached me today, just as I came in, all covered with mud. We have indeed had some good times, & what is more, we will have other & better I hope, when this upheaval is ended. So cheer up, my dear, & let us just look forward quietly to that time, whether this year or next or the year after.

I know nothing of course, but should say that Fritz meant to go back to shorten his line by some 100,000 men, & to delay our own push; but though he had the devil's own luck, in the way of mist, to cover him, he was caught, & had to go much quicker than he meant; & though he is now on the line he means to fight us on & has saved his 100,000 men, his people must be down in the mouth about it, & of course the French & our own men are full of joy & confidence, & are already strafing the new line, & the summer will no doubt bring tidings.

I went yesterday to Clery & from there walked into Peronne. Clery is on the Somme & all smashed to bits, but a lovely place once; chalk country with a wide river, half reed bed. The road to Peronne is pretty flat & much dug about by Fritz, who was holding it only 8 days ago. Away to the left, on very gently rising ground, you see what looks like a Roman camp rather built on & shaded by trees, & very much dug about by shells. This is the famous Mont St Quentin, of which you may have read these last days. Nature made it a very strong place, but the enemy had encircled it with several lines of trench, each line protected with walls of wire, & up on the top he had his observation posts, watched the land for miles round, & telephoned the news to his batteries.

His trenches were in first rate order, & his rubbish was still fresh; German books, bombs, wire, shells, notices, duckboards, rags, caps, uniforms, rifles & graves; & the road quite beautifully kept; rather a change from the poor old shell blasted road to Miraumont, through which I have so often ploughed, over the ankles.

Nearer to Peronne, there were some of his dead, & then we saw Peronne, & longed to have him by the throat. It was a fair little town, say like Bury St Edmunds or Hereford, with Vauban fortifications & a quite exquisite toy cathedral, about the size & beauty of St Margaret's Westminster, & all surrounded by the chalk river moat, & like a little jewel. These damned dogs had blown up the cathedral & pulled out the front of every house by teams of horses & had pillaged & sacked & taken away & defiled, till the town was like an earthquake & a debauch, & no whole house or tree or thing left in it.

Before that, we passed through Combles, which is, as it were, Mitcheldean blown to pieces. In the chalk at Combles there are dene holes, which they call catacombs, & I went down into them a long way, & saw where Fritz had housed 200 soldiers in the bowels of the earth. Fritz likes to get well under the ground. The hole slants down fully 50 yards before there is a shaft, & there are rooms, r & l, possibly passages.

Today, I went out to Hamel & Anchonvillers, to the left of the battle, & saw where our men failed to get through in July. No troops in the world could have done better, & our graves are all over the hills there, some hundreds of them, & there are stray heads & feet & hands lying about, & terrible rags of bodies. On one poor body there was a bit of prayer book with a Psalm for the 17th day, with a verse which struck me very deeply, something like:– 'Thou hast broken his hedges, thou hast torn down his strong places.' The poor man had been killed only a few yards from our line, but the enemy's hedges are gone from there, & in all those rolls of blasted moor there is no living enemy at all. I put up a rabbit in our old lines, & any number of partridges. Now I must stop my dear dear heart. Bless & keep you, & kiss little Tim & dear Nana from me.

Your old love
Jan

---

[122]                                                                    27. III.

Dearest heart,

We are in rather late tonight although we started early, so this will only be a scrap I'm afraid. I've been worrying all day, thinking of you with all the worry of moving & me not there to help. I do hope that it is going well, & that it has not all been one long strain & nuisance.

The people in the invaded districts, now liberated, say that the enemy is really short of food & that he has already eaten all the cats of N France. You need not believe this. It probably only means that the cats were killed as a part of Kultur[1], or for not saluting, or for night-wandering or something; or that they were only killed in one district, for fear of the mange, or because the Kommandant disliked them. I don't see any sign of the Boche being short of food. The newly taken prisoners are well fed & burly, & from the look of their dug-outs, which are always exceedingly good, but not nearly so good as the French ones, they seem to be doing themselves well still. He is short of india rubber, which makes him use carts instead of lorries, & this saves his roads, even if it multiplies his transport.

Today we went to Hamel & walked along the old lines to Beaumont Hamel, which the Boche used to think impregnable. Near Hamel, we came on the dead of our early July fighting there, which failed, & on our way we passed & trod on the relics & remains of hundreds of English soldiers, who are buried just as they fell. They had about 200 yards to go, across No Man's Land, & they were caught by machine guns placed so as to sweep whole stretches of these approaches, & there they fell, & there they lie, partly buried & partly not, & the rats burrow in them & their heads lie all over the place & their boots & feet & hands.

Further on, we saw the immense & awful crater of Beaumont, which is 100 yards long, 20 deep and 50 across, but though it is very terrible, it is less imposing than the Boisselle one, because it is not one vast white hole, but streaky, red & white, & so looks like a butcher's shop instead of an immense white sepulchre.

By Hamel Church we saw 2 paysannes & their man digging in the ruins of their home to find some papiers which they had buried there 2½ years ago. I do hope they found them. Poor souls, their village was smashed to smithereens, & their house was 3 parts of walls, with a bit of floor on top of them, under which I have often sheltered from the snow, & a cellar where 2 soldiers have their dugout.

Beaumont Hamel lies in a ravine, with ravines leading out of it & into it, &

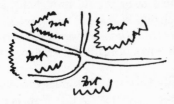 high ground between each ravine. It was nearly impregnable, but we shelled it a lot, & then attacked at dawn in thick mist & caught every soul in the place. That was really the break up of the battle. Fritz has gone back steadily ever since, & hasn't won a yard of ground anywhere.

Dear love to you my darling. Kiss dear Tim & Nana from me.

Your old love

Jan

1. Like the French Revolutionary 'Virtue' this is difficult to translate in one word. It implies rather more than 'culture': a compression of all the German civilised values, achievements, ideals, and general superiority. When used by British and French writers, the tone is usually sardonic.

---

[123]                                                  March 29. 1917.

My dearest heart,

Alas, very different this year from last, when I was just back from A, full of a mission well accomplished, & happy to be among you all again. There is the same war & the same beastly weather, exceeding cold & wet, but my dear love's away, & no near prospect of home yet.

Now as to letters. W.H. may do *Good Friday* for autumn if he likes, as the Somme book can hardly be ready in time, as far as one can see it from here. Eagle[1] as far as I can learn, is either W. H. Squire, a tenth rate parodist, or Gerald Gould[2], who married the Ayrton woman. Take no count of him, in either case. What do you read the N.S. for anyhow? It is a dull thing, written, apparently, by a suffragette, an unseated liberal member, two C.O.'s an undergraduate, & an office boy. . . .

You will be having dear Na tomorrow. Would to God I could be there to bring her home. Tell her that I have been rather chatty, in spite of the cold, but think that all my little friends are now nipped in the bud. One cannot avoid chattiness on the battlefield & sleeping in these camps & places. Mine were little piebald ones, very frisky in front, but rather sedate abaft the beam. However, if I have the eggs still on me you will no doubt see them for yourself. Please God, however, they may be gone now. I went out to A today in a succession of lorries, getting off when one stopped & taking another as soon as it came along. It was a beastly cold wet muddy day. In A, I heard two soldiers talking about the smells of war. One said

'Now the spring's coming along we'll begin to smell the old Boches again. They're a lot buried just round our place.'

'Yes', said the other, 'I expect they'll be a bit Camemberty.' I walked out to the old front lines near La Boisselle & had a look at Fritz's old stronghold, & the immense crater, in snow-white chalk, which blew so many of him to pieces. The shaft of the mine was 470 yards long, & 70 tons of powder were exploded, & a pound of powder used to cost a shilling, & a foot of shafting used to cost a pound.

I came back partly in a lorry, partly in an ambulance (which is much quicker & not so jolty) & am now safe at home. No news here, except that Fritz is in very good spirits, well-fed, & very confident of victory; different indeed from the old Pozieres time, when he had had enough. Still, I suppose he will soon be shaken up again, & if he didn't like our shell fire then he will like it less now. Our shell fire is hell itself; there has been nothing more terrible in the world.

The corn is a shade greener, & there is a bud or two on rare bushes; but it is still February here. I'm afraid it must be the same with you. Dear love to you, my dear heart.

Kiss little Tim & my darling Nana from me & give them both my love.

Your old love
Jan

1. 'Solomon Eagle', the name adopted by J. C. Squire, for his 'Books in General' column in the New Statesman. Sir John Collings Squire (1884–1958) was a poet, journalist, critic, editor, and founder of the cricket team featured in A. G. Macdonnell in *England, their England*. He had already published a poem *If Wordsworth had written the Everlasting Mercy* which Masefield might not have appreciated, and had several times mocked his verse, before admitting that, with *Reynard the Fox*, Masefield had 'pulled it off'. The original Solomon Eagle was a seventeenth-century religious fanatic who would stride naked through Charles II's London foretelling the Apocalypse and the destruction of the sinful capital.

2. Gerald Gould (1885–1939), poet, critic, journalist, associated with the Daily Herald and Georgian verse.

---

[124]                                                                    30 March.

M.D.O.C.

. . . My days are crowded & tiring. Up at 7, break 7:30, off in a car at 8, on the field about 10, wander & plod in the slough & plough & shellholes & trenches all day long & get back, dead beat, nearly always too late for tea, at about 6 or 6.30; then back to my little room over the railway to write a letter to you, & at 7.15 I change & go to mess, which lasts from about 8 to 9.15 or so, as there are long pauses between courses so that the servants may wash the very limited number of plates. After dinner, we have all to wait for what is called the conference, when the orders for the cars for next morning are given out, & when this has been settled it is time for bed.

My poor darling Na's letter wrings my heart. It seems we wring poor little Na's gentle soul whatever we do.

The German prisoners are generally glad to get out of the firing; but a few officers & n.c.os, to whom the army was the life's profession, are grieved & do not settle down well. They all say that our shell-fire was hell on earth, & that if all our shells had burst the war would have been over. They think that we cannot possibly beat them, & that at the end of this year we shall realise that & come to an arrangement, & that then, after a few more years of preparation they will destroy us, root & branch, & sow our sites with salt.

I was in High Wood today at about the time little Na came in to L'pool st. It is still full of German dead. They must have lost very very heavily there; & the position is very strong, & they had been cunning with it. They had a small concrete fort in the middle of it, for one big gun, & all sorts of hidden machine gun lairs. Up in one corner we had blown them up with a mine. It is clay soil there, so there was this great clay grassless bowl, 30 yards across, with dirty water at the bottom, & German corpses & hands & skulls & books & rags all littered down the sides. All that corner was a pash of dead men, & outside there were endless shell holes, full of stinking water, & rags hanging in barbed wire, & blasted ground. Away by Achiet I saw an observation balloon blown away in the gale. It went up on its end into the clouds & I never saw it again. Coming back I made the 25 miles in 6 different lorries; rather a feat.

Dear love to you my Darling, & to Tim & to Na.

Your old love

Jan

---

[125]                                                          31st March.

M.D.O.C.

This at least is the end of March; one of the coldest, wettest snowiest & beastliest months I ever remember to have spent; the world is all February here; & we have pouring rain with hail. Day by day, the month has made me hate the war & curse it more & more bitterly; but it is no use cursing. I'm afraid we must just grit our teeth & prepare for another two years before the real danger, the peace, can begin. I don't know what you think of states & the world now, but I say, with Raleigh, 'give me my pilgrim's scrip of quiet', & let me be free of both, with my Con & my little ones, forever & ever & ever.

I've been out ever since & this morning, & it is now nearly 7. I have the colour & the hunger of a ploughman, from being out in the air thus, 11 hours a day, but the mud takes the edge off the keenness; 11 hours in the mud is enough.

I know nothing of where you are nor what you are doing & suffering (quite enough, I fear, with all these troubles on you) but I hope (from the silence) that you are actually en route for the new house, & perhaps even getting in to it, with Timcat & little Na. Would I were making a 4th.

We went today to B'mont Hamel again, up a deathy gully called Y ravine, & so to the big crater, which looks like a pit of dirty putty smeared all down with blood, & with chemicals brewing in little pits at the bottom, as though the little pits were lice upon it. From there we went into B'mont, where we saw a Boche dugout, of the usual superior kind; smart, fashionable Boche wall paper, 'tapestry on the walls', the sergeant called it, cretonne ceilings, 'good' furniture, electric fittings, 'a ball-room, three storys down' (the sergeant again, probably meaning the men's quarters) & a little kitchen near the door. It was dark & dirty; & anyhow, these dugouts, however splendid, are all alike, & not one of them is as convenient, nice, or attractive, or as possible for human life, as the larder at Lollingdon or the area at Well Walk[1]. To the devil with all this talk of Boche efficiency. War is a degradation of life, & these 'splendid' dugouts are fit only for the degraded beings who like war. Paupers would refuse them in time of peace.

I cannot make any estimate of coming home yet. The field is really a vast one, & very very confusing, being, in a way, so like, now that it has been so devastated. Then I am worried as to the permanency of my appointment, now that the usual two-monthly man-panic has begun again; though not very much. . . .

By the way: Do you know if they *did* censor G.B.S.[2] & what he said about it all? He was much liked over here & I believe entirely won the heart of the C-in-C, but then the C-in-C is a wonderful man himself & would know his brother.

After leaving Beaumont we went to Miramont, whence I walked alone, across a prairie of bedevilled mud, sprinkled with graves & rags & wreck, past the smash of Pys to the abomination of Courcelette, & from there to the filthy ghost of Martinpuich & so to Bazentin, where I met the car again & came home. I don't think I saw anything interesting, except some little rifle grenades of the enemy's, which seemed neat. The day was wild, stormy & very clear, so that one had a good view of the field. If you go to Pozieres on a clear day, you can really see the whole field: Albert, Sailly, Bapaume, Miramont, Puisieux, Mesuil: & that is very wonderful. Alas, it is dress time, being almost mess time. Dear love to you, my darling, & dear love to Nana & Tim.

Your old love,<br>Jan

Please stablish my credit anon.

1. The street in Hampstead where the Masefields had a house. The well water had

alleged medicinal properties, which resulted in a brief attempt to make eighteenth-century Hampstead a fashionable spa.

2. In February, 1917, Bernard Shaw, invited by General Haig, and conducted by C. E. Montague, toured Flanders, visiting the Somme front, Ypres, Arras, Vimy Ridge and talking in many messes. In 1914, his 'Common Sense about the War', published by *The New Statesman*, written in the teeth of the prevailing, though temporary, war hysteria, angered many people, and must certainly have irritated Masefield.

---

[126]                                                    2nd April. 1917.

My dearest heart,

I couldn't write at all yesterday, as I was in the car from 8 a.m. till 9 pm, & got home, on a broken car, dead beat, at about 11. All the same, it was a rather wonderful day. . . .

About yesterday. We went first to Sailly Sallisel, on the east of the battlefield, a crest of moor once very important, as it commanded a huge tract of landscape, & gave direct observation over it. It once had a famous road along it, said to be the finest road in France, used for motor trials; but the whole crest has been so shelled that the road is not distinguishable now from the other mud, & no known motor could go a yard on it anywhere. The ground there is littered with the beastly little blue egg bombs used by the French, & if these were not very conspicuous by their colour the walking in those parts would be dangerous.

As we got there, we saw one of our 'sausage' observation balloons going up from the valley. They are tethered balloons, & they are let out by a winch to 1000 or 1500 feet high or so, & 2 men sit in a basket under them & spy out the land with strong glasses, magnifying 8 or 10 diameters. This balloon was, I suppose, about 2 miles from us, & far down below us.

He had not been up 5 minutes when we heard our anti-aircraft guns giving out a furious strafe in the valley, & I saw shrapnel bursting not far from this balloon; & someone cried out 'By God, there's a bloody Boche aeroplane'. In another second, I had my glasses out, & just as I got them on, the balloon burst into a mass of flames, & I saw first one & then the other observer hop over the car's side with his parachute, drop like a stone, & then steady out beautifully, like a little slowly descending white mushroom. The balloon burnt furiously for some 5 seconds, like a vast sausage of fire, & then collapsed down & I was afraid would fall on the parachutists, but it missed them both, & I think (but am not sure) that they reached the ground safely. At the same instant, while the heaven was all one flame & smoke there, the Boche aeroplane wheeled out & was off & got clear away, & I must say deserved his luck, for it was a most dashing piece of work, & the speed of his wheel away was superb. The whole thing only took about ten seconds, & we, as Chaucer says, were not worth a bene & might go blow the bukkes home. It was the Boche's game.

After this, we went on in the rain & the mud to Peronne, where we went in the rain & the mud to the top of Mont St Quentin, where we stood in the rain & the mud & cursed them both. It is all smashed to mess, but was a fortress fit for the Romans, as strong as even the Boche could make a place. We heard that Poincaré[1] was coming to Peronne, so we waited for him there, & so did a lot of poor soldiers, for 2 full hours in the rain & the mud, in the public square there. I expect in a few days the *Graphic* & *Illustrated*[2] will have pictures of the ceremony, & you may perhaps see me, in front of the church, near the plinth of the broken statue, which the Boche, by the way, indecently defiled, she being a lady. The show only lasted 2 minutes, as P only stuck on 7 or 8 medals & then came away. He didn't even kiss the recipients or give a discours.

There were a lot of eminencies around. I always feel on these occasions what I feel in a theatre when something big is being played, that the actors need the cothurnus & the mask, to make them seem as big as the destinies they fulfil. Coming back, our springs broke, so we came home at about 5 miles an hour. It is now snowing very hard, this being 2nd April, & no trace of a flower nor a bud. Dear love to you & to my little Na & to dear Tim. Bless you all my darlings.

Your old love J.

1. Raymond Nicholas Landry Poincaré (1860–1934) was at this time President of France, and, with Clemenceau, urging the most rigorous war-effort, and harsh treatment for the defeated.
2. The *Daily Graphic*, and the *Illustrated London News*.

---

[127]                                                                April 3, 1917.

My old darling Con,

I am so awfully grieved & upset by all your troubles, & I do wish that I could get back to help you through them. I am heart-broken about Na[1], but God knows we did it to save her from an evident misery. Perhaps no-one can be wise about another, I don't know what to say or do. She *was* very unhappy & the place was & is a dangerous place. It was wise, I think, to take her from such a place for this coming period of the war; & to get through that period, somehow, all more or less well & complete, is as much as any of us can look to do. All making & tending of life will have to come after; so much seems clear. She will cheer up, perhaps, with the new house & Timcat; & by the end of this week, as I hope, things will not be so black for you. It will be the hell of a move, I'm afraid. Bessie[2] is a shattering blow; but I hope she will be happy. She deserves to be, she has made our little Tim so happy. But it is a black outlook for you, except that you have the children.

I can't say anything to comfort, except that. We are now in the black period of the war, & if we can get through this, then probably a brighter time will begin. After all, we are alive, & not in any great misery & danger, only troubled & worried & lonely & perplexed; it is not so bad. I saw men marching with their packs & rifles (over their ankles in mud) towards the line today, & tonight they'll be in the mud of the line, being killed & maimed, & some of them had wives & children no doubt, & our lot is paradise to theirs.

I think, from all that I can hear & from all that the Boche have done in the past, that the next Boche blow will be either Holland or Italy. The Boche find it easier to knock out the weak than to butt against the strong, & so Holland or Italy will probably be attacked in force before many weeks are out. Here, the Boche fall back still, or are pushed back, & have lost rather heavily, & have felt the retreat a good deal. One regiment (about 3000 men with the Boche, I believe) was told to evacuate Beaumetz, & was kicked out of it before it could do so, & fell back a long way, & was then told to go up again & retake it, so went up & got a devil of a mauling & had to fall back again quite broken. It is only a straw of course, & makes very little difference immediately, but it is a fair sample of what has happened on the Cambrai road since Bapaume. We are getting up to the Hindenburg Line now, & I gather that it isn't any great shakes of a line naturally; nothing like his devilish perch on the Somme here; so be of good cheer my darling heart. All this misery may come to a final end this year of years.

N. L is very bitter about Willy[3]. He says he heard Willy make a speech in a theatre once after a play of his. He began 'We po-uts'. N. L said 'My son, if I had a rotten egg here you should have it'.

It snowed very hard yesterday, & today all the battlefield was covered; & not even a coltsfoot is in blossom yet there. I saw a rabbit in the old Boche citadel at Fricourt (now K. George's Hill) & at an Army H.Q. I saw the very loveliest bit of house & garden planning I've ever seen. It was Louis Seize, & rather overgrown & neglected & so quite quite exquisite, lovely. I did wish you could have seen it. A lovely old brick house with classic trimmings & a bulge, then grass, then a big basin of water, then a formal clipped hedge 20 feet high & a wood cut into alleys just beyond. My dear, Kendal's was gross & plebeian beside it.

Dear dear love my darling to you & all of you.
Your old love
Jan

Is there any chance of getting Adeline even as a companion to Jude & Tim?

1. This paragraph continues with the difficulties of Judith's change of school, already mentioned.
2. In her diary, 4 January 1916, Constance Masefield mentions 'our dear little nurse Bessie and our old grumbler, Annie.' She had now fallen ill and presumably taken to hospital.
3. William Butler Yeats.

[128]                                                                April 4. 1917.

[in margin at top, in lines diagonal to other writing, appears this postscript]
By the way, the enclosed very loving letter (rather an interesting one) came
through yesterday from Mrs F. Lamont. Today we hear the news of U.S.
declaring war; or being asked to do so, which is rather a different thing. F.
surpasses herself.


My dearest heart Con,
   It is snowing so hard that I've decided not to go up to the field today, but to
stop in my billet & try to write. There is no car for me anyhow, so I could only
go out by lorry, which has its drawbacks. To go by lorry, one begins by walking
2 miles to a place called the Barrier, where passes are examined. There, in the
grimy suburbs, under the shadow of the jail, one stops a lorry. 'W. D. Load
not to exceed 3 tons.' If lucky, one gets a seat in front with the driver & his
friends, & tastes the fresh air, & hears the news. If unlucky, one only gets a seat
behind, where the stink of dust & petrol, mixed, is blinding, & the jolting
prevents conversation. So then away you jog to a beastly respectable little
town, where there is a sort of H.Q. & where everybody is a sergeant of strict
Church of England principles, an awful picture of what England may become.
This place is about a third of the way along, & a beastly junction, for here, in 9
cases out of 10, one has to leave one's lorry, & wait for another. Presently
another comes, & takes you out, in the same way, another third of the distance;
then it, too, turns off, & leaves you in the road. You walk a while, & see the cars
of the great, whirling past, in mud or dust, according to the weather, generally
mud, with lots of room in them, but no charity. 'D—n them', you say, with
Shakespeare, 'the d—d uncharitable dogs'; & then along comes a lorry, & takes
you on to the battlefield. Then, when you have walked enough on the
battlefield, you reverse the process, & get home, but if very very lucky one
sometimes gets a lift in a real car, especially if the car is in charge of a private or
a subaltern. Once I came home from Pozieres in 5 lorries and 1 motor, making
6 stages in all, sandwiched in between walks.
   I am upset, thinking of you at Loll, in weather probably exactly like this, &
quite unable to get moved. O Lord, O Lord, my poor old heart.
   The feeling here is, that the next enemy blow will be against Italy. Here, as
far as one can see, the enemy aim is to retire. The Hindenburg Line[1] is mainly
bluff, I think, & not very strong, &·I shouldn't wonder if he really means to try
to hold the line with the scum of his army & a lot of machine guns, while he falls
on Italy, or Holland, or both, with what he calls his Sturm troops; that is, the
survivors of his picked men, specially brigaded, led and fed. I'm afraid he
might scupper Holland[2], & might, conceivably, destroy Italy, but if he leaves
both countries alone & has a go at Russia I think the distances will defeat him,

while if he has a go at us or at France he will probably be blasted to hell by a preponderance of guns.

We do not hear your rumours of revolutions in Germany & do not in the least believe in them. There is a feeling in W Germany that Prussia is the devil, but that is far from being a revolutionary feeling. The sheep has always done as much as that against the wolf. The recent prisoners have said that they long for an end of the war, they don't care what end, but then, if you saw the mud & misery & the awful tumult of our fire, you would understand why they say that. Don't you think that it will be almost impossible for a revolution to take place in Germany while 9/10ths of the men are under military control? It is not so in Russia, where I suppose 3/5ths of the men are still free, if not 4/5ths, or even more. Of course, the Socialist party in Germany is a very strong, sensible, level-headed, well-educated, & moderate body, corresponding, perhaps, to people like ourselves in England, or nearly so, & it has now a great chance, & seems to be using it both wisely & nobly, as far as one can judge. I think we all ought to play up to that body, by stating that we will not treat for peace with any Hohenzollern[3] or any member of the military caste. This may make a revolutionary feeling begin, & at the same time turn it towards the Socialist party, which is really not a Socialist party as we understand the term, but a party of sensible idealists. I wish that our press would have a little political wisdom & try to give these German thinkers something of a backing, instead of ranting & raving & foaming at the mouth, by & large & across & on again. Naturally, while the socialists think that Germany is to be devastated by fire & sword, whatever happens, they hesitate to weaken their only means of protection.

Dear love to you my darling & I do hope that the move has really been done, without too much worry & strain.

Kiss dear Tim & darling Nana. Your old love

J

1. This ingenious defence in depth, lines of fortresses, wire, redoubts and general blockage was the German answer to the Allies' partial success on the Somme, which compelled a German withdrawal and, for some months, a more defensive attitude. This withdrawal, conducted with method and purpose, was much derided by allied journalists for propaganda reasons. Masefield's belief that the Hindenburg Line was 'mostly bluff', though sincere, was very mistaken. The finest German military engineers designed it. It was actually breached by the British, September 1918.

2. Holland was neutral throughout the war, and instead of being scuppered, received the defeated Kaiser Wilhelm after his flight in 1918, and there he died, still exiled, in 1941.

3. In fact, President Wilson declined to treat with the Hohenzollerns and Habsburgs, insisting that they be replaced by democratic regimes. Had he lived to 1933, he might have questioned his own wisdom.

April 5. 1917.

My dearest heart Con,

I don't know what to do or say. I'm heartbroken about J. If we spoil her happiness she will never forgive us, & if we send her back to St F. we shall have the same anxiety all term through, & the same requests to be taken away for the first fortnight of term. I suppose she had better try Mayorborne[1], with home leave twice a month, if that can be managed, & then after this summer we may see how the war shapes & what is likely to happen.

But don't be discouraged about the war, & do not feel that the news is bad, & do not think (above all things) that the Boche fell back of set design to fulfil all sorts of occult plans. I was over the scene of his last big stand (along the Bapaume Ridge) today, & you may tell everybody that he fell back because he was kicked back, & blasted back, & defeated back, & jolly thoroughly beaten back. And what he got there he is getting now, only worse, & he is being beaten further back. He has been licked everyday for 9 months, & is now beginning to go back quicker & to leave guns & men behind. It is true, we lose aeroplanes. If he had as many as we have & risked them as boldly, he, too, would lose them. They went over today, in the sun, & jolly well routed out the hornet's nest, & blew up his balloons & generally bedevilled him.

It is surely to the good that A comes in. If it brings any sort of rapprochement between us & A it will surely help us in the difficult times after the war. Really, my dear heart, with A in with us & Russia becoming a democracy, I have more hope for us & the world than I have had since this devil's time began. So be of good cheer my Darling & hope for the best. Please God this lovely weather may hold & let you move in peace.

Margaret[2] sent me a note that she has been having German measles, & will only be out of hospital today. I have not got any measles, but am still a bit chatty, not with real lice, because I have killed all those, but with a kind of harvester which one gets on the battlefield. He is what H James[3] would have called the Invisible Playmate. He gets under the skin at the belt & ankles, just like harvesters, & nearly all the field is chalk, pretty well stirred up, so I suppose they are out & hungry. He dies under ointment; that is the best thing about him: but then one gets new ones next day.

I saw a pathetic thing today on the field. One of our men had been hit, & had fallen in exactly the attitude of the Dying Gladiator. Evidently he had felt no pain, for he had taken out his pipe, matches & tobacco, & had then died from loss of blood; but he was still sitting up, propped with one hand, & must have died gently, thinking of his smoke. There were many dead there, ours & the enemy's, & the rats live inside their bodies, & pop in & out of them; & although I'm pretty callous now I can hardly keep from crying when I see these dead. I go over parts of the field where no-one ever goes now, & I send in reports & get these poor bodies buried. I think, if Germany is really punished for this war, by defeat & a change of heart, it will be a sign that a Justice directs this world. . . .

Begin a crusade, dear heart, against the use of the word Tommy[4]. They are not that at all. They are wonderful men, & I have had so much kindness & fun from them that I cannot think of them without deep feeling.

Kiss my beloved Na & dear dear Tim. And I kiss you too my dear

Your old love

Jan

1. Isabel Fry's school.
2. Margaret Bridges.
3. Henry James, the American novelist, who had become a British citizen in 1915.
4. 'Short for "Thomas Atkins", a journalistic name for a private soldier from one T.A. who mythically distinguished himself at Waterloo; or perhaps a formal name on documents like "John" and "Richard Doe". Never used by English troops except derisively or when imitating the style of a newspaper or a charitable old lady. Used by Australians and New Zealanders . . . Picked up by the French and Germans from newspapers.' (Brophy & Partridge) The term was popularized by Rudyard Kipling's 'Barrack-Room Ballads', particularly during the Boer War.

'Yes, makin' mock o' uniforms that guard you while you sleep
Is cheaper than them uniforms an' they're starvation cheap;
An' huslin' drunken soldiers when they're goin' large a bit
Is five times better business than paradin' in full kit.
Then it's Tommy this an' Tommy that, 'an Tommy 'ow's yer soul?
But it's 'thin red line of 'eroes when the drums begin to roll–'

[130]                                                              Ap. 10.

M.D.O.C.

It is still snowy weather here, so I suppose it is with you, & that you are still at Loll, & all my last week's letters will have missed you, but as I have nothing from you later than 3rd I am hazy about your whereabouts.

The enclosed[1] pretty much speaks for itself. You might have it typed & send it round to special friends, such as John & Ada, Bobby & Lion, Lucy (to whom it might do good) & the Bridges, if you like. The frostbitten man, being the older of the two, had had a very bad time. He looked like one of the corpses I find on the field. His face was all drawn & his eyes fallen in & his legs like sticks, and he had suffered a lot too much to have any bitterness or anger or real suffering; the thing had happened so for 3 months of his life & that was all that he could say. The other man, a lad, naturally much stronger, was in fair trim, except for the boils on his head. They were in billets, with lots of blankets & a stove, & the Australians, who are noble fellows, were being jolly good to them.

I do not doubt that the thing happened exactly as they told it. It was rather hard, God help our frailty, to come out from such a story on a Boche road-gang, fat & merry & well-clad, with waterproofs in case of rain, & half of them not working & the rest of them joking with the guard, & their nice snug huts & blankets & kitchens, & real good silver pay, two or 3 francs a day no less, to come to when the day is over at 4 or half past. But God deliver me from trying to make a prisoner's life harder. There is something about a prisoner, I don't know what it is, something in the back & in the hang of the head, that is hell; and they have a sort of slow slouch back to camp, with their picks & forks sloped on their shoulders, & all in column of fours, their non-coms leading, that is like the song of all the prisoners that ever were; it is like the pilgrim's song in *Tannhauser*.

Well, the battle continues much in our favour; & it seems now pretty clear that the Boche cannot possibly succeed against us here, because he hasn't the guns for it. He is going to stand on the Hindenburg or Siegfried line, whichever they call it; but he is getting anxious, & is always patching up new dodges. You remember the dodge of covered pits used against the English cavalry at Bannockburn? He is covering pits busily against our cavalry now. Let him that diggeth a pit fall into it, saith the Psalmist. There is no doubt, Vimy was a sharp knock to him. It began as you know at dawn. Just before dawn the larks began to sing & there was quiet, except for the usual desultory crash, & the whole world was gray, & the sky dark, & then suddenly every gun opened & the sky became one run of fire & the hill rose up red & white & brown & gray, blown up bodily in heaps by our shells; it was the worst shell fire ever seen. Lots of the enemy said that they were kept in their dugouts for four days before the battle by our barrage, as it was certain death to go out of doors; so they had no food & drink for the last day or two.

I believe the Somme was child's play to Vimy. What the later Somme was I saw. God help the Boche if this were worse.

I must stop.

Dear love to you & to Timcat & lovely dear Nana; oh I do rejoice at her comparative good cheer.

Bless you my darlings

Your old love

J

1. Some atrocity or horror story.

---

[131]                                                        April 11. 1917.

M.D.O.C.,

Very heavy snow is falling now, so I suppose you will still be at Loll, unable to move, & the prospects of peace for you drift away again. The spring has surpassed even last year. I have known no March bleaker than this April, & I have seen many Februarys further forward, in the way of greenness & sun. It looks as though it would snow all night again.

In spite of it all, the roads & battlefield are much less quaggy than they were. There is some sort of an improvement, though not one that we can feel. I have been lately on roads that were awful six weeks ago, & even the worst of them, though very holey & one sided in places, were no longer bogs of mud. The road gangs have done wonders with them. Of course 6 weeks ago these roads were being shelled & had only just been blown up by the Boche. Now our men have repaired and relaid them, & made them 6 or 8 feet wider, & dug deep pits beside them to take the main swim of the filth when it comes on to rain.

Today, as there was no car, all the cars being needed to take the foreign journalists to the Arras battle, probably in full flame today, I set out by tram car & lorry, & reached Avelny, & the place on the Ancre called Crucifix Corner, in the 6th stage, having had lifts from 3 lorries & 3 cars. It is odd how a little alliteration catches people. Very many of our soldiers believe that the battle of the Somme began at Crucifix Corner; which is, I may say, at least 1/4 of a mile from our front line as it then was.

That eastern bank of the Ancre is often very bold & steep, & runs for stretches of a hundred yards at a time in a kind of cliff like the railway cutting at Pangbourne. We were on the top of one of these banks near Avelny, looking down over the flat marshy flooded Ancre-valley, with its trees up to their knees in water & the water as blue as the sky. Men had dug out all manner of dugouts all up this cliff, & there was a path at the foot, on the lip of the blue water, & all the dirty tumble down dugouts & the mess, & the path & the dazzling water looked so exactly like Anzac cove that it came just like a blow, & I could have stood there & gazed & gazed for hours, & then looked up to see Imbros, & looked again to see Sari Bair. However, we were on the Ancre, & went on a little, & saw the Leipzig salient above us, & crossed it, & a beastly strong Boche fort it was, & the bones of the men who took it were lying all over the field, & presently we came to Ovillers, which is gone from this earth, & holes left where the houses were, & there were more bones, picked clean by the birds & rats & dogs, & if ever there were the bones of brave men those were they, for Ovillers was a hell on earth. It is on one side of a narrow valley, about 150 yards across and at most 100 feet deep, quite a narrow shallow place, but all be-Boched & mined & enfiladed, as well as trenched & ranged on, till it was as strong as death. After this we came home in 1 lorry, 1 car & 1 light car, & got in just before the snow & got your letter. There is no telegraphic address for me, I'm afraid, except the full postal one. I am writing to thank the Ambassador & say why I didn't turn up. Probably he wanted me to write a Hail Columbia poem to appear on the day A declared war. Well, he won't get.

The Arras news is nice. 100 guns means the artillery of some 30 or 40,000 men at one swoop. A few more wallops like that & Fritz will go back again.

Dear heart I wish you could get your move done & so be settled. I am glad to

have Na away from Southwold. It will quite surely be shelled this summer.
Bless her & you & Timcat.

Your old love<br>Jan

---

[132]                                                                Ap 12. 1917.

My dear old heart,

. . . It is not true that Germany's army is bigger than it ever was before, and
even if it were true, it would mean nothing, for it is nothing like so strong, &
the men are not fighting so well. I see no end to the business, for I really don't
see how it can be ended except by beating Germany. The only good we can get
from the war is the ending of the immediate fear of war which made life a
nightmare for all our lives. I myself think that there is a chance of beating
Germany in the West here this year. If we fail, as we very likely may, then I
think it will have to stop, though that will be a very tragical thing; the burglar
will remain in power with all that he fought for & all the swag he wanted; the
dead will be dead & the maimed halt & France & Belgium sacked, & ourselves
mined; & the threat of another war will be just as great as it was in 1913; or
greater, for there is hatred now to fan it. As you know, I hate war, & think it an
infamy & folly; but when men are fighting, they fight to a definite end, of
victory, defeat, or exhaustion, & so far I see no definite end; I wish I could.

We did very well at Arras. We knocked out 2 German Divisions, say 30,000
men, & took all their guns, which run to some 3 or 4 to every 1000 men. One
Canadian Brigade took 33 guns. It entrenched in the dark on captured ground
& in the morning found that they were right under the muzzles of these guns,
so they rushed them & took them. The enemy had a fearful time in his
trenches, 'covered with lice & blown to bits' one of their letters said, & half or
wholly starved, for no food could come up to them for the last 8 days, so that
they made but a poor fight & surrendered freely. Still, though these men were
said to have been most pitiful creatures, it may be that Fritz has divided his
army into Holding Troops, who are just cripples with machine guns, &
attacking, or Sturm Troops, who are his picked men. We shall see very soon.
Meanwhile, it is Boche weather, snow every day, bitter pelting rain, & howling
wind, so that guns can't move, aeroplanes can't observe, & troops can't attack.
Our gas is said now to be A 1; & something the Boche can't stand; & we have
also a flame thing which is said to work wonders. Imagine, our writing like this
3 years ago.

Food is being cut here, but not harshly yet. We don't get Army rations, but
are catered for in the town, & we get an odd kind of meat, which I cannot at all
place, but it isn't bad. Some say it is horse, but I think it is really French
mutton. We get eggs & bread & jam, oranges from Algiers, & a kind of local

fish from one of the countless branches of the Somme which make Amiens a kind of Venice. We are well fed, though a bit monotonously, & I hate to have food here while you are starved in England. Still, courage, I think the tide has turned. Fritz doesn't want the war to go on any more than we do.

Dear dear love to you & Na & Tim cat.

Your old lover

Jan

---

[133] April 13.

M.O.D.C.

Your letter of Sunday just in; thank you so much.

About the Boche in occupation. I should have thought that that was by this time fairly plain. He comes into a town & placards it with notices that no-one is to go out after dark nor to do any human act (pretty well soever) without permission, on pain of being shot. Frequently he shoots a few citizens to shew them that he means what he says; then he deports the young men, makes the elder men dig trenches, debauches the girls, terrorises the women, fines the community, pillages the houses & at last destroys them. I have not been much in the occupied districts, but I have never yet heard of any other procedure than the above, & everybody agrees that the Boche have been everywhere harsh, cruel, pitiless & overbearing, & that their rule has been a rule of terror. Every French person in the occupied districts is half starved, & wholly cowed, except perhaps some bold curé or so. The legacy of hatred left in France by them is something you cannot realise until you meet it. . . .

I think they did defer to public opinion on those points, but they have been everywhere cruelly harsh, & they are devils unhung to our prisoners, & their going has been simply the going of brigands. It is true, no armed occupation could be pleasant to the French; & war anyhow is a going back to criminal times & standards. Perhaps no armed occupation would have been 'better'.

I went up today to Hébuterne, where Edward was for so long. It is on one side of a sort of valley, with very gentle slope down & then a very gentle slope up, & a great Boche line, of awful strength, on the slope up; the very devil of a place; quite the strongest of all the beastly places he had on that line. He had put about 30 yards of barbed wire in front of it, & then in front of that he had a lot of low wire, just high enough to trip you & throw you. Then in front of that, he had made a few neat little nests for machine gunners, & on a bit of rising ground, some 5 feet higher than the rest, he had dug a few pits for snipers. He had terrific trenches (15 feet deep) behind all this array, with the usual deep dugouts in them, & there he could sit & drink his beer (which he did, by the thousand bottles, evidently) in practical safety, while 20 men could destroy & did destroy any attack sent against them. Of course, in the Somme battle, our attack at this point was said to be a 'containing attack' to keep the enemy engaged there while he was broken elsewhere. We lost very heavily there. Our dead were everywhere. And the worst of it was, that in just one bit of the line, the Germans had behaved well. They had buried some of the London Scottish in front of their wire & had put up crosses over them.

Hébuterne itself is a sort of French Prestwood, but bigger & better built, & more compact, & of course all shelled & strafed & broken & ruined & without roofs & walls. But as long as our men weren't attacking, it was probably not a bad part of the line, as such things go.

I was in very late tonight & must now change for mess.

Kiss my darling Na & my dear Timcat, whose cold I hope is better.

Dear love to you my darling

Your old love

Jan

---

[134]                                                                     16 Ap. 1917

My dearest heart Con,

The day before yesterday I could only send you a note, & today I have to make up for yesterday, when I could not write at all, as I was out till after 8 p.m. & had then to go to mess & to the conference, & the post goes out at 8.30. It was not a very joyous day as it never ceased to rain all day, & I was at Monquet Farm, which is one of the damnedest bits of smash in all this accursed field. The worst of this life is not knowing even where you are. From the letter I got yesterday I think you may be moved now, either by Baugham or Heelas [?], but I cannot be sure. The weather here has been of a big system type & probably has affected you with as much mud & swill as it has ourselves; so this will go to Loll, & I hope will reach you.

I forget what I have told you & what I haven't. Did I tell you of the shell fire at Arras? In one sector, 5 kilometres long, south of Arras, & therefore comparatively mildly handled, in the 4 days preliminary bombardment, we dropped 18,000 tons of shells of all calibres, from the 18 pounder to the Granny[1] (which is about as big as a boiler & weighs a young ton). In all, we fired 750,000 rounds of shell onto that 5 kiloms, & followed it up with bombs & bullets. It was intenser fire even than the Somme. Our gas, both cylinder & shell gas, was both new & good, quite the best gas in use on the front. It is very strong & quite smell-less & invisible, & the first symptom of its use is the man collapsing. It kills through the respirator, & at present the enemy has no guard & no protection against it.

In the counter attack, further to the south, where the enemy gave us a nasty knock, since more than amply avenged, a funny thing happened which I shall write about. A patrol of 9 Australians went out & got into a fight with an enemy patrol, & got rather the better of it. Then the enemy was reinforced, & brought up a machine gun, & the Australians got cut up, 3 killed & 4 wounded. Many Germans had been wounded, & the Germans busied themselves with looking after these wounded & getting them sent in. While they were doing this, the 2 surviving unwounded Australians, crept round & stole the machine gun. They didn't know how to work it, but they picked it up & crawled from shell hole to shell hole with it, & at last brought it safely in. The Australians are the best men out here, pretty well. They aren't such heroic and beautiful natures as the English perhaps, but they are daredevil, resourceful, hardy souls, with a kind of wicked wit about them which is very engaging; & then they are such splendid fellows to look at.

Their pioneer[2] badge, of a rifle crossed with a spade, is very very like the General's badge of 2 crossed swords. A General passing an Australian was not saluted. In a very mild & friendly way he asked the Australian 'If he did not even salute a General. The man stood to attention, saluted, & explained, "I thought you was one of those bluidy Pioneers, & I wasn't going to salute one of those swine."'

I don't believe that anyone can have a clear idea of what the Somme fighting really was. I am beginning to grasp the ground now, & to see clearly the enemy's theories, & the depth of our own supineness & stupidity before the war, & the inadequacy of our thought. At least, our best thought was probably always better than anything the enemy ever had, but you see, our best thought was never used. We preferred our second best, & so the enemy prevailed, for all this time & at all this cost.

Monguet Farm stands in a hollow at the apex of a valley, which runs roughly speaking, between Pozieres & Thiepval, parallel to the Ancre. Before I do this book, I must get a lot of wax or putty & make moulds of the field or parts of it. It is a bit like this:

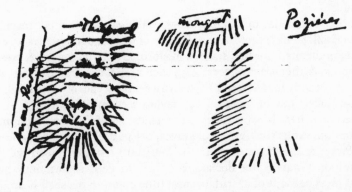

It does not look to be a very strong place, but it was enormously strong as a support to Thiepval, & exceedingly difficult of approach. If you came up the valley to it you were flanked by the fearful fortresses, the Leipzig, Wunder

Werke & Thiepval, & got scuppered, & if you came by Pozieres you were
flanked by the guns further to the north. So the only thing to be done was to
smash it to smithereens & then bomb & crawl your way into it; & this was done;
& now it is a big heap of splintered brick in a collection of pits, most of which
contain skulls, ribs, heads, feet, old tins, general litter, filthy water, bombs,
shells, broken rifles, bayonets, leg bones (literally everywhere, often with
putties on them) helmets, & rags both of leather & of cloth. But it cannot be
described. This desolation & damnedness must be seen.

Now dear love to you, my darling & to my sweet Nana & Tim. Marg B sends
the enclosed. Poor lamb; she has now got pleurisy.

I hope you'll have her to Sandpits when she goes back.

Dear love.

Your Jan

1. Before 1916, a particular 15-inch howitzer, but by now any of the bigger guns.
2. Units sent out before the main troops to clear the foreground of all obstructions –
wire, mortars, etc.

---

[135]                                                                  17 Apr.

My dearest heart,

After a chapter of accidents on the road, I've come in too late for the post, for
the 2nd time this week. I'm awfully sorry, but it can't be helped; you will get
double allowance next day, & it is this Boche god who makes the weather that is
to blame.

I've got your letter of 12th & am so grieved about your disappointment about
the move again; alas alas my dear you are having a sad time & I can do nothing
to comfort.

I've been out all day in blinding snow, walking miles, & at last reaching the
town of Guillemont & the village of Ginchy of which no solitary trace remains;
both are obliterated; for they had the misfortune to be on a crest, & crests give
observation & the means of correcting shell fire, & command vallies, so they
are always bitterly fought for, & these two were the scenes of bloody fighting, &
are now collections of holes. After having seen my bellyful, of the usual
smashed trenches, broken rifles, feet, hands, heads, bones, equipment &
ammunition, skulls sticking out of graves, & legs cocked up out of trenches, I
came away, & at last got down to the Maricourt road, & passed the famous
ammunition dump that the Boche aviator blew to pieces some months ago (& a
famous mess he made of it) with his neat little bomb on the shell-heap. Then I
got a lift on a lorry loaded with old salved rifles, ours & Fritz's, picked up on the
battlefield, & sitting on the rusty barrels of the same, I came to Albert, & got
another lorry, going near home by a round about way. I was late in leaving

Albert, & the detour made me later still, for we got onto a bad bit of road & stuck in the mud. There was an Australian officer with me, who had been in the Landing, or said he had, but he was a little drop takenish, or so I thought, & as his conversation was mainly about the Boche prisoners he had massacred (some hundred or two, to his private account) I did not pay much attention to him. He smelt like a rum-vat.

As we were in the mud, I collected some big rocks, as big as I could carry, & plomped them into the quay; & though they disappeared, they did the trick & just got us out; which was one to me, though the A took the credit. After this, all went well, till the lorry went off to its billet. It was now 7 p.m., & we had still 6 miles to go or more, & most of the traffic had stopped for the night, & we were preparing to walk the 6 miles, weary as we were, when a general's car came bowling along. I keep clear of generals myself, but the bold A had rum in his head, & he stopped the general, & we got in & came all the way home. The A explained things to the general, with his balmy breath, 'No cheek, no Xmas pie;' which is certainly a motto to act on on these roads. . . .

I believe M Bridges goes home today. I wish I could come.

Dear love to you & to the dear babes.

Your old love

Jan

---

[136]                                                                    Ap. 18.

M.O.D.C.

Two lets today, hurray; but alas I missed the post yesterday, owing to the mud.

My poor dear heart, I do grieve for your troubles in moving. It has rained or snowed hard every day this week & Loll must be a quagmire, so I fear you won't get off on Monday. Alas alas. (Heelas, as the French say). I don't know what to say about Na. I would be glad to have her out of St Felix this war time, for I think it is likely to be a dangerous place, & we have no right to let a child run the risk of terror & maiming, which is a real risk there from now on. You must tell her this, and ask her to be brave & good about it & to put up with Mayortorne for a term or two, till the danger is past. She shall go back to St Felix as soon as possible, & perhaps if Mayortorne is hateful she shall stay at home; but I believe S' wold to be dangerous, & I am glad to have her away from it. Boche ships are sure to shell the place within the next few weeks, & naturally they will aim at the biggest buildings there. So Na must be kept away from it. You know very well that if she were to go there she would be deathly homesick the last week of holidays & the first fortnight of term. It is quite impossible to be wise about a child, but it is at least possible to be prudent in a time of danger, & though the removal may be a mistake in some ways, it is not mistaken as an attempt to keep her in safety. The enemy fleet is certain to come out this summer[1], probably in May or June, & in fine weather haze (if we ever have any) these coast places will be strafed. So thumbs down, bleeding heart though it be to say it.

I wish I could see about getting home. If I only had a car, or a billet in Albert again, I could finish this month; but I can't possibly as things are. Getting to & from takes such ages, and then the mud is so fearful it is impossible to walk a mile on the field in less than an hour, and the actual field is about 20 miles by 6 miles, or at least as big as from Goring to Oxford, & the roads are foul & the land is shell holes. I go out every day & try to get done, but I have still a whole heap of places to try to get the hang of. You see, in G. I had Ian, & could go ahead, but here I am not going to have anybody, & must depend solely on what I can pick up here by myself. It is the devil, & damnably costly, & my boots have gone in the mud (the old ones) & my oilskin-Burberry is the devil, & it rains all day, or snows, & I believe I've got lousy again from one of these filthy lorries. I must beg for another 20 pug, & with that I may be able to manage to get through.

I saw a lot of prisoners from Vimy ridge today. They were all very young or very old & they hadn't got over the shelling, & a more heart-broken lot you never saw; not one head up in all the hundreds I saw. They will probably be in road gangs tomorrow, having a nice easy slack time, without any shell-fire, & with comfortable billets to go home to, & a system of work that says, 'one shovelful a minute, & then a long thought about the next one.' There is no doubt, they got a fearful licking at Vimy. If the weather would only be fine, clear & dry, they would get another & another, but this everlasting cold & mud spoils everything. I'm afraid Russia[2] is done for. I think she will make a separate peace, & so seal the knell (or sign the death-bell) of Italy & Salonika, & make the war last another 3 years. One cannot be sure of this, but I don't see what else she can do. One knows nothing about her & judges her revolutionary party by what such a party in England would be, Saleeby[3], Ponsonby,[4] H.W.N.[5], Keir Hardie[6], Shaw, Mrs Pank[7], & the staff of the Red Tie. Just such a party began the French Revolution, with a lot of slop and fine phrases.

Why do you doubt our holding the Vimy Ridge & taking Lens & beating the Boche. Can you not see that he got a fearful hiding at Vimy, a hiding as complete as the Marne & nearly as bloody, & that Lens is bound to fall as soon as the weather changes. The Boche is beaten. He has won nothing in the way of ground for a year, & he has been beaten & booted out of nearly a third of the France he has defiled. Could not Harley come to Oxford to see you. Surely you need not have all that gad to see him.

Now my dear love to you & Na & Tim. I must stop.

All blessings & love to you.

Your old love
Jan

1. Actually, after the Battle of Jutland, a disappointing encounter for Britain, the German fleet never reappeared, save to surrender, and mutinied when ordered to do so in the last days of the war.

2. On his taking dictatorial, one-party power, Lenin made peace with the Germans and withdrew Russia from the war later in the year.

3. Dr Caleb Saleeby, a well-known, popular science writer of the time.

4. Arthur Augustus William Harry, first Lord Ponsonby (1871–1946), politician, diplomat and author, always vehemently opposed the war, urging a negotiated peace. Prominent in Labour of overments and oppositions after 1918, having deserted the Liberals.

5. Nevinson.

6. James Keir Hardy (1856–1915), miner, journalist, labour leader, first leader of the Labour Party in Parliament, 1906–07, MP 1900–1915. Opposed the war. Arnold Bennett met him, a member of the Union of Democratic Control, a pacifist-socialist group, and described him as 'a pale, light, large-foreheaded man. Seemed surprised when I said that Germans would be beaten, and that Government would stand. All these chaps have twisted minds.'

7. Emmeline Pankhurst (1858–1928). Militant suffragette, several times imprisoned, though suspending her direct action policy during the war.

---

[137]                                                    Ap 19.

Dearest heart Con,

On getting back last night I had to tog up & go to a state dinner given by N.L.[1] to the Fr Ambassador from Paris, the United States Ambassador, I mean, Mr Sharp, & his allies Bliss[2] & Coolidge[3] whom I met in Paris last autumn. The 3 Americans, N.L. & myself, made the party, & we dined on duck at the Rhin. I don't know that anything wise or witty was said, but I was very glad to see Coolidge again, & this morning I got up early & caught them all at their petit dejeuner, & gave Coolidge some war trophies which I had spent half the night polishing, this being Welt politik; consequent collapse of Coolidge & envy of the other 2; so N.L. & I are going to load them with trophies from this time on. However, as they were finishing their coffee, N.L. came in, looking most splendid, as he always does, in his red staff cap & a kind of gorgeous piebald goatskin that he wears, & old Mr S began to talk. He is a Wilsonite, & a bitter opponent of Boche devilry, & he was very interesting. He said that when the peace conference begins, it would begin with the proclamation that it was going to begin the Hundred Years Peace, & make it impossible for any war to break out for a century, that it would suppress all use of submarines & aeroplanes in war, & take certain steps to make sure that Germany came into line with the rest. He struck me as being sanely pro-English, which is a very rare thing in an American. He said that it must be seen to, that the two Anglo-Saxon races have a union, to defend the peace of the world, & that with such an union, war will be impossible henceforth.

After this, they went out to have a go round the field with N.L., all vowing that they were going to give us a go round Paris as soon as they could get us leave to come. But be this as it may.

I must now stop, but I may have time for a 2nd note this evening.

Dear love to you & to all; Nana & Timcat.

Your old lover

Jan

Don't type the enclosed.

1. Neville Lytton.
2. Tasker Howard Bliss (1835–1930), American general, professor of military science, diplomat, Chief of the General Staff 1917–18, American representative on Supreme War Council in France, 1918, and delegate at the Versailles Peace Conference, 1919.
3. Calvin Coolidge (1872–1933), American lawyer and politician, and at this period Republican Lieutenant-Governor of Massachusetts. President of the United States 1923–29.

---

[138]                                                                     20 April.

My dear heart,

. . . I saw a lot of the Vimy prisoners yesterday, close to, & they haven't got over the shelling yet. They are the sick & the old & the dead; you never saw such specimens; broken, dejected, hang-dog; were these the blonde beasts & supermen that were to bring Kultur to the world. They looked as like lice as men can look. There were a few of the old armies among them, but not many, & I have no doubt that Fritz simply parts his armies into sheep & goats, lets the sheep be massacred & sacrificed, & saves his goats for any real job he wants to do. The goat army is no doubt ready for some devilry, & may ever be already engaged. As rumours are going round that the Italian scheme has been abandoned, it is likely that they are now there, beginning.

I'm afraid that a war, like a work of art, must have a definite end, & if it be possible to get a decisive end to this one, it were well to get it; but the cost seems pretty high. The German losses since the beginning of the war must be terrific, & I suppose they have lost altogether in this last push not less than 120,000 men, counting in the French toll as well. If we could only have 2 months good, really beautiful, dry clear weather, we should see our way perhaps. But the mud never dries, & the land is still bleak February, with no sign yet even of March, and the rain & the cloud prevent observation.

It was rather touching (& I am writing to Ian to tell him). I was in Albert the other day, & a lot of Australians were there, peering into passing cars, & I asked an officer, what they were doing. He said, 'Ian Hamilton is here on a visit. He has been seen here, so we are come around to give him a damned good cheer when he comes through.'

I don't believe it was true that he was there, for most war rumours are false, but he would have been pleased had he come through while they were waiting. The Australians always speak highly of 'Iron Hamilton', & the English, as a rule, belittle him. The Australians only see his positive quality, of romantic courage, & the English only his negative quality, of not being true to type.

This morning by a bribe of 2 francs I got into the _____ where there are some 7 or 8 big frescoes by Puvis de Chavannes[1], the glory of Amiens; & indeed it was very glorious of a provincial town as big as (say) Preston, to give a young man such a chance. The frescoes are pseudo classical, milky young artists' models, very cold without their clothes, emptying fruit out of baskets to signify peace & plenty; & looking rather mad in front of some fire to signify war; & then being just naked & aimless & one of them flinging a stick, while the ladies sit naked on the grass talking to some old men devoid of passion, to signify (I think it was called) physical exercise. It was the work of a tame pale soul, with good taste & good feeling stronger in him than delight and power. He had evidently never seen naked flesh exposed to wind & sun. His people looked to be made of bled veal.

I haven't gone to the field today, as I've been trying to do something for this Russian business.

Dear love to you & Tim & Na, & I trust to God the worries are now letting up on you & that the warmth has come.

Your old love<br>Jan

1. Pierre Cécile Puvis de Chavannes (1824–98): he developed novel styles of fresco painting, and Masefield is referring to the 'Peace' and 'War' frescoes with panels painted in 1862.

---

[139]                                                                April 21.

My dearest heart,

I am thankful to have your note dated 18th & to think that perhaps you are now into H.C.[1] & perhaps finding it not so vile. I do trust that it is not proving hopeless. After all, it is bigger than the farm, where we were so happy, & peace cannot be very long delayed. People here think this year, & though that is a bold line to take, there is no doubt that Fritz is not the man he was, & has lost heavily (terrifically at Reims, where the French put a barrage right into his army massed for an attack), & his letters home all say that they have 'no hope of victory now', only the hope of holding on till the submarines starve us into terms. By the sound, he is getting a hammering now. May the dear god of the English let there be dry clear warm sunny weather for a couple of months on end, barring such refreshing showers as may bring forth the fruits of the earth; & then peace will be 6 months nearer I should reckon.

I went today to the northern battlefield beyond Hébuterne. Really, I need not have gone so far, for the battle's northern limit is opposite Hébuterne; at a place called Gommecourt, a Boche salient, stronger than anything in his line. Six weeks ago, he was in Gommecourt, being shelled & shelling back, & now he is all those miles away, & the No Man's Land is a kind of almost green & the villages Fonquevillers, Hebuterne & Gommecourt are more desolate than you can imagine. It is like coming to complete Uriconiums². It is just as it must have been at Uriconium after the sack. Ruts in the roads, every house a ruin & a smash, & cats wandering everywhere, but no man, woman or child, & the magpies picking in the streets. One expected to see perhaps a madman singing, but there wasn't one, so I went out into the No Man's Land, & along, between the wires, to the Gommecourt salient, where, in the wreck of a trench, a fat & happy cat was sleeping, probably on a meal of man.

Fritz had a lot of artillery against us up there in July, & I don't think we ever had the ghost of a chance there as long as he was fairly secure further to the south. Nowadays, when we attack, we do not lose so many men by two thirds. We blow Fritz & his line to pieces together & leave none of either before we start the advance.

Leaving Gommecourt & those strange, sad, romantic villages of the dead, all so like the deserted towns I used to imagine as a child, I went on through B'mont Hamel, where the other day I found the village blacksmith trying vainly to piece out where his house had been, so that he might dig up his papers, & so down the Ancre to Thiepval. You know the deep gully under the wooded combe, going up to the Roman house from Aston. If you can imagine the gully a village street you have the spit of B'mont Hamel before the war. Now, not one stone remains in place, & not one blade of grass grows, nor any bush or shrub. It is all bald broken earth & chalk & holes & ruinous mess, shards of iron, splinters, mud & bedevilment.

At Thiepval there was an old Tank, just salved from the mud & going home, after a winter on the hill. She was a cheery old thing, labelled 'We're all in it', but much too slow to be terrible, though pretty to see the way she went into a crater & out. They may someday get a workable kind of Tank. This kind is too slow, & her tracks are too vulnerable, & she weighs too much & I daresay has other faults. Sooner or later, land wars will be fought in Tanks, so I was respectful to her. She was rather like Winston to look at, a big slow aggressive louse-shaped lump of a thing. She would have been the very thing to move a poor family from Lollingdon. No upset about her.

There is a terrible man here who knows Lollingdon.

N.L. has telegraphed about Peter, but no answer yet.

Dear love to you & to Tim & to darling Nana.

Your old lover<br>Jan.

1. Hill Crest, Boar's Hill.
2. Uricon. Remembered for the verse in A. E. Housman's *On Wenlock Edge*:

'The gale, it plies the saplings double,
  It blows so hard, 'twill soon be gone:
To-day the Roman and his trouble
  Are ashes under Uricon.'

Masefield wrote in 1963, to Miss Napier-Smith, 'Did you ever go to Uricon? There is a vast heap of basilica or forum wall in the midst of grass. The forum must once have been just about the measure of Birmingham Town Hall; & the city about a mile across; & the lovely brook once its drink & its bath now romping free to the Severn.'

Housman's work meant much to Masefield. To the same friend, he had written, 1956: 'I love you to love A. E. Housman, for I have loved him deeply for 58 years now: & tho I did not often see him, I admired him deeply.'

And again: 'Please do you know AEH? Probably you do: but they come, away back, just at the very time when they could be all the world to me: and for years they were. I have his poems on the table always, and as Ben Jonson said of WS "I loved the man . . . on this side idolatry"'.

---

[140]                                                            April 21.
                                                                Sunday.

My dearest heart,

    . . . N.L. very kindly telegraphed to Mr Baring[1], who is a sort of Military secretary to the Flying Corps, & late last night the following answer came about Peter. It says nothing, probably, that the Warrens do not already know:

    'Lt Warren left aerodrome 10.30 a.m. 2.IV.17, engaged hostile aeroplane about 11.10, & was last seen by pilots in a spiral but under control east of Vimy & disappeared into the clouds still under control.' I'm afraid I've no hope really. I was afraid he would be killed, poor boy, but the telegram, as you see, makes it possible that he brought the machine down within enemy lines; in which case he will be a prisoner, wounded or not, & word will someday come through. But there was a fatality about him, as about Rupert[2], and I'm afraid I've neither hope nor doubt; poor beautiful boy.

    There is not much news, except the glorious improvement in the weather, which is drying up the mud, & the accursed filthy pools up on the braes. I know now what is meant by the graves & the sea giving up their dead; for half these filthy pools have bodies under their water; & now that the water goes the bodies appear, just as they fell, in July & November & in the recent fights; and one sees the pity of awful bloody war as no man can describe it.

    I was up today between Beaucourt & Hebuterne, in some of the most smashed of all these ruins of hills, & I suppose there was no human being within a mile of me in all that desolation; & I stood on the crest, where the enemy had an observation post, just in front of his quite invisible battery positions. With even my glass I could see about a mile of English front line (as it was in July) with its communication trenches, & parts of the villages behind them. No wonder our poor men had no chance there. A man with a telescope could have sat in a chair there, & no doubt did, watching our men massing for the attack, & at the critical moment he had only to sing out, & about a mile of batteries could plaster any point he chose. Just those places visible from that point, as I noticed on my way home, were those where our losses were worst. That was the point which made me keep my head down when I went to Mesuil in October. Now it is just the usual smash, with nobody anywhere near it, ever. A curlew was crying there, which was beautiful, & made me feel that perhaps now, in their burnt bald heaps, these hills are a little like Parkmore, or liker that than any thing. I ate my lunch at Serre, a Sodom & Gomorrah of a place, where I went when it was still being shelled, at least they shelled it while I was there, early in March, & a ghastly place of death it is, & our losses there in July were sad to see, but it is quiet enough, except for rats, today.

I believe we & the French have put 160,000 enemy out of action since last Monday week, the 8th; & this with light losses to ourselves. That is more than the number of men engaged at Waterloo, & about as many as surrendered at Metz in 1871. The enemy has had a mauling, which is still going on. The cannonade is terrific all along from Arras to Cambrai, & it goes like drums night and day, all guns, little & big: & at Reims the French guns are doing the same. I am thankful I'm not an enemy soldier in any of the front lines. I don't think I do wrong in telling you this, for the enemy must know what kind of shelling he is having.

Dear love to you & darling Na & Timcat. Kiss them both from me.

Your old love

Jan

1. Maurice Baring (1874–1945), wit, poet, novelist, diplomat, special foreign correspondent; air force officer, 1915–19. His *Anything to Declare?* (1936) is one of the best anthologies. Frequently read still, is Hilaire Belloc's Cautionary Tale, *About John: who lost a fortune by Throwing Stones*, which contains:

'Like many of the Upper Class
He liked the Sound of Broken Glass'
with its footnote:
'A line I stole with subtle daring
From Wing-Commander Maurice Baring.'

In 1959, Rupert Hart-Davis wrote to George Lyttleton, 'I think it was Maurice Baring (but you will correct me) who said he had decided that the Iliad and the Odyssey weren't written by Homer, but by another man of the same name.' Baring knew Russian well, and his anthology includes some of his Pushkin translation. The National Portrait Gallery has James Gunn's painting of Baring standing above Belloc and Chesterton seated at a table, in which he looks like a seasoned man of the world watching the cautious manoeuvres of two card-sharpers.

2. Rupert Brooke. In Brooke's last letter to Eddie Marsh, 9 March 1915, he asks Marsh to give his love 'to the New Numbers folk, and Violet (Asquith), and Masefield and to a few who'd like it. Masefield in previous correspondence with Brooke had always been generous in his appreciation of the younger man's poetry, and other work. However in earlier correspondence with Edward Marsh, over his project for an anthology of Georgian poetry, Brooke did not reciprocate Masefield's appreciation of his (Brooke's) work but wrote rather condescendingly of Masefield's writings. Jealousy of Masefield's success as a poet and writer at the time may possibly have had something to do with it.

---

[141]                                                    Ap 23.
                                                        Mon.

My dearest heart Con,

. . . I've been out 11 hours today & am only just back in time to wash for mess. I've been out through Bapaume to the front, & seen the battle a little from various holes in the ground, & then I saw Birdie[1], who is like a very bright small intelligent Hobart Hampden, hopping & twitting like a little bird, very shrewd & sharp & nice, & his chief, too, a very bright-eyed pleasant man, said to be the genius of the war by his admirers. I should say a genius of sorts. Now I must stop & wash off my dust & run for mess.

Dear love to you & to all.

                                    Your old love
                                    Jan

There is a very able Russian here who thinks Russia will certainly carry on the war to the end, & is sure that with the Rev party[2] she can do this

1. William Riddel, Field Marshal Lord Birdwood, (1865–1913), commanded the Anzacs at Gallipoli and, at the end, all the land forces. He led the victorious 5th Army in 1918. Master of Peterhouse 1930–38.

2. The Russian revolutionary government was dominated by the lawyer, Kerensky, the Menshevik leader, who had promised the Allies to continue the war and develop a new offensive against the Germans. He was soon, however, to be ousted by Lenin and the Bolsheviks, dedicated to bring Russia out of the war.

---

[142]                                               Ap 24. 1917.

My dearest heart Con,

I could only send you a scrap yesterday, as I had rather a field day. You ask how the Boche could know what we were up to at Arras. It is really not so uncanny as you suppose. No man can hide very large bodies of soldiers, still less the waggons & horse teams which supply them. Men from the top of the Vimy Ridge could see easily that there was treble the traffic behind Arras, & draw their own conclusions. A trench must be visible from higher ground.

Besides, they have quite extraordinarily good photographic lenses (infinitely better than ours I believe) & take photographs from incredible altitudes in aeroplanes, & these photographs are said to be marvellous, & to show men & guns & everything; & although we kept most of his aeroplanes behind his lines, some came over, & no doubt got some information by photograph in spite of the bad weather. And although he does not get great hauls of prisoners, he gets some, in every fight; as must happen always; & all prisoners give away a certain amount of information, even if it be not very valuable. So on the whole, I don't think the Boche did so marvellously strangely; & anyhow, the weight & numbers of our guns took him entirely by surprise. Those had been screened & hidden & camoufle'd in protective colours, & dummies rigged up to draw his fire, & when the fight began he got something he had not expected & could not endure. They all say that it is now infinitely worse than the Somme, & speak of it as unendurable.

Now as to yesterday: we went out (N.L. 2 Russians & myself) in the early morning, along the familiar Roman road, to a certain place, where we met Bean (the correspondent attached to A.N.3.A.C. Hq.) He was in a little camouflé hut in a hollow, & the Australians had 'conveyed' a lot of box and primroses & daffodils & planted them about his hut, & there were now in blossom. Bean is a fine fellow, very shrewd & generous & cool, & speaks exactly like Murray. He has a car of his own, into which I got, so I then had a long talk with him about the Australians in the Somme fighting, & escaped my two Russians, one of whom (whose name is Hindenberg or something like it) I call the Hindenberg limit. The other is a clever fellow & rather nice. We went out to Bapaume, which is the usual scene of smash, indescribable & very hideous, & then, oh Lord, the change, we passed into open, green, unbedevilled country, with real spring & real trees & horses grazing, & none of the smash & horror & mud of the blasted & awful field of hell between Albert & Bapaume. It is very graceful big plain gentle country in a big expanse with wide horizons, & long slow graceful folds of hill with little red brick villages on them, such as Ovillers & Pozieres & Fricourt must once have been. We went out to a place to a hole in the ground, where we sat in the most infernal racket you ever heard. Machine guns clacking like blazes at aeroplanes, & a heavy battery roaring like hell, & the hell of a terrific roaring blazing battle like the surf of hell, making a tumult & dizziness as far as one could see. The battle had a kind of angel of wrath above it, a mist or darkness, sometimes reddish, when a house blew up into it, sometimes black from mud, sometimes just duncoloured, with awful flickers & blinks of a most dazzling reddish fire, from guns & shells. Most of all this was coming from us to them; & it was terrible; a noise like a terrific surf, & this mist or dimness, which was not smoke, but dust of blown earth & blasted houses, floating over half a county. Nearer at hand was the enormous Hindenburg line, of 150 yards of the thickest possible barbed wire; a belt of wire as broad as from 13 W W[1] to the Heath. And in & beyond this wire our shells were falling &

bursting like geysers; wallop, & then a spout of whiteness & blackness, as thick as a devil, with black clods & bits flying out of it, & then wallop again. I could see a Boche position in a village, & while I was watching it, a shell hit a house, & the whole house became a pinkish mist a hundred feet high of splintered dust of brick & then disappeared. Soon after that, I saw a German run across an open space as fast as he could pelt, & I thought 'My son, how desire doth outrun performance.' The air was wavering & shaking across my glasses, so that it was not easy to see, and I suppose this was due to the battle. Without glasses one could see better, in a dazzling clear April sunlight which showed up everything clearly & sharply. Once every 5 minutes some punctual Fritz led off a solitary shrapnel shell, which burst high up in a certain place in the air. He was doing this all the time, punctually, with 5 minute intervals, keeping to the very second, & what he hoped to accomplish by it God only knows, unless to mark his joy at being 5 minutes nearer peace. Long afterwards, we saw this 5 minutes shell punctually popping in the same bit of air. Perhaps he had read Bertie Russell, & had calculated, that in time it would happen that an aeroplane would cross that bit of air at the moment of the burst of the shell & that then he would get the iron cross. The Boche is like that in his mind, when he is educated & loves his Kaiser.

After this we went back to the cars & ate our lunch away from the racket, near a line that the Boche had wired but had not held. When he prepares a line, he first of all digs his dugouts, 30 feet deep, with 3 storeys, as usual, then puts up his wire, & then digs his trenches. Here he had not dug his trenches, but he had traced them, & had scattered the earth broadcast so as to leave no trace. I gather that the H line, which is of course, enormously strong, is still not quite wired in, nor dug, so that if he can get walloped out of it in these next days he will feel a little homeless, which God grant.

After this we went to tea with Birdie (of whom I wrote last night), a thoroughly nice tea, & a charming host or hosts; & so, after saying goodbye to Bean, we came home. Bean is going to take me over the line of the Australian advance at Pozieres; & he says that the Australian Govt. will let me see the picture postcards of Pozieres taken before the war. It once stood near a good sized wood, & was itself a big village, probably as big as Missenden, if you can imagine Missenden planked down at Prestwood. Well, I don't believe any tree of the wood is now more than a 2 foot stump, & of the village, 3 things remain, an iron gate with 86 holes in it, one bit of concrete wall about 7 feet × 12 feet, & the mound where the windmill stood. The rest is simply big holes in the ground.

I must stop now. The enclosed *may* give you some idea of the battlefield, but I'm afraid will not.

Dear love to you & Nana & Tim. Kiss them from me.

Your old love
Jan

1. 13 Well Walk, Hampstead, which leads to the Heath.

———————

[143]                                                                          26 Ap.

Dearest heart Con,

I have had a very piteous letter from Nana, begging to be sent back to St Felix, & my heart is wrung, for she is suffering cruel grief, yet all solutions seem hopeless. If she goes to Southwold[1], she will almost certainly be shelled during the term & perhaps killed, or maimed, or driven half mad with terror, in which case we should never forgive ourselves. If she doesn't go, she will break her little heart in secret, rebel against Isabel, & take half her confidence from us, & never really forgive us. The shelling is a probability, the other, I'm afraid, a certainty; but with this critical summer before us I am dead against Southwold, and so I say thumbs down, and I am writing a thumbs down letter to her. It is a cruel position, & I wish we could have Adeline to soften it, & it leaves me in the case of hoping there may be a shelling to justify me. I'm afraid of her suddenly putting roots into school life, just as I did at her age, & for many reasons I have always been bitter at being dragged away then; but I went to the *Conway* & to a way of life I loathed, & she may possibly like Mayortorne & can anyway go back to St Felix as soon as it is safe. She is specially heart broken at missing the dear summer term.

She must miss it. The coast is certain to be shelled, & I will not be a party to letting her run the risk. This is the critical time of the war & I think everything will have to be tried by both sides within the next 6 months. The enemy fleet will come out, & there will be raids on the coast & every kind of devilry. So whatever you do, do not let J go back to St Felix. One small shell in that place would burn the whole house.

You will know what a pain it is to have to give this pain to Nana, but it must be. She doesn't know the risk & doesn't mind it. She sees only the pain. If need be, keep her at home this term.

I had your 2 letters, postmarked 22nd & 23rd, today, with their enclosures & the violets. Here there are no violets, but I see a daffodil or two & a celandine or two & some wood anemones & a kind of cowslip that is really a primrose.

The enemy is fighting very stubbornly on his line, but it is thought that he is going further back to another line before long. He has lost at least 250,000, since April 9th, & a vast proportion are dead, for it is most bloody & awful fighting. As long as he has any leaders he will come on just as of old. When his leaders fall he seems all at sea & surrenders. Out of a trench, as long as he has no machine guns, he is not worth the sixth part of one of our men. Latterly he has been driven desperate by our shell-fire, & will attempt anything rather than stand still under it. Yesterday, 300 of them made a bolt to desert to us. They came over like a charge, so our gunners gave them a 'creeping barrage' & then machine-gunned them, so only two got across to us, & both of those were quite mad. In another attack, three told an Australian cook to surrender. The cook took the rifle from one of them & shot him & then took the other two prisoners. Still, they attack & attack, because they cannot endure the shelling, & the Lord only knows what the end will be. I don't think we shall break them & I don't think they will break, & I don't think Russia will do anything, but of the three, our breaking them is the likeliest. We shall at any rate cause them the most appalling losses. They are losing literally thousands on this front every day, nearly a division a day; from 10–15000 K.w. & prisoners.

I must stop now. Dear love to you my dearest heart, & I hope the hill is not so vile really.

Dear love to the babes.
Your old love
Jan

1. This town, which has been mentioned previously, had suffered a Zeppelin raid on 15 April 1915, and, like all eastern coastal towns, was dangerously exposed. During the Great War, Britain suffered 111 air raids, with 1413 dead, with 720 German losses in aeroplanes and airships.

---

[144]  Ap 27. 1917.

My darling Con,

You are right about J. She must not go back to St F till the danger clears a bit, & if M is hopeless for her the sooner she leaves the better. This great tangle makes so many lesser tangles that there is no peace on this earth, but that at least seems the wise thing, if anything can be wise. My heart bleeds for you & her & I wish this wicked war would end; only I see no end. Sometimes it seems to me certain that the next generation will be one of continued awful war, as it was a hundred years ago.

There is not very much news. The shelling of the line continues, & we kill great numbers of the enemy, & I suppose we shall go on shelling till the line is sufficiently pulped for us to attack, & then we shall repeat Vimy & send him back further. All enemy documents speak of our fire as very hell on earth, & of fearful losses, heavier even than at the beginning, but all the prisoners seem convinced that they can hold us back until we are starved into making peace; so there the matter rests. Still, if he goes on losing 30 divisions a month, as he is losing now, his army must break by July; so it is like to be a close finish. I really do not see how an army can lose 1,000,000 in 3 months & still remain an army. For every division broken, two divisions are shaken; and how 3rd line troops can stand what these fellows are getting is one of the mysteries of the war. We may really be near a dramatic end.

I sometimes see cavalry, & feel in the Middle Ages again. You see a man on a horse, with a gun & a lance & a sword & a bag of oats & a bag of hay & a horsecloth & a picket pin & rope & a water nosebag & a horse gas bag and spare shoes & curry comb, & the devil knows what beside, as well as all the man's kit, & you say 'My son, one lousy Boche in a shellhole with a 3 legged mitrailleuse, would shoot your regiment dead from 2000 yards away.'

War now is an affair of trenches, heavy unlimited artillery, & machine guns. The only possible cavalry henceforth will be swift tanks or armoured cars. Farewell my Arab steed[1].

The Boche were right in their analyses of modern war. But don't for a moment think (with Willy) that they were right because they used their imaginations. They were right because they used our imaginations. Wells foresaw the machine gun. Major Redway foresaw the trench, 35 years ago at least. The big gun ought to have been plain to our men after South Africa, & I think was, to our best men. I try to see why it was that we were so out of it, & it seems that we have a way of stablishing a vested interest so as to ensure our having the second best; & the way out of this I cannot see. We have been up against so many vested interests, fine old crusted ones, & here one sees the results, lying in the mud.

The enemy captured a company of Australians a few days ago, & disarmed them, took them into a quarry, & shot them with a machine gun, all except one, who managed to escape. If ever the Boche did a damnable deed that was damnably silly that was the one. I pity any Boche troops who come in front of the Five Divisions after this.

I am much with Australians here, for they are in this sector, and are almost the only troops here. It is odd, that both here & at Anzac I should be with them & not with English troops, & that I, by my life, should be so much more in sympathy with them; for I am.

I've passed the last 2 days on their amazing battlefield of Pozieres, & that is a place almost like Troy to me, with a kind of daze of beauty about it; for it was the crown of all the Somme battle; and it has a unity, that none of the other bloody ghastly blasting & death comes near to having. It is a small plateau, 500 yards square, & in its important part 200 yards square, & 10,000 men were killed in that plateau & buried & unburied & buried & unburied till no bit of dust is without a bit of man upon it.

Dear love my darling
from your old love J.

1. A quotation from Caroline Norton's poem 'The Arab's Farewell to his Steed'.

---

[145]  Ap 28

M.O.D.C.

. . . Am very glum today, it being dear Na's birthday & the first time I've ever been away for it.

I am dead against her going to St F for ½ a term. S'wold will be a dangerous place this term, highly dangerous, & the school specially so. We have no right to send a child to a frontier of the kind. Do not do it. This summer will see more desperate & devilish doings than have yet been done, & there may even be some attempt at a landing. Judith must not go to St Felix while this danger threatens. The danger is greater than you can imagine, & though it is not a national danger, only a local one, it is very real & very terrible, & J must not be exposed to it. At whatever cost of pain to her she must be kept out of it.

There is a lull in the actual battle & no news has been coming through. The cannonade is very heavy. I believe 5 English shells burst every second, or 300 a minute, or 18000 an hour, on our line of about 100 miles or so. It works out at about 1 for every 10 yards every hour, if I do the sum rightly, so that each yard of the line gets 2⅓ shells per day. Perhaps it doesn't seem much; but as most of the shells fall like rain on certain chosen spots, it works out as a good deal. We fire 3,000,000 a week, & perhaps 2 of the 3 millions will go upon one 5 mile sector; & God knows the effect it has. I have been fairly often under shell-fire, once very heavy, and it is a devilish thing, & it makes good troops bad troops & it drives bad troops mad. How the enemy can stand his present gruelling I cannot imagine. The firing is the heaviest ever known.

I went out today over Thiepval hill to Monquet Farm, which is one of the terrible places here. It stands at the head of a valley, & looks down the valley, & was once, a rare thing, a lonely French farm, looking down a lonely glen. Behind it is gently rising down, & in front of it, beyond the glen, is another gently rising down, with no other house in sight. It had vaulted brick cellars & was built of reddish bricks & had a court or dungyard, with a pond, open towards the glen. I don't know any place like it, but there must be some in Wilts, where the chalk slopes are gentle.

It does not look strong, except that you can only get to it by walking down an open slope & then walking up an open slope; and as you cannot walk in any open place near a machine gun, the enemy filled it with machine guns, perhaps a dozen, & defied us. So we blew the farm & the bricks & the pond & most of the dungyard & all the trees & all the fields to dust & rags & holes, till this is all that can be seen.

Corpses, rats, old tins, old weapons, rifles, bombs, legs, boots, skulls, cartridges, bits of wood & tin & iron & stone, parts of rotting bodies & festering heads lie scattered about. A more filthy evil hole you cannot imagine. Near it, in Pozieres, I saw 2 weasels hunt & kill a field mouse, & another weasel tackle, but fail to kill, a huge army rat, 11 times his weight. The weasel jumped, missed his tip, & the rat squealed & fled, shouting Kamerad.

Dear love to you my dear heart & to dear love Na & Timcat.

---

[146]                                                                 April 29.

Dearest heart,

. . . It is difficult to form any view of the war out here. Sometimes a thing occurs, & we feel that the war will end in the autumn: then something doesn't occur, & we feel that it will run another year. The submarine thing will make things awkward, but not impossible, so have no fear as to that. With a stout heart that can be won through easily enough. As to the enemy in the field, I doubt if he will be done for this year, judging by the way the war has gone hitherto, but there is a chance of it. Russia may increase the chance or lessen it but there is a chance. It would be rather a score, if we finished the war before any Americans have enlisted. They are a slow-moving race, for all their talk, & now the world will see them, what they are. The enemy fight very well. While he was up there, one of our aeroplanes dropped a bomb on one of his ammunition dumps, & blew it up, with the entire village, & killed a fearful lot of his men, but he was unfortunately not near at the moment.

If there were only some means of destroying or getting past machine guns. The war is held up by enemy machine guns. If we had 50,000 swift small 25-knot tanks with quick firing guns in them we could end the war next week. I believe that alone is the way to end the war. But as such things don't exist we must even be patient.

The enemy is very clever in hiding his machine guns. He makes the neatest little dodges, & uses 3 or 4 different kinds. In one, he has a tiny concrete fort just big enough for the gun & the man. This is immensely strong, & so buried & covered that it looks like the rest of a trench-parapet. In another, he has a small underground room, with a square opening, like a small well, just big enough for him to poke the gun through. In a third, he has just a shallow hole for the man to lie in, & a turf rest for the gun to fire over. One gun has as big a fire as 500 men; as I should think was plain to anybody, not a professional soldier. Yet at the beginning of the war, when Wells wrote on this point, a professional soldier replied, that Wells should write about things of which he really knew, & leave the use of machine guns to soldiers, who knew their limitations, etc. I don't know why; but that kind of a critical ass has more power in England than in other countries.

I hope to go out to see Birdie again before long. I love little Birdie his heart is so warm, & when I ask Birdie for information he asks me to tea, which is not the way with some I could name.

Dear love to you & to Nana & to Timcat. I wish his cough were better.
Your old lover
Jan

---

[147]                                                              April 30.

Darling heart Con,

. . . Not much news these last few days, except the usual reports from prisoners, that our shelling is more than man can stand. It must be something like that, & if it goes on much longer we shall get the H line (we already have parts of it) and apparently all Germany has been wagging that the H line is impregnable. It is tremendously strong, but no line can stand artillery if artillery is put in in sufficient weight, so before very long the H line will go, & Germany will get a very bad shock. Our 'offensive' hasn't begun yet. We are only sparring. So when we begin, & the H line goes, & the Germans realise that it has gone, they will be forced to try coups de theatre, & the fleet will come out or Holland will be overwhelmed.

They are beginning to use the class 1919, & the prisoners say that though these boys aren't very good they are good enough for 'cannon fodder'.

The other day up at Thiepval hill, a mounted policeman held me up, on suspicion, & examined me. Four prisoners had got away & had been traced to Thiepval, & the question arose, was I one of them; but I passed on my face alone as obviously not Boche; the police rode off to beat other coverts. Later, I heard that only two were prisoners escaping, the other two were spies of a very dangerous kind, who had come over dressed as a smart, elderly, Lieut Colonel, & his orderly, with every little particular complete & bright, & the orderly the exact shade, a little like a butler who still calls his lady friends bloody bits of all-right.

Now it is the very devil running down men like that. If you arrest the wrong man you had as lief cut your throat, & if you arrest the right one he shoots you through the head. And it is almost impossible to prevent that kind of thing; though less of it occurs than formerly. Probably we have a few of the devils own who do the same daily in the enemy lines. It must be tremendously exciting & interesting & quite unlike anything else in war, & no doubt it attracts people; but I believe it is like fighting in the air, the nerves don't stand it for very long & the people have to give it up.

In the old days, I had often thought, 'How could people be so cruel as to inform against poor, escaping prisoners?' I used to think it the vilest meanness. But now I joined in the hunt at Thiepval & beat a whole hill with the trackers & jolly well hoped we should catch the fellows, who were supposed to have gone to earth in some old dugouts. I suppose there are some thousands of deserted dugouts out Thiepval way, & any amount of bully beef tins in case they should be hungry, so they might well lie there for weeks, & steal new uniforms, & become sappers or railwaymen or labour battalion & so creep off. We did not catch them & I've not heard of their being caught, but I hope they will be caught; for a man who walks through our lines picks up too much to be safe thereafter. He sees where guns & ammunition are, where troops are billetted, & where the roads are busy, where H Quarters are, & where the troops are concentrating, & then, when he gets home, the guns are turned on, & our poor men are slaughtered.

I've been working at the battle of Pozieres for some days, & have now got it fairly clearly into my head; but of all the vast confused devilries the battle of the Somme is about the wildest.

Bone is here. We are to go to Monquet Farm tomorrow.

I don't think there is any more news, except (as I think I told you) we blew up a big enemy dump the other day. Of course he gets big dumps of ours from time to time, but this was as big as any he has had of ours.

Dear love to you & to my darling babes.

Your old love<br>Jan

[148]                                                                      May 1st.

M.O.D.C.

I'm so late tonight & so weak & weary I shan't be able to write a proper let. though I have yours of 27 & 28, one of them enclosing a batch of rubbish from various people. Many thanks for doing the money for me.

That d——d Scotch etcher was the man who made me late today. He has a car, & took me out to Pozieres, where I guided him to Monquet so that he might draw the place, while I got the hang of the lines on the crest above it. When he had drawn Monquet, & he only drew the cellar or tank laid bare by a shell, not the ghastly & heroic heaps which killed our men, he wanted to do Thiepval, so I took him there & left him on the castle ruins (a heap of earth). It was now 1, & time for lunch. He had left his lunch in the car 2 or 3 miles away. There was nothing for it but to give him half mine, which I did. We agreed to meet at 3.30 at a dump in the valley, so that I could get home for tea & do some writing later. I went up to see the Stuff redoubt, which wasn't much of a place, & the Hohenzollern redoubt, which was the devil of a place, all sunken concrete machine gun emplacements as wicked as hell, well up above Monquet, so as to kill anyone whom Monquet missed. Then at 3.15 I went down to the dump & waited. The d——d Scotch etcher never turned up till 5.15, so I lost half my lunch, all my tea, & nearly all my time for writing; so you may guess the mood I was in. However, he will not catch me like that again; never again, if I can help it, does a Scotch etcher make me wait 2 hours on a dump.

Just before I got to the dump a man had blown his thumb off by playing the fool with an improperly burst shell. It hadn't burst, but had partly broken, so he gave it a friendly jounce inside to see what would happen, & there came a bang, & his thumb went off, & the shrapnel coming out just missed his head. A head of that type is really better off, one would say.

While I was there, a Boche aeroplane came over, got up like one of ours, so I had an interesting view of this perky devil 3 miles up or so, being shot at & missed.

I don't know much about the Vimy battle. It was brilliantly successful, & now, I think, it is over, & we must wait a month or two for anything more. Personally, I don't think the Boche will do us by submarine, but they very nearly will, & I don't think we shall do them on shore, but we very nearly shall, & I don't think America[1] or Russia or Italy will count for a row of pins in the future fighting; it is a matter of ourselves mainly, with our ally France.

Now I must stop.

> Dear love to you & to the babes.
> Your old love
> Jan

1. Masefield under-estimated the physical and moral power of the arrival of American troops in France, likewise the Germans sneered at the Yankee 'red necks'. But the French knew better. Jean de Pierrefeu wrote, 'Everyone felt that the Americans were present at the magical operation of blood transfusion. Life arrived in torrents to revive the mangled body of a France bled white by the countless wounds of four years.'

---

[149]                                          May. 2nd or 3rd.
                                                Wed?
                                          Date & day forgotten.

Dearest heart Con,

 . . . It is mighty hot now & the roads are dusty, but the mud is dry. You cannot imagine what it is to have no mud. Shade in the desert, a well in the summer, a green fig tree anywhere, are all beautiful; but to have no mud is better; it is as good as to have leisure & a faithful friend. The only drawback is, that our service cap[1], which I always said was idiotic, is really a damnable thing. It gives no shade to the eyes, & no protection from rain or snow or sun, & to go out on a sunny day into a chalk country where the chalk is all laid bare, & no grass is growing & every tree is either dead or a stump, with this absurd thing on your head, is to be almost blinded with the glare of the ground. I do not know who invented the cap, which has no single thing to recommend it. Probably it was a job between some listed general & a tailor. I know of no more silly thing in all our equipment.

The colour of our khaki is a good thing, & far better as a colour protection than the grey the enemy use. The grey is the result of a great deal of thought &

patient labour & consciousness (Willy's[2] bellyful of all three) & probably our khaki was taken without any thought at all from some Indian costume. The grey, when you see it, seems perfect as a shade for colour protection, but when you watch it, you find that it remains visible for a long long time, & stands out vividly when the man moves. When you see khaki, you think, 'that will be conspicuous'; but it soon disappears into a background, & at even a short distance is invisible. You only see the movement & the man's face.

Two days ago I was in Sausage Valley, where the Australians formed for their attack on Pozieres, & up at the valley-head there is a little graveyard, as there always is where the field dressing stations were, & (as I always do) I went round the graves, to note what battalions were cut up & the dates. One of the graves contained five men, among whom was Gunner F. Crommelin[3]. 106 Howitzer Battery. Aust. 1. Force. Killed in action. Aug 7. 1916 (in the Pozieres fighting).

Do you know who this could have been? The grave was very carefully made, & had a cross of shell-caps upon it, & some cowslips in flower, & the word ANZAC worked in cartridges.

I went today up to Mametz wood, where a German machinegunner once had a nest in a tree. He was killed in his nest & stayed there till he fell to bits, but his nest is still there & two kestrels have built in it, & there are violets in blossom below & wood anemones. I believe every tree & nearly every bush in that big wood is dead, & the same in every wood in the battlefield; most of the big trees cut down by the fire & the rest blasted.

I'm afraid the last enemy we shall defeat is the English press. It is pitiful to see it, howling & foaming, playing the enemy's game whenever it might be helping to depress them. Every day, I see some sickening howl: 'We are being defeated by the submarines'. Even if it were true, why in God's name cheer the enemy by saying so? Such cries from us are the *only* solace Germany has now; literally the *only* one; & it is ghastly that it should be allowed, while the Nation gets suppressed for being simply silly. I think we will give up having papers.

Dear love to you & to Nana & Timcat.

Your old love,<br>Jan

We are moving billets again, & are living in a queer world of mess & litter. One of these damned foreign correspondents stole my gloves (a new pair) out of my cap last night. D—n his eyes say I.

1. Another writer, Sir Arthur Conan Doyle, had brooded over caps, incessantly urging the introduction of the 'Tin Hat', for which many soldiers were initially ungrateful.
2. Kaiser Wilhelm's.
3. Mrs. Masefield was a de la Cherois—Crommelin.

[150]                                                      May 3rd.

Dear heart,

. . . We are in to new billets today, & my little attic is like to be no great
shakes, but at least infinitely better & quieter than what I've been having near
the railway. In a way, I like this foreign correspondents' mess, although one of
the swine stole my gloves on me, but in other ways I hate it like the devil, &
long to be back in Albert, where, though there was no privacy, I could at least
talk every evening with Australians, about Anzac & Pozieres. But Albert,
though it is near my work, is now occupied by more important souls than
myself, & the club is closed. We have men of all races here, & of all of them, the
Italians alone seem universally competent & charming; the Russians have been
duds, & the French (as perhaps they really are to us) distasteful. It was one of
the two minor Frenchmen who pinched my nice gloves.

Today I went out to the famous Butte de Warlencourt, which I have seen in a
sort of blazing rain of shells & is now quite quiet & deserted. Perhaps no part of
all the filthy field has been so terribly shelled as the ground near the Butte; &
there the pools are still full of water & the water full of corpses, & the Boche
trench lines frequently filled in & obliterated. Lots of dead are lying there still,
& a kind of mess of equipment, such as lies everywhere all over the field. The
waste of war has to be seen to be believed. The dead were all Boche, most of
them quite young lads.

From the Butte I went down a blasted ally of dried mud where bits of barbed
wire was the only vegetation, & came to a nightmare town of broken firewood,
brick, pits, old girders & scraps of tile. This was Eaucourt l'Abbage, a little
place, as big as Kendals[1] with the front garden added, & all desolate &
deserted. Martinpuich, beyond, was the same. It was a populous town 3 weeks
ago, now the satyr goes there, & the dragon has his habitation there, & the
whole straggling village, as big as Missenden, is ruin & silence. Some of the
Boche concrete still stands there, & mighty strong it is. From Martinpuich I
came home in a tender, which is a sort of swift errand going car which does the
shopping for particular services, such as aircamps & artillery. They are
jolly good things to catch, for they whisk you in in no time. So this one did
me.

There is fierce fighting again, & things are being attempted & some things
are being done; one knows not with what success.

I'll send a note to Cross. Of course we must do the repairs. I told Munday to
do them as far as I can recollect.

Dear love to you & to Na & Tim.

                              Your old love
                              Jan

I hope to be done at the end of this month, if all goes well.

1. The home of Bobby and Lion Phillimore.

---

[151]                                                                    May 4. 1917.

M.D.O.C.

Will you, when you next write, please send me Mrs Warren's address. I will send her a few words if I can. . . .

Could you have Dorothy Warren for a night? I think she will feel Peter's loss more than anyone, & I feel she would be touched, for she thinks the world of you, as everybody does who is worth anything. I don't blame people for sending him into the air service. Surely he chose his service? It is one only of the countless wastes & wickednesses of this damned crime, the war. There was more in him than in Rupert, & much more purpose. There is just a chance that he is alive: & though I have no hope, we need not feel that he is gone until we are sure. The worst of it is, that this will be going on for another year at least, & then the cleaning up of the mess will have to begin; God knows what that may bring.

I'm writing this in my new little billet, which is rather dark & rather hot & rather smelly, & rather noisy from the singing of the orderlies in the offices below. I get wafts of 'Stony Nat Tony', 'A beautiful Rose' & other ditties, & now & again a bit of a sad, rather noble tune, which I first heard in October, from troops marching up to the line in Albert, & which is now well known & popular here, though I never heard the words. It reminds me a little of the old song of Greensleeves; & it has all the meaning of what the war now is in it.

The good Bean came in last night & we went into the question of the Germans killing the Australian prisoners in a quarry. Something of the kind happened; but just what, it is impossible to say, as we have only one witness, who is badly wounded. It is just possible that the thing was an accident, or that the men came under our own fire, nobody really knows. Of course, in a war like this, individual devils do get chances of being devils, & behave like devils of hell.

I look forward to hearing spicy scandal of Mrs A[1], & the full story of your jaunt to Harley.

Do you never receive any letters ever? You have only sent me one that has come to you since I came here. I get very few letters, as America has practically ceased to write; nothing even from F now. These submarines are responsible, & I wish they were in Jonah's belly[2]; which is like to be fuller than our own during the next few weeks.

It is very hot here & very dusty; but one would not mind these things if only we wore a kind of hat that would screen the eyes. The men wear their caps, peak at the back, which at least tends to screen them from sunstroke, but the eyes get no cover whatsoever. Here we see the professional soldier, sacrificing everything to appearance in time of peace, & thereby risking everything in time of war.

Well, dear love to you & to dear Tim & darling Nana.

A kiss to you all.

Your old love

Jan

1. To the reader's regret I have not unearthed this story, which is obviously connected with the circumstances of the Granville-Barker divorce.

2. Another example of Masefield's cavalier use of allusion and quotation. Jonah was imprisoned in the belly of 'a great fish'.

---

[152]　　　　　　　　　　　　　　　　　　　　　　　　　　　May 6. (or 5)

Sat.

M.D.O.C.

I have yours of the 1st with Mrs Webb's[1] enclosure. Alas, alas.

But I see no way of stopping until the war is over. This war is not over, nor anything like over. A certain conception of a State is being pitted against all other conceptions of a State, & when that happens, as it has often happened before, it goes on, till there is either victory by one party or a change in the other. If we were to have peace now, the German machine would make another bid five years hence; I cannot but feel sure of that. They hate us & mean to knock us out. Our conception of life is simply hateful to them. They think us fools & gentlemen, & I don't know which kind of us they despise the more. We have no knowledge of how they hate us. It is a bitter raging hate, & while that exists I don't see any possibility of the war's stopping or of peaceful relations beginning. They are brutes to our wounded, they are beasts to our prisoners, they would wreck all our towns, sink all our ships, plunder all our homes & ravish all our women, & if we don't stop them from doing this in this war be quite sure that they will try again in another.

I hear that the brutes have begun systematically to pillage the towns of N France, & what they call 'the plunder of war' is being packed up to go to Germany. I believe that this is true, & if it is, it is a sign that its line is to be abandoned soon, & another falling back is preparing. He is being shaken on H's line, as you will have seen. You may possibly hear stirring news this month.

It is a blessing to be in this new billet, out of the whistling of the trains, which used to go on all night, ten times an hour, just under my window in the old one. I am getting arrears of sleep now.

Today, I travelled in a lorry with a French interpreter officer, & talked about books with him, & he said that it was the first time he had ever met an English officer who had read not only a French book but any book of any kind, except perhaps a novel by Mr Garvice; so you see, I shall soon be a legend in the French army, as the one & only.

My darling old Con, it is no good using anything but mild & loving joking with Na. You can coax her into being a saint, but that is the only way. Alas for your poor toothbrush.

Dear love to you my darling & to my dear loves the babes.

Your old love<br>Jan.

1. Beatrice Webb (1858–1943): it is unlikely that Masefield, despite his concern for under-dogs and the poor, would have had much in common with the celebrated Fabian sociologist, political scientist. Three days later at the Yacht Club, London, she said, 'Poetry means nothing to me. It confuses me. I always want to translate it back into prose.'

---

[153]                                                                    May 6.
                                                                       Sunday.

My dear heart Con,

I was greatly pleased by Mr Tim's noble writing. He tokens his pasture & is indeed a credit to you. I have duly written to him a letter of thanks by this post. *Please let me know if it reaches him.* . . .

I've been going into reckonings, & think I had better have an extra ten pug to my credit. I shall not need it, probably, but it will be safer, for the journey back is always costly, & life here is what France always is, & worse now than ever. If you will do this for me, probably I shall not have to bother you again in this way for this time.

In a few days time, I shall have to go north to Anzac H.Q. to stay with Bean for a couple of nights, to complete my Pozieres. There is talk of my going to other H Qs, but let the circumcised believe; I don't expect for a moment that that will happen. The work does not seem to get any unity in my head, but rather tends to split off into four or five quite distinct battles. The fight for Fricourt-Mametz, the battle of the big woods, the fight for Pozieres, Monquet Farm, Thiepval & St Pierre Divion; there are 6 already. I shall have a hot & dusty fortnight in London, I'm afraid, grubbing in the records.

One very dreadful thing about the battlefield is that it is quite without shade. All the trees are killed (I think quite without exception) & all the houses are laid flat, so that on a hot day one's only chance is to find an old bomb-proof or magazine or hut, & crawl within like a cave-dweller.

Today I went out to Le Transloy, where, only a few weeks ago, I saw the enemy walking in the street. I walked up the street where I had seen him walking down, & looked at the general smash, & the corpse of one of the last squads of enemy to come there, perhaps one of the very squad I saw. He was lying on his face, with a tattered German testament blowing all about him, &

his new pair of boots cocked up into the air. I walked back to Griedecourt, a big smashed village in big smashed trees, with a lot of our dead just outside it, & there I ate my lunch, while some Australians sang & chatted in the ruins. Then I walked over real grass to Flers, which I last saw when all the field was mud, & when that lonely village in the mud was like Sodom & Gomorrah mixed. Today, it was quite deserted; I was the only person within a mile of it; and it gave me a feeling of romance & strangeness, as though I had done that thing before, as I have, often, in imagination, come to a deserted town. It is a fair size, (as big as Missenden proper) & all its big trees are killed, & most of them smashed, but there is a kind of spring there all the same: some onions are pushing & there are currant bushes, primroses, two daffodils, some gooseberries, & a little rhubarb. God help us, this war is hell.

No news particularly this time, but fierce fighting is going on, & that is all that we shall hear for a while. The French are said to have done well. Perhaps this month will shew us what Russia can still do. Probably Russia's real need is educated men. She has never had many, & most of those she has are exiles. Now she wants 300,000 trained minds or so in a hurry & very rightly scraps the cause of the lack. When the Revolution took place, the Boche held up a notice in their eastern trenches. 'You have sacked your Czar. Now Make Peace.' The Russians in reply held up a notice 'We have sacked *your* Czar. Now look out.'

Dear love my darling.

---

[154]                                                    May 7.
                                                         Monday.

My dearest heart Con,

Thanks for your let of 3rd.

I hope to be back about 30th, if I can only get at these corps commanders. It is not at all like a year ago, when the commander was only too eager. These commanders are all conducting operations & have no time whatever to spare to anybody, least of all to a sub, who drives up in a lorry, to the horror of the sentries at the gate.

I've been making enquiries about the enemy's habits, & it seems fairly certain that the enormous piles of beer bottles near his trenches are not beer bottles, but soda water bottles. He makes all his men drink a kind of soda water, aerated not far from the front, & each man going into the line brings up 2 or 3 of these bottles, fills them with soda water on his way, & takes them into the trenches & throws them away when empty. Old beer bottles are used because they happen to have lots of them. The cognac bottles, which also abound, are said to be found only on the sites of field dressing stations. I don't think they could say the same of our whiskey bottles.

There is no doubt whatever that they are a fine sturdy lot of men, whenever they are men at all. They are very depressed at being driven back so often & at losing so many men; but they are all confident that we cannot break through, & that the submarines will starve us long before we can starve them. It is certain, that one Prussian regiment of veterans mutinied a few days ago, & said that it was sick of the war, & had fought long enough, & wasn't going into the trenches again. The regiment was rounded up by hussars & taken off to hard labour somewhere. They no longer shoot mutineers, but put them to hard labour for long sentences. They have 180,000 mutineers & deserters now in their military prisons, so we must not call him a servile being, as the press delights to do. He has plenty of the adventurous criminal in him, as the world has reason to know. He is a sort of cormorant Japanese.

I think he is a little anxious about his man-supply, for although he has many men, they are getting spent at a great rate, faster than our ships; so I suppose it is now a race. He is fighting very bravely & skilfully. I'm afraid his military mind is more flexible than ours.

Today I went again to Serre, where we lost very very heavily in July. I was also at a cruel place called the Hawthorn Ridge, where our men fell dead in platoons, & where the enemy turned machine guns on the wounded & the stretcher bearers, & then hoisted the Red Cross flag while they went out to rob them. This at least is wholly true, for I have it direct from truthful eye witnesses who were in our lines at the time.

Of course, the Boche say, 'we are not fools nor gentleman, & we make war like the clever cads we are. If you like to be such fools as to try to be gentlemen in war, you may try it, & when it is too late you will find it doesn't pay.'

Orpen[1] is out here, painting. He gave me a lift in his car both today & yesterday. I've not seen any of his work, but it is probably better than anything that has been done so far. (This is another jab at the Scotch.)

I send you Mrs Coolidge's letter. Her husband was here, you may remember, a few days ago, with the Am Amb.

Dear love to you & to Nana & to Timcat.

Your old love<br>Jan

1. William Orpen (1878–1931), portrait painter, first to be sent to France as an official war artist. Knighted 1918.

---

[155]  1.(d).   c/o R.T.O.
A.P.O.S. 37.
B.E.F.
May 8 (or 9)

Dearest heart,

I'm late again, as I had a long day, & was late getting into Albert, & should be on the road still, but that Orpen came along, for the 3rd day in succession, & gave me a lift in his noble rich car.

I've got your let of the 6th. . . .

I keep trying to get some accurate idea of the war into my head, but I haven't got John's just mind[1], nor his legal grasp, & I cannot. I feel this, that we have never yet tried Imagination & the New Thing, & that the Germans have succeeded simply because they have. They tried barbed wire & the howitzer & the machine gun. I believe that if we tried the aeoplane we should succeed. I don't mean the 'squadrille' & the 'flight'. I mean the aeroplane by the Division & the army corps, 20,000, & 100,000. It is true, we tried the tank, but it seems to me that we tried it much too much as an experiment, & too little as a weapon certain to have some success.

Now it seems to me fairly clear that the war can hardly be won by fighting. Even if we break the line, he will still have more machine guns than we, & there is no getting past a machine gun. He will fall back on another line, & there will be a delay, while the guns are brought up to blow him out of it. Then when he is blown out of it, he will fall back on another line, & there we shall be again. Meanwhile our ships will be being sunk & his populace will be getting resty. I sometimes almost think the quarrelling nations will repudiate their governments & their armies & conclude some sort of an independent arrangement, as I fear Russia may.

The present fighting reminds me very much of Napoleon's later indecisive battles, Lützen, Bautzen, & Eylau, if those were their names, in which he avoided disaster & lost whole hecatombs. As far as I recollect, they were followed by Leipzig, which really settled his hash, but we can hardly expect Leipzig this year. Fritz has an easier task than Boney & a much sounder position. From 1 or 2 small signs, I conclude that the Italians are going to attack. The Italians here are very remarkable men, & remind me of the Medici; if their army is of the same quality they ought to achieve something. But *we* are the mainspring of this war, I have no faintest doubt of that. It rests on us or on no-one.

Did I tell you, that I may go to Paris for a night? It seems there is a big French Bureau, with wonderful photographs of all the battlefield *as it was before the war*, so that I shall be able to see Pozieres, & the Farm of Monquet, & Beaumont Hamel & the damned & bloody corpseyard of Serre, all in green leaf, with cows in the meadows. My God, it will make me weep like a child. I may not be able to obtain access, but I hope to do so, & one of the Frenchmen here says I could even obtain duplicates free of charge. Mon Dieu, mon dieu, moi qui n'a pas even a car nor a postcard.

Dear love to you & to the babes & forgive a stupid letter.

Your old lover<br>Jan

1. John Galsworthy had trained as a lawyer, and was called to the Bar in 1890.

May 11.
Friday.
M.O.D.C.

. . . Yesterday I was taken out to Pozieres in the early morning, & met Bean, & went with him over the eastern half of the Pozieres Battle, which of course he saw, & we finished up, as the first half of the battle finished, on the high road from Albert to Bapaume. We then walked down to a hut & had some lovely stew with bread & jam & a quart or so of tea. After this, we walked up over the western half of the battle, from the road to Monquet Farm, which was mighty hot work, & we ended at Monquet in the old enemy dugouts, which are deep, pannelled rooms, & passages far under ground. They fought with machine guns down in the passages, & all the panels are cut & gouged & scored with the bullets. Even after Monquet was taken, the enemy who knew the passages (& God alone knows how far they may go) used to come along them with machine guns & shoot our men in the back & then escape. It is all a kind of rabbit warren, & I do not know at all how soldiers can deal with a warren of the sort. They seem to be shellproof (more or less) & gasproof; & I don't see how they can be treated.

It came on to rain as we reached the car, from Monquet, so we went back to the hut & had another quart of tea with bread & jam, & then pottered about & got cool & looked at Dyson's drawings (which are rather good, D being official artist there, & the old cartoonist of the early war-time). Then we had dinner, with more bread & jam & another quart of tea, & so out to different huts to sleep. There were no ghosts, that I could see, but from my hut I watched for a long time the flashings of the guns over the crest, like a continual blinking of summer lightning.

This morning, after a quart of tea & some bread & jam, we went out to Flers, which was once a sort of hell on earth in a sea of mud, besides being pretty dangerous, but is now a quiet ruin in a field already partly green, though smelling fearfully of dead men & horses. We went into a kind of famous Australian tunnel there, which runs 1000 yards into a hill, but was never finished. It was as good as any tunnel cut by the enemy. It was cut to provide a safe road from near Flers to Griedecourt, & then, when it was nearly ready, the Boche withdrew & went back to beyond the ridge.

After this, we went back to lunch at Mametz, with a very interesting, clever, nice & rather famous Australian, who happened to be there. We had sausages & bread & jam & a quart or so of tea, & talked about events of the war. He said that in some of the recent fighting on the H line, he saw 4 Boche prisoner stretcherbearers carrying in a wounded Boche, shoulder high, to our lines, while 4 Australian stretcher bearers walked alongside them carrying a wounded Australian shoulder high. A Boche shell came over some 60 yards from them & burst. The Australians never turned a hair but walked on with their load. The Boche flung their man down on the ground & bolted into shell holes. He said, he thought the Boche were like that always, whenever they had no one to command them; but that as long as they had a corporal or someone to beat & kill & curse them they would be as brave as lions.

A few days ago, an Australian officer went into a Boche dugout with an electric torch. He turned into a side room & flashed his torch, & saw five Boche there. He nipped back, drew his revolver, shoved the revolver in at the door & fired 2 shots, & heard some groans & loud cries of Kamerad. As all the 5 surrendered he marched them in to prison & then went back to the dugout, where he made himself at home & ordered food. While he was eating his food, a little mild voice of Kamerad came from under the table & scared him out of his wits. By a great effort of will be managed to get up & look under the table, & there he found a sixth Boche who had been there all the time. After this, Bean drove us back to A, & here I am writing this.

I got Lew's little letter, thanks, & have written to him.

I've not seen RB's[1] sonnet but may be able to find it in *The Times* here.

Dear love to you & to the babes.

Your old love<br>Jan

1. Robert Bridges.

---

[157]                                                                          May 12.

M.O.D.C.

Thanks for your letters of 8 & 9.

I can't well fix any day or even week yet; but I hope to be back this month. The battlefield is fairly clear in my head now, & I need not go there much more, or not very much, & my application to see the Paris records is in the hands of Lord E, & is likely to go through fairly soon. The Paris things are photographs & ought not to take very long to study, & some Frenchmen here think that they will give me duplicates to take away, which is not at all my conception of Frenchmen nor of Government Institutions dealing with a writer, but if they do thus madly, blessed may they be. It is likely that the Australian Govt will give me facilities; but I put no faith in any Govt; we have put spokes in their wheels; they may do the like by us.

I am concerned about what you say of food, but perhaps we may be able to manage. I think at a pinch this country could ration us, & during the winter we could make a Channel tunnel probably & so be a little free of this eternal ship business, so wasteful of time & labour. The enemy will sink every ship she sees, Vaterland or not, & will be jolly glad to sink Vaterland to spite us. She is out to destroy us as a nation, to kill as many of us as she can, & to pillage, ravish & enslave the rest. That is her conception of war, & the only possible way to stop her is to kill & enslave her first; or to change her mind somehow, into some way of thought less given to war; & how to do that without first beating her I do not see, nor how to beat her[1]. I really don't see how there can be peace before 1919. People here say 1920. And thinking that, I don't see how any peace could be more disastrous; so there we are.

Today, I took a dud Russian up to B'mont Hamel, Thiepval & Monquet. Like half these creatures, he had no nails in his boots, & lay down with his tongue out after half a mile, so he spoiled my day, which was a pity, as I had a car to myself on condition that I took him, & could have done a lot by myself. Corpses seemed to fascinate him. Some say that they fascinate animals, but I think they frighten animals, as I have often seen horses shy at them, or at the smell from them. He used to stand at gaze & say, 'C'est un cadavre?' 'Oui, c'est ca. C'est un Boche.' Then he would gaze some more & reluctantly come away, with his head over his shoulder, still gazing. I think, like a true Russian, he was getting a true impression of it.

Coming back, we saw 6 naked Australians bathing together by the road in a shellhole which still held water. It was about 7 feet across, so a tight fit, but well worth it on a day so hot.

There aren't many troops in the Ancre valley now, so all that jolly bathing country runs to waste as far as I can see. Some of the trees there are not quite dead, as there will be a kind of a browny green-ness there after all. There are about 200 green leaves & a sprout of pampas grass even in Pozieres, but beyond that is almost perfect death.

As far as I can see, I shall be about free to get back in the last week of this month, unless they devise some new stunts or want me at HQ or something.

One feels a beast to be going back to Blighty, while these men remain, to work on & to face danger; & one feels sad to leave these Australians, who have been jolly good fellows to me, knowing that I shall never see them again, for many will be killed & the rest will go home & I shan't see them again anyhow. I'll try to give their battle of Pozieres a story.

Now dear love to you & to the babes.

Your old lover<br>Jan

1. Writers as politically diverse as H. Rider Haggard and H.G. Wells would have agreed with Masefield's fairly representative loathing of Germany. Bernard Shaw, Gilbert Murray, Bertrand Russell would not.

---

[158]

May 13.
Sunday.

M.O.D.C.

Alas, alas, no let from you today, & not any time for me to write to you.

I've had to go to a duty tea with a Major, & some Fr ladies were there, & they played & sang to us, & it was not etiquette to leave till they did, so here we are. One song they sang was very lovely. It was an old nursery rhyme of 'Au clair de la lune'. I wish that I could sing, even with no voice. At Oxford, where one learns all things, perhaps someone will teach me that.

Now at Oxford, where one learns all things, I want you to learn some things for me, if so be as you can.

Can you get at the Oxford Dictionary & at Johnson's Dictionary & send to me, out of them both, the accepted spellings of the word skilful or skillfull, or skillful. There is a bold & noble general among the Australians who has a bet on the point, & I've been asked to decide it.

I am still Pozieres-popeyed, & go there every day, & try to get the hang of it all in an intimate way. It was a kind of Troy, & has a unity in it, & will make a brief book by itself. I wish you could see it.

That army is a little like Napoleon's old army. The bravest officers in one of the Brigades were, in civil life, a working wheelwright, a carpenter, & a hair-dresser.

There is the bell for mess, & I am not unbooted or nothing.

Dear love to you & to Tim & Nana.

Your old lover

Jan

---

[159]

14. May. 1917.
Monday

M.O.D.C.

Yours of 10th came today. Gracias.

I am delighted about Peter; it is splendid; & I am writing to Mrs Warren. He will probably be safe for a time, & afterwards doubtfully safe, though perhaps as safe as he would be at the front. The Boche will probably kill most of their prisoners if we put their men in hospital ships, as I hope we certainly shall, & if they start doing that, the bloodiness & savagery of the end of the war will be without parallel. Then, again, I think they will take to shooting flying corps officers if we bombard their towns in reprisal again, as we did Freiburg. The only reason why, till now, they have been polite to RFC men, is simply that they want our airmen to continue being 'polite' & the rest of it, & to refrain from bombing their towns, which they are terrified of. All our bombardments of the German towns have produced immense effects on the national mind, & 'if I were etc' I would see that those effects were rubbed in in these critical days of the war. Still, the main thing is, that Peter is at present safe. We must all get his address & write to him.

Who are the people who are delighted, at my doing the Somme?

I don't really know O, who is a Major. There is no real intercourse between Ms & Ss. The whole business is the devil & silly & farcical, & smacks of

Bochery & the early Georges, & all this damned tomfoolery that would fain
have the varnish of Bochery with none of its industry. However, all this can
wait.

Our armies are having some successes at the moment. Fritz is supposed to be
packing, to go back to a new line, the Wotan or Gotterdammerung or Wiener
Schnitzel line, whatever it may be called. Any other armies would be dis-
pirited, but I believe these enemies enjoy digging, & rather look forward to
making another line. He is using all our prisoners very brutally & away up
under fire; & our men are growing weary of the big fat squads of Germans who
idle away 8 hours a day on the roads here in safety. It is really farcical. The
squads stand about the roads & pat them with picks, & then stand aside to let a
car pass. Then they pat them again & stand aside to let a lorry pass. Then they
all draw up to let some troops pass. Then they gather round to enjoy the latest
joke of their guards, & then they knock off for lunch.

Today, a certain, who has a car, took me to B'mont Hamel. I started in joy,
thinking, hurray, I have a day with a car, & shan't have to ask for a lift. But my
happiness was soon turned to acute misery, which has lasted all day. 3 nice
Australian officers asked for a lift up to Albert, & we could easily have taken 2,
though not the 3rd, & I was so eager to repay the many many lifts Australians
have given to me. But to my horror & anguish, the certain, whose car it was, &
who is my superior officer, refused, O God, on the plea that he hadn't room. So
I had to sit still & blush with shame & agony & to see what those Australians
thought of us, & to feel that I was in the same condemnation with the certain. I
shall never forget their faces, nor the faces of the men at the barrier who heard
my man's excuse. My God, I've blushed & suffered all day long at it. It was a
damned thing to have done. I don't know how I shall ever ask an Australian for
a lift again; nor anybody else for that matter. I've never known such a thing on
these roads. It was a wicked thing. There were two seats plainly vacant. I shall
never forget it; but nothing but an order will ever take me with that man again I
hope.

B.H. is much as usual, a desolate cross gully full of blasted tree
& broken brick. We were beaten there, with many casualties, & then we were
triumphant there with hardly any, & afterwards the mud there was something
to remember, & now, like so many other places, it is 'a back-area'; that is,
deserted, save by a policeman at the cross & some salvage men, who fish out old
equipment from the shellholes, & say 'I got a bloody trout or something ere,
Bert'; & then dump it down by the road till somebody else removes it.

I've heard nothing yet about going to Paris, that beastly hole. I prefer this
place to Paris. The country people have a rather noble & simple carriage & are
genuinely nice. I see our men walking out on Sundays with perhaps two girls &
their mother, & talking perhaps two phrases of French 'Na poo'[1] & 'Bong'.[2]

The folk go back to Albert daily, & they have even ploughed 2 fields beyond
it.

Dear love to all.

Your old lover

Jan

1. War-time expression, derived from attempts to pronounce 'il n'y en a plus', meaning 'it's finished', 'all gone', given by bar-men and store-keepers, but extended to cover most branches of service life in which expectations and supplies are exhausted.

2. 'Bon' was one of the four French words actually understood and used by British troops, and 'bonne bouche' was corrupted to 'Bongo Boosh'.

---

[160]                                                             May 15.

M.O.D.C.

Your letter of 12th came & filled me with sorrow for poor Bessie, who is better now I hope. Poor little Lew will be in a sad state about her. I hope that the Oxford doctors & people are nice & understanding & pleasant to deal with.

As far as I can make out, I am to go to Paris next Monday, if the thing can be arranged. No doubt it could be arranged; but some months of experience of these people make me very doubtful if it ever will be. However, it seems probable that the Australian Govt has got duplicate photographs of some of these places, & so far the Australians have proved pleasant & easy, so that if Paris falls through, as it may, I may manage with the Australians.

By a curious chance, I saw a squadron of Indian cavalry passing an Australian battery this morning. The Indians looked like philosophers & the Australians like the rather tough bartenders in a mining camp. It was a contrast of east with west, but one had no hesitation in choosing which unit one preferred. Afterwards one had a kind of awe, in thinking that we were responsible for both types; & then I thought, 'How, in God's name, & who does these things?' For we do not know anybody who does these things, we have not met them, nor dealt with them in our official dealings; far from it. Yet here are these results; wonderful, in their way.

Thought about the war changes & is vague, up & down the road, & is today a little pessimistic, & 1920-ish, whereas a day or two ago it was October. We shall go on thus for a while. The main thing is to cook the goose of the submarines, & probably before that is done we shall have the H line. With the goose cooked & the line taken, Fritz's tail will be down & there will be a chance of bringing the thing to an end. If it is to be settled by fighting, 1920 will be the date, roughly speaking.

Na's letter troubles me. She talks of going back to St Felix at ½ term, just the dangerous season of the year. Surely this is not what you have planned?

I met a gunner going up today, & travelled in a lorry with him. He said, that he had been censoring his battery's letters, & had come upon one letter which said 'The enemy are shelling terribly as I write & I may be blown to pieces at any moment, but I would not be anywhere else. I am proud to be out here, doing my bit for England.' The man had never been under fire, & was writing in a base, & 'his bit', that he was so proud of, was cleaning latrines, he being useless at anything else.

Coming back in a lorry there were two Australian lads of the Light Horse, whom I judged to be recent drafts & new arrivals. I have noticed that all these recent drafts allways [sic] swear that they fought all through Gallipoli, & were the sole survivors of their regiments after the taking of Pozieres. We were passing through Pozieres & I asked them if they had been in that fighting? 'Oh yes, they had, all through it, all the time.' I asked, where their regiment had been, & they were flummoxed at this, so I asked, 'on which side of the road were they engaged?' This settled the more innocent of the two; but the other, after a little thought, said 'We were pretty near in the middle & the rest were just about all round.' I thought this a magnificent reply for a lad of about nineteen.

I have not looked at an English paper for about a fortnight now, nor at any book for about a month. It is terrible, that our press should be what it is, & have such power.

Now I must stop. Dear love to you & to the babes.

Your old love
Jan

---

[161]                                                                  May 16.

M.O.D.C.

Once again I curse your Oxford Sunday that gives me no letter on Wed; besides it is wet again & mud is forming.

Here, with the low barometer, the talk is naturally of Russia, & not much faith is put in her, & still less hope, & no great amount of charity. The question arises, what will happen, if she makes a separate peace.

It seems (to me) probable, that the Boche already count Russia as out of the war, & are moving troops from the Eastern front to the H line, & that that is the reason why the H is proving such a job. Austria, doing the same thing in Italy, is holding the Italian thrust. The Enemy general staff would not risk this adventure without good reasons; they are much too good soldiers; so that there is at least a strong likelihood of Russia standing out.

If she stands out, perhaps this would be the normal result, or the likely result: Germany, eager, really, for peace, & not likely to secure a better occasion for treating, would say to France: 'We will evacuate N France if we may return to the status quo ante, with some safeguards as to Belgium & the Balkans, & some commercial arrangements not hostile to ourselves.'

This seems to me more likely, on the whole, that that she should bring over her eastern armies & try to overwhelm us here. Even if she tried that, she knows enough now of defensive war to know that she would not succeed for a year, & that by that time some few American troops would be in France, say, perhaps, 100,000; with more coming.

So that on the whole, if Russia treats & stands out, it brings up an occasion & opportunity for 'collective bargaining', & perhaps a better one than some think, if much less good than was hoped. Anyhow, the old 'end of war' idea has no chance. The nations will be as armed as ever. The most we can hope for, is, that, England, France & the United States may league themselves to prevent war, & arm themselves up to the eyes to enforce their words.

Failing this, & if Russia is out of it, the war must go on for another 18 months[1] & I doubt if any combatant wants that.

Our Russian here, who is very critical, & often shrewd in his criticism, says that on the Eastern front they charge trenches with cavalry & that the cavalry take the trenches.

It is all very well, but the trenches there must be very different from these. I do not see how cavalry could either assemble to take these trenches or go across to take them, over our lines of trenches, through our wire, over no man's land, through the enemy wire, over the parapet, into a ditch perhaps ten feet deep, perpendicular at the back. Fancy putting a horse at such a succession of obstacles, under a barrage & machine guns.

It is possible, that if ever we really rout Fritz, cavalry may be of great use in pushing the rout; but I contend that the horse belongs to a past age in war, with the battleaxe & the British cocked hat; & that the thing now is to use cavalry in the skies, & to have whole vast divisions of aeroplanes; enough to terrify & ecraser & aneantir, & to hunt & bedevil & blind; & that that is what we ought to bid America to do, as she has so many mechanics; viz: to train an army of fliers, 50,000 strong, & to put all her energy into that, & to have them out here by September, ecraséing the infame. Peterkin[2] would.

Cavalry do get chances in modern war, I admit; especially in following up a really successful attack. But one never knows when the attack will be successful, & until it has been proved a success the cavalry cannot assemble anywhere near the place without being blown to pieces. So that they have to keep well back, & are not up in time when their chance comes. So there you are. They look pretty, & they clink, & catch the ladies' hearts & all the rest of it; but time has passed; & though soldiers naturally are loth to give up so many helps to attracting female interest, the sight of a cavalryman today ought to be limited to outside the good old war museum in Whitehall. There they would be in place & would be worth the 6$^d$.

It is terrible to see that the world has gone on 100 years without the soldier noticing.

Dear love to you & to the babes.

Your old love

Jan

1. Here Masefield was prescient: the Great War continued until November 1918.
2. I cannot identify Peterkin, unless it is a not wholly apposite reference to the Dutch boy in Robert Southey's verse, *The Battle of Blenheim* (1798):

'And every body praised the Duke
    Who this great fight did win.'
'But what good came of it at last?'
    quoth little Peterkin.
'Why that I cannot tell,' said he,
'But 'twas a famous victory.'

[162]
                                                    May 17.
                                                    Thursday.
M.O.D.C.

No letter from you again, which is very worrying, as the last I had said that Bessie was ill. I hope that she is better & that tomorrow I may hear so. Perhaps the delay is only due to your country Sunday post.

There is not much news today, except accounts of desperate fighting. An officer came in to tea. He was just back from Russia, which he had left, of course, before the Revolution broke out, but only just before. He said, that things there were very bad indeed, & had been made, for the moment, much worse by the Revolution, but that he thought there would be an improvement soon. At present, the troops desert a good deal, & each army & corps & brigade & regiment is forever engaged in forming committees to choose their officers. Then, the men fraternise with the Boche a good deal; there is hardly any fighting; & a Boche has come over with terms of peace & been allowed to go back. The Boche is evidently thinning his eastern line to hold this line. It is still too early to do any fighting on that front, but, if the weather keeps good there, fighting will be possible by about the first of June. Until then, we shall not know which way Russia will turn. She is in a difficult place, & unless the Boche does something silly, or some man arises who can direct the country as Napoleon directed France, the committee habit will probably land her in a peace.

Yesterday, coming back from my wanderings, I came through a village, where, in the days of Louis XIV, there was a certain lady loved by the King. The King built a chateau & laid out the grounds for her, & employed Vauban, the fort-maker, & made him build the chateau as a miniature fort. So there it is today, in quite wonderful old redbrick, with parapets of stone, & covered ways & entry ports & re-entrants & all the other things; except that the lady's family seems to have come down in the world & sold some of it at a bargain & turned the rest into a villa. It must once have been a very noble place. Blossom was out all over it; but the spring here has no sort of feel; the war is on it all.

An American, who was in Germany in Sept, says that Germany is sick of the war but is not going to give in till she is beaten to the world, & that she has plenty of food, as indeed I always supposed she had, though possibly short of certain things. He says that she (I here mean America) is building wooden ships, to go (I suppose) by oil engine. This she ought to be able to do pretty quickly, for in the old sailing days she used to turn out smallish wooden ships, say 6 or 700 tons, able to carry, say, 8 or 900 tons cargo, in a very short while. They were stuck together by hairpins & did not last, but profits were so big then that it was worth while. She is also hard at work, or soon going to be, mobilising mechanics for war work. She has some ships over on this side now, as you know. I think, that she is a mechanically-quick & mechanically inventive nation, & that that, apart from finance, ought to be her contribution to the war. Let her invent the damnable & bloody machines that she alone can invent, & then let her make them by the hundred thousand, & let them be deadlier than hell, so that Fritz may get them on his vitals.

I was out yesterday at Morval, on the east of the battlefield, & today at Martinpuich; both busy places when I was here first & noisy with cannon & none too safe, but now as quiet as tombs, utterly deserted wrecks & ruins of pleasant little towns, Morval on a hill top, like a little Troy, & M'puich along a ravine, like (I suppose) Nineveh. It is not possible to describe either place. They are both collections of big holes, with shattered wood in them, & a sort of mound in each, where the church was. In M'puich there were a lot of the cure's sermons, in script, lying in the mud, all about Jesus & the holy Marie, & a lot of rather blasted gardens, with currant bushes & May flowering tulips. But no man can describe them. They have to be seen. Once they must each have had 3 or 400 souls in them, with homes & smoke & fires & dinner times & beasts in the stable, & now, my God, they lie out in the blasted field, unvisited by man, & they look like the cities of the plain, & the corpses' knees & hands & boots stick up out of the mud at one as one goes by, & the rats come out sick over one's feet.

No more news.

Bless you all & my dear love to all.

> Your old lover
> Jan.

---

[163]                                                                    May 18.

My dear heart,

I have your letter of 13th with Lady H's[1] paper, which shall be dealt with. You do not say how Bessie is, but I conclude she is better.

It is early days for CB[2] to begin telling us what society is to be after the war. I wish it were the time for that; but it is not; nor nearly. The war is pretty well certain to go on for another two years, or more, if Russia comes out of it now;

anyway her collapse makes it almost impossible for it to end as we had hoped & planned; & the kind of end can no longer be foretold.

The societies that have survived great wars in the past have (I think) always been exhausted, disappointed, embittered & impoverished, even after success. As for great & ennobling ideas coming out of clever talk to kindle the world, he might as well go put his head in a bag. The world is not prone to kindle at clever talk, except with anger. The world has always said to the talker what the little boys said to the prophet, 'Go up, thou baldhead'; and neither you nor I can remember any sentence or saying spoken by any clever talker in our own time or the world's.

It was said by someone that C.B. is in the army. If that be so, it is hard to understand what he means by saying that society will end with the war or how he comes by it. He must surely have met some deep & thoughtful men, among these hosts of officers, whose opinions are wise & ideals fine. There must always be some such in any community, & I here have been much struck by the number of them in our army. We have the other kinds as well, the man of tiny wit & many regulations, the jovial ass, & the empty, plucky ready lad, who says Tophole and Right Oh (& nothing else ever) & sings 'My little grey home in the West'[1], & then goes out & wins the Military Cross. It takes all kinds to make a world.

We have won a good stretch of the H line, & the chances are that Fritz is about to go back to the line behind it, if not already going. He will have held this 'impregnable' line about a month or five weeks, & is now being booted out of it, after all his bluff and brag, & after many desperate & bloody attempts to hold it or to get it back.

I do not know; but it seems fairly evident that he is going to fight on this system all through the summer. Prepare a line, fall back to it, fight on it, delay our taking it for as long as he possibly can, at almost any cost, & then fall back to another line. It is is [sic] a plan of fighting delaying actions & then delaying our advance by poisoning waters, blowing up roads & laying mines, while he consolidates a new position a few miles further back, & hopes to get it done before we can bring up our guns. At this rate, I should think that he will be back some ten miles by the end of the summer, but will also be without the men to delay us further. We got a prisoner the other day, a boy of 18, who reached the front at midnight, was put into an attack at 12.30, was wounded immediately, & was a prisoner at 1 o'clock. His military career was briefer than the summer flower.

The devil of it is, that if Russia comes out, as we must expect, Fritz will have more men than he can spend, to throw against us, & although we have ample guns to kill them all, it will be a slow business, & he will be able to hold each line at least a month longer. It looks as though he had drawn half his army from Russia already.

The cinema man was here last night. During the Delville wood battle he was up in Trones Wood in a dugout, getting what pictures he could. One night as he turned-in in a dugout he noticed an evil smell in the place & complained of it. A young officer who was sleeping there (& in fact lived there) looked up & said 'Oh yes, that's those Boches. It was draughty in here so we blocked the passage with them. Never mind, they won't bite; go to sleep.'

The cinema people are about the worst daredevils in the army. They go into the thick of every fight & run more risks almost than the infantry men themselves. The best films they take are censored, so God knows why they are taken, & they themselves have a way of dealing with their passed films that drives me, the historian, to despair. They film a world-shaking attack, & then chop it up to introduce some soldiers eating stew & stealing each other's caps, & then. . . .

Dear love to you & the babes

Your old lover

Jan

I believe I'm to go to Paris on the 25th.

1. Lady Hamilton.
2. Curtis Brown?
3. The troops had their own versions of this sentimental ditty.

'In my little dug-out in the West,
Where of shrapnel we have such a feast . . .'
or
'There's a little wet home in the trench,
that the rain-storms continually drench;
A dead cow close by, with her hooves in the sky,
And she gives off a beautiful stench . . .'

---

[164]                                                    May 19.

M.D.O.C.

No let from you again, for the 3rd day this week. Is Bessie ill or what?

Today I had a rather dotted kind of a day, going to a place near Albert, & then going across country to another place to see some Australians. I found them engaged in making a report on the bloody & bitter battle of Bullecourt, now more or less over, & they were busy with the following question:– 'If a battalion goes up to hold a position, & loses half its strength, & is reinforced by another battalion, & then loses most of its survivors, & is reinforced by a third battalion, is it entitled to say, that it held the position? Is the second battalion entitled to say, that without it, the first battalion would have been destroyed? And is the third battalion entitled to say, that it saved the situation?' You have

no idea, how bitter these arguments may be among the men of the battalions, &
how they wrangle, as to which really deserved the prize.

They were full of praise for the carriers in this last battle. A modern fight is
mainly an affair of carriers, & the people who can bring up enough bombs &
explosives to the front line quickest are the victors. We have a weapon called a
Stokes bomb, which is fired from a special gun, so rapidly that 8 may be in the
air at the same time. Its range is only about 400 yards, but it is a devilish thing,
for when it bursts it makes a terrific bang & sends out flakes of jagged steel
which account for anything standing within 50 yards. The bombs are longish
ugsome cylinders on stalks, very heavy, & 6 are reckoned as a man's load. The
men of the Stokes gun squads all carry up 6 when they go up to the line, &
carriers bring up more, & any man, going up to the line, is generally caught by
trained watchers (like the poor devil Simon who had to carry the cross) &
compelled to carry up a few more. In the Bullecourt battle a Stokes gun was in
action but ran out of bombs. The gunners sent back for some by telephone, &
the carriers went out with some, but were all brought down by machine gun
fire. The gunmen waited a long time, & at last concluded that the carriers had
been hit, & so decided to go out & find their bodies. They went out, under
machine gun fire, to search for the bodies & presently found them with the
bombs. They loaded themselves up with bombs, & each man managed to take a
double load of twelve, & then they went back to their gun & fired them off.

In the same fight a machine gunner was out with a Lewis gun & two other
machine guns & their crews. The 2 other guns & crews were knocked out, &
this man was presently left alone with his gun. He used up all his ammunition
& then, as he was useless, he decided to go in, taking his gun with him. These
guns are fearfully heavy, but he carried it as far as he could, & then, seeing that
he would be cut off if he carried it any further, he buried it in a shell hole, all
except the lock, which he took off & pocketed. He marked the shellhole, so
that he would know the place again, & then returned to his own lines, & all this
under fire.

These things may seem tame, written down, but they are wonderful, when
one considers what fire is.

I've been thinking again, what may happen if Russia comes out. I fear it will
be a bad business in Mesopotamia, & a great heartener to the Turk & the Bulg
& the very devil in Salonika. We are in a rotten position there & have no
business to be there. The poison of that insane move on Gallipoli[1] is eating into
our vitals there. Having gone, I presume our men will stay there till they are
kicked out, & then, after having failed to save Serbia & failed to help
Roumania, & tied up shipping & wasted men we shall come away, & Greece
will join the enemy.

I am inclined to think, that if Russia comes out, Japan also will come out &
turn against us. I believe that she has helped to let Russia down, & she is the
Germany of Asia, & by no means a trustworthy friend; and with her against us

it will be complete, & we shall have all the reactionaries & devilries against us, which is as it should be. I don't think they can do us; but we must now just grit our teeth; make up our minds that there must be at least 2 years more of war, & that we are the main prop of all our side, & the real backbone of the struggle.

It is strange, that all this welter has failed to produce even one remarkable man in any country, & that no country has a leader, or a voice, or a mind, or a figure; they have politicians & journalists & big military systems; nothing focussed or kindling.

Dear love to you & to the babes

Your old love

Jan

1. Masefield seems to have altered his views since writing *Gallipoli*. Either by now he knew more of the political and military facts, or original reservations were blocked by censorship, or consideration of the need to impress neutrals, notably America, with the overall strength of the Allied position. It is only fair to Churchill's memory to remember that though the campaign was disliked from the start by Admiral Fisher, Churchill's First Sea Lord, condemned afterwards by Lloyd George, and mocked by E. M. Forster, it had its defenders from reputable military historians. Captain Liddell Hart wrote in 1938: 'Everyone save the wilfully purblind now realises that, in the words of the German official account, "Churchill's bold plan was not a fine-spun fantasy of the brain", and that the real sufferers from delusions were the commanders on the Western Front . . . We too now know, as the Germans did in the War, how feasible was the Dardanelles project, and how vital its effect would have been.' Clement Atlee, who fought at Gallipoli, wrote to Churchill in 1954, 'You had the conception of the Dardanelles, the only imaginative conception of the war.' Field-Marshal Sir William Robertson, Chief of the Imperial General Staff 1915–18, wrote in 1926: 'The advantages to be derived from forcing the Straits were perfectly obvious. Such a success would, as the advocates . . . said, serve to secure Egypt, to induce Italy and the Balkan States to come in on our side, and, if followed by the forcing of the Bosphorus, would enable Russia to draw munitions from America and Western Europe, and to export her accumulated supplies of wheat. There is seldom any lack of attractive-looking schemes in war. The difficulty is to give effect to them, and one of the difficulties in the Dardanelles scheme was that nothing really useful could be achieved without the assistance, sooner or later, of troops, and, according to the War Minister (Kitchener), no troops were available.' Masefield, though stoical towards himself, was hypersensitive to the sufferings of others, which, of course, he had seen at first-hand, and these must have remained with him long after the early promise of Gallipoli had faded or soured. Sentences by Major-General Fuller, another military expert and historian, would have deeply grieved Masefield. 'Meanwhile the force at Gallipoli expanded, but never quickly enough to grasp its fleeting opportunities. This was attempted in August . . . the conjunction of elderly generals and raw, untrained soldiers, under a "permissive" C-in-C like Hamilton proved fatal.' Fuller concluded in words that Masefield might have felt supported him: '410,000 British and 70,000 French soldiers had been landed, of whom 252,000 were killed, wounded missing, died of disease or evacuated sick. The Turkish casualties amounted to 218,000, of whom 66,000 were killed. The booty left behind was immense: "It took nearly two years to clean up the ground."' Fuller's editor, John Terraine, rates it 'one of the greatest disasters in British history, and one comparable with the Siege of Syracuse in 415. BC, because its root cause was

the inability of democracy to conduct a war. As Mr Churchill has pointed out: "No Man had the power to give clear, brutal orders which would command unquestioning respect. Power was widely disseminated among the many important personages who in this period formed the governing instrument."'

---

[165]                                                                   May 20.

M.O.D.C.

I have had nothing from you in the last five days but one brief note of the 15th, & your letter with Lady H's appeal.

I'm afraid you are jumping to the conclusion that I shall be back almost at once. I may be back in about two weeks from now, but the bother, worry & delay of getting back make it seem an age hence. My going to Paris has been delayed till Friday next, the 25th. It will take me all the 25th to get there & all the 26th to get permission to see the records; the 27th is Sunday, when the records will probably be closed, so that I may not really begin. It will be a little like your move from Loll.

An agricultural officer took me out today to Nerle, which the Boche occupied & hadn't time to destroy. We had lunch there with two liaison officers, one of whom said, that he had had to go to an English Brigade, & found there a French interpreter, who knew only 8 words of English. 'Yes. Quite so. As a matter of fact.' He had at once written to the Interpreters' corps & told them to send another interpreter, but in a day or two he received an appeal from the Brigade, which said, 'It is quite true that the old interpreter's knowledge of English is elementary, but we should like to keep him as a mascot.'

From Nerle, where the inhabitants, though only just released from bondage, had quite grasped the idea that the Anglais were there to bring them in a little dew of heaven, we went on to Roye. I suppose these dirty devils the Boche had cut down every apple & pear & plum tree between Nerle & Roye; & the sight of those trees, in blossom, though cut through & lying on the ground, made one's blood boil. You have not seen it & cannot imagine it, but the effect it has upon one is not easy to describe. You feel that you could cut a Boche throat & desecrate a Boche grave & bomb a Boche town, & get a Boche officer down & gouge his eyes out.

Roye had once a very very lovely old church, rather obscured by houses but most beautiful & full of fine old glass. These devils put a mine under the chancel, & blew the inside, & the roof, & the glass, to smithereens, out of dirty devilry & malice; & then cleared out of the district.

All that ground, Amiens-Roye-Nerle, is the French battle of the Somme. They had an easy task, for the ground is flat, & they met Fritz on even terms, & that is why they progressed so fast. We had to go up hill all the way to Pozieres, & afterwards all the way up hill to Bapaume.

I found a French bayonet that had been used as a hammer, a poker, & a rake; so I have now English, French, Austrian & Boche bayonets.

In one of the camps, I met a Major who knew Bobby Masefield[1] & had served with him. He said that the French are the limit for greed. They have been asking us to leave 100 tents with 200 people's rations for a fortnight, in each recaptured French village, so that they may bring back the civilians at once. There are some 200 villages (at the least) in our recaptured territory, so that this is asking us to lodge & feed some 40,000 strangers, some of whom are quite certain to be spies.

Somebody brought a big crate of strawberries for tea. They tasted more like lemons than strawberries, & we ate them with little sour cream cheeses & made pigs of ourselves; though they weren't really nice. I'm afraid men degenerate, my sweetheart, away from their lovely dear wives.

Did Murray[2] or Raleigh[3] never call? I will d—n them in a poem if they didn't. I am much concerned, that the people are being so dull for you.

I can't write intimately, because one never knows now.

Dear love to you & the babes.

Jan

1. Major Robert Masefield of the Kings Shropshire Light Infantry was killed in 1915. He was a distant cousin of John Masefield.

2. Professor Gilbert Murray (1866–1957), classical scholar, translator of Greek tragedies, fervid internationalist, one of the Masefields' new neighbours at Boar's Hill.

3. Sir Walter Alexander Raleigh (1861–1922), literary critic and scholar, first Professor of English Literature to be appointed at Oxford (1904).

---

[166] May 22.

M.O.D.C.

. . . I am sending with this what the photographer calls a Wiew of Morval, which is out on the east of the battle & is the hell of a desolate place on a hill, exactly as you see it in the print. The background has been shelled a good deal since we took it, & the distant church is now only a mound of brick from which you may survey the landscape.

I was there again today. Just below it, only about 300 yards away, is another (bigger) village called Les Boeuss, which is even worse, though perhaps no more desolate looking. Les Boeuss Church is now exactly like a tumulus, & on the very top of it is the church-bell, not even cracked, for all the fire. A lot of sodden old books lay about in the ruins, mostly church & school books (as they would be in so tiny a place) & the account-books of the village shops, from 1827–1830, & some farmer's plans for the year, & some old newspapers of 1870. It was the hell of a desolate & ghastly ruin, with no living being, except magpies, within a couple of miles, actually no human soul, & the rain was falling & the dead were rotting & the mud was squelching, & after a time I felt the grue of it & went back to Morval.

The road between the two places is a lane in what the French call a deblai or space between two lynchets. The Fritzes had had a battery in the deblai, & our shells had caught it & smashed it to bits & had killed all the gunners, & there they were in the mud, heads & hands & legs, with a whole squad of helmets sticking up out of the filth, & a broken machine gun, & about a ton of Fritz shells, & a lot of broken harness & equipment. It had been raining hard for many hours & all this mess lay in the muddy pools.

Up in Morval, there were marks of the French, who had joined on to us there, & wherever the French have been it is well to walk carefully, for though our men & the Fritzes are careless of bombs the French are reckless with them. Sure enough, I soon saw the blue egg bombs lying half buried in the mud, & by & by came on another kind, very evil looking, rather like penny inkpots, & soon afterwards on some hundreds of cricket-ball bombs, so placed that half of them had been buried by splashed filth from the road. Going round these I came on a great heap of little black egg bombs, like black artificial eggs, & thought my last hour had come, for they littered the landscape & it was a job not to tread on one. There is a yet more deadly kind, flat, called the oyster bomb, but I didn't see this kind today.

Some people collect these things. They rush on to them & snatch them up & screw their heads off & pour out the explosive, rinse them in a shellhole & carry them home. Others delight to make them explode. A lonely old dump-guard at Thiepval has some means of exploding dud shells, & in the daytime he collects these damnable things; in the evenings, when he settles to his loneliness, as the only man within a mile, he brings them out, one by one, & bangs them off on his hilltop, to Baal or Ashtaroth or some other devil, & I suppose dances naked, with a necklace of Boche skulls or so.

I suppose the lonely men in the camp near Pozieres see the flashes of the bursts & think that the ghosts of the old attacks are riding the night there.

I would fill this last page with indecencies of an outrageous kind but had better forbear. The thought of coming home has turned my brain.

Dear love to you my darling & to my dear babes.

Your old love<br>Jan

---

[167]                                                        May 23.

M.O.D.C.

I have an undated note from you, presumably Saturday's or Sunday's. This should reach you about Monday, which should be one of the last days of this stay. Unless delayed (which is quite possible & likely) I ought to be home one day next week. It is not possible to be more precise than that. Paris is a dark horse, GHQ is a dark horse, the boat is an exceedingly dark horse. All may & all may not help or hinder.

I don't look forward to foul London & the record office after so much out of door life. To be out of doors from 8 till 6 & not to read or write at all is pleasanter than to sit in foul air, stewing over papers.

I probably know more of the Somme field than any of the soldiers who fought there. Parts of it do not attract me, parts repel me, some of it is romantic, some strange, some unearthly, some savage. The north is rather hateful, then comes an interesting bit of Pozieres, & from P eastward for a mile, an extraordinarily romantic piece, then come the dull woods, Bazentin, Mametz & Fricourt, then lousy Carnoy & dirty Montauban, then Delville wood, which has its interest, & the dead & corpsy Guillemont, Ginchy bit. The outer fringe, towards Bapaume, is all rather attractive; but nothing is like Pozieres; that is the real place.

I see Pozieres as a unity. The rest is somehow scattered. At P, they did send one body of men at one place, & kept them there till they got it; elsewhere, this unity is less apparent.

Love to all,
Your old love
Jan

# Appendix

The first result of Masefield's Somme explorations was *The Old Front Line* (1917). Its quality can be judged by these extracts.

Before the battle, the British pounded the enemy with two million shells.

The shelling continued all that day, searching the line and particular spots with intense fire and much asphyxiating gas. Again the enemy prepared for an attack in the morning, and again there was no attack, although the fire of preparation still went on. The enemy said 'Tomorrow will make three whole days of preparation; the English will attack tomorrow.' But when the morning came there was no attack, only the never-ceasing shelling, which seems to increase as time passed. It was now difficult and dangerous to move within the enemy lines. Relieving exhausted soldiers, carrying out the wounded, and bringing up food and water to the front, became terrible feats of war. The fire continued and increased, all that day and all the next day, and the day after that. It darkened the days with smoke and lit the nights with flashes. It covered the summer landscape with a kind of haze of hell, earth-coloured above fields and reddish above villages, from the dust of blown mud and brick flung up into the air. The tumult of these days and nights cannot be described nor imagined. The air was without wind, yet it seemed in a hurry with the passing of death. Men knew not which they heard, a roaring that was behind and in front, like a presence, or a screaming that never ceased to shriek in the air. No thunder was ever so terrible as that tumult. It broke the drums of the ears when it came singly, but when it rose up along the front and gave tongue together in full cry it humbled the soul. With the roaring, crashing, and shrieking came a racket of hammers from the machine-guns till men were dizzy and sick from the noise which thrust between skull and brain, and beat out thought. With the noise came also a terror and an exultation, that one should hurry, and hurry, and hurry, like the shrieking shells, into the pits of fire opening on the hills.

And still the enemy waited for the British, until, at 7.30, on a summer day, there came a whistling and a crying. The men of the first wave climbed up the parapets, in tumult, in darkness, and the presence of death, and having done with all pleasant things, advanced across No Man's Land to begin the Battle of the Somme.

The soldiers who held this old front line of ours saw this grass and wire day after day, perhaps for many months. It was the limit of their world, the horizon of their landscape, the boundary. What interest there was in their life was the speculation, what lay beyond that wire and what the enemy was doing there. They seldom saw an enemy. They heard his songs and they were stricken by his missiles, but seldom saw more than perhaps, a swiftly moving cap at a gap in the broken parapet, or a grey figure flitting from the light of a star-shell. Aeroplanes brought back photographs of those unseen lines. Some-times, in raids in the night, our men visited them and brought back prisoners; but they remained mysteries and unknown.

In the early morning of the 1st of July, 1916, our men looked at them as they showed among the bursts of our shells. Those familiar heaps, the lines, were then in a smoke of dust full of flying clods and shards, and gleams of fire. Our men felt that now in a few minutes, they would see the enemy and know what lay beyond those parapets and probe the heart of the mystery. So, for the last half-hour, they watched and held themselves ready, while the screaming of the shells grew wilder and the roar of the bursts quickened into a drumming. Then as the time drew near, they looked a last look at that unknown country, now almost blotted in the fog of war and saw the flash of our shells, breaking in little further off as the gunners 'lifted', and knew that the moment had come. Then for one wild confused moment they knew that they were running towards that unknown land, which they could see in the dust ahead. For a moment, they saw the parapet with the wire in front of it, and began, as they ran, to pick out in their minds a path through that wire. Then, too often, to many of them, the grass that they were crossing flew up in shards and sods and gleams of fire from the enemy shells, and those runners never reached the wire, but saw, perhaps, a flash, and the earth rushing nearer, and grasses against the sky, and then saw nothing more at all, for ever and for ever and for ever.

It was a day of intense blue summer beauty, full of roaring violence, and confusion of death, agony, and triumph, from dawn to dark. All through that day little rushes of the men of our race went toward that No Man's Land from the bloody shelter of our trenches. Some hardly left our trenches, many never crossed the green space, many died in the enemy wire, many had to fall back. Others won across and went further, and drove the enemy back from his fort, and then back from line to line and from one hasty trenching to another, till the Battle of the Somme ended in the falling back of the enemy army.

One need hardly look at the ground to know that the fighting here was very grim, and to the death. Near the road and up the slope to the enemy the ground is littered with relics of our charges; mouldy packs, old shattered scabbards, rifles, bayonets, helmets curled, torn, rolled, and starred, clips of cartridges, and very many graves. Many of the graves are marked with strips of wood torn from packing cases, with pencilled inscriptions, 'An unknown British Hero;' 'an unknown British soldier;' 'a dead Fritz'. That gentle slope to the Schwaben is covered with such things.

Long after we are gone, perhaps, stray English tourists, wandering in Picardy, will see names scratched in a barn, some mark or notice on a door, some signpost, some little line of graves, or hear on the lips of a native, some slang phrase of English, learned long before, in the war-time, in childhood, when the English were there. All the villages behind our front were thronged with our people. There they rested after being in the line and there they established their hospitals and magazines. It may be said that men of our race died in our cause in every village within five miles of the front. Wherever the traveller comes upon a little company of our graves, he will know that he is near the site of some old hospital or clearing station, where our men were brought in from the line.

★   ★   ★

Here the legion halted, here the ranks were broken,
And the men fell out to gather wood;
And the green wood smoked, and bitter words were spoken,
And the trumpets called to food.

And the sentry on the rampart saw the distance dying
In the smoke of distance blue and far,
And heard the curlew calling and the owl replying
As the night came cold with one star;

And thought of home beyond, over moorland, over marshes,
Over hills, over the sea, across the plains, across the pass,
By a bright sea trodden by the ships of Tarshis,
The farm, with cicadae in the grass.

And thought, as I: 'Perhaps, I may be done with living
To-morrow, when we fight. I shall see those souls no more.
O beloved souls, be beloved in forgiving
The deeds and the words that make me sore.'

JOHN MASEFIELD

Faces – passionate faces – of men I may not know,
They haunt me, burn me to the heart, as I turn aside to go:
The king's face and the cur's face, and the face of the stuffed swine,
They are passing, they are passing, their eyes look into mine.

JOHN MASEFIELD

# Bibliography

*The works of John Masefield referred to in the text*

*Salt Water Ballads* 1902
*Sea Life in Nelson's Time* 1905
*The Tragedy of Nan* 1909
*Lost Endeavour* 1910
*My Faith in Women's Suffrage* 1910
*The Everlasting Mercy* 1911
*The Widow in the Bye Street,* 1912
*Dauber* 1913
*Gallipolli* 1916
*Lollingdon Downs and Other Poems with Sonnets* 1917
*The Old Front Line* 1917
*The Battle of the Somme* 1919
*Reynard the Fox* 1919
*Recent Prose* 1924
*Sard Harker* 1924
*Odtaa* 1926
*The Midnight Folk* 1927
*Badon Hill* 1928
*Midsummer Night* 1928
*The Wanderer of Liverpool* 1930
*A Tale of Troy* 1932
*The Bird of Dawning* 1933
*The Taking of the Gry* 1934
*Victorious Troy (or The Hurrying Angel)* 1935
*Live and Kicking Ned* 1939
*Basilissa* 1940
*Conquer* 1941
*The Nine Days Wonder* 1941
*A Generation Risen* 1942
*Wonderings* 1943
*The Lost Childhood* 1944
*Badon Parchments* 1947
*So Long To Learn* 1952
*Grace Before Ploughing* 1966
(All published by Heinemann)

*Letters to Reyna* (edited by William Buchan) 1983
(published by Buchan and Enright)

*Other references*
*Apart from Masefield's own works, I have drawn heavily on the following:*

BABINGTON SMITH, CONSTANCE, *John Masefield*, Oxford University Press, Oxford, 1978

BETJEMAN, JOHN, *Selected Poems of John Masefield*, Heinemann, London, 1978

BUCHAN, WILLIAM (ed), *Letters to Reyna*, Buchan & Enright, London, 1983

FISHER, MARGERY, *John Masefield*, Bodley Head, London, 1963

HASSALL, CHRISTOPHER, *Edward Marsh*, Longmans, 1959

LAMONT, CORLISS, (ed), *Letters of John Masefield to Florence Lamont*, Macmillan, London, 1979

—, *Remembering John Masefield*, Kaye and Ward, 1972

MITCHISON, NAOMI, 'John Masefield' in *Twentieth Century Children's Writers* (ed Daniel Kirkpatrick), St James' Press, 1983 edition

REID, MARGARET J. C., *The Arthurian Legend*, Oliver and Boyd, Edinburgh, 1938

SPARK, MURIEL, *John Masefield*, Peter Neville, 1953

STRONG, L. A. G., *John Masefield*, British Council, 1957.

# Index